CHINA'S RISE, RUSSIA'S FALL

Also by Peter Nolan

CHINA'S ECONOMIC REFORMS IN THE 1980s: The Costs and Benefits of Incrementalism (*editor with Fan Qimiao*)

GROWTH PROCESSES AND DISTRIBUTIONAL CHANGE IN A SOUTH CHINESE PROVINCE: The Case of Guangdong

INEQUALITY: India and China Compared, 1950–1970 (*with T. J. Byres*)

MARKET FORCES IN CHINA: Competition and Small Business – The Wenzhou Debate (*editor with Dong Fureng*)

RE-THINKING SOCIALIST ECONOMICS (*editor with Suzy Paine*)

STATE AND MARKET IN THE CHINESE ECONOMY: Essays on Controversial Issues

THE CHINESE ECONOMY AND ITS FUTURE (*editor with Dong Fureng*)

THE POLITICAL ECONOMY OF COLLECTIVE FARMS: An Analysis of China's Post-Mao Rural Economic Reforms

THE TRANSFORMATION OF THE COMMUNIST ECONOMIES (*editor with Ha-Joon Chang*)

China's Rise, Russia's Fall

Politics, Economics and Planning in the Transition from Stalinism

Peter Nolan
Fellow and Director of Studies in Economics
Jesus College, Cambridge

St. Martin's Press   New York

St. Martin's Press, Scholarly and Reference Division,
175 Fifth Avenue, New York, N.Y. 10010

First published in the United States of America in 1995

Printed in Great Britain

ISBN 0–312–12714–6

Library of Congress Cataloging-in-Publication Data
Nolan, Peter.
China's rise, Russia's fall : politics, economics and planning in
the transition from Stalinism / Peter Nolan.
p.   cm.
Includes bibliographical references and index.
ISBN 0–312–12714–6
1. China—Economic policy—1976–   2. China—Politics and
government—1976–   3. Russia (Federation)—Economic policy—1991–
4. Russia (Federation)—Politics and government—1991–   I. Title.
HC427.92.N65   1995
338.951—dc20   95–33089
                                                       CIP

For Siobain

Mao Zedong on the Great Leap Forward:

'The chaos caused was on a grand scale and I take responsibility. Comrades, if you have to shit, shit! If you have to fart, fart! You'll feel much better for it.'

(Mao Zedong, from his speech at the Lushan Conference, 23 July 1959, translated in full in Schram, 1974)

Contents

Preface

I wish especially to thank my colleague Geoff Harcourt, who read through and commented on the entire manuscript. He has been an inspiration to countless colleagues and students.

I am also most grateful to the following people who have contributed in diverse ways to the ideas in this book: Paul Aiello, Amiya Bagchi, Bob Ash, John Barber, Chris Bramall, Trevor Buck, Vladimir Busygin, Terry Byres, Ha-Joon Chang, Dong Fureng, John Dunn, John Eatwell, Michael Ellman, R. Fenton-May, Igor Filatochev, Laurence Harris, Alan Hughes, Jiang Xiaoming, Grigorii Khanin, Mushtaq Khan, Michael Landesmann, Cyril Lin, Liu Xiaofeng, Geoff Meeks, John Sender, Albert Schweinberger, Ajit Singh, Dmitri Slavnov, Michael Twohey, Wang Xiaoqiang, Gordon White, Peter Wiles, Robert Wilkinson, Keith Wrightson, and Zhu Ling. Thanking them in no way implicates them in the views expressed in this book.

I am grateful to those who participated in seminars given by me on various topics covered in this book at the following places: Aberdeen University; Australian National University; St Petersburg University; Hong Kong, Conference of Africanists and Orientalists; University of Konstanz; University of Venice; Cambridge University, Faculty of Economics and Politics seminar at Queen's College; Cambridge University, Social and Political Science Faculty, 'Revolutions' Seminar; London School of Economics and Political Science.

PETER NOLAN

Abbreviations

CCP	Chinese Communist Party
CPSU	Communist Party of the Soviet Union
EBRD	European Bank for Reconstruction and Development
FT	*Financial Times*
IHT	*International Herald Tribune*
ILO	International Labour Organisation
IMF	International Monetary Fund
NEP	New Economic Policy
OECD	Organisation for Economic Co-operation and Development
SMEs	Small and Medium Enterprises
SSB	State Statistical Bureau (China)
UNDP	United Nations Development Programme
USCJEC	United States Congress, Joint Economic Committee
WB	World Bank
EBRD	European Bank for Reconstruction and Development

1 Introduction

1.1 FOCUS OF THE STUDY

The contrast in the outcome of the reform process in the two giants of communism has arguably been the most important event in international political economy in the last quarter of the twentieth century. The contrast will have consequences that will resonate well into the next century. In this book I attempt to explain the reasons for this remarkable contrast.

In the period since the collapse of the Soviet state, this book focusses on developments in Russia itself, since the problems of analysing such a diversity of experience as is encompassed by each of the newly independent states that were formerly within the USSR is simply too complex. Despite some hopes of system reform upon Gorbachev's election to the post of General Secretary of the Communist Party of the Soviet Union in March 1985, little changed in Gorbachev's first year in office. The start of system reform in the USSR is properly dated from the summer of 1986, when Gorbachev first enunciated *glasnost* as a distinct policy. The start of system reforms in China is usually identified as December 1978. However, the reforms began almost the moment Mao Zedong died and the 'Gang of Four' was arrested in the Autumn of 1976. Thus the period of system reform in China has been at least double that in Russia.

1.2 SIGNIFICANCE OF THE STUDY

Large size of the events studied

The history of the twentieth century has been hugely affected by the rise of communism and is now being powerfully affected by the consequences of its transformation. The two countries analysed in this book were the giants of the world communist movement. The USSR was the first socialist country, the nature of whose ideas and institutions profoundly affected all subsequent communist states. China is much the most heavily populated country in the world. Between them, China and the USSR accounted for over one quarter of the total world population, and around nine-tenths of the world's population living

1

under communist regimes.[1] To a considerable degree, the history of the rise and fall of communism is a history of these two countries.

Each exerted an especially powerful impact on the communist countries in their own region of the world. This was true not just for the period of relatively stable communist rule, but also applied to the epoch of the decline of communism. It is not too fanciful to speak of an East Asian and a European path to the end of the communist system – one evolutionary, the other revolutionary (see Chang and Nolan, 1995).

This is the first book-length study which compares the reform process and its outcomes in the these two countries. The subject matter of the book is recent, and only a small literature so far exists. It is likely that this will grow at a fast rate in the coming years.

Significance for the citizens of China and Russia

The contrast in outcome is of the highest importance to the large number of people who live in these two countries. The lives of the bulk of the population of them each of them have moved at high speed in different directions over the past decade and a half. If someone, fifteen years ago, had predicted the scenario that has come to pass he/she would have been dismissed as hopelessly eccentric.[2] In fact the contrast has produced the sharpest possible difference in the results for the citizens of the two countries in terms of most important aspects of their lives, from personal safety, job security and national pride to personal income, the distribution of wealth and economic power.

Significance for international political economy

The impact on international political and military relations has been profound already, with many important consequences still waiting to be worked out. Because of China's vast population size, should it grow successfully to upper middle income income level and beyond, it would, at some point in the twenty-first century, become the most important economy in the world. If India's pace of growth were to continue to be significantly slower than China's, then China's dominance of the world economy could conceivably be even greater than that achieved by the USA in the middle of the twentieth century. It is hard to predict how this would affect international politics. However, it is certain that its effect would be large. On the other hand, the collapse of the USSR leaves a vast zone of instability from Europe through to the Far East.

Significance for the study of economics

The dramatic and almost entirely unpredicted contrast in outcomes, has already had some impact, and is likely in the future to have even more impact, upon the study of economics. The 1970s and 1980s saw the rise to dominance of both free market economics and confidence in the ability of economic 'science' to understand and predict economic events. The dramatic contrast in outcomes has thrown a shadow over the more extreme versions of these points of view. A great deal of attention is likely to be devoted in the years ahead to absorbing the. significance of these contrasting events for economic theory and policy. They are likely at the very least to increase strongly the impact within the subject of the importance of the study of institutions in understanding economic performance. It may make economists more aware of the limitations of their discipline. It will, hopefully, also make all economists involved in policy-making less confident about recommending large 'revolutionary' changes in policy in countries they are advising.

1.3 THEMES OF THE BOOK

The importance of policy decisions in determining the outcome from reform

It has been argued, by most of those who have made more or less explicit comparisons between reform in China and Russia, that the main cause of the contrast in the large differences in the system which the 'reformers' in each case were bequeathed. It is argued that the main cause of the difference in outcome lies in such factors as the relative levels of industrialisation, of income, or urbanisation, of the importance of state industry, or the role of ethnic minorities. This book examines these propositions in detail. There were, indeed, large differences in the initial conditions. However, there were also strong common similarities, as well as differences which in each case could have supported accelerated growth along different paths. In both cases there were large possibilities for rapid economic progress if the correct policies had been chosen. It is not obvious that in either case, the reform process should have been followed by a phase of deep decline in output and living standards. I argue instead that the main reason for the difference in outcome is the difference in the policies chosen.

The importance of planning in the transition from the communist economic system

Most analysts considered the transition from communism to be essentially about the transition from 'plan' to 'market'. This book argues that this is an incorrect way to think about the process. The communist economies were not 'planned' economies. Rather, they were more correctly described as 'command' economies. Indeed, they were at least as anarchic as the pure form of capitalism. Once the huge changes involved in the first five-year plans had been completed the communist sytems were almost wholly incapable of shifting towards goals that policy-makers widely agreed were desirable, such as faster technical progress, a shift away from heavy industry ('removing the steel blinkers'), improved product quality, faster growth of living standards, and less environmentally damaging growth. This book argues that in the transition from a command economy to one with a greater role for markets, there are likely in principle to be large areas in which markets left to themselves will fail to produce desirable outcomes in respect to economic growth. Nor will they produce widely desired outcomes in terms of poverty alleviation or the distribution of income and wealth. Therefore, it is an apparent paradox that in the transition from a 'planned' economy, a central condition of success is the ability of the state to plan effectively. In fact, this ceases to be a paradox once one recognises that the communist economic systems were not planned economies at all. Success in the transition was conditional upon learning how to plan, as opposed to giving orders.

The importance of politics in the economic transition

Both inside and outside the communist countries, the analysis of the role of politics in the transition was heavily influenced by ideology, and the oppression endured under the communist political system. A large body of intellectuals found it hard to imagine any desirable alternative to the policy of supporting the overthrow of the communist system. This was frequently buttressed by arguments about the alleged advantages for the economy of supporting such an overthrow. This book argues that such arguments were erroneous and irresponsible. They underestimated the importance to the achievement of socially desirable goals of maintaining an effective state apparatus during the long and difficult transition period. They underestimated the difficulty of creating an effective state system after the collapse of the communist party. They underestimated the degree to which it might be possible for a communist party to allow a move towards a market economy and allow a gradual change in the nature of communist rule from totalitarian to authoritarian, and lay the foundations for eventual transition to democratic political institutions. In analysing large issues of system change, in which all the parameters of socio-economic life are altering, proper policy requires political economy, not merely the separate 'sciences' of economics, politics or sociology. It is their interaction in a complex, indeed, organic structure that is the key to devising correct policies.

The causes of the selection of contrasting reform policies

Reform policies could not be selected from a menu, from which one set of leaders chose more wisely than the other. There were complex determinants beneath the apparently simple matter of 'choosing policies'. The international setting faced by the two countries' leaders was different. The USSR was in the frontline of international military competition, and was subjected to intense pressure from the USA. China was not. However, China was strongly affected by the approach towards political economy in the surrounding Asian capitalist states, especially those with strong Chinese elements in the population and leadership.

Events within each of the communist giants reacted back upon the choice of policies in the other. The emergence of a 'transition orthodoxy' in the late 1980s, which favoured revolutionary change in both politics and economics, was hugely influenced by a perception that the Chinese reforms were failing. The radical Russian plans of 1990, for example, made specific reference to this apparent fact. The Chinese leadership's fear of the consequences of large scale political change was hugely intensified by the acceleration of political disintegration in the USSR in the late 1980s, and by the collapse of communism in Eastern Europe in 1989. Increasingly, the collapse of the USSR provided a source of confidence to the Chinese leadership that their incremental reform path was broadly correct and that they had been correct to avoid the alternative of rapid system change. Moreover, the historical background within each of the countries helped shape a different choice of policy. China's turbulent modern history, with long periods of anarchy, made its leadership acutely aware of the possibility of anarchic outcomes to over-hasty system change. The Soviet leadership in the 1980s could look back upon a long period of political stability, stretching back to the 1920s. Moreover, the possibility of disintegration of the nation-state seemed remote in a country which had experienced national unity for several hundred years.

1.4 STRUCTURE OF THE BOOK

The first task of this study is to set out briefly (in chapter 2) the main areas of the contrast in results under reform policies. This demonstrates the most remarkable divergence of paths under reform. Almost every significant indicator moved in opposite directions in the two countries. The rest of the book is devoted to attempting to explain this contrast.

One approach towards the former communist economies was to argue that systemic problems were greatly exaggerated. It was argued that in the last resort these were the product of ideologically motivated criticism from the representatives of an opposing system. Chapter 3 examines these propositions in relation to China and the former USSR. It finds them to be severely wanting, and argues that mere tinkering with the respective systems was not enough. Whatever the ideological motivation of much of the criticism of the performance of these systems, it contained a core of truth. Fundamental reform of the system of political economy was necessary in order to improve economic performance and popular welfare.

As the communist economies began seriously to investigate ways of improving system performance, a consensus built up about the desirable path to be followed. The consensus grew stronger in the late 1980s as the Soviet system entered *perestroika* and most commentators considered that the gains from Chinese economic reforms were exhausted. The high point of the consensus about the desirable path for post-communist system reform were roughly 1988 to 1991. In these years, the communist system was in its death-throes in the USSR. China appeared to be in the deepest political economic crisis in 1989 with the Tiananmen massacre. Few commentators thought that the communist regime could survive in China. Still fewer thought it could prosper. In 1989 communism was overthrown in eastern Europe. A massive consensus built up among both external and internal critics of the communist system that only simultaneous revolutionary change in both the economic and the political sphere could produce a desirable outcome to the transition from communism. Chapter 4 describes this consensus, the 'transition orthodoxy', and evaluates it. It finds its logic and judgement to be seriously deficient.

This book is one of the first attempts[3] to systematically compare the reform process in China and the former USSR. While none of those foreign advisors who helped shape the reform process in the former USSR has undertaken a full length study of the comparison, most of them have commented upon the contrast.[4] The strong consensus is that the reasons for the difference are not to be found in the policy contrasts, but rather in the different starting points from which reform set out in the two countries. It is, of course, important for them that this should be so, since insofar as the reason for the profound contrast is found to lie in the realm of policy choice rather than system difference, it places responsibility upon their shoulders for providing bad advice. Chapter 5 analyses the nature of the two systems of political economy at the start of their reform process. It confirms that there were many large system differences. However, in some important respects these differences were to the disadvantage of China. Moreover, it identifies important system similarities which in both cases made it possible for well constructed reform programmes to have produced rapid economic progress. In other words, a comparison of the starting points of reform suggests that policy choice rather than system difference was the main cause of the difference in outcome from the respective reform processes. It suggests that it was unnecessary that system reform be accompanied by a massive economic downturn in the USSR, and that it was far from an easy matter to obtain rapid advance from the command economy in China.

Chapter 6 examines the course of reform in China. It describes firstly the way in which the Chinese leadership resisted the transition orthodoxy in the West (and increasingly in China among intellectuals) on the need to undertake rapid political democratisation. Instead they concentrated on trying to improve the performance of the huge centralised political apparatus, giving high weight to the maintenance of political stability and the avoidance of *da luan*, 'political turbulence'. It then describes the careful, experimental way in which reform proceeded in every area of the economy. At the end of this process, public ownership remained a central feature of the property rights regime in every sector. The economy remained highly protected from the forces of international competition. The state remained at the centre of the economic process, having fundamentally shifted its approach away from economic commands towards economic planning which worked in tandem with market forces. In every major area, China pursued a reform strategy which ran counter to the transition orthodoxy. In terms of the conventional wisdom of the late 1980s about how to reform a Stalinist system of political economy, China got all the main policies wrong, yet it was the world's most dynamic economy in the reform period. This suggests that were serious problems with the methodology underlying the transition orthodoxy.

Chapter 7 analyses the reform process in the USSR. It argues that the key to the disintegration of the Soviet economy lay with the disastrous decision taken by Gorbachev and his close advisors at the end of Gorbachev's first year in office to pursue *glasnost* and *perestroika*. These policies led rapidly to the collapse of the communist party without replacing it with an effective alternative government. Moreover, they led to the disintegration of the Soviet nation-state. For a brief period the Gorbachev government attempted to put into effect a cautious programme of experimental, evolutionary economic reform. In its fundamentals it was similar to the Chinese programme. However, its potential effects were swamped by the consequences of the political reforms. Moreover, support for a more radical programme of 'shock therapy' quickly gained ground in the centre of power, strongly affected by the rapid growth in influence of Western ideas as political and cultural liberalisation gained pace.

The Gorbachev period bequeathed a political and economic disaster to the successor government under Yeltsin. Given the political framework, it proved impossible to control the rate of inflation. For most of the reform period, other policies were put into effect against the greatly disadvantageous background of extremely high rates of inflation. Law and order collapsed. The economic philosophy of the government was powerfully influenced by the Bretton Woods organisations. Its central planks were: a largely failed attempt to control the rate of inflation; a radical price reform, put into effect in 1992; a largely liberalised international trade and foreign investment regime; and, most importantly, rapid privatisation of state assets. The logic of the economic programme was deeply questionable. Attempting to put it into effect under such adverse political conditions as those in Russia after 1991 helped produce a disaster. A poor economic performance under Gorbachev became a complete disaster under Yeltsin. Moreover, the reform period witnessed a profound restructuring of the ownership of assets. The process of primitive capitalist accumulation had been crushed into the space of only two years, under conditions likely to produce extreme inequality of outcomes. These outcomes were the parameters, the 'givens', within which Russian economic life would be conducted for many decades to come.

Chapter 8 summarises the main conclusions of the book. It indicates

also some implications for economic theory and policy of this extraordinary contrast. Above all, it suggests that modesty is in order in
looking back at the experience of 'transition'. Western social science
failed badly in this period. It formed the intellectual foundation of the
advice given by the Bretton Woods organisations, and it played a large
role also through the myriad of contacts that developed between the
Russian and Western intellectual communities. The transition orthodoxy quickly and confidently built up in the 1980s. It had a profound
impact upon the way the 'transition' problem was viewed within the
reforming countries themselves. However, it was deeply flawed. The
advice which flowed from this orthodoxy contributed substantially to
the Soviet disaster. The decision not to follow it helped the Chinese
achieve enormous success in their transitional programme.

2 Economic Performance during the Reform Period in China and Russia

2.1 INTRODUCTION

The death of Mao Tsetung and the arrest of the 'Gang of Four' in the Autumn of 1976 ushered in a period of huge change in China's political economy. Although important changes occurred in the first two years after Mao's death, most observers date the beginning of reform as the Third Plenum of the Eleventh Central Committee of the Chinese Communist Party in December 1978. Gorbachev's election to the position of General Secretary of the Soviet Communist Party in March 1985 raised hopes that serious system reform would begin. However, it was not until the summer of 1986 that the distinctive features of the policy of *perestroika* could be seen. The subsequent period of 'reform', already much longer in China than in the former USSR, produced strikingly different results.

2.2 CHINA

Output growth

China's economic growth record under reform policies placed it in the front rank of growth performances during the relevant period. In the 1980s and early 1990s it was one of only three economies whose growth rate of GDP was reported to have been over nine per cent per annum. It also attained one of the fastest growth rates of exports, with a real growth rate of almost 12 per cent per annum from 1980 to 1991 (Table 2.1): the value of China's exports in US dollars rose from ten billion in 1978 to 92 billion in 1993 (SSB, *ZGTJZY*, 1994, p. 105). Behind the growth of total output there was a massive accumulation process, with huge additions to the stock of capital goods. China's capital goods industries grew in leaps and bounds to feed the appetite of overall economic growth (see Chapter 6). The leading edge of Chinese indus-

10

Table 2.1   Comparative performance of the Chinese economy, 1980–91

	China	India	Low income countries[1]	Middle income countries
Av. annual growth rate, 1980–91 per cent:				
GDP	9.4	5.4	3.7	2.3
Agriculture	5.7	3.2	2.5	n.a.
Industry	11.0	6.3	4.0	n.a.
Services	11.2	6.7	4.8	n.a.
Av. annual rate growth rate of exports, 1980–89 per cent	11.5	7.4	3.3	3.4
Av. annual growth rate of population, 1980–89 per cent	1.5	2.1	2.6	1.8
Av. annual real of inflation, 1980–89 per cent	5.8	8.2	23.4	67.1
Debt service as per cent of exports of goods and services				
1980	4.4	9.3	11.6	23.9
1991	12.1	30.7	25.0	20.3
Food production per capital (av. annual growth rate, 1979–91)	3.0	1.6	—	—
Daily calorie intake (per capita)				
1965	1931	2103	1960	2482
1988	2632	2104	2182	2834
Crude death rate (no./1000)				
1970	8	18	19	11
1991	7	10	13	8
Infant mortality rate (no./1000)				
1981	71	121	124	81
1991	38	90	91	38
Life expectancy at birth (years)				
1981	67	52	50	60
1991	69	60	55	68

Note: 1 Excluding India and China.

Source: World Bank, *WDR*, 1983, 1991 and 1993.

try was modernised rapidly with imports of high technology products, and the capital goods produced by modernising domestic factories.

Consumption

The improvement in economic performance was achieved through a sharp improvement in overall economic efficiency, reflected in the fact that the growth of output was accompanied by an extraordinary surge in living standards in the 1980s (Table 2.2). China's economic performance in the 1980s was much better than that in the most relevant comparator country, namely India, and was immeasurably better than virtually anyone in the late 1970s could have hoped. The level and structure of food intake greatly improved. Huge new consumer durable industries sprang up in the 1980s, with a 'first wave' of goods such as bicycles, watches, TV sets, fridges, and washing machines, followed by a more complex array of goods in the 'second wave', including products such as motor cars, motor cycles, and video recorders (Table 2.2). A massive housebuilding boom took place over the reform years with space per person more than doubling.

Welfare indicators

China did well at raising the incomes of the poorest 40 per cent of the population. This was reflected in the improvement in already extremely favourable 'basic needs' indicators (see Table 2.1). Judith Banister, the most respected analyst of China's demography, concluded that between 1981 and 1990, there were 'real improvements in mortality . . . especially for females above infancy and for children of both sexes' (Banister, 1992, p. 12). She notes: 'it is impressive that the rural population of China has experienced measurably lower mortality in only nine years, especially since the Chinese countryside had already achieved rather advanced mortality conditions for a developing country rural area by 1981' (Banister, 1992, p. 12).

Poverty

In China on the eve of the reforms the worst concentrations of poverty were found in the countryside (Table 2.3). A variety of factors combined to produce a remarkable reduction in poverty in the reform period. These included trickle-down from rich regions, explicit government policy to assist poor regions, rapid growth of non-farm employment, and fast income growth in the countryside at large. The World Bank constructed a constant poverty line for China from the later 1970s through

Table 2.2   Changes in the material standard of living in China, 1978–92

	1978	1992
Index of real per capita consumption	100	252
Consumption per capita of:		
grain (kgs)	196	236
edible oil (kgs)	1.6	6.3
pork (kgs)	7.7	18.2
fresh eggs (kgs)	2.0	7.8
sugar (kgs)	3.4	5.4
aquatic products (kgs)	3.5	7.3
cloth (metres)	8.0	10.7
Ownership of consumer durables (no./100 people):		
washing machines	—	10.0
refrigerators	—	3.4
tape recorders	0.2	12.2
cameras	0.5	2.3
TVs	0.3	19.5
sewing machines	3.5	12.8
bicycles	7.7	38.5
radios	7.8	18.4
watches	8.5	51.6 (1990)
Retail outlets and food and drink establishments (no. per 10,000 people):		
establishments	12	101
personnel	57	249
Health provision (no. per 10,000 people):		
hospital beds	19.3	23.4
physicians	10.7	15.4
Housing space per capita (sq. m.)		
cities	3.6	7.5
villages	8.1	20.8

Source: SSB, *ZGTJZY*, 1991, p. 42; SSB, *ZGTJZY*, 1994, pp. 48, 51; SSB, *ZGTJNJ*, 1993, pp. 279, 283–4.

to the late 1980s and estimated that the total number in poverty fell from around 270 million in the late 1970s to around 100 million only one decade later (Table 2.3).[1]

Inequality

Undoubtedly, the growth of market forces produced large new inequalities in China during the reform period. The absolute gap between regions widened. Inequality in some aspects of income distribution did increase

Table 2.3 Poverty in China, 1978–1990 (percentage in brackets)

	1978	1985	1990
Total population (m.)	963	1059	1143
Urban	172 (17.9)	251 (23.7)	302 (26.4)
Rural	790 (82.1)	808 (76.3)	841 (73.6)
Average per capita income (1978 yuan)			
Urban	—	557	685
Rural	134	324	319
Poverty line (current yuan/year)			
Urban	—	215	319
Rural	98	190	275
Incidence of poverty (million)			
Total	270 (28.0)	97 (9.2)	98 (8.6)
Urban	10 (4.4)	1 (0.4)	1 (0.4)
Rural	260 (33.0)	96 (11.9)	97 (11.5)

Source: World Bank, 1992b, p. v.

Notes: After three years of apparent stagnation in real rural per capita consumption, a substantial further growth occurred in 1991 (SSB, *ZGTJZY*, 1992, p. 42). Had the 1991 data been made available to the World Bank, it is likely that there would have been some further reduction reported in rural poverty.

substantially compared to the Maoist period. However, during the reform period, in contrast to most developing countries, China's rural population experienced faster growth of income than did the urban population.[2] During the reform period there occurred a massive, egalitarian land reform. Moreover, the vast bulk of national assets remained in some form of public ownership, with ownership rights residing in the hands of either the central state, the city, the county, or the village community, thereby severely limiting the possibility for wealth accumulation by private individuals. The government at different levels maintained a relatively effective tax system.

Psychology

China experienced around one hundred years of national humiliation, beginning in the 1840s with the Opium Wars, extending through to the chaotic period of the Warlords from 1911 to 1927. For a brief interlude of around ten years (1927–1936) there was some semblance of national progress under the Guomindang (KMT), but the modernisation effort was retarded by the Japanese occupation from 1936 to

1945. In 1949, there was enormous popular enthusiasm for the leadership of the CCP, under whom Mao Tsetung claimed the Chinese people would 'stand up' at last. Despite large achievements, the policies of the CCP produced the disaster of the Great Leap Forward in which as many as 30 million people may have died from starvation and related illness. The Cultural Revolution in the late 1960s and early 1970s brought anarchy to much of the country, damaged the economy and caused great suffering to a large number of people.

The massive success of the economic reforms brought a renewed sense of national pride. The fact that the reform programme was carried out under the communist party, with only gradual change in ideology, produced only a limited sense of mass psychological disorientation.

Human rights

Throughout the reform period China remained a one party, authoritarian state. It also remained one with an extremely tough legal system, with several thousand executions in an average year (Amnesty International, 1987). This presented profound ethical and philosophical dilemmas. There is a spectrum of 'human rights' and it may not be possible simultaneously to achieve improvements in all of them.

If one looks beyond the right to vote in an election, to a wider range of human rights, then the situation in China improved drastically during the reform period (Nolan, 1994a). There was an explosion in the provision of a wide range of 'human rights', including improved health, education, freedom to migrate, huge increases in employment opportunities, better food, clothing, housing and a greatly increased range of cultural products. China's system of basic needs provision had enabled it also to achieve very low death rates for its level of income. By the early 1980s, China's death rate had fallen to an exceptionally low level for a poor country. The decade of economic reform in China saw no trend deterioration in China's exceptionally low death rates (Table 2.4). Indeed, careful analysis by Judith Banister shows that death rates fell for all age groups beyond the age of one (infant mortality rates rose for females for special reasons associated with the 'One Child Family Campaign'), a remarkable achievement for a country with such low death rates as China. Life expectancy rose from an already exceptionally high level for a poor country (Table 2.5).

China's Rise, Russia's Fall

Table 2.4. Crude death rates in China, Russia and selected groups of
countries (no./1000)

	1960	1970	1982	1991	1993	1994
China	10.0	7.6	6.6	6.7	—	—
Russia	7.4*	8.7*	10.5*	11.4	14.4	16.2***
Low income countries**	24	19	16	13	—	—
Middle income countries	17	11	10	8	—	—
High income countries	10	10	9	9	—	—

Sources: Bergson and Levine, Table 3.4; SSB, *ZGTJNJ*, 1992, p. 78; Ellman, 1994;
and World Bank, 1984 and 1993.

Note: *RSFSR
**Excluding China and India
***first quarter

Table 2.5 Life expectancy in selected countries and groups of countries

	1970	1982	1991	1993
Low income countries				
men	46	50	54	
women	47	52	57	
Middle income countries				
men	58	58	65	
women	62	62	71	
High income countries				
men	68	71	73	
women	75	78	80	
China				
men	61	65	67	
women	63	69	71	
Russia				
men	61 (1979–80)	62	63	59
women	73 (1979–80)	74	74	73

Source: World Bank, 1984 and 1993, Ellman, 1993; and *Observer*, 13 March 1994.

2.3   RUSSIA

Output

Soviet economic performance under Gorbachev was poor. After the collapse of the communist government a poor performance turned into a disaster (Table 2.6). The disintegration of the USSR in the late 1980s led to a collapse also of proper statistical reporting. Any estimates are of only the roughest magnitude. Table 2.6 provides an extremely crude view of the picture as portrayed by standard sources. It shows a crisis of massive proportions, comparable in scale to the awful downturn in production in China after the Great Leap Forward.[3] Grigorii Khanin's meticulous estimates show a decline in national income of 34 per cent from 1989 to 1991, which was 'comparable to the decline national income in the United States and Germany during the crisis of 1929–32, which was the worst in the history of capitalism' (Khanin, 1993b, p. 7). However, much worse was in store with a decline in national income of a further 30 per cent in 1992 and 10 per cent or so in 1993 (Table 2.6). Moreover, 'utilised national income' fell by an estimated 40 per cent in 1992 (Khanin, 1993b, 17) as 'enormous inventories' accumulated, with enterprises producing unwanted output to keep afloat. Capital accumulation in Russia collapsed in the early 1990s (Table 2.6).

Furthermore, the decline gathered pace into 1994, with net national product estimated to fall a further 25–27 per cent in 1994 alone (*Transition*, July–August, 1994). Moreoever, due to the disastrous foreign trade performance, the capital stock was unable to modernise quickly through import of foreign technology. While a huge new capital goods industry was growing in China, the capital goods industry in Russia in the early 1990s was simply disappearing. In the single year of 1994 alone it was estimated that output of the Russian machine building industry would fall by 42–45 per cent (*Transition*, July–August, 1994). Because the decline in output had been so large few people imagined that this rate of decline could continue much longer. However, there is no economic law which says it cannot be sustained for a substantial period even beyond this catastrophic fall.

Consumption

Bare statistics fail to capture the massive extent of the dislocation and suffering. Despite the paucity of hard data, it cannot seriously be disputed that for the vast bulk of the population real incomes fell significantly in the late 1980s and drastically in the early 1990s. It is true

Table 2.6. Selected economic indicators for the former USSR (all data are indices at constant prices, except where indication is to the contrary)

	1989	*1990*	*1991*	*1992*	*1993**	*1994**
Net Material product (i)	100	96.0	80.7	64.5*	58.1	48
(ii)**	100	—	66	47	—	—
Gross industrial output	100	98.9	90.9	77.3*	68.0	50
Gross agricultural output	100	97.7	87.9	80.0*	75.2	—
Retail trade turnover	100	110.4	99.4	59.6*	53.6	—
Gross fixed investment	100	101.0	89.2	49.1	—	—
Volume of foreign trade						
Exports	100	86.9	85.2	63.0*	—	—
Imports	100	98.6	90.8	70.8*		—
Foreign trade (index of value in current US$)						
Exports	100	95	72	54	54	47
Imports	—	100	64	58	47	47
Foreign debt (billion $)	60	61	65	76	—	—
Consumer prices (per cent change on previous year)	5.0	8.0	150	2,500*	1,000	—

Notes: *estimates, for Russia only

Source: Economist Intelligence Unit, Country Report, CIS (formerly USSR), no. 4, 1992; United Nations Economic Commission for Europe, 1993; Khanin, 1993b, pp. 7, 12(**); *Transition*, July–August, 1994; Smith New Court, 1994.

that every variety of foreign luxury suddenly was available in the shops, and, of course, one did not need to queue for most of these products. However, simultaneously large falls were taking place in the consumption of most foodstuffs, and consumption of basic non-food items fell even further (see below, Chapter 8). For example, physical output of textiles and shoes fell by around one half or more between 1991 and 1993 (Chapter 8). In the single year of 1992/3 cotton textile output (in square meters) fell by no less than 38 per cent (IMF, 1993, p. 87). In the first half of 1994 output of textiles and shoes fell by a further 'one-third to one half' as the final *coup de grace* was delivered to Russian industry (see Chapter 8). Such devastating declines in output of basic industrial products cannot be consistent with anything other than a very large fall in income for a large proportion of the population. Khanin estimates that personal consumption in 1992 alone fell by over 30 per cent (Khanin, 1993a, p. 17).

Welfare indicators

One of the most important consequences of the economic collapse was the disintegration of the health service, which was already experiencing serious problems in the Gorbachev epoch. This, and the sharp rise in poverty were the factors that caused an 'explosion of morbidity' (Murray Feshbach, quoted in Ellman, 1994). In 1993 it was revealed that alarming increases were occuring in infectious diseases such as measles, whooping cough, tuberculosis, and syphilis (the rise from 1990 to 1993 were 142 per cent, 72 per cent, 34 per cent and 300 per cent respectively) (Ellman, 1994). Large rises were reported also in diptheria, dysentery and typhoid.

Moreover, the breakdown of government was accompanied by a very large increase in crime. Murders rose by a reported 42 per cent in 1992 and a further 60 per cent in the first half of 1993 (Ellman, 1993). Russia's murder rate for the first half of 1993 stood at 25 per 100,000 people placing it firmly in the category of 'high homicide' countries, with rates well above most other 'high homicide' countries – countries such as Mexico (20 per 100,000) and Brazil (15 per 100,000) (Ellman, 1994).

Psychology

The consequences of the collapse are not just economic. It involved too, the deepest sense of national humiliation in this country which for most of the twentieth century considered itself to be the leader of the world's socialist nations.

The sharpest change in social values occurred in a breathtakingly short time, away from collectivism and egalitarianism to rampant individualism. It was widely observed that for most ex-Soviet citizens their sense of 'social coherence' had been smashed. A nationwide condition of *anomie* was brought into existence with a complete absence of reference points for the individual psyche.

The sense of personal uncertainty greatly increased, especially because the changes since the mid-1980s occurred against a background of extremely high levels of security about most fundamentals, such as employment, personal safety, education, health and housing. The mood of national despondency and humiliation in the late 1980s and early 1990s was comparable to that of the 'three dark years' in China in the early 1960s.

Poverty

A mass of evidence supports the conclusion that, for a large fraction of the population, probably well over one-half, the period since the late Gorbachev years has seen a serious deterioration in living standards, alongside a large rise in income for a small fraction of the population. One serious, though extremely rough, estimate was carried out by Russian Statistical Office (Goskomstat) together with the World Bank to estimate the level of poverty in Russia in 1992–3. In this study, 'poverty' was defined as an income which would allow a level of food consumption adequate to maintain a normal body weight at an average level of activity. It suggested that around 37 per cent of the Russian population was now living in poverty (quoted in Ellman, 1994). The situation was worse for children. In 1992 46–47 per cent of all children below the age of 15 were living in poverty (Ellman, 1994). An estimate of poverty by the Living Standard Centre of the Russian Ministry of Labour, using a somewhat lower poverty line, calculated that 29.4 per cent of the population was living in poverty in the fourth quarter of 1993. However, it showed a frighteningly rapid deterioration of the situation in 1994, as the proportion of the population in poverty rose to 30.7 per cent and then again to 38.5 per cent in succesive quarters (*Transition*, July–August, 1994).

An important aspect of the impoverishment was the deterioration in diet. In 1992, according to household budget surveys by Goskomstat, the consumption of meat and meat products fell by 11 per cent, of milk and milk products by 16 per cent, of fish by 19 per cent, of vegetables by 10 per cent and fruits and berries by 15 per cent. On the other hand, the consumption of bread rose by 3 per cent and potatoes by 9 per cent (quoted in Ellman, 1994).[4]

Inequality

Alongside the spiralling collapse there took place a massive redistribution of income and wealth. It is frequently the case that when disastrous collapses of output occur, such as in wartime, the hardship is shared relatively equally through rationing and direct state controls over production to ensure that basic needs are met for the poorest members of society. In the early 1990s in Russia the reverse happened. The dramatically declining average income was distributed grotesquely unequally.

In the chaotic economy of the early 1990s Soviet citizens had vastly different capacities, related to age, political position and connections, and initial capital endowments, to benefit from the 'privatisation' of assets: in just two years, the vast bulk of state assets was 'privatised' under lawless conditions. This was the process of 'primitive capital accumulation', which in the West took place over centuries, being conducted at the highest possible speed. A new 'aristocracy', often building on the old positions of power under the communist party, was created at high speed, rapidly accumulating a large share of the newly 'privatised' assets. The situation was analogous to a famine. Poorer people disposed of assets, however pathetic these might be, at a high rate in order to survive. This led to a decline in their real price, enabling those who possessed financial resources to accumulate resources at an especially fast rate.

Income distribution shifted at high speed. According to the journal *Trud*, the ratio of the income of the top decile to that of the bottom decile was in the order of 1:5.4 in 1991, and had risen to 1:8.0 by the end of 1992 (result quoted in Weir, 1993, p. 2813). The Russian Centre of Living Standards concluded that the growth rate of inequality was sharply accelerating in 1993–4 alongside the further stage of economic collapse. It concluded that there was a 'dramatic increase in the purchasing capacity of the wealthier strata of the population', alongside 'even further decline' in that of the poorer segments of the population. They estimated that the ratio of the income of the top decile to the bottom decile had risen at an alarmingly rapid pace, from 1:9.0 in the first quarter of 1994 to 1:13.0 in the second quarter (*Transition*, July–August 1994).

Human rights

While China's economic prosperity and widening process of marketisa-
tion was steadily leading to the inexorable democratisation of daily life
under the umbrella of one party rule, Russia's disastrous economic
performance continued simultaneously with a slide back towards authoritarianism. If one constructs a balance sheet of 'human rights', then
one has to offset the fact that Soviet citizens gained the right to vote
and to speak freely, against the huge deterioration in other 'human
rights' for most people, including the right to live safely, to employment, to decent food, to a decent education, housing and health service. Moreover, there was a hugely unequal capacity to benefit from
the new 'negative' freedoms (e.g., freedom of speech, freedom to accumulate capital), as were gained after the mid-1980s.

An alarming rise in death rates was the most powerful symbol of
the deterioration in human rights under Soviet and post-Soviet reform.
In the early 1960s the USSR stood proudly as a country with one of
the lowest death rates in the world. By the late 1970s the USSR's had
begun to rise ominously, reflecting mainly an increase in death rates
among working age males. By the late 1980s, Russia's death rate had
risen above the level for middle income countries. However, the most
remarkable development was to occur in the post-Soviet period. By
1993 Russia's death rate had risen above even the level of low income
countries (Table 2.4). Russia's death rate now stood on a par with that
of such countries as Bangladesh, Nigeria, Sudan and Togo,[5] a dreadful
testimony to the awful results of the reform process.

The human right to employment was eroded rapidly. Already in July
1994 the number of unemployed was estimated at around 10 million,
or 13 per cent of the economically active population (*Transition*, July–
August, 1994). If bankruptcy provisions were strictly applied, then it
estimated that around 5 million more would overnight become unemployed (*Transition*, July–August,1994). However, the concept of 'unemployment' was rapidly losing meaning. A large porportion of those
'employed' in the state sector were receiving no pay for long periods
on end. The real value of government unemployment pay was falling
rapidly alongside the collapse in real government expenditure. Fewer
and fewer unemployed people were bothering to register as unemployed.
As in the Third World, there was a rapidly rising 'informal' sector in
which a large proportion of the 'self employed' worked at any kind of
'business' however low the returns per hour. Far from heralding excit-
ing new opportunities and signalling income growth, the explosion of
these forms of informal sector 'service' activities reflected rapidly grow-

ing poverty and a drastic shrinkage of full-time employment opportunities in the formal sector.

2.4 CONCLUSION

The contrast in performance that accompanied the reforms in these two countries could not be greater. The impact on the daily life of the citizens of the two countries was dramatically different. The contrast is all the more striking because it was not predicted by anyone, least of all the leaders who initiated the reforms. Neither the speeches of Gorbachev in mid-1986, nor those of Deng Xiaoping in late 1978, when the two reform programmes began in earnest, anticipated this extraordinary outcome. Nor did any foreign social scientists predict this result.

What caused this dramatic and unpredicted contrast? The literature on the subject is still painfully thin, in part of course because the experience is so recent. In part also, however, this may be because of the discomfort caused by the role played by foreign advisors in each case. In the Soviet case, their influence was intially indirect, but still important. The direct influence rose steadily over time. In the Chinese case, foreign advice was accepted only selectively. China's reform programme was largely shaped despite, not because, of foreign advice.

The main line of argument that has been advanced to explain the contrast has been to suggest that the prinicipal reason for the contrast lies not in the policies themselves, but, rather, in the different starting point from which the reforms proceeded. The main foreign advisors to the Russian government have exhibited no humility in respect to their contribution to the disaster that has befallen that country. One imagines that they would have been pleased to take the credit if their policies had brought success, rather than to attribute the succes to the underlying conditions. Notable among the advisors is Anders Aslund, advisor to both Gorbachev and Yeltsin. He was asked in late 1992 as the disaster was unfolding, whether he 'would do anything different now'. He answered: 'Not really. I have been in favour all along of a very liberal solution for Russia. And the failures suggest that one has to go in a more liberal direction, as quickly as possible' (*Transition*, November, 1992, p. 5).

The rest of this book attempts to indentify the degree to which the contrast in outcome was attributable to policy choice and how far to the underlying conditions of politics and economics inherited by the reforming governments.

3 The Need for Reform of the Chinese and Soviet Systems of Political Economy

3.1 INTRODUCTION

It might be thought odd to write a chapter such as this. There are two reasons for doing so. The central theme of this book is the shortcomings of the orthodox approach to reform of the communist system of political economy. I wish to make it unambiguously clear that I am not implying that the alternative was remaining with the Stalinist system. It needed fundamental reform both in China and in the USSR. The question is not 'whether' but 'how' and 'towards what'? Many of those who opposed the wild stampede to the free market in Russia had no illusions about the communist system. Indeed, among the most vociferous critics of the Russian reform strategy were people who had been sentenced to internal exile for opposition to the Stalinist system.

There was a small but significant group of critics of the path of transition in both countries, who did, indeed, believe, that the communist system of political economy needed only tinkering with in order to produce greatly improved results. One such thesis was that greater 'pressure' of the 'Andropov' type would be able to improve substantially the performance of the system. Another was that limited introduction of market forces would be sufficient to improve substantially the performance of the system. Indeed, there still is a remnant of analysts who believe that the Soviet and Chinese path under communism was superior to that under any sort of market system. This chapter disputes the validity of these approaches.

24

3.2 POLITICS

3.2.1 Similarities

Internal party organisation

The key features of centralised Party organisation had been established in the former USSR during the War Communism period (1917–21) under a *de facto* monopoly of political power exercised by the communist party. They were further reinforced during the key period of transition from War Communism to New Economic Policy.

Simultaneously with the introduction of the market-oriented measures of NEP, a sequence of measures was adopted by the Bolshevik leadership which greatly strengthened both the degree of centralisation of Party organisation and its dominant position in society. Dissemination of a separate programme of a group within the Party, such as the 'Workers' Opposition' which had criticised the Bolshevik leadership, was declared incompatible with party membership. 'Factionalism', or the adoption of a separate 'platform' within the party, was banned. Once a Party decision had been adopted, members were obliged to give unconditional obedience to it. An inner core of party leaders, the Politburo, was established. E.H. Carr comments: 'It seemed necessary and reasonable at the time . . . but the vesting of what was in effect a monopoly of power in the [central organisation] of the party was to have far-reaching consequences'(Carr, 1979, p. 34).

By the start of the NEP period in the USSR the characteristic features of the communist party dictatorship had been established and were to be replicated in China, with the establishment of its own communist party in 1921. In each case after the revolution the communist party remained a small 'vanguard' party with a monopoly of political power. Even after its large expansion after the death of Stalin, the Russian Communist Party in the late 1970s still was composed of only around sixteen million people, or about 6 per cent of the total population. In China in the early 1970s, the party was even smaller in relative terms, amounting to just 3 per cent of China's huge population. In absolute numbers it was huge, totalling 28 million members in 1977. In both cases, the communist party penetrated deep into the formal apparatus of state at every level, including the legislature, the bureaucracy, the armed forces and the judiciary. The party's unassailed leading position was formalised in both countries in successive constitutions:

The Communist Party of China is the core of leadership of the whole Chinese people. The working class exercises leadership over the state through its vanguard, the Communist Party of China. (*Constitution of the People's Republic of China*, 1975, article 2)

The Communist Party of the Soviet Union is the leading and the guiding force of Soviet society and the nucleus of its political system, of all state and public organisation.... The Communist Party armed with Marxism–Leninism, determines the general perspectives of the development of society and the course of the home and foreign policy of the USSR, directs the great construction work of the Soviet people, and imparts a planned, systematic and theroretically substantiated character to their struggle for the victory of communism. (*Rules of the Communist Party of the Soviet Union*, 1961, Preamble)

Party and society

It is hard to dispute the use of the term 'totalitarian' to describe the political structure of the USSR and China prior to the respective modern reform movements. The communist party in both cases stood at the centre of the whole socio-economic system from the highest to the lowest levels:

The key to the operation of the system ... was the crucial role of the Party. Authority and power were effectively concentrated in the Party as an institution, and it was able to exercise firm control over the entire system. Consisting of a carefully recruited, thoroughly indoctrinated, and highly disciplined elite, the Party penetrated every area of the country and every sector of society, down to the lowest grassroots level, and at every level its authority as the ultimate center for decision making was unchallenged. (Barnett, 1974, p. 37)

The extent of socio-economic control was greater than that excercised under most late twentieth century dictatorships, most of which are more accurately described as 'authoritarian' rather than 'totalitarian'.

War was important in both China and the USSR in shaping the evolution of internal Party oganisation as well as the Party's relationship to society. During the civil war in Russia (1917–1921), restrictions on civil liberties and political rights had been tolerated in the interests of achieving military success. However, the conclusion of hostilities resulted in an outpouring of opposition to the Bolshevik rule, which crystallised in the Kronstadt uprising of 1921. The Kronstadt revolutionaries attacked the socio-political nature of the regime from a left perspective:

> In making the October Revolution, the sailors and Red soldiers, the workers and peasants spilled their blood for the power of the soviets, for the creation of a toilers' Republic . . . The Communists first removed from power the socialists of other tendencies; then they pushed the workers and peasants themselves from the helm of the ship of state, all the while continuing to rule the country in their name. . . . [T]he Bolsheviks proceeded to nationalise the factories and shops. From a slave of the capitalist the worker was transformed into a slave of state enterprises. . . . The whole labouring peasantry was declared the enemy and identified with the kulaks. . . . The life of the citizen became hopelessly monotonous and routine. One lived according to the timetables established by the powers that be. Such is the shining kingdom of socialism to which the dictatorship of the Communist Party has brought us. We have obtained state socialism with soviets of functionaries who vote obediently according to the dictates of the party committees and its infallible commissars . . . ('Socialism in quotation marks', March 16 1921, translated in Avrich, 1970, p. 244).

The response of the Bolshevik leadership was to supress the uprising brutally.[1] The political consequences were huge. They included the banning of all other political parties. After a period of relative relaxation of Party control during the middle of NEP, the shift in the second half of NEP towards increased use of the command mechanism in economics and the gradual imposition of control over 'petty capitalist' elements, was accompanied by a simultaneous tightening up of Party control over society: 'The year 1928, which followed the defeat of the opposition, and was marked by the growing pressures of industrialisation, witnessed throughout the Soviet society the imposition from above of a powerful and despotic authority, of a rigid orthodoxy of opinion, and of the harshest penalties against those who offended against it' (Carr, 1979, p. 122).

The basic principles of the Chinese Communist Party's relationship with society were laid down during the long struggle in the revolutionary base areas before the completion of the revolution, with much input from Soviet party ideology. The classic statement on these issues still remains Liu Shaoqi's speech of 1945, 'On the Party', which outlined the way in which Party members should lead the mass of the population in the struggle to create a better society:

> Only under the firm and correct leadership of our Party and only by carrying on the struggle on the political lines laid down by our Party can the Chinese people achieve their complete emancipation. . . . [T]he vanguard of the masses must establish proper and close relations with the masses. . . . [S]ome comrades yielded to the backward ideas of the masses and reduced themselves to the level of an ordinary worker, a peasant or even a backward element, thus abandoning their vanguard role. . . . The task of leaders and leading bodies is to exercise correct leadership, have a correct idea of the situation, grasp its essence, set forth the tasks, make decisions, and mobilise and organise the masses to carry out these decisions and supervise the work. (Liu Shaoqi, 1945, pp. 206–26).

In both China and the USSR, tight Party control over socio-economic affairs had intrinsic negative consequences as well as negative economic results.

In both the USSR and China under communism, the attempt to 'emancipate all mankind and bring humanity into a world of happiness, radiating with beauty such as it has never known before' (Liu Shaoqi, 1939, section 5), produced great personal suffering for large numbers of people at the hands of the Communist Party. These ranged from tight cultural controls, so that the diversity of freedom of expression was dramatically reduced compared to capitalist society, to widespread persecution of political opponents and the incarceration of large numbers of people in prison camps, often under awful conditions, to periodic large scale executions for 'political crimes'. Mao Zedong put the position clearly in 1949, on the eve of the founding of the People's Republic of China:

> 'You are dictatorial'. My dear sirs, you are right, that is just what we are. [The people], led by the working class and Communist Party, unite to form their own state and elect their own government; they enforce their dictatorship over the running dogs of imperialism – suppress them, allow them only to behave themselves and not to be unruly in word or deed. If they speak of act in an unruly way they will be promptly stopped and punished. (Mao Zedong, 1949)

Under communism in both China and the USSR the stultifying uniformity of 'socialist realism' was imposed on all forms of culture, reaching its greatest intensity during the Chinese Cultural Revolution, when only a tiny range of plays, art, films, and music, was deemed politically acceptable. Despite the post-Stalinist 'thaw', Soviet culture throughout the communist years followed a similar line, the fundamental position being that laid down by Zhdanov in his famous speech to the first All-Union Congress of Soviet Writers in 1934:

> Under the leadership of the Party, with the thoughtful and daily guidance of the Central Committee and the untiring support and help of comrade Stalin, a whole army of Soviet writers has rallied round the Soviet power and the Party. . . . Comrade Stalin has called our writers engineers of human souls. What does this mean? What duties does the title confer upon you?. . . . [T]he truthfulnes and historical concreteness of the artistic portrayal should be combined with ideological remoulding and education of the toiling peoples in the spirit of socialism. This is what we call the method of socialist realism. (Zhdanov, 1934)

In the 1970s it was estimated that there still were around 70,000 people in the USSR who were employed under the Central Comittee in censorship (Lane, 1978, p. 259).

In both countries a *samzidat* culture survived which was deeply critical of the Party-imposed uniformity. It could be seen in the form of the content of public works whose real essence escaped the censor, such as the desparate intensity of the music of Shostakovich. It sprang to life at the slightest sign of relaxation, as in the *glasnost* movement in the USSR in the late 1980s, and in the thaw in the late 1980s in China, out of which sprang the democracy wall movement:

> Whoever has lived in China under the dictatorship of the proleteriat and who is at the same time willing to examine carefully the thinking and spiritual condition of the people, will certainly feel most acutely the turbidity and oppressiveness, the quite suffocating atmosphere. The people have been cut off from the outside world for years, cut off from history and no-one is allowed to think freely. From the cradle to the grave, people are only allowed to believe- indeed must believe in one 'ism'. All else is criminal except to read the one type of philosophy, to laud one type of system, to fawn on one leader and to curry favour with one political philosophy. . . . How can [China's youths] understand human life and the world we

live in with its boundless variety? Even the cut of one's clothes, the tunes of songs, the contents of books, the time and place of one's romantic liasons are all monopolised by the CCP and made the subject of regulations. . . . The scars left by a forcible education in Marxism Leninism's great unity are evident in every debate, every argument and every attempt to be serious on the part of Chinese youth. ('What are the implication of China's democratic experiment?', May, 1979[2]) (quoted in Goodman, 1981, p. 134)

Much more serious than the cultural unformity of totalitarianism, was the physical persecution of a huge number of people in both countries. A succession of 'rectification' movements occurred in China both before and after the revolution, each of which resulted in great suffering for those labeled as class enemies. The families of those who were labelled as 'bad elements' were discriminated against in innumerable ways. During the cultural revolution, political struggle intensified, and it is thought that 'hundreds of thousands of people' died as a direct result of this movement (Rodzinski, 1988, p. 127). However, the scale of suffering in Maoist China as a result of direct brutality by the state was much less than that experienced in the USSR under Stalin.

In the USSR during collectivisation, around five million *kulaks* and their families were deported to prison camps. One recent estimate is that as many as eleven million people may have died as a result of collectivisation, either directly through execution, but more typically through death in the harsh conditions the prison camps to which they were sent (Conquest, 1986, p. 306). During the Great Purge of 1936–8, as many as eight million people may well have been sentenced and imprisoned for 'political crimes' (Lane, 1978, p. 74). The size of the prison camps shrunk drastically after the death of Stalin. However, on the eve of Gorbachev's accession to power many people still languished in the Soviet gulag: Amnesty International estimated the number of 'prisoners of conscience' to be around 10,000 (Lane, 1978, p. 269).

Many of the political dissidents in both countries were subjected to a variety of lesser, but still serious, penalties, including demotion, transfer to distant places to work, humiliation and criticism from party cadres in their place of work, poor housing allocation, and social stigmatism for their family.

In both countries political rule by the highly centralised communist party had strong negative economic results. The system had the capacity to make large errors. This stemmed from the absence of a framework of wide discussion among independent experts, and the existence of a large capacity to issue orders centrally which affected the economy. The most important examples of such policies were the Soviet collectivisation campaign and the Chinese campaign in 1958 to undertake a 'Great Leap Forward'. These both resulted in disastrous declines in output. Moreover, the ill-effects of the output collapse were compounded in both cases by extreme government secretiveness to the outside world about the extent of the consequent agricultural problems. In both cases massive loss of life stemmed from these policy-induced errors. In the Soviet case, the famine caused as many as seven million 'excess deaths' (Conquest, 1986, p. 306). In China's famine, the figure may have been as high as 30 million 'excess deaths' (Banister, 1987, p. 85). Much the most severe famines of the twentieth century have occurred in communist countries. Without these famines, the century would have a witnessed a steady decline in the total loss of life due to famine as a result of growth in the stability of farm output, growth of incomes in poor countries, and large improvements in transportation and communications (Nolan, 1993c).

A less dramatic but still important impact of the totalitarian political system upon the economic performance of China and the USSR was the tight constraints on the range of discussion among economists. Under Stalin and for long periods in Maoist China, the 'liquidationist' view of economics under 'socialism' was dominant. In this perspective, the advent of 'socialism' eliminated the need for 'economics'. Planning was thought to be able to allocate resources without reference to the fundamental concepts of economics, such as price, costs of production and profits: the science of 'collectively organised production' was thought to have replaced 'the theory of political economy' (*Novaya ekonomica*, Moscow, 1926, quoted in Nove, 1968, p. 302).

After Stalin's death and in those brief periods in Maoist China when more liberal attitudes prevailed, economists were able to investigate a much wider range of ideas. These incorporated many concepts from market economies under the heading the 'law of value', which encompassed all those concepts associated with exchange relationships. Economists such as Liberman, Nemchimov and Novozhilov in the USSR, or Sun Yefang, Chen Yun, and Dong Fureng in China, opened up new avenues in analysing the economic problems of the communist countries, using concepts close to those used by economists in capitalist economies (Nove, 1968, Chapter 11, and Lin, 1981). However, even in the periods of greatest liberalism, economists in the communist countries still operated under tight Party control in their institutions, with their work vetted by Party cadres. Moreoever, the overall framework of thought still was tightly circumscribed by a basic commitment to the 'planned' economy and public ownership of the means of production.

Much of the most creative work in the USSR was devoted to attempting to simulate the market, endeavouring to calculate resource allocations using shadow prices, rather than devising ways of introducing a real market economy with genuine competition. In both China and the USSR the most advanced thinkers were not permitted to go beyond conceiving of reforms in terms of the provision of greater initiative for enterprises within a closely circumscribed framework of 'planning' and public ownership. A typical formulation is that of Kashin, the Soviet economist, who spoke of a new environment with 'a plan providing just a frame, a kind of crystalline grill for the national economy, which offered enough space for the deployment of free initiative by enterprises, workmen, collectives, and localities, [such initiatives] flowing freely betwen the economic partitions which remain centrally planned'(quoted in Lewin, 1975, p. 166). Moreover, even the most creative work, such as that of Liberman (1971) still required a constant reference to the Marxist classics as the analytical framework and for the language in which economic issues were discussed.

Economists in neither pre-reform China nor the USSR developed skills in controlling the movement of a market economy. Practical economics was closer to accountancy than to economics as understood in the West. Indeed, for ten years in the USSR (1931–1941), the Central Statistical Office was renamed the Central Office of National Accounting, because "statistics" was 'regarded as a word suggestive of the measurement of random, haphazard events, and therefore unsuitable for a planned economy' (Nove, 1968, p. 302). Moreoever, 'political economy' was simply the teaching virtually by rote of selected aspects of Marx and Lenin. It was the most boring and least developed aspect of economics. Thus, the economics profession of the communist giants came to the reform both singularly ill-equipped for the analysis of the complex tasks of political economy and applied economics which would lie at the core of devising a successful economic reform strategy.

A further problem stemming from the nature of the political system was the large power granted to the Party committee in enterprises in both town and country. The promotion of Party cadres in both cases depended only partially on technical abilities. Therefore, in both systems a wide range of decisions was affected by Party members who lacked the appropriate technical capacities.

3.2.2 Differences

In the USSR the most extreme period of inner-Party struggle and Party-led violence towards the non-Party population occurred under Stalin. After his death the CPSU formally accepted that class struggle had ended in the Soviet Union. The political system moved towards increased pragmatism, routinisation, and steady progress towards the emergence of a better educated, technocratic elite. The ten years preceding the reform in China witnessed the utmost political turbulence. It is difficult for those who now do business in China, and those who only recently have gained acquaintance with China, to realise the full extent of the political storm that shook China for the ten years of the Cultural Revolution.

Mao used his immense personal power to launch a massive attack on the apparatus of Party and government:

> Mao believed that representatives of the bourgeoisie, called counter-revolutionary revisionists, had infiltrated the Party, the administration, the army and academic circles in large numbers. This meant that the leadership in a majority of organisations was no longer in the hands of Marxists and of the people. . . . Mao believed that the power of those with capitalist tendencies could be recaptured only by carrying out a great cultural revolution, by publicly and unequivocally encouraging a mass movement from below to expose the dangers threatening socialism. (Zong Huaiwen, 1989, p. 127)

Massive nationwide turmoil resulted as millions of Red Guards swept the country, attacking the authorities at every level. Local government disintegrated as 'revolutionary seizures of power' took place all over the country. Enterprise management was overturned and revolutionary committees replaced them:

> The nation was in chaos. By early 1967 nearly all Party and government organisations had been deprived of their power or drastically reorganised. Public security agencies, the procuratorates and the courts ceased to operate, while violence and civil strife ravaged the country. Production in factories, mines and other enterpises crawled to a halt, and communications and transportation systems were seriously interrupted. (Zong Huaiwen, 1989, p. 141)

Eventually order was restored through the Army, and slowly in the early 1970s, the Party apparatus was reconstructed. Unlike the Great Purges of the USSR under Stalin, Mao's attack on the Party and government was an attack on the basic institutions themselves: 'Where else had a supreme leader of a revolution not only purged the majority of his former colleagues, but also incited sweeping attacks on the basic structures of a regime that he himself had done so much to conceive and build?' (Barnett, 1974, p. 39). Recovery from the disruptions of the 1966–68 period were painfully slow. Writing in 1974, Doak Barnett commented: 'conditions of instability may continue for some years . . . China still has some way to go before it can achieve a degree of insitutional cohesion comparable to that of the pre-1965 period' (Barnett, 1974, p. 36).

The economic consequences of the Cultural Revolution were large, and ranged far beyond the short-term disruption of production. The drastic attack on the Party and administrative structure played a large part in causing the policy of local 'self-reliance'. To a large degree, there was little option, since the capacity to co-ordinate economic activities had been reduced to little more than an ability to arrange interprovincial transfers of major commodities. The Cultural Revolution raised the cult of personality to new heights. Even more than in the USSR under Stalin, scientific work was guided by the 'thoughts' of the leader.

The effect on economics was devastating (see, especially, the account in Lin, 1981). In the early phase of the Cultural Revolution, the attack on economics focussed on the Economics Research Institute (Chinese Academy of Social Sciences), which was labelled as a 'bourgeois domain'. The attack widened to include the economists and planners in government departments at all levels: 'The government planning and management machinery ceased to function when their personnel were dispersed to the countryside for reform-through-labour and "criticism–struggle–transformation" exercises, and planning became pretend-planning' (Lin, 1981, p. 36). Economics only began to recover in the late 1970s after the fall of the Gang of Four. One perceptive account has argued that during the decade of the Cultural Revolution China remained fundamentally committed to the Stalinist planning system, but ideology (e.g. the attack on material incentives and the profit criterion) and shortage of personnel meant that the Stalinist material balance operated even less well than in the pre-reform USSR.

In the USSR during Stalin's 'mass attack on the party' the whole swathe of the top leadership, and indeed the lower levels of leadership, was executed by Stalin. Of 1,961 members at the seventeenth Party Congress of the CPSU 1934, no less than 1,108 were arrested on charges of 'counter-revolutionary crimes' (Schapiro, 1970, p. 421), and 'tens if not hundreds of thousands' of Party members were arrested during the Great Purges of 1936–8 (Schapiro, 1970, p. 420), of whom a substantial proportion died in the *gulag*. Of the 139 members of the Central Committee of 1934, it is probable that 98 were arrested and executed (Schapiro, 1970, p. 420): 'between them they represented a substantial concentration of power within the party apparatus, in the national economy, in the government apparatus and in the army' (Schapiro, 1970, p. 420).

Many of China's leading political figures died during the course of the Cultural Revolution, including Lin Biao, Zhou Enlai and Liu Shaoqi.[3] However, in the sharpest contrast to Stalin's 'assault on the party', in China's Cultural Revolution, despite the great violence and suffering, the bulk of the first generation of local and national leaders was not executed. Zhou Enlai estimated that the Cultural Revolution had resulted in the 'permanent ousting' of only one per cent of the total party membership (Barnett, 1974, p. 56), and most of the key national figures who had opposed Mao, such as Deng Xiaoping, Chen Yun, and Tan Zhenlin, survived the Cultural Revolution, and returned to positions of power even before Mao died (Barnett, 1974, p. 57). China's capacity to reintegrate villified leaders into the national leadership continues to the present day, with the tentative re-emergence of Zhao Ziyang onto the political scene in 1994. Zhao had been attacked heavily by the Party leadership during the Tiananmen demonstration, and appeared to have departed from the political stage permanently.

3.3 ECONOMICS

3.3.1 Fundamental problems of the Stalinist command economy

From the late 1920s to the mid-1980s, the Soviet economy was run along non-market lines with the whole economy 'planned' as a single factory. The Chinese economy followed the Soviet pattern closely. The basic stuctures of the command economy were set up during the First Five Year Plan (1953–7) under Soviet tutelage. In both economies, the vast bulk of industrial assets was nationalised and most rural assets were transformed into either state or collective ownership. 'Collectives' were far removed from genuinely co-operative forms of ownership. Prices quickly came to be set almost entirely by bureaucrats. At the heart of the system was a comprehensive material balance supply system, which controlled the allocation of all major products.

The classic statement of the goals of communist 'planning' is found in the *ABC of Communism*, by Bukharin and Preobrazhensky, published in Russia in 1920:

> The basis of communist society must be the social ownership of the means of production and exchange. All these means of production must be under the control of society as a whole, and not as at present under the control of individual capitalists or capitalist combines. . . . In these circumstances society will be transformed into one huge organisation for cooperative production. There will be neither disintegration of production nor anarchy of production. In such a social order, production will be organised. No longer will one enterprise compete with another; the factories, workshops, mines and other productive institutions will all be subdivisions, as it were of one vast people's workshop, which will embrace the entire national economy. (Bukharin and Preobrazhensky, 1969, p. 114)

During the War Communist period in the former USSR (1917–1921) the first example of a nationalised command economy was put into place. The system was hailed by most Soviet economists as a desirable system in its own right, not simply as a system that might enable the fledgling Soviet state to survive a desparate civil war. Larin, a leading member of the Supreme Council of the National Economy, wrote in 1920 while this transformation was under way:

> With the socialised organisation of production – and to the extent of its realisation – an ever greater naturalisation of the national economy as a whole will unavoidably occur. Above all the transition will take place from an uncertain market to a socially recorded production 'on order'. . . . [T]he various branches of the national economy will work according to a uniform plan, centrally determined and coordinated in all its details. . . . [E]very enterprise in these economic branches is now owned by a single proprietor: the state. These branches now all become, as it were, plants or workshops of the same enterprise, and within this enterprise there is no place either for 'the spontaneous play of blind economic forces' of the old bourgeois society, or for commercial relations between individual workshops. (Quoted in Szamuely, 1974, p. 37)

The adjective 'planned' is inappropriate to describe the Stalinist system of state ownership and commands deriving from the construction of material balances. Rather, the system was an 'administered', an 'instruction' or a 'command' rather than a 'planned' economy (see especially, Zaleski, 1980). The central elements of 'planning' are 'looking ahead', 'co-ordination', and 'the attainment of deliberate aims' (Tinbergen, 1964, p. 44). A key goal in the construction of the communist planning system was the attempt to overcome the anarchy of the market. The competitive struggle for profit under capitalism resulted in dominance of the profit motive over human being's lives. This was so both in a simple economic sense, with an inability to produce socially agreed outcomes such as full employment and sustained steady growth, and in a deeper sense of the creation of a corresponding culture geared to selling for profit rather than production for human fulfillment. The desire to overcome this 'alienation' of people from their true 'species being' as purposive producers (*homo faber*) was a central motive in the heroic attempt to construct a 'planned' economy in the Soviet Union. In March 1926, the Soviet economist Pyatokov described the beginnings of 'planning' in the following terms:

> We are setting ourselves a task, we deliberately depict a model of industry to ourselves as we want it, so that it may be brought into existence; in other words, we set ourselves a definite purpose and a task dictated by our will; *we free ourselves to a considerable extent from the clutches of what is given by history*; we break the old bounds and gain a considerably greater creative freedom. (Quoted in Carr and Davies, 1969, p. 840) (Emphasis added)

A great paradox of the 'planned' economy in China and the USSR is that the system of commands issued to enterprises failed to establish an economy which was any less anarchic and therefore any less alienating. As under capitalism human activity created the economic system. At least as much as under capitalist competition the system that people themselves had created exercised control over them. It remained, in a fundamental sense, anarchic. Kritsman recognised this possibility very early on in the 'planning' process:

> In our proletarian-natural economy exploitation and the market were overcome without overcoming the anarchy of economic life. . . . *As is well known, commodity economy is anarchic economy. It would be incorrect, however, to conclude, from this that a non-commodity economy, i.e. a natural economy, is necessarily a non-anarchical*

economy. . . . For an economy to be anarchic it necessary and sufficient for there to be a multiplicity of (independent) economic subjects (Kritsman, 1924, quoted in Ellman, pp. 47–8). (Emphasis added)

The problems of the state administered economic system have now been widely documented, and it is possible to realise just how perceptive Kritsman's comments were. Instead of working as a 'team' pulling towards common goals, agents at different levels of the 'planning' system struggled to maximise individual self-interest and failed to provide truthful information to higher levels of the 'planning' system. In the absence of market information the task of checking the information provided by agents at each level became impossibly complex. Moreover, even if all agents had provided planners with truthful information, the iterations and feedback effects involved in constructing a material balance plan were impossibly complex.[4] Consequently, as is well known, the administratively 'planned' economy had built into it permanent imbalance of supply and demand (see e.g. Kornai, 1980). As Shmelyev and Popov expressed it:

In an economy with rigidly planned proportions, . . . production disproportions and shortages on the one hand and overproduction on the other . . . are not the exception but the rule – an everyday reality, a governing law. The absolute majority of goods is either in short supply or in surplus. Quite often the same product is in both categories – there is a shortage in one region and a surplus in another. But the needed amount is almost never present in the needed region in the needed amount. (Shmelyev and Popov, 1990, p. 89)

The resulting systemic shortcomings have been analysed in a wide array of sources. A high degree of self-sufficiency was produced at every level of the system: 'Our factories have turned into the most "all purpose", the most unspecialised. Striving to have everything at hand and not depend on producers for trifles, the directors of enterprises "naturalise" their economic operations. . . . It is much easier . . . to produce the needed nuts oneself than to arrange for their delivery from specialised factories that are often non-existent' (Shmelyev and Popov, 1990, p. 118).

The system resulted in a pervasive tendency towards hoarding, with a vicious circle of 'suction' and hoarding feeding off each other in an atmosphere of great uncertainty about supplies of intermediate inputs (for the classic analysis, see Kornai, 1980). The advanced capitalist economies were reducing inventories per unit of final product, culminating in 'just-in-time' supplies of needed inputs. The Soviet economy experienced rising stocks of inventories per unit of final product: by the end of 1985 it was reported that inventories in the sphere of material production amounted to no less than 90 per cent of the national income produced in that year (Shmelyev and Popov, 1990, p. 133). In China in 1980 it was reported that the value of stockpiles of machinery and equipment was greater than that year's total capital construction investment, and almost a full year's supply of steel had been produced in unneeded varieties (Riskin, 1987, p. 172).

The system produced little interest among producers in the usefulness of their output. The pervasive atmosphere of shortage meant that there existed a seller's market for a large proportion of output. Specification of output targets in simple physical terms led to a pervasive tendency towards the narrowing of product range towards those products which were easiest to produce. Thus, the mix of consumer goods notoriously failed to respond to consumer signals and there was a high rate of breakdowns of consumer durables. The real welfare provided by a given bundle of consumer goods was much less than might have been the case under competitive conditions. Moreover, throughout the system, capital goods were unsuitable to the task for which they were supplied and/or broke down frequently.

A deep paradox for 'planners' and policy makers in the communist countries was that, far from overcoming the key shortcomings of the capitalist system, the communist 'planned' economy produced many of these shortcomings in an even more acute form. Far from abolishing waste it produced waste on a grand scale. It abolished production for profit but was unable to replace it with production for use. It abolished the short-termism produced by competitive capitalism but substituted for this an even more profound short-termism of current plan fulfillment. It steered economic activity in directions that were widely acknowledged as being socially undesirable, but was unable to shift away from this pattern of economic behaviour. In sum, it was a system that was more 'anarchic' than competitive capitalism.

3.3.2 The intensification of economic problems in the USSR

Demographic crisis

The Soviet path of growth was 'intensive', relying on increases in inputs of labour and capital, with only small improvements in factor productivity. In the 1930s the main source of growth in labour supply in the industrial sector had been the transfer of labour from low productivity agriculture to the non-farm sector. This source of labour supply increasingly dried up in the post-war period. The problem was compounded by the fact that the rate of growth of the population and the labour force began to slow down. The average annual growth rate fell from around 2 per cent in the 1950s to around one per cent in the 1970s and 1980s. Moreover, in the RSFSR the growth rate was even lower, leading to a net decline in the working age population in the 1985–1990 period.

Capital accumulation crisis

Capital productivity deteriorated alarmingly in the USSR from the mid-1950s onwards. Western estimates show a sustained decline begining in the late 1950s which continued right through to the 1980s:

> The USSR's record with respect to capital productivity is really is extraordinarily poor and difficult to explain on traditional economic grounds. . . . Negative trends [in capital productivity] such as those exhibited in the USSR imply falling rates of return on investment. In a market economy falling rates return would trigger a reduction in investment and hence in the accumulation of capital stock, thereby arresting the fall in capital productivity. (Cohn, 1982, p. 174)

By the 1980s, the slow growth of output meant that even high rates of investment were failing to generate large increases in total investment. The average annual rate of growth of total investment fell from around 13 per cent in the late 1950s to around 2 per cent in the early 1980s (Cohn, 1982, p. 171).

Output growth

Despite continued high rates of investment, the alarming long-term deterioration in capital productivity, combined with the slow down in the rate of addition to the labour force helped produce a steady decline in the growth rate of national product. Official estimates of the growth of net material product show a fall from over seven per cent per annum in the late 1960s through successive Five Year Plans, reaching only around 3 per cent in the Eleventh Five Year Plan of 1981–85. Moreover, unofficial Soviet estimates suggest that the growth rate had fallen to virtually zero by the early 1980s (Agenbegyan, 1988, p. 2).

Standard of living

Soviet living standards declined severely during the early 1930s. By the late 1930s they had more or less recovered to the position of the late 1920s (Chapman, 1963). Naturally, a collapse occurred during the Second World War. From the early 1950s to the late 1970s a large improvement took place. The best Western estimate is that there was a growth of real average consumption of around 3.7 per cent per annum from 1951 to 1978 (Schroeder, 1983, p. 315). Major advances occurred in both food and consumer durable consumption.

However, there still were large problems with progress in Soviet consumption standards. Firstly, the rate of growth of real average consumption slowed down markedly to less than three per cent per annum in the 1970s, and in the early 1980s little, if any, growth occurred. Secondly, the base from which post-war Soviet consumption growth began was low. Moreover, the slowdown in Soviet consumption growth coincided with an epoch of continued strong growth of real incomes in the advanced capitalist countries. By the mid-1970s, careful estimates of comparative consumption levels based on purchasing power parity dollars showed that Soviet per capita consumption levels were only 34 per cent of those in the USA, 50 per cent of those in France and Germany, and 69 per cent of those in the UK (Schroeder, 1983). Thirdly, comparative studies fail fully to capture the contrast in quality and variety of products consumed in the Soviet Union and in the West. Poor performance in industrial technical progress in the USSR coincided with a surge of technical progress in the West in the nature of consumer goods and services, ranging from an explosive growth in electronics and motor vehicles, to a revolution in the provision of financial services. Soviet reform efforts in the later stages of the communist command economy focused on more 'pressure' rather than introducing market forces (see below). This contributed to a widely acknowledged deterioration in the quality of consumption goods, a reverse process to that taking place in the advanced capitalist countries.

Fourthly, a much analysed deterioration began to set in Soviet performance in respect to mortality rates. A major area of Soviet success was in the provision of health services and basic needs of food, employment and shelter. By the 1950s these had helped to produce a decline in the death rate to low levels for a country of the USSR's income level. However, in the 1970s the death rate began to creep up alarmingly, against the trend of the advanced capitalist countries. Between the 1960s and the early 1980s the crude death rate had risen

from 8 per 1000 to over 10 per 1000. In part this was due to ageing of
the population. However, an important part of the story was changes
in age-specific death rates. A sharp rise occurred in infant (i.e. between 0 and 1 years of age) mortality rates in the 1970s, 'to the point
where on a comparable basis, it might be now be over three times that
of the United States' (Feshbach, 1983, p. 90). Moreover, a 'remarkable' rise occurred also in the death rates of males in the 20–44 age
group, with reasonable evidence that much of the increase was due to
a rise in alcohol intake (Feshbach, 1983, p. 90).

Fifthly, despite having the world's most sophisticated environmental legislation, the Soviet 'planned' economy proved incapable of controlling environmental pollution. In the late 1980s under Gorbachev's
perestroika, a 'green' movement quickly emerged and demonstrated to
the world the full extent of the Soviet environmental crisis. Again, the
Soviet 'planning' system proved incapable of ensuring that the economic system functioned in order to enforce agreed socially desirable
outcomes: 'We haven't had a case in our history where a minister has
been sacked for polluting the environment.... There are plenty who
have been dismissed for not fulfilling the Plan' (Shmelyev and Popov,
1990).

International relations

It was obvious by the early 1970s that the Soviet economic system
was ailing seriously. An explicit part of the Cold War conflict strategy adopted by the Western powers, and accentuated by President Reagan
with the strong support of Mrs Thatcher, was the intensification of the
arms race. The final element in this was the 'Star Wars' strategy. Already in the 1970s a large proportion of the best Soviet resources were
devoted to the defence sector. In the decade or so before Gorbachev
came to power, and during the course of his administration, the proportion of resources allocated to this sector grew in response to the
intensification of the Cold War. This had serious consequences for the
system's capacity to generate efficient growth in the civilian sector.

Reform efforts

Soon after the death of Stalin in 1953 debate began about the defects
of the Soviet planning system. The decline in growth rates alongside
the unanticipated dynamism of world capitalism prompted an intensified search for ways to improve the functioning of the system. Three
successive reform programmes were introduced. However, none of these

attempts changed the fundamental principles upon which the system operated.

The first occurred under Khrushchev between 1957 and 1965. The Khrushchev reforms 'decentralised' many planning functions to the level of the Republic. However, they produced no change at all in the setting in which the enterprise operated. Indeed, in certain respects the reforms made planning harder by fostering a spirit of regional loyalty that made inter-Republican economic relations more difficult to coordinate. The reforms were abandoned formally in 1965.

The second reform wave was introduced in 1965. At first sight it sounded as though fundamental system reform was being proposed, with discussion about introducing balance sheet profit as the key 'success indicator' for enterprises, increased enterprise autonomy in decison making and reliance on bank credit with a positive rate of interest for finance. However, the reform did nothing to undermine the dominance of the material supply system, which was the heart of the 'planning' structure. A US expert on Soviet planning commented: '. . . after seven years of the reform, economic methods, or 'levers', have been effectively converted into administrative 'levers' . . . As a consequence centralised planning and administration are even more entrenched' (Schroeder, 1979, p. 36).

The third wave of reform in response to growing recognition of systemic problems began in 1979. The explicit goals of the reforms were to limit enterprise demands for labour, to force enterprises to economise on the use of material inputs and energy, to improve product quality and stimulate technical progress. As with the previous reform wave, no fundamental attempt was made to introduce the market mechanism. Instead it became clear quickly that the reforms amounted to no more than an attempt to improve their efficiency through greater 'pressure'. For example, the efforts to raise the efficiency with which enterprises used material inputs and energy and to reduce their hoarding of labour involved an extensive revision of planning norms for input–output coefficients, and raising the relative price of these inputs but without introducing the complex of reforms that would have led enterprises to respond to these market signals:

In no sense do the working arrangements set forth in the July 1979 Decree and its successors constitute a genuine reform of the economic system. Quite the contrary. Planning is *more* centralised, rigid, and detailed than ever; the scope for the initiative of production units is *more* circumscribed; producer goods are *more* tightly rationed;

administratively set, inflexible average cost based prices are retained; and intricate incentive systems are tied to meeting plans for many potentially conflicting variables, with priority given to production plans expressed in physical units. These changes move the system in a direction opposite from what most Western (and some Soviet) observers agree is needed – decentralisation, flexibility, and introduction of market elements. (Schroeder, 1982, p. 82)

Far from improving the functioning of the 'planning' system, these changes actually made the situation worse. They bound the enterprise in 'an even denser thicket of targets, norms, rules and incentive schemes than did the previous working arrrangements' (Schroeder, 1982). Moreover, the greater 'taughtness' in the 'planning' system increased the intensity of 'shortages' and bottlenecks. The system became even more prone to 'suction' and 'hoarding', and even more a 'seller's' market in which quality and technical progress were sacrificed to meeting the current plan. The increased stress was easily visible in a deterioration of the quality of consumer goods in the early 1980s.

The system might have staggered on for a substantial period of time. However, by the mid-1980s, there had been three successive failures to improve the functioning of the system through half-hearted reforms. These reforms had worsened rather than improved the problem. The 'old' methods of achieving growth were even less able to be sustained than in the past due to the stagnation in the size of the labour force in European Russia and the slow-down in the rate of addition to the capital stock. A major reason for the election of Gorbachev as General Secretary of the Communist Party in 1985 was a wide recognition that fundamental system reform was necessary. The issues were: at what pace? towards what goal? and with what relationship between political and economic reform?

Crisis of leadership confidence

A combination of factors produced a severe crisis of confidence in the Soviet leadership by the mid-1980s. The facts of worsening economic performance were becoming increasingly obvious and the successive reforms had simply worsened these problems. Stagnation or possible retrogression in living standards alongside continued powerful growth in the West undermined the legitimacy of the Soviet 'planned' economy.

Finally, the Soviet Union was apparently losing the Cold War, being outpaced by Western technical progress symbolised by the 'Star

Wars' strategy. It was in this atmosphere that Gorbachev assumed power. The Soviet Union was subjected to a bombardment of hostility in international relations, much more intense than that experienced by China. It was the USSR that was regarded as the 'Evil Empire' by President Reagan. It was the USSR that was regarded as the greatest threat to Western interests because of its military might.

3.3.3   The intensification of economic problems in China under Maoist planning

There is much confusion outside China about the degree to which the 'Maoist model' differed from the Soviet model of 'planning'. The fact that the Soviet Union split so violently from China in 1960 led many commentators to asume that there was indeed a basic difference of approach towards economic matters. This idea was reinforced by the Chinese use of concepts such as the 'mass line'. Moreover, during the Great Leap Forward (1958/9) enormous changes occured within both collective farms and industrial enterprises. After a retreat from these massive experiments in the early 1960s, similar revolutionary changes again were put into practice in the mid-1960s during the Cultural Revolution.

During the Great Leap in a large part of rural China, collective farms introduced highly egalitarian methods of work remuneration, frequently adopting payment 'according to need', in the belief that China was able to 'leap' directly into the realm of communism. Having painstakingly learned from the Soviet Union's 'cold grim experts' (Schurmann, 1968, p. 247) how to set up an effective system of industrial enterprise management, division of labour and remuneration, during the Great Leap and the Cultural Revolution, Mao and those around him encouraged the overthrow of these painfully acquired systems. A Soviet textbook on the Maoist economy despairingly described these changes as follows: 'The workers drew up their own plans and set their own rates; decided on the technology to be used, making changes wherever they pleased; subsitituted metal grades or materials as they saw fit; made their own designs or altered the drafts and projects they had been given; and controlled operations, technical standards and accounting' (Korbash, 1974, p. 54).

These massive changes constituted a huge affront to the Soviet Union, since they effectively constituted a rejection of a large part of what the Soviet experts had taught the Chinese about how to 'build socialism'. These large disagreements were a major part of the Sino–

Soviet dispute. In important Party speeches made in the late 1950s, and early 1960s Mao developed a powerful critique of Soviet 'revisionism'. He argued that Stalinism had left the USSR with a sharply stratified society in which individual incentives played a central role in work motivation, rather than the selfless labour for the community ('serve the people') which he regarded as the essence of a communist society:

> The Soviets believe that technology and cadres decide everything. They emphasise specialisation, not redness, cadres but not the masses. . . . In China the cadres take part in labour; the workers take part in management; the cadres are sent down for tempering; the old regulations and systems are destroyed. . . . Though he [Stalin] urged selfless labour, they would not work even one extra hour and could not forget the self. . . . Bourgeois rights must be destroyed, destroyed every day, such as the emphasis on qualifications, the emphasis on grade levels. . . . The grade system is the father–son relationship, the cat–mouse relationship. It must be destroyed continuously. . . (Mao, 1959)

In addition, China experienced two long cycles of centralisation and decentralisation of economic decision-making (Table 3.1). Even in a relatively poor economy such as China, the task of enacting a large proportion of planning decisions centrally was extraordinarily difficult, with large problems in collecting and transmitting information and inflexibility in dealing with the special features of different localities. However, attempts at decentralisation produced their own set of problems of lack of overall co-ordination. China oscillated between centralisation and decentralisation with a long-run pattern of 'centralisation–rigidity–criticism–decentralisation–chaos–centralisation' (Yu Guangyuan, 1984, p. 76).

However, neither radical changes within the enterprise nor periodic bouts of decentralisation led to a substantially greater role for the market. With the exception of a brief period of disintegration of planning altogether in 1958–9, the material balance planning structure remained intact throughout. Almost all output was produced in accordance with plan instructions and handed over to state wholesale agencies. Almost all investment decisions were taken by planners rather than by enterprises. Almost all profits were handed over to planning bodies:

> For a long time many people considered that socialist planning and

Table 3.1 Cycles of centralisation and decentralisation in China

	1953	1957	Dec. 1958	1963	1971–3
No. of enterprises under direct central control	2,800	9,300	1,200	10,000	2,000
No. of materials subject to unified distribution by central departments	227	532	132	500	217

Source: Yu Guangyuan, 1984, p. 76.

regulation through the market opposed each other. They considered that in socialist economies all activities should be subordinate to the state plan. If enterprises had their own plans and market regulation were permitted, the result would be anarchy, and the interests of the state as a whole would be undermined. They believed that such could not be considered a planned economy. As a result, all enterprises had to obey the state plan rigidly with no room for independence and initiative. (Xu Dixin *et al.*, 1982, p. 41)

Results

Superficially, the Chinese economy under Maoist planning performed well. China's average annual growth rate of GNP per capita from 1960 to 1981 placed it among the ranks of the best performing developing countries: official World Bank data show China's growth rate in this period to have been 5.0 per cent per annum, compared to 0.8 per cent per annum for low income countries excluding India and China, and 1.4 per cent per annum in India, in many ways the most relevant comparator country (World Bank, *WDR*, 1983, pp. 148–9). China's growth rate of national product placed it close to the rate achieved in the fastest growing developing countries in this period. However, closer examination reveals deep problems with the nature of the growth performance. Chinese economists writing in the late 1970s almost all spoke of the deep shortcomings in the Maoist growth pattern, and the need to take fundamental policy measures to rectify these.

The pattern of growth was erratic, with two large policy-induced recessions punctuating the long-term growth trend. Official data revealed that there had been a massive decline in national output in the late 1950 and early 1960s, real national income reportedly falling by 35 per cent from the peak of 1958 to the trough of 1962 (SSB, *ZGTJNJ*,

1993, p. 34). Moreover, after 1976 it quickly became apparent that this downturn had been associated with a huge loss of life, with perhaps as many as 30 million excess deaths because of the famine. While not as severe as the earlier crisis, the Cultural Revolution was also associated with a large drop in output, with a decline of over 13 per cent in national income reported for the years 1966–68 (SSB, *ZGTJNJ*, 1993, p. 34).

There was a long-term trend deterioration in economic performance. The average annual rate of growth of 'national income' (net material product) fell from 8.9 per cent in the first Five Year Plan (FYP) (1953–7) to 5.5 per cent in the Fourth Five Year Plan of 1971–75 (SSB, *ZGTJNJ*, 1993, p. 35). The effectiveness with which resources were used declined over the long term: official statistics show that incremental output to capital ratio ('increase in national income per 100 *yuan* of accumulation') fell from 0.32 during 1953–7 to only 0.16 in 1971–75 (SSB, *ZGTJNJ*, 1988, p. 69). Careful studies of the state industrial sector have shown a steady long-term trend deterioration in capital productivity.[5]

In a poor country agriculture is the basis of the economy, not only because food is such a large share of consumption, but also because a large part of light industry depends on raw materials from the farm sector. In China in the late 1970s more than 80 per cent of the raw materials used in light industry were from the farm sector (Dong Fureng, in Xu Dixin (ed.), 1982, p. 97). In the first FYP, the agricultural growth rate (net value) was 3.7 per cent per annum, almost double the population growth rate, but by the Cultural Revolution decade (1965–75), the agricultural growth rate had fallen to 2.8 per cent per annum, only fractionally ahead of the growth rate of population, at 2.4 per cent per annum (SSB, *ZGTJNJ*, 1993, pp. 34 and 81).

The industrial growth rate (net value) had slumped to less than half of its growth rate in the first FYP, from 19.6 to 8.5 per cent per annum in the fourth FYP (SSB, *ZGTJNJ*, 1993, p. 35). The rate of growth of net output in the construction sector had slumped from 19.4 to 5.2 per cent, that for transport, from 12 per cent per annum to 5.3 per cent, and that for commerce from 8.5 per cent to just 2.1 per cent per annum (SSB, *ZGTJNJ*, 1993, p. 35).

The rate of growth of consumption also slowed down markedly, from an annual average growth rate of 4.2 per cent during the first Five Year Plan to 2.1 per cent in the fourth FYP (1971–75). Indeed, official data on physical consumption show that in the Cultural Revolution decade (broadly defined), there was no perceptible increase in per capita

Table 3.2 Changes in consumption per capita in China

	1952	1957	1965	1975
grain (kgs)	198	204	183	191
edible oil (kgs)	2.1	2.4	1.7	1.7
pork (kgs)	5.9	5.1	6.3	7.6
beef, lamb (kgs)	0.9	1.1	1.0	0.7
chicken (kgs)	0.4	0.5	0.4	0.4
eggs (kgs)	1.0	1.3	1.4	1.6
aquatic products (kgs)	2.7	4.3	3.3	3.3
sugar (kgs)	0.9	1.5	1.7	2.3
cigarettes (packs)	10.9	16.9	16.2	26.2
alcohol (kgs)	1.1	1.4	1.3	2.2
tea (kgs)	0.1	0.1	0.1	0.1
cloth (m.)	5.7	6.8	6.2	7.6
shoes (pairs)	0.2	0.3	0.5	0.8
watches (no./100 people)	negl.	0.2	0.3	0.9
bicycles (no./100 people)	negl.	0.1	0.2	0.6
sewing machines (no./100 people)	negl.	negl.	0.1	0.3
radios (no./100 people)	negl.	negl.	0.1	0.8

Source: SSB, *ZGTJNJ*, 1988, pp. 803–4.

consumption of most important items, and most of the reported small increase in the value of consumption was attributable to improvements in the stocks of high priced consumer durables, though levels were still low (Table 3.2). Moreover, the range of output was narrow and the quality poor.

Maoist policies were outstandingly successful in reducing levels of poverty as reflected in social indicators. By the late 1980s China's levels of infant mortality and child death rates had fallen to exceptionally low levels compared to other developing countries. Infant mortality rates had fallen to 71 per 1000 compared to 124 in low income countries (excluding India and China), and reportedly were even below those in middle income countries (81 per 100) (World Bank, *WDR*, 1983, pp. 192–3). Life expectancy at birth, arguably the most important single indicator of well-being, had risen from 36 years pre-1949 (World Bank, 1981d, p. 5) to 71 years in 1981 (World Bank, *WDR*, 1983, pp. 192–3).

It is a paradox that social indicators can improve simultaneously with a constant or even rising headcount of poverty. This applies, for example, to much of Africa since the 1960s and to India also, if one accepts those who estimate that the absolute numbers of people below the poverty line has risen in the recent past. Raising incomes is more difficult than improving social indicators. The latter can be achieved relatively cheaply, as Maoist China demonstrated, whereas the former requires above all the creation of non-farm employment opportunities. China's pattern of growth was poor in generating such employment increase. Although the absolute growth of industrial employment in China was large, rising from 14 million to 43 million between 1957 and 1978, this less than doubled the share of industrial in total employment (from 7 per cent to 12 per cent) (SSB, *ZGTJNJ*, 1984, pp. 107–9).

It is unlikely that the proportion of the population in poverty can have declined greatly from the mid-1950s through to the late 1970s. The World Bank estimates that still in the late 1970s, the income of no less than 28 per cent of the total population, totalling around 270 million people, fell below a poverty line roughly comparable with that which the World Bank has used to analyse poverty in other developing countries (World Bank, 1992b, p. ix). It is almost certain that the proportion of the population below a similar poverty line fell sharply in the early years after the revolution on account of land reform, rationing and the greater equality of income distribution in the collective farms. It is likely, however, that the absolute number of people below the poverty line grew over time under the Maoist system. If one makes the bold assumption that the proportion of people below the poverty line fell from around 50 per cent in 1949 to around 30 per cent in 1957, then the absolute numbers below the poverty line would have fallen from about 270 million in 1949, to about 190 million in 1957, but would have risen again to the figure of around 270 million in the late 1970s.

China's economy was characterised by a series of imbalances stemming from the peculiarities of the Stalinist system of command economy in its Maoist variant. The economic pattern was widely referred to by Chinese economists as 'disproportionate' in many different respects.

A first aspect of the disproportionate pattern was the balance between consumption and acumulation. The profligacy in the use of investment was reflected in a high and rising rate of investment. The rate of 'accumulation'[6] rose from 24 per cent during the first FYP to 33 per cent in the fourth FYP (1971–75) (SSB, *ZGTJNJ*, 1993, p. 43): 'If we had paid greater attention to the efficient use of the accumulation fund, we would not only have ensured a fast rate of growth and saved much waste, but we also have achieved a rapid improvement in levels of consumption' (Dong Fureng, in Xu Dixin (ed.), 1982, p. 93). The World Bank estimated China's gross investment rate in 1981 to be 28 per cent, twice that of other low income countries (excluding India as well as China) and above that even of upper middle income countries (World Bank, *WDR*, 1983, pp. 156–7).

A second aspect was the balance between sectors in investment allocation. China under Mao allocated a strikingly small proportion of investment resources to the 'non-productive' sectors,[7] including housing, health and education. Their share of state investment in fixed assets was squeezed drastically, from one third of the total in the first FYP, to only 16–17 per cent in the third and fourth FYPs (SSB, *ZGTJNJ*, 1993, section 5). As the market economy began to take effect in the 1980s, the share altered sharply, rising quickly, to over 40 per cent of state fixed investment in the sixth FYP (1981–85) (SSB, *ZGTJNJ*, 1993, section 5). Housing, in particular, had been squeezed severely, to only 4–5 per cent of the total in the third and fourth FYPs, but then rapidly increased its share to 21 per cent by the sixth FYP (SSB, *ZGTJNJ*, 1993, section 5). The share of heavy industry rapidly rose from 36 per cent of total state investment in the first FYP to around one half in the third and fourth FYPs, while the share of light industry languished at only 5–6 per cent (SSB, *ZGTJNJ*, 1993, section 5).

A third aspect is the disproportionate growth of output in different sectors and sub-sectors. The growth rate of agriculture lagged far behind that of industry. The net value of farm output per capita stagnated over the long term, growing by just 0.3 per cent per annum from 1957 to 1975 (SSB, *ZGTJNJ*, 1993, pp. 34 and 81). Moreover, within the agricultural sector, the share of crop production remained high, at over 70 per cent of the total value of farm output. Furthermore, within the crop sector grain remained massively dominant: in 1982 it still accounted for 49 per cent of the total value of farm output (Ministry of Agriculture, *ZGNCJJTJDQ*, 1949–1986, 1989, p. 106). As the farm economy began to be reformed in the 1980s and the impact of market forces started to take effect, a sharp alteration occured in the structure of the farm sector reflecting the increased efficiency with which farm products were supplied as well as the growth of income and demand for a much wider variety of farm produce (see Chapter 6).

By the mid-1970s, heavy industry accounted for 56 per cent of gross industrial output (SSB, *ZGTJNJ*, 1993, pp. 58, 60), reflecting what many Chinese economists regarded as a 'vicious circle' of capital goods production. The command economy produced persistent 'investment hunger' and the investment goods sectors were themselves large users of capital goods inputs: 'Theoretically, it was more than once pointed out that the relations among agriculture, light industry and heavy industry must be handled correctly in socialist construction. However, in practice, both agriculture and light industry were ignored in favour of the development of heavy industry' (Sun Shangqing in Yu Guangyuan (ed.), 1984, p. 179). At the end of the Maoist period, the share of heavy industry in total industrial output was very high for a developing country, especially one in which passenger vehicles were weakly developed, and stood close to that of the advanced industrial economies. The World Bank estimated that the share of heavy industry in Chinese industry in the late 1970s was around 64 per cent compared to 67 per cent in the UK, and 70 per cent in the USA and Japan (World Bank, 1981, p. 16). The share of machinery, equipment and metal products in total industrial output was large (30.3 per cent) compared to other developing economies, and the share of food, beverages and tobacco was exceptionally low (12.5 per cent, compared to 44 per cent in Indonesia, and over 30 per cent in Egypt and the Philippines) (World Bank, 1981b, Table 1.8). The share of machinery, equipment and metal products was much above even that of India (21 per cent), a country which had followed a capital goods oriented development strategy.

3.4 CONCLUSION

Neither the Chinese nor the Soviet system could have continued indefinitely without fundamental reform. In the Soviet Union by the early 1980s growth had virtually ground to a halt. The Chinese economy under Mao was growing faster than the late Soviet economy. However, even in China there were serious problems, stemming mainly from the same set of shortcomings associated with the command economy. In China economic performance was also worsening. In both economies, the rate of growth of personal income had declined to a low level, possibly stagnation, even perhaps some degree of decline in both cases if living standards are properly measured. Fundamental economic system reform was necessary in both cases in order to produce better results from available resources and to generate faster growth of income.

Not only were the economies performing poorly, but both countries faced deep political problems. In both cases a wide range of human socio-political rights was denied. It became increasingly difficult to sustain the legitimacy of this denial in the face of stagnation in economic performance. In both cases the totalitarian political system prevented an open-minded search for a solution to systemic problems. However, on the eve of reform the degree of political repression was much greater in China than in the USSR. Moreover, the Chinese Cultural Revolution's attack on the Party and government left China with a much weakened administrative capacity. The core institutions of the state had been attacked in a way that had never occurred in the Soviet Union.

The deep systemic problems in China and the USSR developed against the background of wider development in the world economy. Economists and politicians in the communist countries had been wrong in their predictions about the fate of the capitalist world. A vast industry of 'economics' in the communist countries had argued that capitalism could not advance beyond a certain point in either the advanced or the developing world. It was believed that within the advanced countries capitalism would suffer a prolonged crisis stemming from over-accumulation and the sapping of the incentive for technical progress due to the growth of monopolies. The developing world was confidently thought to be incapable of 'catching-up' due to the drain of capital to the advanced countries and the deleterious effects of inequality in international trade.

These views became increasingly unsustainable in the face of the obvious facts of the continued dynamism of capitalism within the core capitalist countries, and emergence of a group of 'newly industrialising countries' countries that had begun to close the gap with the advanced industrial economies. They cast a deep shadow over the poor performance of the communist countries, since they raised the conterfactual possibility that things might have been a great deal better under a non-communist system of political economy.

Were the systems both in a state of crisis? They each had deep systemic problems that required fundamental system change. However, neither system was on the verge of collapse. In the absence of fundamental system reform it is most unlikely that either system would have soon entered a phase of rapid decline in output and income. Rather there would in all probability have been continued slow growth or stagnation.

4 The Transition Orthodoxy and its Problems

4.1 ABSENCE OF A THEORY OF THE TRANSITION FROM COMMUNISM

The rise and decline of communism was compressed into a relatively brief period of time, essentially from 1917 to 1989. Looking back at the literature on the communist countries, it is striking how little attention was devoted to the problems of the transition away from the command economic system or the totalitarian political structure. To a considerable degree this was a product of the ideological confrontation between the two systems.

In the non-communist world there existed a vast intellectual industry devoted to criticising the manifold defects of communism. Most of this literature took it for granted that a more or less free market capitalism was the alternative to communism. Little of it simultaneously was critical of the ethical basis of capitalism. Not a lot of it viewed capitalism as defective in its ability to generate stable long term growth with full employment and social justice, and without destruction of the physical environment. Moreover, such approaches, with their emphasis on the necessary functions of the state in the economy, became increasingly unfashionable.

Prior to the 1970s only limited attempts were made to reform the communist system gradually. Knowledge of some of the most important such experiments was slight in the West and, perhaps, even less in the communist countries themselves. In the USSR, for example, the main protagonists of a 'socialist market economy' had been executed in the 1930s, and their writings banned. In China, those who had argued for introducing market forces to improve the functioning of the command economy were heavily attacked, deprived of power and a public forum, and, typically, were sent down to live for extended periods in the countryside. Within the communist countries, neither the political nor the economic system were items for discussion. They were ideological 'givens', which left the countries poorly prepared for dismantling the system.

54

The best-known attempt in recent times to introduce a gradual reform in the communist system was the Hungarian New Economic Mechanism. In fact, the Chinese experiments of the early 1960s, China's 'New Economic Policy' (Schurmann, 1964), were at least as important but were far less well-known outside China. The most influential writing on the Hungarian experiment, most notably that of Janos Kornai (1986), was comprehensively negative in its evaluation. This negative evaluation had a strong influence on the way in which the possibility for gradual reform in the communist countries was considered. This was so even among many economists in China in the 1980s, where the lessons from the Hungarian experience were much discussed. Throughout the 1980s, the Chinese incremental reforms were widely and with increasing confidence interpreted as reinforcing the view that incremental, 'half-way house', 'Third Way', 'market socialist' reform was a dead end that did not work. This view reached a crescendo around the period of the Tiananmen massacre, the collapse of the USSR and the 'Velvet Revolution' in Eastern Europe. Very, very few economists dissented from this position.

When social scientists were forced to think about the problem of 'transition' in the mid-/late 1980s, a large part of the analysis was, unsurprisingly, given the absence of serious prior discussion, simplistic. Moreover, it continued to bear the marks of ideological conflict. This chapter evaluates different aspects of the 'transition orthodoxy' which rapidly came into being in the 1980s.

4.2 COMPREHENSIVE REFORM OF THE SYSTEM OF POLITICAL ECONOMY

4.2.1 The 'Big Leap' in the socio-economic system

The benefits of creating the institutions of political economy de novo

There has been a greatly increased interest in the relationship between institutions and economic performance (Olson, 1982; Reynolds, 1985; and North, 1990). One approach to the reform of the former communist countries was to argue that the end of communism provided the opportunity to construct the economic and political institutions of these countries from scratch, learning from the accumulated wisdom of Western social science research, and avoiding the mistakes that many countries have made. This can be called the institutional 'advantage of the latecomer':

Big leaps can only occur in the aftermath of destruction of an ossifed and non-performing system. . . . In history, major dynamic rebirths have only occurred after catastrophic destructions. . . . Like Western Europe after World War II, Eastern and Central European Countries now have the historic opportunity to create *ex novo* optimal economic and social institutions and thereby free their latent energies. . . . [W]e argue in favour of an approach which we have christened 'big bang' . . . A 'big bang' approach may have an unpleasant ring about it and therefore requires definition. The essential feature is comprehensiveness, immediacy and irreversibility with the objective of establishing a democratic, capitalist society with a human face. This excludes 'la grande illusion' of a 'third way' because it does not exist outside of utopian visions. (Steinherr,[1] 1991)

Most proponents of the systemic Big Bang recognised that there would be a great deal of 'pain' in the course of the transition. This curiously parallels the 'historicist' propositions of those who, earlier in the century, had advocated a revolutionary leap into communism. For the earlier generation of communist revolutionaries, the pain of the revolutionary transition and the hard climb to socialist industrialisation were all justified in the belief that today's suffering would create the possibility for future prosperity.

Problems with a 'Big Leap' in the system of political economy

It was noted above that there existed no theory of the transition from the command system. This alone should have argued for great caution, since the problem was being encountered for the first time. Moreover, it ought to be self-evident to any social scientist that the system of political economy is an immensely complex integrated fabric of politics, economics, ideology and social relationships. Successful improvement of the functioning of such a mechanism is likely in principle to be slow. Karl Popper long ago identified the dangers of attempting to make great leaps in the whole system of political economy:

Every version of historicism expresses the feeling of being swept into the future by irresistible forces. . . . Contrasting their 'dynamic' thinking with the static thinking of all previous generations, they believe that their own advance has been made possible by the fact that we are now 'living in a revolution' which has so much accelerated the speed of of our development that social change can now be directly experienced within a single lifetime. This story is, of course, sheer mythology. (Popper, 1957, p. 160)

He argued for the application of scientific principles of careful experimentation in socio-economic policy as much as in the natural sciences. He cautioned that rushing into huge system change in the hope of 'leaping' into the millenium was the 'historicist' fantasy of which Marxism was the biggest example. The non-experimental historicist pursuit of a fantasy was now being advocated by the reformers of a large number of communist countries.

An important strand of the new institutional economics, the evolutionary approach, emphasises the role of knowledge in economic life (Nelson and Winter, 1982). Ultimately, economic activity is undertaken by individuals with limited information. An economic system is a complex network of knowledge lodged in individuals' minds. Destroying existing institutions has a high cost in that it takes time for individuals to reconstruct their knowledge about the workings of the economy (Murrell, 1992).

A major problem with large leaps of policy across many areas simultaneously, is that it may be impossible to reverse unanticipated, undesirable results. Paradoxically, these were exactly the kind of losses that the command system regularly caused. A small policy error can always be followed by a change of policy direction and minimisation of losses to the system from that error. A widely applied error before experimentation has occurred can lead to huge, irreversible system costs before the policy can be altered:

> Sudden action is for those who do not themselves suffer, do not think before acting, who proceed by formula, not fact. Only if time is allowed can there be time for thought – the thought that is attuned to pragmatic result and not to primitive ideology. (Galbraith, 1990, p. 96)

4.2.2 The role of the state in the transition from Stalinism

Arguments for a minimal state

It was seen in Chapter 3 that the Stalinist state 'failed' in fundamental respects. It is unsurprising that post-Stalinist governments should have had a strong desire for a 'small state'. In the immediate post-communist period individual rights were strongly emphasised relative to the necessity for the observation of wider duties in order to achieve common goals. This was expressed powerfully in the writings of Janos Kornai:

> [My approach to reform is that of] liberal thought (using the term 'liberal' in accordance with its European tradition). Respect for autonomy and self-determination, for the rights of the individual, is its focus. . . . [I]t advocates a narrowed scope for state activities. It recommends that citizens stand on their own feet, and rely on their own power and initiative. Perhaps the role of the government will be reconsidered at a later stage. *But right now, in the beginning of the transformation process, . . . it is time to take great steps away in the direction of a minimal state.* Perhaps later generations will be able to envisage a more moderate midway. (Kornai, 1990, p. 22) (Emphasis added)

The introduction of a liberal, capitalist system with a small state was argued as providing the people with real liberty, without the directing hand of the monolithic state. The Shatalin 500 Day programme in Russia put the populist hope thus:

> The [reform] programme plans to move towards a market-oriented economy at the expense of the state but not at the expense of the people. For a long time, economic policy did not consider the people's interests. The state was wealthy while the people were poor. . . . Everybody has a right to choose, guided by his own wishes and capabilities whether to become an entrepreneur, an employee of the state apparatus or a manager at a stock company, to engage in individual labour, or to become a member of a co-op. . . . It is freedom of choice which is the basis for personal freedom and for the realisation of individual creative potential. (Yavlinsky *et al.*, 1991, p. 88)

A further aspect of the argument for a minimal state in the 'transition' period was the poor quality of the existing state apparatus. Even though it was acknowledged that there might be large 'market failures' in the transition, it was argued that the state was so inept that a free market was preferable to state incompetence and corruption:

> The bureaucracy provides an extraordinarily important practical argument for radical free market policies, even in circumstances where 'market failures' exist and pure theory might suggest more nuanced

policies. It is naive to think of the existing bureaucracy as equipped, professionally and temperamentally, to implement sophisticated policies based on Western-style theories of the 'second best'. The bureaucracy cannot be relied for efficiency in regulating monopoly prices, promoting infant industries, or implementing industrial policy. (Lipton and Sachs, 1990a, p. 35)

The arguments for a strong role for the state in the transition period

It is precisely during a complex process of transition from one kind of socio-economic system to another, simultaneously with large stuctural change in the economy, that 'market failure' could in principle be expected to be especially large.

This is likely to be a time of great economic uncertainty. Hence, it is likely that investors' time preferences will be strongly oriented towards the short term. Consequently, it may be especially important for the state to intervene in capital markets to ensure that investments which yield their returns over the long term are undertaken at a socially desirable level.

As the economy moves away from Stalinism, great personal uncertainties arise. There are certain to be huge changes in the system of pricing and consumer goods supply, in the system of welfare provision, in the ownership and organisation of housing and large movements of people from one region, sector and occupation to another. If the state simply steps out of these areas, great social dislocation will result. There is a strong argument for extensive state action in these areas during a substantial transition period to reduce the shock of the transition process and guarantee a social safety net for all citizens. Since the absence of a social safety net will mean large suffering for the most disadvantaged groups in society, there is a strong case for incrementalism and extensive state action in this area above all.

Ownership rights over huge amounts of assets are certain to be altered greatly. The manner in which the reallocation of property rights occurs will determine the future class structure of the country. If the state abdicates from control over the process, then it is very likely that a highly unequal structure of asset ownership will emerge, with the outcome strongly related to initial inequalities in financial resources, power and access to information.

Economists almost all concede the case in favour of state intervention in favour of infant industries. Reform of the Stalinist economies present an extreme form of the 'infant industry' argument. In the Stalinist economies in most sectors, not only the technical level, but also the whole institutional organisation, involving labour markets, capital markets and the ownership structure, placed these economies at a disadvantage compared to competitor countries. Extensive state action was needed to construct a competitive industrial sector.

It is incorrect that only a bureaucracy trained in sophisticated Western neoclassical economics is capable of implementing successfully policies to step in where markets fail in the transition. Many of the most important interventions require common sense and experience rather than a high level of economic theory. Moreover, the bureaucracy of the communist countries was not especially incompetent in technical terms, albeit that their efforts had been grossly misdirected under the command economy. The prevailing orthodoxy among the successful East Asian industrialising countries, including Japan, Taiwan, and South Korea, in the early phase of their industrialisation was not neoclassical economics, but rather an eclectic blend of Marxism and the economics of List and Schumpeter, which seemed much more relevant to the 'catch-up' task that these countries faced.[2] The fact that they lacked a high level of knowledge of 'Western-style theories' may not have been a large handicap to intelligent intervention. It may even have been a help, since their intellectual background inclined them not to regard the economy as a simple mechanism akin to perfect competition, but rather a sphere of struggle between interest groups in which capital acccumulation was the at the centre of the growth process.

4.3 POLITICS

4.3.1 Arguments for political democratisation

Virtually no one dared to question the simplest proposition of the transition orthodoxy: a revolutionary overthrow of the communist party was intrinsically desirable and functionally useful to economic progress. A number of arguments were advanced in support of this apparently uncontentious proposition.

Democracy is foremost among the fundamental human rights

There is a growing body of opinion which argues that democratic institutions are the most important developmental goal in their own right.

Many commentators have argued that democracy is at least as important a component of welfare as material aspects. The work of the UNDP over the past few years has been strongly oriented towards monitoring different countries' human rights records and criticising human rights failures. This has taken the form most notably of the annual publication of the UNDP *Human Development Report*. The UNDP's 'human development index' included 'political democratisation' as one of the variables. So deeply has concern over 'human rights' penetrated the international institutions that in many instances in recent years, the World Bank and the IMF have attached political democratisation as a condition of development assistance.

'Democracy' involves more than simply the right to vote in elections. It involves also a wide range of civil rights, of which arguably the most important is the right of labour to organise 'freely'. A major part of the activities of international human rights activists such as Amnesty International and of the ILO has been to monitor the degree to which the labour force has the right to organise 'freely'.

Democratic institutions are inseparable from private property

For markets to function effectively, it is, indeed, necessary that there be a system of clearly delineated property rights. The emergence of stable property rights from their insecure position under feudalism, was a central element in European capitalist development (North and Thomas, 1973; Rosenberg and Birdsell, 1986). This was associated with growing demands of the newly emerging bourgeois class for political representation in Parliamentary institutions. It is regarded as self-evident by many commentators that democracy and capitalist property rights emerged simultaneously in the Western world. Take, for example, Milton Friedman's proposition espoused in his many lectures and interviews in the reforming communist countries:

> Historical evidence speaks with a single voice on the relation between political freedom and a free market. I know of no example in time or place of a society that has been marked by a large measure of political freedom, and that has not also used something comparable to a free market to organise the bulk of its economic activity. . . . The nineteenth century and early twentieth century stand out as striking exceptions to the general trend of historical development. Political freedom in this instance clearly came along with the free market and the development of capitalist institutions. . . . *[T]he expansion*

of freedom occcurred at the same time as the development of capitalist and market institutions. (Friedman, 1982, pp. 80–1) (Emphasis added)

A totalitarian party cannot preside over the transition to a market economy

There was wide disbelief that a totalitarian communist party could lead a movement towards a market economy sufficiently far to cross a minimum 'threshold' level of market activity. No one argued this position more forcefully or influentially than Janos Kornai. He deeply criticised the 'naive reformers' who believed the party could itself bring about a successful reform:

> The reform [in Hungary] is a movement from 'above', a voluntary change of behaviour on the side of the controllers and not an uprising from 'below' on the side of those who are controlled. There is, therefore, a stubborn contradiction in the whole reform process: how to get the active participation of the very people who will lose a part of their power if the process is successful. (Kornai, 1986, 1729)

He urged other reforming socialist countries to learn from the Hungarian experience which showed the apparent logical impossibility of a communist party leading reform from 'above'. A *political revolution* which overthrew the communist party was seen as an essential precondition of successful transition away from the Stalinist system of political economy:

> The collapse of communist one-party rule was the *sine qua non* for an effective transition to a market economy. If one proposition has been tested by history, it is that the communist parties of Eastern Europe would not lead a process of radical reform sufficiently deep to create a real market economy. (Lipton and Sachs, 1990a, p. 34)

Gorbachev was regarded as a hero who overthrew communism and provided the citizens of the communist countries with a 'free political choice', the essential condition for 'real', radical economic reform:

> Mankind has experimented with a great many third road solutions. The reform of the socialist system, directly affecting the lives of almost 1.4 billion people, is the biggest third-road undertaking so

far. . . . [T]his gigantic experiment has failed up to now. . . . [T]he incoherence, internal contradiction, and lack of stability in the reform of the socialist system suggests that it is not lastingly viable. The process of reform yields a heteromorphic formation that contains the seeds of its own destruction: an inner tension that builds up until it busts. One alternative by which these can be relieved is for the possesors of power to combat the discontent of the people with violence and lead society back to the second road. *The other alternative is that the reform process transforms into a process of revolutionary political changes. That offers the opportunity of free political choice, in which case the majority of the public choose the first road. In my view, historians will view Gorbachev and all others who initiated and supported the process of reforming the socialist system as people who earn undying merit.* (Kornai, 1992, p. 574) (Emphasis added)

Foreign investors will not invest substantially in a country still ruled by a communist party

This proposition was regarded as self-evidently true: 'The low regard in the West for the communist goverments, [makes] it impossible for them to mobilise the international financial support vital for the economic transition' (Lipton and Sachs, 1990a, 34).

Democracy does not harm growth and may well promote it

An important strand of academic research supported the proposition that greater democracy would not harm and might well accelerate the rate of growth of income in poor countries. The work associated with WIDER was important in this debate. Dasgupta (1990) was especially influential. Dasgupta's article analysed cross-sectional data from a large number of developing countries, and presented the important empirical finding that greater democracy in developing countries did not apppear to harm growth performance:

> [The] choice . . . betweeen fast growth in income and . . . negative liberties . . . is a phoney . . . choice. . . ; statistically speaking societies are not faced with this dilemma. . . . Political liberties . . . are positively and significantly correlated with *per capita* income growth. (Dasgupta, 1990, pp. 27–8)

Moreover, it was but a short step to the argument that democracy *benefits* growth of per capita income. This view rapidly entered the mainstream of development studies in the early 1990s as if it were a proven fact.

4.3.2 Problems with political democratisation in the transition

Mass democracy typically followed rather than preceded or accompanied industrialisation

Hardly a single country grew from low to high income in a democratic framework. None of the advanced economies had mass democracy in the early stage of modern economic growth. During the take-off phase virtually all of them were governed by liberal principles which granted political rights to property holders, but did not mostly allow political power to the urban or rural proletariat, to impoverished racial minorities, or to women. The development of mass democracy followed rather than preceded the take-off. This has been the case too in successful industrialisers in the late twentieth century:

> Bourgeois democracy, in the same way as its Athenian predecessor, first arose as a democracy for male members of the ruling class alone. Only after protracted struggle were these rights extended to the ruled and exploited classes as well. Sometimes the ruling class of these early regimes was extremely narrow. . . . Sometimes it was fairly broad. . . . But in every case the propertyless were excluded. (Therborn, 1977, pp. 33–4)

The late eighteenth century and early nineteenth century liberal philosophy was in no doubt that the wide divergence of interests between socio-economic groups made it impossible to obtain a democratically worked-out compromise consistent with advancement of the national economy (Hirschman, 1977). Class conflict was at the heart of the conflict of interests between capital and labour. In the early stages of industrialisation, the poverty of the working class means that it values current income highly relative to the prospect of future income which might result from its restraint in exercising its monopoly power. Moreover, its poverty and class distance from the owners of the means of production reduces its trust of the capitalist class. A democratically-based co-operative solution to the need to sustain a high rate of investment and to establish a flexible labour market is difficult to achieve in the early stages of industrialisation. Polanyi expressed this view with harsh clarity in relation to early British industrialisation:

When the Chartist Movement [in Britain] demanded entrance for the disinherited into the precincts of the state, the separation of economics and politics ceased to be an academic issue and became the irrefragable condition of the existing system of society. It would have been lunacy to hand over the administration of the New Poor Law with its scientific methods of mental torture to the representatives of the self-same people who for whom the treatment was designed. . . . In England it became the unwritten law of the constitution that the working class must be denied the vote. . . . The Chartists had fought for the right to stop the mill of the market which ground the lives of the people. *But the people were only granted rights when the awful adjustment had been made.* (Polanyi, 1957, p. 266). (Emphasis added)

Even the archetype of Western liberal democracy, the USA, initially was founded in the late eighteenth century upon the same liberal principles, of voting based upon a property qualification, as Britain, the country from whose shackles it had liberated itself: 'It was not a purely fortuitous circumstance that, when the crisis between Britain and the colonies rose to its climax, the Continental Congress should appeal to the mother country in the language of the freeholders: "Why should not the freeholders of America" demanded the Congress, "enjoy the same rights enjoyed by the freeholders of Great Britain?"' (Williamson, 1960, p. 19). The elimination of property qualifications to vote was not accomplished finally until 1860, and even then suffrage was denied to women, and most of the black and native Indian population (Williamson, 1960, p. 278). Indeed, the Southern USA from the Civil War to World War II may be best described as a 'landlord-dominated authoritarian political system' (Rueschmeyer, 1992, pp. 122–32).

The state and economic growth in the Asian NICs

The Asian NICS are the most recent recruits to the ranks of the advanced economies. Much of the recent research on the East Asian NICs attributes a substantial part of the explanation for these countries' rapid growth to the 'relative autonomy' of the state:[3]

In the context of economic growth it is . . . the capacity of the system to insulate economic management from political processes of distributive demands, rent-seeking and patronage disbursement that makes the crucial difference. . . . The single-minded pursuit of growth goals of the Korean leadership has been protected by authoritarian executive dominance, with the legislative and judicial branches of the government being largely irrelevant and the influence of labour unions negligible. (Bardhan, 1984, pp. 72–3)

The governments of the East Asian NICs, following the Japanese path, were committed to the profit motive and the market mechanism. However, they recognised that in the real world domestic and international markets are highly imperfect, and a large amount of state intervention often is necessary if a poor economy is to harness the dynamic power of market forces.[4]

In the East Asian NICs the relative autonomy of the state enabled it to put into effect a succession of policies that placed national growth above powerful vested interests. Vincent Siew, Chairman of the Taiwanese government's Council for Economic Planning said bluntly in 1994: 'Democracy makes the economy more transparent and fair, but less efficient. . . . In the days of martial law, we just did what was right for country. It is much harder now to push through decisions' (quoted in *Financial Times*, October 10, 1994). Under East Asian authoritarianism, the governments of the East Asian NICS carried out sweeping land reforms. Each of them allocated state resources generally to good effect, e.g. they were successful in building up sectors with high positive external economies. They set the exchange rate at, or close to, free market levels. They intervened flexibly in protecting domestic industry, not often sustaining protection indefinitely in response to domestic lobby pressures. They used methods of protection that would have the minimum of distorting effects upon domestic resource allocation i.e. tariffs generally were preferred to quotas, and exporters generally were able to obtain protected inputs at world market prices. They were successful also in controlling the rate of growth of the money supply and keeping inflation under control. They did not generally allow loss making state enterprises without strong positive externalities to continue in operation for long.

Democratic institutions and economic growth in developing countries

India is virtually the only example in the developing world of long term commitment to democratic institutions. The need to maintain the political support of vested interest groups whose voice could be expressed through the ballot box and whose financial support enabled elections to be fought, contributed to the long-term maintenance of policies which hindered Indian growth. Protectionist barriers were retained in many sectors much longer than was useful. The exchange rate was maintained at a level that damaged exports. The state failed to impose hard budget constraints on state enterprises in many cases where this would have helped better use of scarce resources. It failed to carry out effective land reform. It allocated much expenditure to projects whose main purpose was to placate regional or class interests rather stimulate national growth: 'It is [the] lack of political insulation from conflicting interests, coupled with the strong power base of the white-collar workers in public bureaucracy, that keeps the Indian state, in spite of its pervasive economic presence, largely confined to regulatory functions, *avoiding the hard choices and politically unpleasant decision involved in more active developmental functions*' (Bardhan, 1984, pp. 38 and 74) (Emphasis added).

Quantitative studies of democracy and growth have serious problems

Careful scrutiny of the data upon which Dasgupta's widely quoted result is based show that much more cautious conclusions are in order, than those which are usually drawn from them, especially if these results are applied to the reforming communist countries.

Dasgupta (1990) provides correlation coefficients for the relationship several pairs of 'development' variables (political liberties, civil liberties, level of income, growth of income, infant mortality, and life expectancy). Several of the correlation coefficients are, indeed, high. Thus, there is a strong or fairly strong correlation between, respectively, civil rights and political democracy, falls in infant mortality and growth of income, rise in life expectancy and income growth, and falls in infant mortality and rise in life expectancy. None of these is surprising. However, the correlation coefficient between democracy and income growth is much weaker (and that between civil rights and income growth is even more so) (Dasgupta, 1990). This is not at all surprising. Almost all developing countries have very low levels of political liberties compared to the advanced capitalist countries (Derbyshire and Derbyshire, 1991, Chapter 3). Hence, it would be improbable to find a strong positive or negative relationship between income growth and democracy among countries that all have only marginally more or less political liberty.

The correlations tell one nothing about the direction of causation. Insofar as there is a correlation between income growth and democracy it is more likely on *a priori* grounds that the line of causation runs from rising incomes to demands for democracy than the other way round.[5] The most striking thing about levels of political liberty is that, with a tiny number of exceptions (e.g. Costa Rica and Sri Lanka), only high income economies have high levels. This suggests a very different line of reasoning for policy. Namely, the best way to establish firmly rooted democratic rights is to first ensure development of the productive forces and increases in income.

Cross-sectional studies which appear to show that there is no negative relationship between the level of democracy and economic growth among developing countries are a poor guide to the impact upon growth of the process of democratisation in authoritarian countries, whether developing non-communist or industrialised former communist. They provide no indication of the effect of introducing high levels of democracy ('advanced country democracy') into poor countries. Moreover, studies such as Dasgupta's fail to differentiate between countries which have a stable level of democracy, and countries which are in the middle of transition from one level of democracy to another. Policies which advocate democratisation of authoritarian countries ought to carefully investigate the *process* of democratisation, in order to see whether those countries which have democratised authoritarian systems grow more or less rapidly.

There is little precedent for the dramatic rupture of political institutions involved in the democratisation of communist regimes, and it is deeply problematic to apply results drawn from very different situations. The best way to analyse such a phenomenon may have been simply to think carefully about historical evidence and the logic of the process. It was not possible to investigate quantitatively a process which had not yet occured.

'Democracy' in the labour market is an ambiguous concept

The concept of democracy is inextricable from that of freedom, but the meaning of 'freedom' in the labour market is complex and ambiguous (Phelps Brown, 1983, Chapter 2). There is a dangerous tendency to confuse the rights of one segment of society, namely the organised working class, with the whole of society. In fact they are far from identical. It is not obvious that the rights of an aristocracy of mainly male labour, the industrial working class, have a morally superior claim to organise themselves at the potential expense of other social groups, which include not just capitalists, but also, much larger numbers of women without wage employment, retired people, farm workers, and the huge numbers working in the 'informal' sector. Protecting the rights of the 'aristocracy of labour' over other social groups may harm the growth process in all sorts of ways, and damage the employment prospects of non-organised workers through raising the real price of labour in the industrial sector.

In the early stages of the history of almost all successfully industrialising countries, whether in nineteenth century Europe or twentieth century Asia, in almost all cases, from the Combination Acts in Britain onwards, the state has intervened to prevent the industrial workforce establishing monopoly powers in the labour market. It is debatable how far formerly Stalinist economies can create effectively functioning markets without also creating competitive labour markets, and in turn it is debatable whether this can be accomplished under democratic institutions. Reforming communist countries face great difficulties in moving away from a system of privilege for the urban 'aristocracy of labour' towards a system of competitive labour markets. The political cost of establishing competitive labour markets may be too high in a democratic setting. A large part of the national budget may end up being spent not in re-training and re-structuring but in subsidies to keep politically dangerous workers quiet in their former occupations.

In a Stalinist economy moving toward a form of market economy, price liberalisation is certain to create demands for compensating increases in money wages. Without some form of incomes policy there is large danger of a spiral of cost-push inflation developing. Moreover, habits of trade unions and government responses can quickly become ingrained so that systems of political economy can find it hard to break out of the wage–money–price supply spiral once the process has been set in motion. The contrast between the Latin American (high inflation) and the East Asian countries (low inflation) in this respect over the past two to three decades is instructive.[6]

It is incorrect that communist parties cannot allow the development of market economy

In principle, it ought to be possible to devise a process of transition of a communist system which was supported by the communist party. The key is to provide most Party members with useful jobs in the transition and provide them with satisfactory financial and psychological rewards in their new roles. Moreover, if the leadership is able to build successfully a prosperous economy under communist party leadership, there is no reason why eventually the communist party might not end up as the dominant political party under a system of democratic elections.

There are important historical examples that support the proposition that it may be possible for a Stalinist totalitarian communist party to make the transition to a 'rational authoritarian party'. In the early 1920s in the Soviet Union, following a period of highly centralised rule in both the economy and politics during War Communism, the Soviet Communist Party was able to maintain tight political control while recognising the need for the country's economic success of a greatly increased role for market forces. In China in 1949 the Communist Party emerged from the civil war as highly centralised and disciplined. It had exercised tight control on all aspects of social and economic life in the Base Areas. In the immediate post-Liberation period, up until the High Tide of Collectivisation in 1955/6, alongside the tight control it exercised over political and cultural affairs, it operated a mixed economy, with guidance rather than directive planning in many spheres of the economy. Finally, in the post-Stalinist period since the late 1970s, not only China but also the communist parties of Burma, Vietnam, and Laos have all led the transition towards a market economy.

If a communist party is able successfully to guide the system of political economy out of Stalinism into a market economy, releasing the huge growth potential locked up in the Stalinist system, then there is a high possibility that it will be able to remain in power in the transition from an authoritarian through a 'guided authoritarian' into a democratic system. This prospect would ensure useful employment to most communist party cadres and help mobilise their support for the transition.

The proposition that foreign investors would be afraid to invest in a country still ruled by a communist party showed little understanding of the forces governing the movement of international capital. The proposition simply looks foolish besides the subsequent fact of the explosion of foreign direct investment in China in the early 1990s, and, latterly, in Vietnam. Both of these countries were still ruled by communist parties. By contrast the flow of direct investment to the post-communist countries of eastern Europe and the former USSR was mostly desperately disappointing.[7]

National unity may be hard to sustain under democratic post-communist systems

Nationalism and 'democracy' have a complex relationship. National unity in many of the advanced capitalist countries did not come about peacefully. In the nineteenth century, both German and Italian unification were only achieved through violent wars. Despite the mythology, the fundamental issue in the American Civil War was not slavery but national unity.[8] The resulting economic entity was doubtless more rational economically, but the unity was maintained at a high price, and through violence, not democratic procedures. In modern-day India, the unified national state was created by British violence in the nineteenth century. Far and away the greatest post-Independence violence by the national state has been undertaken in order to maintain national unity, with large violence directed by the central government against separatist movements, with large loss of life, most notably in Kashmir and Punjab.

In large formerly Stalinist countries the forces of nationalism and regional separatism are especially difficult to deal with. Under Stalinism, national minorities' consciousness within the overall nation-state was supposed to have evaporated with the creation of a new communist person. Paradoxically, capitalism proved much better at accomplishing this than the non-market Stalinist economy, with its constraints on the movement of peoples and its isolation of the population from homogenising forces in international culture embodied in internationally-traded goods and services. National minorities' consciousness was kept in the deep-freeze by Stalinism. Once the tight constraints of Stalinism were relaxed, these forces erupted. Succesful economic growth out of the Stalinist system, providing opportunities for different ethnic groups, and through the homogenising power of the market, could have been a powerful force reducing ethnic conflict.

A rapid change in national boundaries in a large communist country with a highly integrated regional structure of production causes large problems. New bases of product exchange have to be created alongside the difficulties of renegotiating international political relationships. The uncertainty alone could be expected to have a large negative effect on output. Where assets in a newly independent country were formerly owned by the central authorities immediate uncertainty arises in respect to property rights, which may take time to be resolved or be resolved in a way that harms growth. The position of much of the workforce is rendered highly uncertain since many of them will now be living in a 'foreign country'. The rupture of the country into a series of new national units is an extreme case of the problems stemming from radical reforms in forcing individuals to discard their old basis of knowledge and learn a complete new set of information about the economic process.

Political stability is an important condition of economic advance

Economic life disintegrates without political stability. Neither foreign or domestic investors have confidence. If politics is unstable, it almost certainly means that the state apparatus is less able to guide economic development. The capacity to collect taxes and even to collect information are reduced. Its energies are diverted away from economic construction towards political struggle. Late nineteenth and early twentieth century China provided a vivid example of this. The collapse of central political power in late Qing China had adverse effects upon economic performance. In the Republican period (1911–1949), the only areas to attain successful modernisation were those in which were established islands of stability amid a sea of disorder over large parts of the country.[9]

There was a high probability that post-Stalinist societies would experience great difficulty in establishing a stable political order in the wake of the communist party's demise. It takes time for a stable set of political parties to emerge which can construct a clear set of policy choices to present to the electorate. The possibility of political disorder is accentuated by the likelihood that a rapid political transition would lead to hasty decisions being taken about the nature of political institutions and rules, such as the method of voting at elections.

'Free and fair' elections are an insufficient condition for democracy

The ability of people to take advantage of political rights depends on their level of culture and on the amount of energy they have to devote to political activity. Like other 'bourgeois rights' the capacity to take advantage of the rights depend on the country's class structure. If the post-Stalinist reforms are accompanied by rapid changes in the distribution of wealth and by new concentrations of administrative power emerging from the old communist power structures, then it is very questionable how much genuine increase in democracy there will actually be. The capacity to benefit from the right freely to organise political parties and contest elections is strongly related to the possession of wealth, and the post-Stalinist regimes are no different. Control over the mass media is especially important in the early phase of the emergence from communism, when the population is still inexperienced in democratic practices.

The 'right to vote' in a 'free and fair' election is only as meaningful as the choices which the electors are given. In elections in the advanced capitalist countries electoral platforms almost always involve incremental changes whose effects are reasonably predictable. The most radical changes in the democratic politics of modern developed countries may well have been those which occurred in the 1980s under Mrs Thatcher in Britain. The main planks of the programme were clearly specified in the Conservative Party's election manifesto, principally trade union legislation and privatisation of the identified sections of the nationalised industries. The outcomes were very much the institutional changes that were predicted.

However, problems for democratic principles arise when the electorate of a reforming communist country is offered a choice of much more radical programmes for comprehensive system transformation. It is impossible for voters to evaluate the probable effects of such programmes. These problems are more serious, the vaguer are the programmes (e.g. 'make a transition to the market'; 'create a capitalist society'). Moreover, the more radical the reforming programme, the less reversible will the policies be. Unfortunately, a majority of the electorate might have become disenchanted with the programme well before the next election, but have no way of giving voice to their discontent.

The most important human right in a poor country is the right to an improved living standard for the masses

The most important goal in poor countries is to raise the material and cultural level of the mass of the population, in other words to provide people with their 'human rights' in terms of a decent standard of living. The most desirable political institutions are those which are best able to assist the attainment of this goal. Even in initially higher income communist countries many social groups, especially poorer people, are more likely to value improvements in their living standard more highly than democratic rights. Moreover, their ranking of the relative importance of these goals could alter sharply as their income level and security changes in the post-communist period.

Countries which successfully raise mass incomes will establish the firmest basis for sustaining democracy in the long term. Indeed, countries which prematurely establish Western democratic institutions from 'above' before mass income and culture have led to their demands emerging in Gramsci-like organic fashion from the masses, run a high risk of political 'recidivism' from formal democracy to dictatorship (as many argue was under way in India in the 1980s and early 1990s) or of unstable oscillations between formal democracy and military dictatorship as in many impoverished Latin American and African countries. It is far from certain that all the former communist countries will avoid such political 'recidivism'. In countries which have raised income successfully, there is less possibility of the mass of the population allowing a return to dictatorial rule.

Large post-Stalinist structural change may be hard to put into effect in a democratic framework

The transition away from a Stalinist command economy is complex not only in the technical sense but also socio-politically. It is a revolution in the system of political economy comparable in scope to the move from feudalism to capitalism. Just as in the latter movement, a wide array of vested interests is directly affected by the transition. The fortunes of different regions, strata, sectors, of the urban and the rural population, even of different age groups, are affected unequally. Reforms offer large opportunities for gain to some social groups and the possibility of decline relatively or absolutely for other groups. Large numbers of workers and managers may have to learn to live with the uncertainty and psychological distress of potential or actual bankruptcy and unemployment.

The possible conflict resulting from the potentially unequal consequences of the transition for different social groups may lend itself to non-democratic political solutions in two different ways, both of which may be termed 'authoritarian', and have often been lumped together under the general term 'new authoritarian'. In fact this term conceals two different approaches to these issues. One version of 'new authoritarianism' justifies the need for a 'hard', undemocratic state in the post-communist period in order to facilitate as rapid a transition as possible to the capitalist economy. Authoritarianism is needed in this approach in order to ride over potential opposition from those who would be likely to lose most from such a transition, and who might under a democratic system be able to halt the 'transition to the market'.

An alternative justification for a 'hard, authoritarian state' in the transition is precisely in order to allow a more controlled, slower transition process. In such a process, the strong state might be better able to use its power to prevent a rapid growth of asset inequality and protect the weaker members of society who might otherwise suffer more during the transition process.

4.4 ECONOMICS

4.4.1 'Shock Therapy' Economics

The revolutions in the communist countries saw a marriage of widespread internal hostility to the state with a similar intellectual climate massively dominant among external policy advisors. In the early postwar period there was great confidence in the capacity of government planning to achieve national goals. The 1970s and 1980s there was a massive intellectual onslaught on the economic role of the state. The earlier naive confidence in the state was replaced by an equally naive confidence in the market. Two important practical experiences contributed towards the policy climate.

The first was the confidence gained from advice given by the Bretton Woods institutions to the developing countries in the 1970s and 1980s. The policy package proposed for the former Stalinist economies by the most influential foreign advisors was similar to that proposed for stabilisation and structural reform packages in poor countries in the 1970s and 1980s: 'How much of what we have learned is relevant to Eastern Europe? Clearly the issues is not to repair the damage to an existing market economy but instead to jump-start one. *Aren't the initial conditions so different as to require a drastically different approach? We do not think so. Most of the standard stabilisation package applies to Eastern Europe as well'* (Blanchard *et al.*, 1991, p. 1) (Added emphasis). The main elements of the stabilisation and structural adjustment package recommended by the IMF and broadly supported by the World Bank for countries in 'economic difficulties' are well-known: instantaneous price liberalisation and reduction of government subsidies; a balanced budget accompanied by restrictive monetary policy; free market determination of the national currency; currency convertibility; liberalisation of international trade, with a rapid transition to negligible tariffs; an undertaking to implement further institutional reform in the direction of a private market economy, including privatisation of banks and industrial enterprises.

The second was the way in which the limited evidence from 'market socialist' experiments was interpreted. The were very few examples of market socialism. The most discussed example was that of Hungary. Largely due to the influential writing of Janos Kornai, this experience was widely regarded as demonstrating that any kind of 'half-way house' solution to the problems of the command economy which tried to combine plan and market was doomed to fail:

In Hungary, and also in a number of the other socialist countries, the principle of 'market socialism' has become a guiding idea of the reform process. . . . Under this principle, state firms should remain in state ownership, but by creating appropriate conditions, these firms should be made to act as if they were a part of a market . . . *I wish to use strong words here, without any adornment: the basic idea of market socialism simply fizzled out.* Yugoslavia, Hungary, China, the Soviet Union and Poland bear witness to its fiasco. The time has come to look this fact in the face and abandon the principle of market socialism. (Kornai, 1990, p. 58) (Added emphasis)

This view became an article of faith at the high point of 'shock therapy' economics in the late 1980s.

It was widely thought among advisors to reforming Eastern European countries and to the USSR that the Chinese reforms provided strong evidence of the impossibility of successfully combining plan and market in some form of market socialism. The views of writers such as Kornai, Gomulka, and Prybyla did much to bolster this perception among Western advisors who were almost as ignorant of China's reforms as those they were advising in the USSR and Eastern Europe:

The sad chronicle of China's post-Mao attempt to introduce a modern economic system contains a useful lesson which others, notably the East Europeans are taking to heart. The lesson is that to address the economic problem in a modern way in the context of a low calibre, inefficient, slothful, wasteful, cronified socialist system, one must go all the way to the market system, do it quickly, and not stop anywhere on the way. To go part of the way slowly, 'crossing the river while groping for the stones' as the Dengists put it, is to end up the creek to nowhere. (Prybyla, 1990, p. 194)

The transition orthodoxy of the irrelevance of a gradualist transformation, the 'halfway-house' of Hungary after 1968, and of post-1978 China was firmly embedded in the Bretton Woods institutions. In their key article in the *IMF Staff Papers* in 1991, Borenzstein and Kumar concluded that while a rapid, comprehensive transition to a market economy was 'bound to be costly, in particular in those sectors where resources have been misallocated to a significant extent', nevertheless this was the much preferred path, since '*a half-way transformation of a centrally planned system can only produce an inferior outcome for the economy as a whole'* (Borenzstein and Kumar, 1991, p. 231) (Added emphasis).

The main economic elements of the transition orthodoxy are outlined in the following paragraphs.

Full integration into the world economy

It was regarded as essential to remove barriers between the 'distorted' communist prices and world market prices. In the orthodox view this needed to be achieved rapidly. It was considered that only a tiny number of sectors should be protected, and even these only for a brief transitional period:

> It is . . . essential to move as rapidly as possible to a transparent and decentralised trade and exchange rate system, in order to hasten the integration . . . into the world economy. . . . The exchange rate [needs] to be moved to market clearing levels. *[Only] a few sectors [need to be shielded] for a short time from intense competition of international markets.* (IMF *et al.*, 1990, p. 17) (Emphasis added)

The need rapidly to liberalise international economic relations and achieve close integration with the world economy was accepted by the 'radical' reformers within the reforming countries. The Russian Shatalin Plan of 1990 for example leaped from the observation that the Stalinist economy economy suffered from isolation from the world economy straight to the proposition that free trade was the best way to relate to the world economy:

> Attempts to build a system screened from the outside world have resulted in the degradation and stagnation of most of our industries. Opening up the domestic market will force our entrepreneurs to compete with cheap imported goods. This will make our economy dynamic and flexible in catering to the market and through the market, to the consumer. (Yavlinsky *et al.*, 1991, p. 219)

In almost the same tones, John Crawford had urged the British Parliament in 1829 to expose India to the full force of international competition: 'Only by the powerful stimulus of competition would India be aroused. The feeble and ignorant must be placed in a state of collision with the strong and intelligent, for this was the only way of sharpening and invigorating their faculties and of raising them in the scale of society. There must be an open assertion of the superior civilisation' (quoted in Stokes, 1959, p. 42).

It was thought essential that full currency convertibility be achieved rapidly in order to ensure that by 'allowing their currencies to be exchanged freely for goods and for foreign currencies' their domestic prices would be brought into line with world market prices (Fieleke, 1991, p. 276). It was argued that foreign investment would be greatly discouraged by the obstacles that prevented foreign investors from earning and repatriating profits in convertible currencies (Fieleke, 1991, p. 277).

Privatisation

Political goals   The Bretton Woods institutions were explicit about the ideological/political goal of rapid privatisation in command economies undergoing system reform: 'privatisation can regarded as an indispensible process by which the very institution of private property in the productive sphere would be reintroduced in the socialist economies' (Borenzstein and Kumar, 1991, p. 230). Moreover, 'from a political perspective, a rapid transformation of the ownership of the means of production is considered to be necessary to ensure a complete break with the old regime' (Borenzstein and Kumar, 1991, p. 231).

The reforming governments pursuing rapid privatisation presented the policy in a populist fashion. Appealing to a bygone age when 'the people' were apparently the owners of the nation's assets, privatisation was to once again allow them to become the 'real owners'. The Shatalin 500 day programme in Russia expressed this populist theme as follows:

> The right to property is realised through denationalisation and privatisation, giving over state property to citizens. By giving property back to the people the social orientation of the economy will manifest itself. This is not an act of revenge but an act of social justice, a way to fix the right of man to his share of the present and future national wealth. Privatisation, it should emphasised is also a way to fix responsibility for the state and level of development of the society to all citizens who choose to accept such responsibility. . . . Property in the hands of everyone is a guarantee of stability in society and one of the important conditions to prevent social and national disaster. . . . *The [privatisation] programme gives equal chances to everybody . . . practically everyone, even if he does not have any considerable initial capital, will have an opportunity to get his share*

of the national wealth. (Yavlinsky *et al.*, 1991, 217) (Emphasis added)

Economic goals   There was an almost universally-held assumption that only private property ownership could provide incentives for those who managed property to minimise costs of production and determine their output mix in response to market signals (Borenzstein and Kumar, 1991, p. 229). Privatisation was to provide the only feasible means 'for owners to monitor, assess, and control the performance of the managers effectively running the enterprises' (Borenzstein and Kumar, 1991, p. 229).

The possibility of 'leaving the enterprises in public hands', but 'requiring [them] to respond to market signals in their operations' was rejected emphatically: 'Both the cumulative evidence from Eastern Europe and theoretical reasons suggest that the answer is in the negative' (Borenzstein and Kumar, 1991, p. 229). It was argued that governments find it impossible not to intervene in the behaviour of public enterprises, in order to pursue wider goals than profit maximisation. Governments were argued to be unable to resist lobby pressure to prevent the imposition of a 'hard budget constraint' and declare loss-making public enterprises bankrupt. Moreover, it was considered that independent public enterprises could only be effectively supervised by a stock market.This brought the argument in a full circle: 'However, the operation of an efficient stock market requires that enterprises themselves be owned, and in fact controlled, by private agents rather than the state' (Borenzstein and Kumar, 1991, p. 230). In other words, private ownership was argued as needing a stock market and an efficiently functioning stock needed private ownership.

With characteristic force, *The Economist* summarised the transition orthodoxy on privatisation: 'The introduction of market forces through decentralisation is a waste of time unless the business environment fosters the right kind of response. To do that, it must provide two things. First, private ownership of capital. Second, hard budget constraints, which in turn require competition, strictly limited taxes and subsidies, and credit only on commercial terms' (*The Economist*, 28 April 1990, 'A Survey of *Perestroika*', p. 15).

'Getting the prices right'

It was thought that price reform should be comprehensive and rapid. Without this no other element of the 'seamless web' could succeed: 'Markets cannot begin to develop until prices are free to move in response to shifts in demand and supply, both domestic and external. . . .

Price decontrol is essential to end the shortages that . . . afflict the economy' (IMF *et al.*, 1990, p. 17). The main dynamic for growth was visualised as the incentives provided by a market in which prices correctly reflected resource scarcities: 'When . . . earning streams are created in response to incentives which more appropriately reflect the trade-offs with which society is confronted, real incomes can grow very rapidly' (Krueger, 1992). For Lipton and Sachs, simply introducing a framework of free markets and private property was seen to be sufficient to ensure the accelerated growth of Eastern Europe:

> If convertibility, free trade, macroeconomic stability, and liberalisation of the private sector are all achieved, the power of natural market forces will reduce the gap between Poland's $1,100 per capita and Western Europe's per capita income more than 10 times that level. (Lipton and Sachs, 1990a, p. 352)

The pace of the transition from central planning needed to be rapid[10]

There was wide agreement that the main elements of the reform package should be put into effect rapidly. It was argued that the need for high speed was dictated by the fact that the reform was an interconnected 'seamless web'. One of the classic statements on the subject was contained in Lipton and Sachs' famous (1990) article:

> Both the economic logic and the political situation argue for a rapid and comprehensive process of transition. *History in Eastern Europe has taught the profound shortcomings of the piecemeal approach, and economic logic suggests the feasability of a rapid transition. . . .* The transition process is a seamless web. . . . The economic strategy must take cognizance of the new political context, which, in our view argues overwhelmingly for a very rapid, straightforward and sharp programme of economic reform. (Lipton and Sachs, 1990a, pp. 34 and 350) (Emphasis added)

A similar view was espoused by the IMF (1990) adding that a rapid, comprehensive reform programme would, by a mysterious and unidentified mechanism, lead to a wider sharing of the costs and benefits:

> Given the linkages in the economy, comprehensive reform increases the likelihood that each element of the program will reinforce other

elements. Moroever, *comprehensive reform helps ensure that the costs and benefits of economic transformation are broadly shared rather than concentrated on specific segments of society* (IMF, 1990, quoted in Fieleke, 1992, p. 274) (Emphasis added)

Lipton and Sachs acknowledged that the transition would cause large problems. They believed that it was politically most feasible to introduce a comprehensive package of changes, lest opposition build up in response to unpleasant piecemeal changes, and cause a reversal of the reform process: 'Fragile governments facing a deep economic crisis are best able to carry out strong measures at the beginning of their tenure. For this reason, Machiavelli's famous advice is that a government should bring all of the bad news forward' (Lipton and Sachs, 1990a, p. 350). They quoted approvingly the analogy: 'If you are going to chop off a cat's tail, do it in one stroke, not bit by bit' (Lipton and Sachs, 1990a, p. 350).

Anders Aslund appealed to 'common sense' in support of a rapid transition. Famously he likened the transition process to crossing a chasm: 'Common sense suggests that if you are sliding into a chasm, you should jump quickly to the other side . . . and not tread cautiously. There is no theory supporting a gradual switch of system' (Aslund, 1990, p. 37).

The small-scale sector offers the key to future growth and prosperity

A mass of evidence attests to the low levels of efficiency in the manufacturing sector of the former socialist countries. Manufactured goods from the communist countries were unable for the most part to penetrate the markets of the advanced capitalist countries. Moreover, where the post-communist countries were immediately opened up to the full force of international competition, notably in the former GDR, a large part of domestic manufacturing industry was unable to survive. There was a strong presumption among much of the advice given to the former communist countries and, indeed, from their own policy-makers, that much, if not most, of the large-scale manufacturing sector needed to close down, especially in heavy industry. Attempting to support and reconstruct the large scale sector was regarded as a waste of resources. Growth was visualised largely as coming from new activities in the small- and medium-scale sector:

For the most part, Eastern Europe's production sector is composed of large, inefficient firms. *Many, if not most, of them will have to close*, and others will need to shed labour on a large scale. *Growth will come largely from the rest of the economy, which exists today only in embryonic form*. Badly needed are small to medium-scale firms, high-tech manufacturing, and most forms of services. . . . The challenge of restructuring will be to efficiently close much of the old structure and allow for rapid expansion of a new one. (Blanchard *et al.*, 1991, pp. 64–65)) (Emphasis added).

Belief in the superiority of small scale business was built into Russia's Shatalin Plan, which stated in populist fashion:

[The state] will support small businesses over big enterprises via reduced taxes and favourable credits. The programme is built on the assumption that society needs small enterprises to orient production to the needs of every person, to fight the dictatorship of monopolies in consumer and production markets, and to create a favourable environment for quick introduction of new scientific and technological ideas (which are best accepted by small and medium-sized enterprises) (Yavlinsky *et al.*, 1991, p. 219).

'Pain' before 'gain'

Advocates of 'shock therapy' recognised that it would cause much 'pain'. Indeed, the advocates of 'shock therapy' waxed lyrical in a variety of metaphors about the eventual 'gain' that would derive from a lot of 'pain'. It was common to compare the choices confronting the reformers with those confronting the surgeon. Like the reluctant surgeon who regrettably has to inform the patient that she/he can only survive with a tough operation, the advisors to the reforming countries informed the bemused governments that only a painful 'operation' could save their economies:

The sum total of ten different kinds of half results is not five full successes but five full fiascos. . . . If the only cure for a person is to cut off his leg, it is still more humane to perform a single amputation with the necessary anesthesia than to schedule a long-lasting operation and cut a thin slice off every week or month. (Kornai, 1990, pp. 159–60)

Stanislav Gomulka's brief, but influential, newspaper article expressed the problem thus:

> The immediate tasks of the new government [in Poland] will be to put out these [inflationary] flames. A tough monetary policy may have to be adopted. The deficits of both the central government and enterprises would have to be reduced as prices are freed to bring supply and demand into balance, and therefore reduce shortages. The freeing of prices and the elimination of subsidies is expected to identify loss-making enterprises, and the next step of the government will be to close down the persistent loss-makers. The result of such structural reform will be greater international competitiveness for Polish industries, but also the emergence of unemployment. . . . *The Polish economy clearly needs a surgical operation to remove the outdated and inefficient industries.* (Gomulka, 1989, 5) (Emphasis added)

Although it was recognised that rapid reform would bring its own set of problems, it was felt that the possibility of large eventual gains justified the risk. Having carefully weighed the dangers of such a path, the Bretton Woods institutions concluded:

> The prospect of a sharp fall in output and rapid increase in prices in the early stage of a radical reform [in the USSR] is daunting. . . . *In advocating the more radical aproach we well aware of the concerns of those who recommend caution.* (IMF/World Bank, 1990, pp. 18–19) (Emphasis added).

It was widely expected that there would be an initial fall in output and living standards if the radical reform package was put into effect. It was thought that, after an initial fall, the stabilisation and structural adjustment programme would within a short period lead to rapid growth. In respect to their recommended program for the former USSR, the Bretton Woods institutions commented:

> *A recovery from the reduced level of output should be able to get under way within two years or so. . . . Further strong growth of output and rising living standards could be expected for the remainder of the decade and beyond.* (IMF/World Bank, 1990, pp. 18–19) (Emphasis added)

4.4.2 Shortcomings of the transition orthodoxy in economics

The theoretical and empirical basis of the policy of economic reform is out of date

It was widely assumed by both advisors and economists within the reforming countries that the accumulated experience of Western economic theory had demonstrated that free market institutions with the 'invisible hand' at its heart were all that would be needed to propel the communist economies into prosperity. This is an old story from economists in the advanced capitalist countries in advocating remedies for the economic ills in other parts of the world. The overall approach towards the fundamentals of institutions and economic development did not seem to have advanced much from the early nineteenth century when an economist such as W. Lester could argue with respect to India:

> The vast peninsula of India has for centuries been harassed by wars and devastation, rendering property very insecure; *but if it becomes open to free trade, under one mild, liberal and effective government, that could protect the property, laws, lives and liberties of the subjects, what a sudden change might we not anticipate?* (Lester, quoted in Stokes, 1959, pp. 38–9 (Emphasis added)

These hopes were a shade optimistic. Under just such a policy regime as was advocated by Lester and other British utilitarian economists the Indian economy grew by only around 0.4 per cent per annum over the hundred years or so it was ruled by the British (Heston, 1983, pp. 410–11).

The conclusions of the accumulated developments in Western economic theory are far from being so strongly supportive of the power of the 'invisible hand' as the transition orthodoxy imagined. More sophisticated analysts recognised that the 'invisible hand' was not the talisman that could solve all economic problems. Hahn's (Hahn, 1984) evaluation of the invisible hand warns of the limited conclusions that can be drawn about its applicability:

> The limitations on the applicability of pure market theory are numerous and many of them quite serious. The exceptions to the beneficence of the invisible hand have been piling up since Adam Smith and, much later Pigou, explored them. Our knowledge of the actual movements of the hand is rudimentary and vastly incomplete. . . .

The Smithian vision still provides a reference point but an increasingly remote one. *It can also be dangerously misleading when this limited role is not recognised.* (Hahn, 1984, p. 132) (Added emphasis)

Moreover, Hahn is highly cautious about the ways in which the doctrine of the 'invisible hand' should be applied. His sage evaluation of the lessons for economic policy from developments in economic theory stands in the sharpest contrast to the naive propaganda about the virtues of the invisible hand which flooded the pages of journals, newspapers and policy documents at the high point of the 'transition orthodoxy':

The predominant conclusion [about the invisible hand] must be that we are quite uncertain of what really is the case. *The pretence that it is otherwise comes under the heading of religion or magic.* Once the uncertainty is recognised it will greatly affect the set of rational or reasonable actions. Traditional theory . . . suggests that exceptional and near-catastrophic circumstance apart, it will not in general be wise to put all your eggs in one basket or to give harsh pulls on levers, unless you are what economists call a risk-lover. . . . *But risk loving itself is unreasonable. . . . [T]hese are the reasons why . . . the wishy-washy, step by step, case by case aproach seems to me the only reasonable one in economic policy.* (Hahn, 1984, p. 3) (Added emphasis)

Hahn observes that 'very few people can live with a shadowy and ill-defined picture of the world', and he therefore 'places no bets on a reasonable approach winning through' (Hahn, 1984, p. 133). The doctrine of the 'invisible hand' offered the comfort of a simple solution to the hugely complex tasks of successfully reforming the communist system of political economy. All that was needed was 'reform' in order to construct the 'free market'.

Hahn cautions against the exaggerated claims being made for the virtues of the free market in Britain under Mrs Thatcher, a period which was a source of deep inspiration to those in the communist countries who championed the cause of 'reform': 'In this country it is very likely that the non-fulfillment of the vastly exaggerated claims for the invisible hand will lead to a reaction in the hand, to our great loss, will be amputated forever. The age of prophets and witches is upon us and such an age is not friendly to reason' (Hahn, 1984, p. 133).

Developments in the analysis of the comparative performance of different countries have led recently to a further large shift in many economists' perception of the role of the state in economic development. In both the US and the UK this changed understanding is filtering through into practical policy, with a much greater preparedness even for conservative parties to consider the need for more powerful government intervention to construct an 'industrial policy' with which to enable manufacturing industry to compete with the emerging industrial giants of East Asia.

In the analysis of developing countries, a string of recent writings has emphasised the centrality of a strong and effective state appparatus in guiding structural change (Amsden, 1989, Chang, 1994, Deyo, 1987, Findlay, 1988, Reynolds, 1985, Wade, 1990, White, 1988). Indeed, even Britain in the late eighteenth and early nineteenth century can now be seen much more clearly to have been the first 'New Authoritarian, Newly Industrialising Country'. The Industrial Revolution in Britain took place under an authoritarian, undemocratic government, which enacted and enforced harsh labour laws, protected domestic producers, promoted exports through a wide variety of 'bounties' and drawbacks, prevented skilled workers leaving the country and supported monopolists.

In planning industrial re-structuring, the former communist countries have much to learn from those countries that have undertaken this task successfully, such as Japan, South Korea, Taiwan, Singapore, Hong Kong and post-war Germany. None of these examples is identical to any one of the former communist countries, but their restructuring problems are much closer to those faced by the former communist countries today than those of the US and Britain in recent years. However, it is economists from the latter group of countries that dominated the provision of advice.

Lessons drawn from stabilisation and structural adjustment
programmes in developing countries were dubious

The impact of the stabilisation and structural adjustment programmes instigated by the Bretton Woods institutions in capitalist developing countries was far from the widespread success that their supporters claimed was the case. Lance Taylor carefully analysed the results of 18 examples of stabilisation in developing countries. He found that the results of the stabilisation orthodoxy were greatly different in different countries. He argued that the 'partially successful cases were all based on stabilisation packages combining price signals and directed state intervention, with getting the prices right playing a secondary role' (Taylor, 1988, p. 168). The stabilisation strategy was most likely to work when there was 'hands-on management of a mixed economic system, and not wholesale liberalisation' (Taylor, 1988, p. 168). He found that 'an austere policy' contained 'no natural transition to development in the long term' once one departed from 'simplistic savings-driven neo-classical growth models' (Taylor, 1988, p. 168). He noted that 'neither savings nor investment is stimulated by stagnation' (Taylor, 1988, p. 168). Most ominously, he warned that 'the risk of economic collapse is non-trivial, if recent history in the Southern Cone, Mexico, and African countries, such as Zaire are taken as a guide' (Taylor, 1988, p. 168).

However, the most important reason for caution in advocating the Bretton Woods package of stabilisation and structural adjustment as the solution to the problems of the transition from the communist command economy, is that the problem is a very different one. It is not just as question of 'jump starting' a poorly performing market economy. The task is a vastly more complex one of attempting to transform the institutional structure of the entire command system.

A high-speed transition is, in principle, undemocratic

The faster the transition process was, the less possibility there was of the population providing feedback. Since the transition was being encountered for the first time, one might expect that the population's views might alter as the results of initial change became clearer, and unanticipated consequences emerged. It was profoundly undemocratic to explicitly attempt to exclude the population from providing political feedback at each stage of the transition, by making the transition so fast that they had no time to comment before the whole operation was completed. A government commited to democratic principles should wish to maximise the involvement of the population in the transition process, giving them maximum opportunity to participate in it and provide feedback on each stage as their views altered, not seeking to exclude them by having only one opportunity for expression of their views, namely the initial election of the post-communist government. Lipton and Sachs were correct to draw on Machiavelli as a source of inspiration for the transition orthodoxy's approach towards the speed of the transition. However, Machiavelli was not a democrat. A communist government which proceeded with a slower transition provided more opportunity for the population to express its views of the transition process through a variety of formal and informal mechanisms, and in this sense produced a more democratic approach to the transition than the Machiavellian stampede.

Market socialism was not a disaster

Careful analysis of other market socialist experiments, such as that of the Soviet Union in the 1920s (NEP), and China in the early 1950s or again in the early 1960s (Schurmann, 1964) would have led to a much more positive evaluation of market socialism than that of the orthodox transition economists. Indeed, the substantial achievements of these periods formed a major source of inspiration to China's leaders in their reforms after Mao's death.

Hungary's cautious introduction of market forces in the 1970s and 1980s produced considerable advance in popular welfare through rapid growth of the non-state sector, especially in services and small businesses. Also the experiments produced widespread understanding of the market and the gradual development of a market culture. These reforms prompted widespread discussion, and it is improbable that in the absence of the collapse of the USSR there would not have been further move towards a market economy in Hungary, albeit slowly. A further large consequence of the long period of 'half-way house' reforms was that Hungary was much the best prepared of the Eastern European countries for the post communist period. Broadly speaking it continued to make relatively cautious changes, refusing for example to enter the road of 'wild privatisation' and allowing only a small role for the stock market.[11] It was vastly the most successful of the Eastern European countries in attracting foreign capital,[12] and it experienced a relatively small post-communist fall in output. Moreover, like China, most of the foreign investment attracted to Hungary after 1989 was direct, hands-on, rather than portfolio, speculative investment.

Growth and efficiency

Economists have become highly expert at measuring the sources of growth, and decomposing it into its constituent parts. However, this is entirely different from explaining what causes these inputs to behave in a particular fashion, why some countries generate higher rates of saving and investment than others, and why some countries use these resources to greater effect. In fact, it is a most complex process, which honest economists of all varieties recognise as a vast gap in their understanding:

[E]conomic theory does not provide an answer to Weber's famous
question why Britain rather than China should have been the first to
have an industrial revolution. Nor indeed has economic theory much
helped in accounting for the Japanese post-war sprint or for the relative
British decline. Plainly, there are here crucial elements which go
beyond market signals and market behaviour. On these grand matters economics is comparatively silent. (Hahn, 1984, p. 131)

Moreover, the most astute analysts recognise that the role of the
state is, in some sense, central to an explanation. Consider, for example,
Reynolds' judgement at the end of his magisterial summary of the
growth performance of a wide range of countries over the past one
hundred years: 'The variables analysts have been unable to quantify
seem largely political – continuity of governments, growth orientation
(or its absence) in the political leadership, administrative competence
of government, effectiveness of policies in agriculture, foreign trade,
and other key sectors . . . For good or ill government seems central to
growth' (Reynolds, 1985, p. 418).

The transition orthodoxy was based on massive confidence that growth
would follow automatically from establishing 'efficient markets'. The
orthodox economists believed confidently that 'inefficient markets',
through such policies as maintaining substantial public ownership, price
control, rationing, subsidies of loss-making enterprises, protection, and
non-convertibility of the national currency, would damage growth.
However, the historical evidence suggests that things are not so simple.
The fact that economists know so little about this, the most fundamental process in the economy, should have suggested at the very least
much more caution about policy formation. The transition orthodoxy
proposed a neat, simple solution to the economic problem of the transition: move as fast as possible towards efficient institutions, even though
this will mean a large contraction of output. In this approach one can
crudely conceptualise that the greater efficiency is achieved by sharply
'collapsing' the production frontier inwards so that the economy moves
closer to the production frontier by contraction, 'cutting out the unwanted bits of the economy' (Figure 4.1).

At least as logical an approach was to try to edge towards a faster
growing economy through cautious institutional experiments and gradually
shift towards greater efficiency, even if this meant accepting the maintenance of many inefficiencies. In the latter path, after a given period,
the economy would somewhat more efficient, somewhat closer to the
production frontier, but the economy would also be much larger. This

Figure 4.1   Stylised two-dimensional representation of alternative paths to reform of the communist economic system

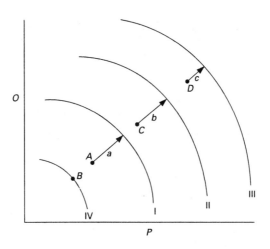

Notes:
$a > b > c$
I-IV Production possibility curves
O and *P* Assorted inputs of human and physical capital
A Stylised starting point of the communist economies
A-C-D Reform through growth, or 'growing out of the plan'
A-B 'Collapsing into efficiency'

path might make it easier to sustain socio-economic support and political stability that is essential for generating growth. In this approach one can crudely conceptualise the economy as moving gradually towards a production frontier that is moving outwards over the reform period (Figure 4.1). This approach has been termed 'growing out of the plan' (Naughton, 1994).

One of the central mysteries in the economics of growth is the way in which self-generating processes of a positive or a negative kind occur. Economies establish a path which it is hard to knock them off. A strategy of 'shock therapy' which causes a large initial decline in output and living standards could set in motion a cumulative process of investment decline, socio-economic instability and government incapacity that could lead to a prolonged period of economic hardship, rather than a 'short sharp shock' out of which the economy quickly emerged 'lean and fit'. The economy might emerge 'lean' but without either demand or supply side conditions that were conducive to large scale non-speculative investment by either domestic or foreign capitalists.

Short-term suffering is a high, certain short-term cost; long-term system improvement is an uncertain benefit

The orthodox transition approach allegedly attempted to liberate the people of the communist countries from suffering endured under political and economic dictatorship. It is odd that something so profound as potential massive suffering from the reforms should have been treated in so cavalier a fashion by those who were not themselves to endure the suffering. Galbraith regarded both the logic and the ethics of shock therapy as unacceptable:

> [A feature] of the flow of advice currently reaching the countries that are now in transition is its casual acceptance of – even committment to – human deprivation, to unemployment, inflation, and disastrously reduced living standards. This is even seen as essential therapy.... Only a few years of sufferring and all will be well. *This, I choose my words carefully, is insanity.* Nothing over the centuries has more often been urged than the social reward of hardship by those who will not have to suffer it.... In the simplest form much of the counsel simply consists in urging the replacement of a poorly functioning system with none at all. (Galbraith, 1990, p. 93) (Emphasis added)

The argument that a period of suffering is necessary before a millenium of happiness and prosperity has a familiar ring to students of the command economies. The slogan of 'bread today, jam tomorrow' was exactly the aspect of the communist drive for 'planned' industrialisation that caused so much anger among anti-communists.[13] The difficulty is that the pain is certain but the 'gain' may not happen or may take a long time to materialise. An important part of the transition orthodoxy was the conviction that the 'gains' would materialise quickly. To the degree that they take longer to materialise, the 'necessary pain' of the reform will have been suffered by one generation in order that a future generation might reap the 'gain'.

There is also the question of the distribution of the 'pain' and the 'gains' among social groups. Unless one could have been certain that 'greater pain' today would have caused 'greater gain' in income for those who had suffered the pain at some not-too-distant point in the future, then it would have been more logical to build a transition strategy around trying to minimise the suffering involved. The more uncertain and the more distant the prospect of 'gain', and the more that the 'gain' might be thought likely to accrue to the non-sufferers rather than to those who suffered the 'pain', the less sensible a strategy built around causing a large amount of pain appears to have been.

While the communist economies prior to the reforms were in deep difficulties (see Chapter 4), the most likely prospect in the absence of fundamental system reform was continued slow deterioration of performance rather than a looming disaster. Moreover, the other possibility – slow 'half-way house' reform – did not produce a disaster anywhere, but rather some certain improvement in popular welfare. The proposition that dramatic, painful reform was a worthwhile risk because of the seriousness of the existing situation and the dangers of the alternative, namely a 'half-way house reform', is not tenable.

Simple institutional reforms in the non-state sector can produce powerful cumulative results

Small non-farm business In all the market socialist' reforms, from Russia under NEP through to China in the 1980s, major benefits stemmed from simply allowing people to set up small businesses which did not threaten the 'commanding heights' of the economy. These businesses tended to be highly labour absorbing. They required little capital. They substantially improved popular welfare by meeting real needs, especially in the long-suppressed service sector. Under 'market socialism' their scope often was allowed to broaden into wider industrial sectors with small economies of scale, such as transport, housebuilding and small-scale manufacturing. In some sectors they were allowed to compete with, or themselves fought the boundaries of state regulations to compete with, the large-scale sector. Their success helped gradually to change the attitudes not just of ordinary people, but also the more conservative, fearful leaders.

Agriculture Institutional reforms in agriculture are easier to accomplish than in large-scale industry. The production process is simpler. The range of products is relatively narrow. There is a much less complex division of labour within the unit of production. The network of input–output relationships with other sectors is generally also less complex, involving less difficult rearrangements of the material balance planning system. The irrationalities of Stalinist institutions probably were greatest in the farm sector, so that the corresponding gains to institutional reforms were the largest in this sector. Successful reform of collective farms which improves the efficiency of food supply has an especially beneficial effect on the lives of the poorest people. It benefits peasant producers directly through improved food supply and improved conditions of work. It also improves the condition of poorer strata of the urban population who spend a large proportion of their incomes on food.

The impossibility of rapid privatisation

There were enormous difficulties in the way of rapid privatisation of state-owned assets in the former Stalinist economies. The pool of domestic savings in most communist countries was too small to enable their citizens to buy the state's assets and the political implications of selling a large proportion of state assets to foreigners (insofar as they were interested in buying them) were unacceptable in most reforming countries.

Valuation of assets was a large problem. Moreover, if all state assets were sold simultaneously, the price was likely to be lower than if a gradual privatisation were pursued, with the result that much of the state's property would be sold at considerably less than its long-term value. To privatise a state industry properly is time-consuming even in a sophisticated capitalist economy. Rapid privatisation is likely to be difficult for governments to control so as to avoid corruption. Government officials themselves may be corrupt. The more rapidly it proceeds, the less possible is it for the general public to monitor, such as through press exposures of scandals. There is a high possibility of 'insider dealing' in which managers, bureaucrats and (less often) workers, may reap windfall gains. They may collude to underprice asssets, have privileged access to share issues either through superior knowledge, or formal regulations which give them preferential rights to part of the share issue. Corruption in the process is likely to be even harder for ordinary citizens to accept during 'shock therapy' in which the reform affects social groups unequally.

In fact, the pace of privatisation in Eastern Europe in the first three years of economic reform was slow. However, the government's commitment to privatisation as a central plank of its reform programme led to great uncertainty over property rights. *De facto* control often passed into the hands of managers and workers in the given enterprise. Uncertain of the long-term future of 'their' enterprise, they had a low incentive to improve its performance, since any improvements might not be reflected in long term advantage to them, but rather to its eventual owners. The workers and managers had a high incentive to consider short term interests and 'mine' the enterprises' assets. It would be hard to think of a worse property rights arrangement.

The only way in which to accomplish high speed privatisation of such large amounts of assets was to give them away in one way or another. This involved collosal loss of potential future income for the state. In its idealised form of equal vouchers to all citizens the disposal of state assets involved substituting ownership by the state with hugely dispersed ownership by a population wholly inexperienced in investment. The vouchers would create the probability of the highest degree of speculative activity, rather than establishing a stable framework of owners interested in the long-run growth and profitability of the firm concerned. If vouchers are simply for rights to buy shares in holding companies, this also creates its own set of problems. Alan Walters, advisor to Mrs Thatcher's privatisation programme, warned that the experience of Britain and the United States 'suggests that such institutional investors tend to be active portfolio managers rather than active and interested managers' (Walters, 1991, p. 261). In Walters' judgement this would be 'a very risky experiment': 'The mind does boggle at the prospect of launching vouchers and an active market in mutual fund shares among the whole populace, where such instruments have been unknown for nearly 50 years. I doubt very much that the market would be at all transparent, and the opportunities for misrepresentation, market rigging, etc., would be enormous. One fears that capitalism would soon be discredited' (Walters, 1991, p. 261). If enterprises were wholly or partially given to incumbent workers/managers this would be hugely unjust, since the value of enterprises would be vastly different from one another. Moreover, a large part of the population was not employed at an enterprise (e.g. housewives and pensioners).

The possibility of improving state enterprise performance

The performance of state enterprises can, indeed, be improved. If management is selected on the basis of business expertise, given operational independence, and managers' remuneration is linked to enterprise profits or reductions in losses, then there is every reason for them to respond to market signals and improve their performance. In order that the enterprises' efforts to increase profits reflect socially desirable goals of more efficient resource utilisation and responsivensess to consumer demands, it is necessary that in most sectors at least prices are moving towards market determination, and that other enterprises are allowed to compete.

The key question is the political will of the government and its determination to improve enterprise performance. A striking example of the capacity of the government to turn around the performance of state enterprises prior to privatisation is provided by the British experience under Mrs Thatcher:

> *The naive belief in the emerging market economies, encouraged on occasion by enthusiasts from the West, is that, with the large-scale state-owned enterprises, all that is needed is to change the ownership from the state to private persons. . . . But this conclusion is a misleading and dangerous simplification. . . .* There was thought to be no point in trying to reform the existing state-owned enterprises while they remained in state ownership. . . . *Under Mrs Thatcher reform of the nationalised corporations was carried through while they were in the public sector.* (Walters, 1992, pp. 102–4) (Emphasis added)

The British experience demonstrated that provided the government was willing to appoint tough managers with a mandate to turn the enterprises into profitable businesses, reduce the workforce, eliminate unprofitable plant and equipment, then it was possible to attain a sharp rise in productivity, product quality and service under public ownership (Walters, 1991, p. 259). Indeed, privatisation in Britain in the 1980s, which was so large an influence upon the transition orthodoxy, 'only took place after all the hard work of reform had been completed' (Walters, 1991, 259).

'Privatisation before improvement' is the easy way to approach reform, since it absolves the government from responsibility and hard work. However, the only way to accomplish this is through rapid, 'wild' privatisation. There is, of course, one powerful argument that helps to persuade a post-communist governments that 'wild privatisation' is desirable, namely, that government officials will be in a position to benefit substantially from the process through insider dealing.[14]

Privatisation did not have to occur rapidly. It was quite feasible to have a process of 'organic privatisation'. As those state enterprises or the subsidiaries which they established became profitable, the ownership structure could alter as ownership shares were gradually acquired

by either foreign capital or domestic capital, including other state enterprises or other state institutions. Nor is the only method of accomplishing a gradual dilution of the state's ownership rights the issuance of
shares tradeable on the stock market. The change in ownership can be
accomplished through a gradual move towards a form of joint stock
company based on a variety of institutional shareholders, none of whom
need necessarily possess rights that are publicly tradeable. Each of the
shareholders would however, have a vested interest in the long-term
expansion and growth of the company.

Dangers of one-cut price liberalisation

Owing to the price policy under Stalinism, especially large price rises
under price liberalisation were likely to occur in basic necessities rather
than luxury items. The poorer sections of the community were likely
to be the most adversely affected by one-cut liberalisation. There was
a large danger that in their enthusiasm to create an irreversible move
towards a market economy instantaneous price liberalisation would be
put into effect before policy makers had time to devise a properly constructed 'social safety net'.

In a setting of political democracy and newly independent trade unions,
there would be large pressures for compensating wage increases which
might in turn lead to a wage–price inflationary spiral as the government was pressured into allowing accomodating increases in money
supply.

One-cut price liberalisation will have a large impact upon the relative profitability of different sectors. Insofar as managers and workers'
incomes are related to enterprise profitability, great inequities in income are likely to result, with these inequalities having little relationship to enterprises' economic performance. A slower liberalisation would
enable the government to monitor enterprise performance more closely,
and to tax windfall profits and assist those sectors which experienced
low profits or losses through no fault of the management or workers.

If price liberalisation happens rapidly at the start of reform then
there is a high probability of monopoly pricing behaviour by as yet
unreformed state enterprises. This is likely to be aggravated by rises
in the price of formerly underpriced inputs which more or less monopolistic state enterprises can pass on in the form of price increases.
This would reinforce already strong inflationary pressures. Given that
enterprise reform is likely to be time-consuming, there is a strong argument for gradual step-by-step liberalisation of input prices alongside rather than ahead of enterprise reform.

The massive network of physical supply material inputs was the heart of the command economy. This could only be eliminated instantaneously at the price of chaos. It takes a long time to build up the knowledge that is involved in the exchange of myriads of products. Moreover, there will be simultaneously be vast excess demands and shortages that will create huge arbitrage opportunities. The only sensible way to reform the material supply system is gradually. This in turn means that the price reform needs to be gradual. A 'free market' price by definition means that the product is not allocated through the material supply system.

Industrial structure: plants, firms, and scale in the reform of manufacturing industry in the communist countries

Absence of firms and the bias towards large plants in the former socialist economies   The communist economies explicitly destroyed the central idea of capitalist industry, namely the competitive firm. Instead, the attempt was made at huge cost to run the whole economy as a single factory, based on administrative orders rather than competitive struggle between rival firms for profits and market share. Under socialist 'planning' all industry was *de facto* or *de jure* state-owned. The 'firm' was synonymous with the Ministry (or even the whole planning system). Large-scale production units were favoured because of the ease of planning a smaller number of units, due to a belief among leaders and many economists in the superior returns to be obtained from large scale units, and reinforced by a bias towards heavy industry with its associated economies of scale. Consequently, large plants played a bigger role in the manufacturing sector of the socialist economies than generally was the case even in the large capitalist countries. The command economies faced a dual problem in industrial reform, namely the construction of competitive firms and reorganisation of the size structure of establishments.

The need to construct competitive firms of different sizes in different countries and sectors, as opposed to privatisation of ownership rights over individual plants, received scant attention in the advice of Western economists to the reforming communist countries. This is ironic, since it is the *firm* rather than the *plant* that is the key location of decision-making and competition within the capitalist economies.

Large firms in the advanced capitalist economies   The role of small manufacturing firms in the advanced capitalist economies has increased in the past decade or so.[15] This increase was associated with new electronic production technologies that allow greater flexibility in manufacturing. Using numerically controlled machine tools, firms frequently have replaced conventional automated production with flexible manufacturing systems.[16] The increased role of small firms has also been associated with a trend increase in contracting out 'service' activities, such as accountancy and cleaning, formerly located within the manufacturing firm. Finally, the early 1990s saw a considerable reduction in employment in large firms, associated with the cyclical downturn in the OECD countries.

However, large firms still occupy a central position in the advanced capitalist economies. Huge corporations with tens or even hundreds of thousands of employees (Table 4.1) stand at the centre of the capitalist system. The large-scale 'modern industrial enterprise' played a central role in the rise of the modern capitalist economy: 'The modern industrial enterprise played a central role in creating the most technologically advanced, fastest growing industries of their day. These industries, in turn, were the pace-setters of the industrial sector of their economies. . . . [They] provided an underlying dynamic in the development of modern industrial capitalism' (Chandler, 1990, p. 593). This institutional form emerged rapidly in the advanced capitalist economies at the end of the nineteenth century, alongside changes in production technology and has remained at its core ever since. There is every reason to think that newly emerging industrial economies can expect that the same institution will play a central role in their own rise to prosperity.

In US manufacturing as a whole, large firms (those with over 500 employees) still account for over 74 per cent of total manufacturing sales (Acs and Audretsch, 1993, p. 70). In the UK 'manufacturing remains dominated by a very small number of large businesses [of over 1000 employees] which collectively produce three-fifths of total net output, and provide slightly more than half of total manufacturing employment' (Hughes, 1993, p. 39).[17] In many small countries like Switzerland, Sweden and Holland the role of large corporations is even greater: in these countries the top 20 firms alone in 1985 accounted for 60, 67 and 95 per cent of total industrial employment respectively (Scherer and Ross, 1990, p. 63).

Large multi-plant firms have been a key element in the process of cost reduction and technical progress. They have benefitted from economies of scale, associated with reduction in unit costs from large plant size. Engineering studies show that in many sectors plants of less than a certain scale face substantial unit cost disadvantages (Pratten, quoted in Jacquemin *et al.*, 1989). In addition large firms often benefit from

Table 4.1   The number of employees in the world's largest one hundred companies (by turnover), 1990

No. of employees (1000s)	No. of companies	Name of the companies
above 750,000	1	General Motors
501–750,000	0	—
249–500,000	12	Ford, IBM, General Electric, IRI, Daimler-Benz, Fiat, Unilever, Volkswagen, Siemens, Philips, BAT Industries, Pepsico
100–249,000	43	Exxon, Royal Dutch Shell, British Petroleum, Hitachi, Matsushita Electrical Industry, Philip Morris, Chrysler, Du Pont, Samsung, Nissan Motor, Nestlé, Toshiba, Renault, BASF, Hoechst, Peugeot, Bayer, CGE, NEC, ICI, ASEA Brown Boveri, Boeing, United Technology, Eastman Kodak, Xerox, Fujitsu, Robert Bosch, INI, Pemex, McDonell Douglas, British Aerospace, Grand Metropolitan, Mannesman, BTR, Sara Lee, Electrolux, Rockwell International, Digital Equipment, Westinghouse Electric, Ruhrkohls, Thomson, Allied Signal,
51–99,000	30	Toyota, Mobil, Chevron, ENI, Honda Motor, Veba, Amoco, Elf Acquitaine, Procter and Gamble, Occidental Petroleum, Daewoo, Mitsubishi Electric, Nippon Steel, Sony, Usinor Sacilor, Volvo, Tenneco, BMW, Pechiney Mitsubishi Heavy Industries, Ciba Geigy, Bridgestone, Hanson, Minnesota Mining and Mfg., Hewlett Packard, Rhone-Poulenc, International Paper
below 50,000	14	Texaco, Total CFP, Nippon Oil, Mitsubishi Motors, Atlantic Richfield, RJR Nabisco, Mazda Motor, Petroleos de Venezuela, Philips Petroleum, Ferruzzi Financiaria, Kuwait Petroleum, Conagra, Perofina, Idemitsu Kosan

Source: European Community, 1991.

economies of 'scope' associated with reduced transaction costs involved in the transfer of goods and services from one operating unit to another (Chandler, 1990). Multi-plant firms may benefit from reduced transport costs, superior research and development, reduced risk, lower capital costs, the capacity to create a brand name, credit provision to customers and after-sales service and repair (Chandler, 1990, p. 200), and in many sectors firms which do not operate several plants may be at a considerable competitive disadvantage.

Large successful capitalist firms do not operate as perfectly competitive units which allocate resources entirely according to the price mechanism. On the contrary, within such firms the co-ordination mechanism is the 'conscious decisions and commands of management' (Scherer and Ross, 1990, p. 109). There are indeed managerial diseconomies of scale associated with large firm size. However, in many sectors the existence of large firm size can be explained by the fact that the cost of organising many activities through direct managerial controls are less than the cost of organising them through a multititude of small-scale complex transactions through the market. Successful large capitalist firms contain some of the characteristics of the planning functions of the Stalinist economy. This is unsurprising, since the orginal notion of the planned economy arose from a generalisation of the planning functions that could be observed in the large firm in the late nineteenth and early twentieth century (Szamuely, 1974).

Despite the heterogenity of experience some patterns can be observed historically in respect to way in which economies of scale and scope affect different sectors. Chandler's analysis of the 401 giant companies with more than 20,000 workers found that in the mid-1970s no less than 72 per cent of them were clustered in a narrow range of industries, namely, chemicals, petroleum, primary metals, and the three machinery groups (non-electrical and electrical machinery, transportation equipment), and food (Chandler, 1990, p. 19). These were mainly capital-intensive industries, predominantly in the heavy industry sector. A major factor underlying this pattern is the sharp difference between sectors in the availability of technical economies of scale (i.e. differences in cost curves associated with the different technical characteristics of the given industry) (Pratten, in Jacquemin *et al.*, 1989).

Policy implications for reforming economies   Post-Stalinist economies should not neglect the large-scale industrial sector. The best policy is not passively to sell off individual plants to private buyers, and try to construct a textbook, perfectly competitive structure of small businesses. It may take a long time for large firms to emerge through the spontaneous play of market forces. In the meantime, in many sectors this will lead to efficiency losses stemming from failure to take advantage of economies of scale at the plant level, as well as economies of 'scope' arising from multi-plant operation. Moreover, if a reforming Stalinist economy fails to produce successful large firms it is likely in many sectors to reduce its ability to compete internationally which will in turn have negative effects on the economy's balance of payments.

A key task of the post-communist governments was to devise policies that would lead to the emergence of 'modern industrial corporations', often in heavy industry, which could form the basis for prosperity in other parts of the economy. This must involve a series of amalgamations, splitting up of inappropriate parts of plants, and mergers of plants, to produce large, competitive multi-plant firms. In order to guide and assist this process, the governments in the former communist countries ought to have looked carefully at the corporate structure of the advanced capitalist countries.

Instead of writing off the large scale manufacturing sector, as could easily happen with free market policies and privatisation under conditions of political and economic instability, a planning strategy was needed to take advantage of the rich legacy of skills that these economies possessed. Careful studies were needed of the existing industrial structure to identify those sectors in which the different countries and regions might in the long-term be able to establish a competitive industry. These sectors then needed to be protected and assisted in a targetted programme of reorganisation, involving operational independence, building a professional management team, and constructing a corporate structure. Such an industrial strategy is built around long-term comparative advantage and requires government intervention.

Much of the growth of small and medium enterprises in the advanced capitalist countries has been dependent directly on contracts with large firms, and indirectly on meeting demands for final products arising from incomes created in the large scale sector. There are strong reasons for the reforming economies to have expected rapid initial growth in employment in the long-suppressed service sector in those areas in which only small capital investments are required. However, it is questionable whether the reforming command economies could expect fast growth of the small scale manufacturing sector in the absence of a dynamic large scale sector.

Heavy industry bias in the former communist countries is not without its advantages

It is by no means the case that heavy industry, in which large firms tend to predominate, plays a small role in the advanced economies. Indeed, the share of heavy industry is not noticeably smaller in these countries from the former communist countries (Table 4.2). This is unsurprising, since these sectors produce the capital goods with which physical investment, capital deepening and increases in labour productivity and income are realised. Indeed, these often 'are precisely the industries where income elasticity of demand is high, technological progress is rapid, and labour productivity rises fast' (OECD, 1972, p. 15, quoted in Wade, 1990, p. 25).

The heavy industry bias of the former communist countries has the advantage that these countries possessed a rich legacy of engineering skills. Shifting to more competitive manufacturing activities is only partially a question of access to new capital equipment. It also requires investment in human capital. An important part of the investment programme of the governments of the Newly Industrialising Countries has been in the engineering skills needed for businesses to make intelligent technical choices in purchasing new capital goods, in operating them effectively and developing new capital goods products. Much of this investment in human capital had already been made in the former Stalinist economies. In market economies there often is a high income elasticity of demand capital goods. Capital goods often experience rapid technical progress and increases in labour productivity. Indeed, Japan's industrial planners gave priority to the development of the capital goods industries in their post-war growth strategy (OECD, 1972, p. 15). The main task of industrial policy in the former Stalinist economies was not to close most heavy industry but, rather, to restructure it into competitive companies which would be the long term basis of profits and rising incomes.

Capital accumulation

In most programmes of Western advice the generation and channelling of savings was an empty box. Financial institutions were to be privatised, interest rates were to reflect market forces, and the rate and allocation of investment was to reflect citizens' individual preferences. In fact, the accumulation and allocation of capital is the central problem in the reconstruction of the former communist countries' economies. An industrial strategy which revolves around restructuring the currently loss-

Table 4.2   Share of 'heavy industry' in gross value of industrial output in different countries, various years in 1970s (per cent)

	China	USA	West Germany	Japan	UK	Italy	Poland	Spain	Yugo-slavia	Korea	India
Total	64.1	69.5	74.2	69.5	66.9	69.0	64.1	68.1	61.8	56.4	61.7
Of which chemicals, rubber and plastics	12.3	10.8	13.5	11.0	12.4	13.9	9.2	13.1	8.6	12.0	14.5
Iron and steel, non-ferrous metals and metal mining	9.0	6.9	9.4	10.5	7.6	9.9	9.9	16.8	11.3	2.7	10.9
machinery, equipment and metal manufacture	27.3	34.2	35.4	35.6	31.0	30.5	32.9	20.4	27.0	20.0	18.8

Source: World Bank, 1981b, p. 16.

making manufacturing sector into an internationally competitive condition which will eventually make profits is precisely the kind of situation in which capital markets will tend to fail. Moreover, in an atmosphere of great uncertainty about property rights (due to governments' widespread commitment to privatisation, but their inability to carry it out rapidly), and in which there is political instability (due in no small part to the social tensions engendered by attempts at rapid economic reform), private investors are even less likely to trust their capital to investments that will only yield their benefits after a substantial time lag. Speculation and the hope of short-term profits are likely to dominate the investment calculation. Under these circumstances there is a strong case for government intervention to raise savings and channel them into reconstruction projects aimed at regenerating the manufacturing sector, either directly or though low interest loans. Unfortunately, in the turbulence of European post-communist politics, it was difficult for the state to raise revenue from taxation with which to finance government expenditure on an industrial strategy. The destruction of the bureaucracy, viewed as the key task in the transition orthodoxy, may bring an increase in personal freedom at the price of failure to achieve socially desirable goals through effective state action.

The importance of demand

Foreign demand　Western policy advice to the former Stalinist economies focussed obsessively on the international economy and was extremely optimistic about trade prospects. Trade is a key channel for growth and technical progress. However, the 1990s will be radically different from preceding periods. The problems of structural adjustment in the advanced capitalist countries will intensify and much hinges on the course of political economy in these countries. The greater the flexibility that they demonstrate, and the faster they grow, the better will be the export prospects for the former communist countries.

However, there is still great uncertainty about the way in which the advanced capitalist countries will respond to this challenge. It would be irresponsible to base an economic strategy around the assumption that there will be no demand-side barriers to exports from the formely Stalinist countries:

> *For Eastern Europe, the EC's half-hearted response to their need for market access provides a disillusioning introduction to the practices of West European capitalism. . . .* The extensive trade liberalisation undertaken by Poland, Hungary and Czechoslovakia suggests that they have swallowed the free trade message. . . . [However], substantial trade barriers will remain against Eastern Europe's main industrial exports for at least the next five years. . . . [The] willingness of [the EC] to bow to special pleading of certain 'import sensitive' industries does not bode well for Eastern Europe's future. (*Financial Times*, 13 April, 1992) (Emphasis added)

Domestic demand　Whatever the export possibilities, the bulk of demand for industrial capital and consumer goods, especially for large countries like China and Russia, Ukraine, Poland and Vietnam, will be domestic. Given that the capacity to increase imports is likely to face constraints through inability to increase exports at the hoped for rate, much of the demand for manufactures in reforming countries needs to be met from domestic sources. Industrial enterprises which are inefficient at competing on world markets may, nevertheless, have a large role to play in satisfying domestic demand. An important function for government planning in a time of such uncertainty will be to assist the restructuring of enterprises by analysing the probable pattern of demand as the economic structure alters. This is a classic function of indicative planning, and one which is needed urgently in a time of such uncertainty. If expectations are formed by government statements along transition orthodoxy lines, then there is a great danger that businessmen will believe the rhetoric which argues that, in the long run, the large-scale manufacturing sector will mostly close down. In fact it will be hopelessly inefficient to produce in SMEs most of the goods needed by the domestic market. The government must try to reorganise large scale industry into structures that can benefit from economies of scale but also behave competitively rather than in an oligopolistic or a monopolistic fashion. Large-scale state industries which are unprofitable in the depths of a post-communist political economic crisis in which, moreover, the government is pursuing a sharply deflationary policy, may well make profits as demand begins to grow. It may be deeply wasteful to allow this sector to be closed down and cannibalised.

It has long been recognised that countries with much lower levels of economic development need to protect their infant industries from more advanced economies . However, the question of what constitutes an 'infant' industry is complex, especially in the reforming socialist economies. An 'infant' industry is not just one which did not exist in any form at some prior point. An 'old' industry which is out-of-date and uncompetitive on international markets, but which is in the process of being modernised and restructured, can be considered to have the same characteristics as an 'infant' industry. It is rational that an industry, or a section of it, which today is uncompetitive and would be bankrupted in open international competition, but which is thought likely to become competitive, be given protection.

Class structure and privatisation

The discussion of privatisation in the orthodox transition literature was, at best, antiseptic and naive. At worst, it was dishonest. The real world of capitalism is not one of equal life chances for all 'economic agents' based on equal opportunities to select ocupations, earn income and accumulate capital. Rather it is based on large differences in life opportunities systematically related to, among other things,[18] class position. The privatisation of asset ownership in the countries in transition from the command system is nothing less than the process of creation of the new class structure of these countries. This is the process of 'primitive capitalist accumulation'. The manner in which the ownership and use of state assets changes during the transition will have a profound long-term effect upon the most fundamental parameters of economic life, the 'givens' of the economic textbook. These are the fundamentals which influence the life chances of different social groups. They will be reflected years later in differences between social groups in income, housing conditions, educational achievement, mortality rates, longevity, occupational position and social status.

It is odd that anyone should advocate a high speed, revolutionary approach to such a fundamental issue which will influence the shape of a society for generations to come. It *would* seem to be common sense to proceed experimentally with something so important as transforming the ownership of almost the entire structure of a country's productive assets. There is a curious symmetry of approach. Throughout the twentieth century the communist governments were attacked ferociously for their revolutionary confiscation of assets. Paradoxically, the orthodox analysis recommended unambiguously a revolutionary disposal of state assets.

The orthodox recommendation of high-speed disposal of publicly owned assets carried obvious dangers. Public rhetoric spoke of the need to 'return assets to the people'. Whatever variant of the privatisation schemes was chosen, the mere fact of the attempt to privatise rapidly was likely to produce highly unequal asset ownership. The faster the process proceeded, the less likely was it that an effective legal structure would be put in place, and the more likely that insider dealing, misrepresentation, and outright theft would occur. These possibilities were greatly increased if the overthrow of the communist party coincided with a phase of political turbulence and outright lawlessness. Moreover, in the early stages of the transition, the market structure is highly imperfect as the shortage economy with its state fixed prices adjusts to the market economy. The long-term value of assets is impossibly hard to evaluate. Even market information is likely to be highly unreliable and hard to obtain, so that those with superior knowledge can rapidly accumulate capital.

This environment offered massive opportunities for speculative gain out of the privatisation process and in its immediate aftermath. Some idea of the practical outcomes of the privatisation process under these circumstances can be seen from the example of Gabor Varzegis. In 1994, he was reputed to be 'Eastern Europe's richest individual'. He made his first, modest fortune as a bass guitarist for Gemini, a 1970s Hungarian rock band. He gave up music to emigrate to the US in 1980, worked as a diamond trader in New York and retained his US citizenship. In an interview with the *Financial Times* he commented: 'Here [in eastern Europe] you can build a serious empire in five to ten years', says Varszegi, *'It's a once in a lifetime opportunity. Part of the world is on sale. It never happened before and it will never happen again.'* (*Financial Times*, 11 April 1994) (Emphasis added).

The problems do not stem simply from the fact of high speed under conditions without effective law and order. The transition orthodoxy also argued for tight monetary polices which it was believed would cause a period of serious economic difficulty.[19] Undertaking privatisation in the midst of a deep recession creates a high probability of the rapid concentration of asset ownership, whatever the method of privatisation chosen. If publicly owned assets are offered for sale to the 'general public', the deeper the recession, the less possible is it for the 'general public' to participate in purchasing the assets. Even if ownership rights were given away to the general public through a voucher scheme, the deeper was the recession, the higher the possibility that the general public would sell their shares in return for current income in order to survive the 'pain' of the transition. The larger the number of people who did this, the lower would tend to be the price of the assets traded. The process is closely analgous to that described by Sen in relation to a famine situation (Sen, 1982). The Chilean privatisation of 1975–78 during a deep recession, though not remotely as deep as the Russian 'recession' of the early 1990s, witnessed exactly this phenomenon.[20] The former Chilean Minister of Finance described the process as follows:

> The First Round of [privatisation] was carried out in the midst of deep structural transformation process, during which there was little interest on the part of foreigners to invest in the country, and which was accompanied by considerable political, social and economic uncertainty. . . . These debt privatisations carried out in an economically unstable environment, contributed to generate a considerable degree of financial asset concentration, financial instability, and some important macro-economic problems. (Quoted in Lipton and Sachs, 1990a, p. 251)

4.5 CONCLUSION

This chapter examined four aspects of the principles involved in the transition from the Stalinist system of political economy. First, I argued that a large difficulty for attaining a successful transition away from communism lay in the fact that neither in the communist countries themselves nor in the outside world was there much prior discussion of the problems of the transition. In both cases the absence of such discussion had its causes mainly in the realm of the ideological confrontation between the communist and the capitalist systems.

Secondly, I argued that an important, if not the dominant part of the discussion about the transition adopted the simplistic premise that the transition of the entire economic and political system was best conducted rapidly and simultaneously in all areas of politics and economics. This was based on an erroneous understanding of the nature of systems of political economy, which can only function with reasonable effectiveness if the knowledge required of the individuals who compose them does not alter too rapidly.

Thirdly, arguments supporting the benefits to be derived from overthrow of the communist system were considered. It is argued by most commentators that democratic political institutions are an instrinsically valuable 'human right'; that private property rights can only be guaranted under democratic political institutions; that totalitarian leaders cannot preside over the introduction of a market economy since this will rob them of the basis of their power; and that the statistical evidence shows that greater democratisation does not harm growth and may even promote it. This chapter argues that the historical evidence does not support such propositions; that there are serious flaws in the quantitative studies of the relationship between democratisation and economic performance; that the idea of 'democracy' in the labour market is highly ambiguous; that national unity may be hard to sustain in the wake of an anti-communist revolution; that political stability is an important condition of economic advance; that 'free and fair elections' are far from a sufficient condition for establishing democracy; that 'human rights' embrace much more than merely the right periodically to cast a vote in an election; and that large post-Stalinist structural change may be hard to put into effect in a democratic framework.

Fourth, it considers the narrowly economic arguments in favour of rapid economic transformation. Much of the confidence of policy advisors to the reforming communist countries stemmed from a positive view of the lessons learned from stabilisation and structural adjustment programmes in developing countries. They reflected confidence that the essential preconditions for successful performance were monetary stability; price liberalisation, including full integration with world market prices; and privatisation of property rights. It was regarded as desirable that there should be a 'surgical operation' in which a large part of state industry should close down under the operation of a hard budget constraint. It was widely thought that the reform package should be put into effect rapidly. This chapter argued that such an approach was deeply flawed in principle. It showed that much of the policy advice was based on an outdated notion of the strengths and weaknesses of state intervention; that simple institutional reforms could produce powerful improvements in economic performance; that rapid privatisation of assets was not practically possible; that state enterprises could improve their performance without outright privatisation; that instantaneous price liberalisation could cause many problems; that restructuring the organisation of industrial assets could produce considerable gains in industrial performance; that capital markets were likely in principle to fail during a transitional period from communist command economy; and that policies which were able to generate steady growth of demand ought to be able to produce large improvements in industrial performance without the pain of more radical approaches.

5 'Catch-up' Capabilities Compared

5.1 INTRODUCTION

The limited discussion of the comparative performance of China and the USSR under reform[1] has mostly assumed that the reason for the dramatic contrast in outcome can be explained mainly by the radically different starting points, with large differences in their respective capacities for 'catching up, forging ahead and falling behind', to use the terminology of Abramowitz (1986). The role of policy choice in politics and economics is given low explanatory weight.

China's 'success' is seen as mainly due to factors such as the low level of industrialisation, its large rural population, the strength of its historical traditions of 'capitalism', and the advantages enjoyed on account of the impact of Hong Kong and Taiwan. The USSR's failure is seen largely in terms of its 'special' problems such as its 'over-industrialisation', the greater strength of nationalism, or the more conservative nature of the communist party. Sachs and Woo have presented the most coherent such argument to date. They argue: 'It was neither gradualism nor experimentation, but rather China's economic structure, that proved so felicitous to reform. China began reform as a peasant agricultural society, EEFSU[2] as urban and overindustrialised. . . . In Gerschenkron's famous phrase [China] had the "advantage of backwardness"' (Sachs and Woo, 1994, pp. 102–4).

This chapter examines these propositions in detail. It concludes that there were large and obvious differences. However, despite these differences the two countries both possessed large 'catch-up' possibilities, many of which stemmed from the common features of the communist system. It concludes that China did not possess greater 'catch-up' possibilities than the USSR.

If this analysis is correct, then the main cause of the difference in outcome must be the differences in policy choice. This applies both to narrowly economic policy and to the wider question of the relationship between political and economic reform.

5.2 ECONOMIC FACTORS

5.2.1 Geo-political location

China is located in the most dynamic region of the world economy, including Japan and the 'Asian Newly Industrialising Countries'. The latter embraces not just the 'Four Little Tigers' (Hong Kong, Singapore, South Korea and Taiwan), but also Malaysia, Indonesia and Thailand. Moreover, the fast-growing economies of Japan and the East Asian NICs started experiencing acute labour shortages, large trade surpluses and appreciating exchange rates in the 1980s, coinciding with China's economic reform. These economies were extremely keen to invest in foreign countries with lower labour costs in less technologically complex lines of manufacturing. China was a major beneficiary from this process.

The core of the Russian economy is located on the edge of Europe. By the early 1990s, major structural problems had appeared in Europe. Growth rates were much below those in East Asia. Moreover, the USSR stretched over vast inhospitable regions in central Asia and extreme northerly latitudes in the Far East.

Trade

The fact that neighbouring economies have fast growth rates may not be as important as it at first sight appears to be. The importance of immediate geographical location can easily be exaggerated. In respect to much merchandise trade, once goods have to be shipped by container on board ships, the impact on costs of shipping them a longer rather than a shorter distance is not great. While Western Europe is growing relatively slowly, the income levels in the region are still far above those in most of East Asia, and the absolute levels of trade are large.[3] The US economy also grew relatively slowly in the 1990s. However, this was the most important market upon which the export success of the East Asian NICs relied, and it became increasingly important for China in the 1980s.[4]

Investment

Physical location *per se* is unimportant in determining international capital movements. The question that has to be answered is: why did foreign investment favour China over other locations, such as Latin America, Africa, and eventually, post-reform Eastern Europe and Russia? Moreover, East Asia itself is brimming with countries wanting to and able to attract foreign investments. The Chinese reform package had to prove itself and gain credibility amongst foreign investors. China attracted substantial foreign investments because it provided political stability, reasonable physical infrastructure, cheap labour costs with a low probability of strike action, and investment guarantees. Moreover, the successful achievement of rapid growth behind high protectionist barriers made China attractive as a potentially huge market both for consumer durables and capital goods, thereby inducing investments by foreign companies in a wider range industries than simply those for which low labour costs are most critical.

China did enjoy an advantage over much of the rest of the reforming communist world in that there is a large amount of capital in the hands of the Chinese diaspora. Other reforming countries also have large diaspora. For example, it is likely that the total amount of capital held by the Indian diaspora greatly exceeds that of overseas Chinese. However, only a small proportion of this has found its way back into India despite the Indian government's commitment to economic liberalisation. Clearly, a diaspora alone is not sufficient. The reforming country has to be successful in establishing a political-economic regime that is attractive to investors, domestic or foreign. Capital is rarely patriotic.

At the start of its reform, the USSR also had the potential to become an attractive investment site. The core of the Russian economy to the West of the Urals was essentially a part of Europe, which was to become the largest single market in the world in 1992. It possessed a labour force which was much more educated and skilled than existed in China. They were prepared to work hard for much lower incomes than comparably skilled people in the advanced capitalist counries. It also possessed a much larger pool of well-trained scientific personnel than China. Moreover, its infrastructure was much more developed than that of China. The fact that it has so far failed to attract a significant amount of foreign investment despite these conditions suggests that there was something deeply unattractive about the investment environment there.[5]

5.2.2 Advantages of the latecomer

In the late 1970s when China started its reform it was much poorer than the USSR. A 'latecomer' country has a potential for a faster growth, as it can draw upon a larger pool of advanced technology than was available for the early industrialisers. Early-developers also have a larger portion of capital stock in older vintage machines, and therefore, once the late-developer builds up its capital stock, it may have a more efficient vintage profile of capital stock. In this sense, it has been argued that China's better performance can largely be explained by a greater scope for catch-up accorded by its greater backwardness. It has also been suggested that it is advantageous for a reforming communist country to have a large share of its population in agriculture. It is argued that agricultural reforms are easier to achieve than industrial reforms. Furthermore, a huge rural labour surplus is said to provide the potentiality for rapid growth in labour intensive industries, which have shorter gestation lags and tend to have more flexible machinery than large-scale industry. However, there are many problems with this argument.

Social capability

Countries which catch up successfully need to possess a certain level of 'social capability' in order to be able to exploit the technology of advanced countries. Very poor economies often do not succeed in catch-up because they lack well-functioning institutions: '[A] country's potential for rapid growth is strong not when it is backward without qualification but rather when it is technologically backward but socially advanced' (Abramowitz, 1986, p. 388). This is expressed in Gomulka's 'hat-shape' relationship between the level of development and the rate of growth, where there is a negative correlation between the two for countries above a certain level of development (i.e., the poorer grow faster, and 'catch-up' occurs), while there is a positive relationship between the two for the least developed countries (i.e., the poorer grow more slowly, and catch-up does not take place) (Gomulka, 1991). When China's reform began, it was much closer to the latter stage than was the USSR, which had completed the minimum necessary institution building process. In the 1970s, immediately before the reforms began in China, the vast bulk of the population was a semi-literate peasantry, over one-third of whom lived in dire poverty. It is difficult to conclude that being more backward gave China a decisive advantage over Russia. Indeed, within Eastern Europe those countries that have done least badly since the end of Stalinism have been those that were most advanced at the end of the communist period. It is 'sophisticated' Hungary, not impoverished Albania or Romania that has attracted the lion's share of foreign investment since 1989. In the 1970s even the latter countries were vastly more advanced than was China in terms of social capability.

Agriculture

Having a large proportion of national output and employment generated in agriculture is not necessarily an advantage for a reforming communist country. Indeed, many economists have argued that a main factor explaining the success of the East Asian 'Four Little Dragons' was precisely the fact that each had a relatively small farm sector at the start of their phase of accelerated growth: 'It is very rare for agriculture to grow faster than 5 per cent in any country where agriculture is an important part of the economy. Therefore, the less important is agriculture, the easier it is to strike up very high growth rates of GDP. This is what people have in mind when they dismiss Hong Kong and Singapore as irrelevant' (Little, 1979, p. 450). Moreover, the capital needs for expanding agriculture often are large, especially in a densely populated economy such as China's, in which yields per unit of farmland in many areas were already very high in the 1970s. Finally, the idea that China's economy was 'agriculture-led' throughout the reform period is incorrect. In the early stages of the reform, the growth rate of farm output was high, at almost the same figure as that for national income. However, in the latter phase, the growth rate of farm output fell sharply to less than one half the growth rate of national income, which remained high despite the drop in the growth rate of farm output.[6]

Capital markets

As the world economy expands, so each successive wave of successful latecomers is able to benefit from ever larger pools of international capital. After the 1970s there was a further acceleration of the globalisation of capital, both through portfolio investment by institutions and direct foreign investment by multinationals. The sheer availability of such pools of capital is not sufficient to guarantee advance. In Latin America, for example, in the 1970s vast amounts of capital flooded into the region, but this did not enable the region to take off into long term sustained growth. However, if developing countries or countries undergoing large structural transformation are able successfully to attract and to employ such capital, then it can assist them to achieve accelerated growth. This is a major factor explaining why latecomers have the opportunity to grow more rapidly than their predecessors.

The nature of foreign investment is especially important in determining whether or not it assists the growth process. Foreign direct investment is especially attractive, since the investor is more likely to have a long term commitment to improve performance in the firm in which the investment takes place. Foreign investment also can make a large contribution to infrastructure building. However, speculative portfolio investment generally makes no contribution to technical progress. Moreover, it can be destabilising by leaving the country at high speed, and even affecting the animal spirits of domestic capitalists so that they to take their financial resources out of the country.[7]

An important part of the growth of foreign investment was in developing countries. For example, the multinationals increased their direct employment in developing countries from 5 million in 1985 to 12 million in 1992 (UN, 1994). The distribution of foreign direct investment between countries and regions was extremely uneven. Many developing countries had declining foreign direct investment in the 1980s, with only negligible inflows by the early 1990s. This was true for large swathes of Africa and many Latin American countries (World Bank, *WDR*, 1994, pp. 282–3). On the other hand, some developing economies, such as China, Indonesia, Thailand and Malaysia, were able to capture a large share of this investment. They were able through this to add significantly to domestic savings, but more importantly, were able to use the globalisation of capital as a channel through which rapidly to upgrade their technological level.

5.2.3 Size

China and the USSR enjoyed a considerable potential advantage compared to the other reforming Stalinist economies on account of their vast size. This meant that they both had a greater possibility to restructure without loss of efficiency behind protectionist barriers. Domestic industries could potentially move towards profitability at world market prices within a relatively closed economy with growing internal competition and yet simultaneously benefit from economies of scale. In this respect they each possessed the potential to take the nineteenth century 'American' way to industrial prosperity behind protectionist barriers producing for a massive domestic market of continental dimensions.[8] In this respect they each enjoyed a large advantage over the other reforming communist countries.

5.2.4 The labour force

General educational level

The socialist ideals of the communist countries was reflected in their deep commitment to the provision of equality of access to education, especially for primary and secondary school age children.

China's level of general education in the 1970s was advanced for a low income country (Table 5.1). Indeed, the proportion of the relevant age groups in primary and secondary placed the country around the middle income level. In the late 1980s the mean years of schooling of the Chinese population aged over 25 stood at 4.8, which was the same level as that for middle income countries, and stood at more than double the figure reported for low income countries (2.3 years) (UNDP, 1992). In normal times,[9] the quality of China's basic education was impressive compared to other developing countries. The World Bank summarised the situation in the late 1970s as follows: 'About 72 per cent of those who enter primary schools in China complete four years of education as compared with 41 per cent in India, 68 per cent in Indonesia, and 38 per cent in Brazil; . . . the achievements of Chinese children in such basic subjects as mathematics are on average ahead of those in most [low income] countries' (World Bank, 1981, pp. 66–7).

The Soviet Union's achievements in basic education compare favourably even with those of the advanced capitalist countries (Table 5.1). Indeed, estimates for the mid-1970s using international purchasing power parity dollars show the USSR to be ahead of all Western countries except the USA in 'consumption' of educational services per capita (Schroeder, 1983, p. 319).

Higher education

China took a strategic decision to place high emphasis within full time education upon the primary and secondary school level. In 1978 only one per cent of the relevant age group were studying in higher educational institutions, compared to 2 per cent in lower income countries as a whole, and 8 per cent in India (Table 5.1). Moreover, during the Cultural Revolution higher educational institutions were closed for much longer than lower levels: 'The Cultural Revolution is estimated to have cost China 2 million middle level technicians and one million university graduates (in addition, only a poor quality education was given to those who did pass through the system during this period)' (World Bank, 1981a, p. 106). In the late 1970s the ratio of scientific and techni-

Table 5.1 Educational achievements in China and the former USSR, 1978

	No. enrolled in primary school as per cent of age group	No. enrolled in secondary school as per cent of age group	No. enrolled in higher education as per cent of population aged 20–24	Adult literacy rate per cent
Low income countries*	74	20	2	43
Middle income countries	95	41	11	72
Industrial market economies	100	89	37	99
China	93	51	1	66
India	79	28	8	36
USA	98	97	56	99
Austria	100	72	21	99
USSR	97	72	22	100

Note: *Excluding India and China.

Source: World Bank, WDR, 1981.

cal personnel to total manpower in the productive sector was low. Even in chemicals and machinery manufacturing, the ratio in China stood at only 4.5 per cent, compared to 5.2 per cent in Brazil, 9.3 per cent in Mexico and 21.1. per cent in the USA.

Moreover, these data 'conceal the poor quality and out-of-date character of much technical knowledge – the result of ten years of educational disruptions and isolation form the rest of the world . . . In relation to China's desire and need to modernise, its supply of skilled manpower is inadequate' (World Bank, 1981a, p. 107). In its evaluation of the key machine building sector, the US Congress Joint Economic Committee Report of 1978 commented: 'China's ability to fully use, copy, or improve on large scale purchases of advanced technology and equipment assigned to the machine building industry is seriously hindered. A major gap in basic research skills, manufacturing know-how, and poor organisation and communication channels argues against China's rapid assimilation of Western technology. *A decade without advanced academic training for an entire generation has created a serious void in China's scientific and technical communities*'(USCJEC, 1978, p. 298) (Emphasis added).

The USSR had a vastly more developed pool of scientific and technical personnel than did China. A consequence of the poor record in utilising scientific skills to produce technical progress was that the USSR allocated a large amount of resources in order to enable the supply of scientific and technical workers to grow rapidly. In the early 1950s the USSR possessed just 15 scientists and engineers per 1,000 people compared to 26 per 1,000 people in the USA. By the mid-1970s, the USSR had overtaken the USA, with the respective figures standing at 66 and 62 per 1,000 people (Bergson and Levine, 1983, p. 55). Moreover, the low effectiveness of Soviet scientific research meant that in the USSR the number of ancillary personnel per scientist and engineer was high, standing at 5.0 in 1970, compared to just 1.3 in the USA (USCJEC, 1979, p. 745). Thus, in addition to its large pool of highly qualified scientific workers, the USSR possessed a large stock of moderately trained scientific workers.

A common consequence of the difficulties of central planning was that both countries possessed a large stock of capital goods per unit of final product. Moreover in both cases, the capital goods were unreliable, with a high propensity to break down. Furthermore compared to market economies there was much less reliability in obtaining spare parts from specialist producers. Thus a striking characteristic of both systems was the high level of engineering ingenuity at all levels. This was reflected, for example, in the huge numbers of general purpose lathes, used to produce a wide range of spare parts that in other economies would be purchased through the market. This was highly inefficient, but it produced a widespread basic engineering capacity.

In neither case was the stock of scientists and engineers used well. The absence of the motive force of competition and profit seeking greatly reduced the incentive of enterprises to undertake technical progress and even led to resistance to technical progress suggested from above the enterprise. The pervasive atmosphere of shortage led to a widespread 'sellers' market' so that in both capital goods and final consumption goods there was little incentive for enterprises to use available scientific skills to improve product quality. In the belief that technical progress was a public good, a large part of scientific capacities were located away from the enterprises. In the USSR in 1973, for example, only about 9 per cent of Soviet scientific workers were engaged in work in industrial enterprises, the remainder being located in higher educational institutions, in the scientific academies or in the branch ministries and other state agencies (USCJEC, 1979, p. 729).

Motivation

A large array of factors combined to produce a workforce in both China and the USSR that was operating much inside its capacity, even given the nature of the available capital stock.

In agriculture, fundamental difficulties arise with production units which employ a large number of workers, such as the collective farm and the state farm. The special nature of the farm work process and the associated difficulty of evaluating work performance means that it is extremely hard to obtain diligent labour.[10]

In the non-farm sector, the penalty of dismissal was virtually absent, which greatly reduced the pressure enterprise managers could exert upon the workforce. Under the material balance planning system, managers had a strong incentive to hoard labour as well as capital, since this made it easier to achieve the key planning targets, namely gross value or physical quantity of output. The administrative planning system found it impossible to obtain timely delivery of needed inputs so as to keep the production process running smoothly at full capacity. Consequently, the workpace was very uneven throughout each production period.

Much has been written of the normally slow pace of work and low work effort which resulted from these factors. However, it is far from the case that this represented a fixed parameter of economic activity. Rather, it represented a huge potential windfall gain if workers' motivation could be harnessed through suitable policies. An important factor which was available to enable this force to be released was the widespread disappointment with the standard of living attained after long years with high rates of saving and investment. Although by the 1970s the absolute levels of the standard of living in China and the USSR were very different, in both cases there was deep dissatisfaction with the poor results that had been produced by the communist planned economy. The introduction of suitable incentive systems could have released a greatly increased intensity of labour, and hugely raise output from existing resources.

5.2.5   Entrepreneurship

China has a much longer tradition of entrepreneurship than Russia. China's medieval technical revolution did not spring out of the heads of inventors independently of economic incentives. Mostly it occurred through the response of producers to practical problems encountered in producing for the market. As early as the tenth or eleventh century AD, China possessed a sophisticated economy, with a highly developed market structure compared to the rest of the contemporary world. It was arguably the world's mostly highly urbanised country until at least the late Middle Ages in Europe. Although China did not make the breakthrough to an Industrial Revolution along European lines, the growth of output, market systems and urban places continued over subsequent centuries. Whether or not one chooses to call this development a process of emerging 'capitalist sprouts', it is clear that China had a highly developed entrepreneurial system for many centuries before the European Industrial Revolution. The most advanced areas by the sixteenth or seventeenth century were those along the Eastern seaboard, and in the Lower Yangzi Valley.

China's capacity to respond strongly to the 'challenge' of the West in the late nineteenth and early twentieth century was inhibited deeply by the lack of a strong central government. By the mid-1930s, China still was an impoverished economy, with the vast bulk of output produced in the traditional sectors, and its exports dominated by primary products. However, in those areas and during those periods in which there was some semblance of political order, notably in Manchuria under Japanese occupation and in the Treaty Ports along the eastern seaboard, rapid progress in the development of modern industry did occur in the first three decades of the twentieth century. This was partially under foreign ownership, but also there emerged a thriving indigenous bourgeoisie. By the 1920s and 1930s, the Shanghai capitalists often had become thoroughly international in outlook, 'capable of surveying equally attentitively the Stock Exchanges of London or New York and the Szechuanese market' (Bergere, 1981, p. 33).

China clearly possessed a powerful capitalist tradition. Moreover, the Chinese revolution occurred relatively recently (1949). Thus, it can be argued that the memory of capitalism was still in the 1970s very much alive.

The Russian picture initially appears very much more disadvantageous. The Russian state itself is a modern construct. As late as the mid-fifteenth century, 'Russia' was a landlocked country of modest size. Over much of the country there were severe natural barriers to the development of commerce and production for the market: 'The fundamental and most stable feature of Russian history is the slow tempo of her development, with the economic backwardness, primitiveness of social forms and low level of culture resulting from it. . . . The population of this gigantic and austere plain, open to eastern winds and

Asiatic migrations, was condemned by nature itself to a long backwardness' (Trotsky, 1977, p. 26). The authoritarian state also presented serious obstacles to capitalist development through its rapacious intervention in economic affairs.[11] Moreover, by 1914, capitalist development had still 'as yet touched little more than the hem of Russia's economic system. The patches of factory industry in the Leningrad and Moscow districts and in the south were no more than industrial "islands" in a vast agricultural sea, bordered to the north by deep forests and to the south by mountain or desert' (Dobb, 1966, pp. 35–6). On top of this, the Soviet Union experienced almost sixty years under anti-capitalist Stalinist 'planning'.

However, the reality is much more complex. A growing body of revisionist scholarship is reassessing capitalist development pre-1914. In European Russia pre-1860 capitalism was much more advanced than was once supposed (see, e.g. Gatrell, 1986, pp. 144–50; Blackwell, 1983). By the late nineteenth century, several major centres of industrial and commercial activity had developed, often building on extensive traditions going back several centuries. The Moscow Region was the most ancient of these, being the centre of an extensive metallurgical industry which began with the formation of the Muscovite state during the Mongol period: 'Generations of such activity provided a pool, not only of artisanry but also of entrepreneurial aptitude and experience' (Blackwell, 1983, p. 16).

From the 1880s to 1914, Russian industry is now thought to have grown at around 4–5 per cent per annum (Gatrell, 1986, p. 143). A powerful group of big businesses emerged benefitting from foreign technology, often involving foreign capital, and frequently in cartelised form. Alongside them went a continued growth of more primitive, small-scale 'kustar' industry involving as many as 15 million urban and rural craftsmen in the 1880s (Gatrell, 1986, p. 154). St Petersburg was the area which modernised most rapidly: 'By the last decades of the old regime, St Petersburg may be considered to be an early version of what is today termed a "world city". . . . The St Petersburg entrepreneurs were involved deeply in foreign trade, but also in highly concentrated industries, with large working forces, corporate organisation, and sophisticated technology'(Blackwell, 1983, p. 17).

It is true that the revolution in China occurred just thirty years before the beginnings of serious reform of the Stalinist economy began. However, in the intervening period there were only limited opportunities for individuals to practise their capitalistic skills. A prolonged 'two-line struggle' affected, among other things, the very existence of the private sector as an ancillary to the socialist sector. During the collectivisation campaign of 1955–6, during the Great Leap Forward and in the Cultural Revolution in the mid-1960s, the private sector in the villages came under heavy attack as a 'snare both to poor peasants and to party cadres who still had bourgeois aspirations' (Walker, 1965, p. 75). 'Capitalism' was likened by the 'left' to a 'dog in the water to be beaten and drowned'. Such tight restrictions were placed on rural commerce and associated activities that the number of people working in 'rural commerce, food and drink services and material supply' fell from 2.8 million in 1957 to only around 0.7 million in the late 1960s and early 1970s (SSB, *ZGLDGZTJNJ*, 1987, p. 80). In the cities, the number of individual workers fluctuated wildly as the campaigns against the private sector waxed and waned, falling from 8.9 million in 1953 to just 160,000 in 1956, expanding to 2.3 million in 1963, before shrinking steadily to just 150,000 in 1977 (SSB, *ZGTJNJ*, 1992, p. 97).

During the early phase of collectivisation in the USSR, the Soviet leadership crudely suppressed the private sector in agriculture. However, the policies were very quickly reversed, and later formalised in the model statute on collective farms (1935). By the late 1930s a large proportion of Soviet livestock were in private ownership, and the private sector was producing an important part of rural personal income. The USSR had no subsequent attack on the private sector comparable to that in China. The legal rural private sector was estimated to be producing around 25–30 per cent of total agricultural output in the early 1980s (Aslund, 1991, p. 155).

The Stalinist command economy produced simultaneous shortages and surpluses without the possibility legally to reconcile them through the market. As a result there was a profound unbuilt tendency for illegal (black) market and quasi-legal (grey) market activity. In Berliner's view, '[m]uch of the activity of the "second economy" consists of entrepreneurship of the classically Marshallian kind – redirecting resources towards an equilibrium state' (Berliner, 1983, p. 196).

Much activity in the second economy involved the provision of personal services or the production of consumer goods. In the USSR in the early 1980s it is estimated that around 50 per cent of shoe repairs, 45 per cent of house repairs, 40 per cent of repairs to private cars and 30 per cent of repair to household appliances were provided by essentially illegal private enterprise (Aslund, 1991, p. 155). In addition there was a large illegal production of output both by enterprises themselves as well as in private illegal factories using stolen materials and often employing many workers.[12] It is estimated that in the USSR in the

1970s between 30 and 40 per cent of personal income came from the private sector. Indeed, it may be argued that due to the pervasiveness of shortages, ordinary individuals had to be far more entrepreneurial in the conduct of their daily lives than the bulk of secure wage earners in the West.

Within the state sector of the Stalinist economies an army of people (*tolkachi*, or 'pushers') was involved on behalf of enterprises in scouring the country to obtain wanted inputs in exchange for unwanted surpluses. In pre-1976 China the planning system produced such 'disconnection betwen supply and demand that enterprises were forced to send people to many parts of the country to get the materials they needed by personal connections, bartering and other unhealthy means. It was estimated that every day there were about three million people who were travelling in the country on an errand to purchase materials' (Liu Guoguang and Wang Ruisun, 1984, p. 97).

In sum, it is hard to argue that China's reforms were more successful than those in the USSR because the inherent capacities for entrepreneurial activity were greater than those in the USSR. China's traditions of entrepreneurship are, self-evidently, of much greater antiquity than those of Russia, but so are they of greater antiquity than almost all other major cultural areas in the world. By the mid-nineteenth century, European Russia had made up a great deal of the leeway in both commerce and industry. For different reasons, neither pre-revolutionary China nor Russia modernised in response to the Western 'challenge' as rapidly as may have been possible under a different set of policies. However, both did achieve considerable progress in certain parts of the country. In post-revolutionary Russia the 'second economy' continued more or less unabated since the command economy began to be put into effect even during the years of Stalin's rule, and was a very important area of entrepreneurship. The Chinese command economy produced the same inherent tendency towards a large second economy. However, it periodically had severe campaigns which greatly increased the risk attached to such activity, and consequently sharply reduced its relative importance in such periods.

5.2.5 Economic structure

It has been asserted widely that the main reason for the failure of the USSR's economic reform is that the Soviet system was 'over-industrialised'.

In terms of the share of output occupied by the industrial sector it

Table 5.2   Economic structure of pre-reform China, the USSR, compared
to the non-communist countries, 1980 per cent

	GDP					Employment				
	USSR	China	LIEs	MIEs	IMEs	USSR	China	LIEs	MIEs	HIEs
Agriculture	16	31	45	15	4	14	71	73	44	6
Industry	62	47	17	40	37	45	17	11	22	38
Services	22	22	38	45	62	41	12	19	34	56

Notes: LIEs = Low Income Economies (excluding China and India).
MIEs = Middle Income Economies.
IMEs = Industrial Market Economies.

Source: World Bank, *WDR*, 1982.

is, indeed, true that in the USSR a large share came from the industrial sector, reportedly around 62 per cent of GDP in the early 1980s,
which is a higher share than even for the advanced industrial economies (Table 5.2). However, China also was 'over-industrialised', in
the sense that the industrial sector reportedly produced a very much
larger share of output than might be expected for a country at its level
of income. Indeed, the World Bank estimates that in the early 1980s,
the share of GDP produced by industry in China was no less than 47
per cent, ahead of any of the major groups of countries, including
even the advanced capitalist countries (Table 5.2). If one accepts that
there were serious inefficiencies in Chinese industry, just as there were
in Soviet industry, then it may be argued that China's 'over-industrialisation' was an even greater burden for China than the Soviet Union's
'over-industrialisation' was for that country. In China's case the 'over-
industrialisation' was in a vastly poorer country, with a much lower
income level from which to generate resources for growth.

A further sense in which it may argued that the USSR was 'over-
industrialised, is that the share of employment in industry was relatively large. It is, indeed, true that in the USSR in the early 1980s the
proportion employed in the industrial sector, probably around 45 per
cent (Table 5.2), was higher than that for the advanced economies.
However, the difference was not large, and it stood at a similar figure
in several of the advanced capitalist economies. Moreover, to some
degree the relatively high proportion employed in industry reflected
the high levels of overmanning in industry in all the communist countries. Suitable institutional reform could raise labour productivity and
release labour from industry to be employed in sectors requiring rela-

tively low capital outlays. In other words this was a form of 'disguised unemployment'.

In both China and the USSR pre-reform there was a large share of the workforce in each case employed in the farm sector. China's employment structure was close to that of a typical low income country, with around three-quarters of the population still employed in agriculture. A large proportion of these were poor and illiterate. It is hard to imagine that this can be considered an advantage for accelerated growth. Although the USSR had a much lower proportion of the workforce employed in the farm sector, the share was still large compared to the advanced capitalist countries. There were large possibilities in Soviet agriculture as in Soviet industry for releasing surplus labour to undertake useful labour in other sectors.

The relative size of the service sector in both countries was much greater than it appeared to be. In both cases official estimates of the share of the service sector were greatly underestimated. In both countries, a large part of 'service' sector activities, which in capitalist economies are obtained from specialist suppliers in the public or private sector, were provided directly by agricultural and industrial enterprises. These included a great deal of health, education, social security, housing provision, food preparation and consumption, and even leisure activities.

5.2.6 Industry

Heavy industry bias

The extreme inefficiency with which the Stalinist economies used investment resources meant that they required a large amount of heavy industrial goods to produce a unit of final product (Table 5.3). The quality of much heavy industrial output, especially machinery, was below that required to compete on world markets. However, a large part of heavy industrial output in most economies consists of intermediate inputs in which the product is more homogenous and quality is a less important element in competitiveness.[13] The high level of development of the heavy industrial sector represented a potential windfall gain for reforming Stalinist economies. If the reforms had been able to generate gradual improvements in the efficiency with which intermediate inputs were used, then these economies should have been able to experience a period of growth with relatively low investment in the heavy industries. Moreover, the capacity to produce large amounts of heavy

Table 5.3   Intermediate inputs per dollar of GNP (1979–1980)

	Steel (gms)	Sulphuric acid (gms)	Cement (gms)	Energy consumption (kgs of coal equivalent)
USSR	136	21	116	1.49
China	146	31	319	3.21
USA	42	17	27	1.16
West Germany	61	7	47	0.56
Japan	109	7	87	0.48

Source: World Bank, 1981a, and SSB, *ZGTJNJ*, 1981.

Table 5.4   Role of very large establishments (over 5,000 employees) in Chinese and Soviet industry

	No. of establish-ment	Employment (Millions)	Employment (per cent)	Fixed assets (per cent)	GVIO (per cent)	Employees /establish-ment ('000)
USSR (1983)	1316	14.4	38.1	46.7	35.9	10.9
China (1987)	885	11.9	16.8	33.9	18.9	13.4

Sources: Liu Nanchuan, 1988, pp. 120, 145 and 436; and SSB, *ZGGYJJTJNJ*, 1989, p. 293.

Table 5.5   Distribution of very large establishments by sector in China and the Russian Federation, 1987

	Russian Federation no.	Russian Federation per cent	China no.	China per cent
Total	952	100	720	100
Engineering	371	39	286	40
Chemicals/ petrochemicals	132	14	62	9
Metallurgy	112	12	118	16
Fuels/energy	100	11	26	4

Source: World Bank, 1992a, p. 83, and SSB, *ZGGYJJTJNJ*, 1988.

Note: In the Chinese case the data refer explicitly to establishments with over 5,000 employees. In the Soviet case, the data are ambiguous but, given that the average size of the 'large' Soviet plants in this table was 8,558, it seems likely that the same criterion was used.

industrial output should have enabled them to be able to grow without quickly encountering a foreign exchange constraint on growth. In the event that the reforming Stalinist economies did encounter a foreign exchange constraint through limitations on their capacities to generate export earnings, then it might have been advantageous to be able to use domestic heavy industrial products, even though their quality might be below those available on world markets.

In both cases there was a huge pent-up demand for the products of sectors that were heavy users of intermediate inputs. These included housing, motor vehicles, and the associated investment in road networks. In both countries, consumption levels of these products were relatively very low. Moreover, a rapid growth in demand for other, lower unit value industrial consumer goods, such as textiles, toys, sports goods, and household electrical appliances, would have created demand for 'upstream' inputs from heavy industries such as power, steel, chemical fibres and plastics. Although the USSR's level of consumer durable and clothing consumption was much greater than that in China, it is likely that there was a high income elasticity of demand for the replacement of old, unreliable and unstylish items purchased in the Soviet command economy period.

Industrial organisation

Similarities In both cases, very large plants (over 5,000 employees) played an important role in the industrial sector (Table 5.4). In the early 1980s in China and the USSR around one thousand very large plants employed 12–14 million workers, accounted for around one-third to one-half of the total value of industrial fixed assets, and accounted for around one-fifth to one-third of the total gross value of industrial output.

In each case the vast majority of very large plants was concentrated in heavy industry (Table 5.5), and in selected light industrial sectors, typically characterised by large plant level economies of scale in all countries. In China, those sectors in which plants with over 1,000 employees produced more than three-fifths of sectoral output value were: tobacco (89 per cent), petrochemicals (96 per cent), chemical fibres (78 per cent), rubber products (62 per cent), ferrous metals (87 per cent), non-ferrous metals (73 per cent), transport equipment (65 per cent), electronic and information equipment (60 per cent) (SSB, *ZGGYJJTJNJ*, 1988). Moreover, the number of giant plants in China was probably greater even than the number in the USSR. As Table 5.4

Table 5.6   Industrial concentration by size of establishment in China
(1987) and the USSR (1983) (per cent)

Size of establish-ment (no. of employees)	Establishments		Employees		Fixed assets		Gross value of industrial output	
	China	*USSR*	*China*	*USSR*	*China*	*USSR*	*China*	*USSR*
under 100	68.5	27.2	14.0	1.6	5.8	1.1	9.6	1.9
100–500	25.6	42.4	32.6	12.6	18.1	8.8	26.6	12.8
500–1000	3.6	13.1	14.7	11.2	12.2	9.0	15.5	10.8
1000–10,000	2.2	16.3	27.5	52.4	38.2	51.8	36.5	54.1
over 10,000	0.1	1.0	11.2	22.2	25.7	29.3	11.7	20.4
Aggregate	100	100	100	100	100	100	100	100

Source: Liu Nanchuan, 1988, pp. 120 and 145; and SSB, *ZGGYJJNTJNJ*,
1988, pp. 7 and 293.

shows, the average size of Chinese 'very large plants' was above that
in the USSR. In the Chinese machine-building industry in the mid-
1980s, the twenty-eight largest enterprises averaged no less than 133,000
employees per establishment (SSB, *ZGGYJJTJNJ*, 1988, p. 299).

If one shifts from very large to 'large' plants, the picture is still one
of strong similarities. In both cases, establishments with over 1,000
employees were massively dominant in relation to the total value of
fixed assets, occupying 64 per cent in China's case and 81 per cent in
that of the USSR (Table 5.6). In China, large plants produced 48 per
cent of the total value of industrial output compared to 75 per cent in
the Soviet case.

In both cases, the share of small and medium plants in sectoral output and employment was generally much greater in light industry, as
is the case in the non-communist countries. In the Russian Federation
in 1987, large plants accounted for less than one-quarter of total employment in 'light industries' (narrowly defined), around 19 per cent
in food products, and less than ten per cent in glass/ceramics, construction materials, and wood products (World Bank, 1992a, p. 83). In
China in 1987, small- and medium-sized plants with under 1,000 employees produced over three-quarters of the value of output in food
and drink manufacturing, garments, wood products, cultural products,
building materials, furniture, arts and crafts, plastic products, and (non-
machinery) metal products (SSB, *ZGGYJJTJNJ*, 1989).

The nature of the large enterprise in the former communist countries needs to be looked at carefully if the structural tasks of reform

are to be understood properly. A major problem of most of the analysis of industrial reform in the communist countries is that this has not been undertaken. For example, the World Bank's report on the Russian economy (World Bank, 1992a) contains one page of text on the 'heritage' of the Soviet industrial structure, and over twenty pages of recommendations about reform policies. What is surprising is how similar are the problems and opportunities that confronted the dominant large-scale state-owned industrial sector in the Soviet Union and China.

In both cases, a striking characteristic of large plants was their high degree of vertical integration. This stemmed directly from the complexity of material balance planning. The difficulties of constructing the 'plan' were greatly reduced by maximising the degree of self-sufficiency of each level of the administrative system. This applied especially to the enterprise, which could not rely on the supply of inputs through the command system. Thus throughout both systems, almost all enterprises in the massive machine building sector produced their own iron and steel rather than purchasing it from specialised suppliers. Thus, in the machine-building industry in former USSR less than 20 per cent of cast iron and steel were purchased from specialist suppliers, compared to over 80 per cent in the USA (Granick, 1967, p. 157). Moreover, in both cases, a large proportion of spare parts and machinery needs was produced within the large plants. A 1978 US Congress Report on the Chinese machine-building industry noted: 'Plant organisation in China is a particularily weak area; factories are vertically integrated producing many of their own parts, and are unable to capitalise on the efficiency of specialisation' (USCJEC, 1978, p. 300). Both countries had a large stock of general purpose machine tools with low utilisation rates used to produce a wide variety of inputs in small batches. A critical Soviet account commented: 'Our factories have turned into the most "all purpose", the most unspecialised. Striving to have everything at hand and not depend on producers for trifles, the directors of enterprises "naturalise" their economic operations. . . . It is much easier to produce the needed nuts oneself than to arrange for their delivery from specialised factories that often are non-existent' (Shmelyev and Popov, 1990, p. 118).

Far from benefitting from large scale specialised production, large Chinese and Soviet plants produced a large amount of small batch output with below optimal scale. For example, in the USSR in 1962–3, 50–60 per cent of all iron and steel castings were produced in small 'shops' within large plants, with an annual capacity of under 1000 tons (Granick, 1967, p. 158). Lifting-transport equipment in the USSR

in the 1970s was produced by no less than 320 enterprises subordinate
to 35 ministries and departments, of which about 250 were in factories
producing the products for their own use: 'Thus much machinery output is produced in small, inefficient shops' (USCJEC, 1976, p. 169).

A good example of a typical large integrated Soviet plant is the
Kirov Engineering 'plant' in St Petersburg. In 1992 this employed around
50,000 workers (including 17,000 in the completely separate Tikrin
site). It embraced a number of semi-independent 'shops' within the
physical boundaries of the 'plant': these included a forging 'shop',
capable of producing a wide array of steel castings, a tractor-producing
'shop', a military tank producing 'shop', a 'shop' which produced
turbines, gears, pumps, main engines for icebreakers and merchant ships,
and a 'shop' which produced a variety of consumer durables, including trailers, aerobics equipment, and body-building equipment (obser-
vations based on the author's personal visit to the plant).

Thus the large scale of the core sections of Chinese and Soviet industry is misleading. Far from being specialist producers on a large
scale, within each of the large 'plants' was a series of relatively small
scale 'shops' performing activities which in a capitalist economy would
mainly be undertaken by separate specialist producers, often on a much
larger scale. Far from there being too few specialist producers, with
large monopolistic propensities, if one 'unpacks' the nature of the large
scale plant it can be seen that the structural problem is the reverse.
Rather, there were, in a large number of sectors, far too many small-
scale producers.

As was pointed out in Chapter 3 a central goal of the communist
command economies was to destroy the basic mechanism of the capitalist system – the profit motive and the market. In doing this the
explicit intention was to unite the whole of industry into a single firm
owned by 'the whole people'. At the heart of the capitalist system is a
relatively small number of large multi-plant firms. An important task
for the communist countries was to construct out of the non-competitive
command system a number of industrial giants that would be able to
benefit from economies of multi-plant operation and compete on international markets. A key part of the task of structural reform was to
reorganise the large number of relatively small-scale in-house plants
producing separately at below optimal scale into large, often multi-
plant companies. This would involve a complex process of horizontal
merger between 'shops' within the shell of existing large plants.

A further element tending to push up the average plant size in China
and the USSR compared to the non-communist countries (Table 5.7)

Table 5.7   Distribution of employment in manufacturing industry by size
of establishment (per cent)

Size of establish-ment	Capitalist countries				USA	India	China	USSR
	Small type		Large type					
	1950	1970	1950	1970	1986	1987/88	1987	1983
10–100	40	35	23	20	31.0	27.6	14.0	1.6
101–500	30	33	30	30	32.0	23.8	32.6	12.6
501–1000	11	13	13	14	11.6	12.0	12.0	11.2
over 1000	19	19	34	36	25.4	36.7	38.7	74.6

Note: 'Independent accounting enterprises' only. In 1978 independent accounting enterprises accounted for 96 per cent of NVIO (SSB,
ZGGYJJTJZL, 1949–1984; 1985, pp. 41–2).

Source: Erlich, 1985, SSB, ZGGYJJTJNJ, 1991, Acs and Audretsch, 1993,
p. 62, Liu Nanchuan, 1988, pp. 120 and 145.

was the large number of non-production functions for which the plant
had responsibility in the communist system. These included workers'
housing, transport services, education, hospitals, canteens, workers' clubs
and even hotels for employees within the relevant ministry.

Differences

Spatial pattern of the distribution of industrial capacity   China's split
with the USSR in 1960 and its isolation from the capitalist world left
it deeply vulnerable in international affairs. A major economic consequence of this intense insecurity was the 'Third Front' policy in industrial investment allocation. The share of total investment allocated
to the inland provinces increased very rapidly, so that the inland
provinces' share of total industrial capital stock rose from 28 per cent
in 1952 to 56 per cent in the late 1970s (Table 5.8). The economic
returns to such investment generally were low (Table 5.8) since the
plants were established far from the main centres of population and
away from the areas with the easiest communications. For example,
the largest truck plant in China was established in a remote mountainous area in the northwest of Hubei province in central China (USCJEC,
1978, p. 288).

Self-reliance   China encountered the usual set of problems faced in a
command economy but these were overlain with a special set of problems

Table 5.8   Distribution of industrial capital, employment, and output
betweeen coastal and inland provinces of China, 1952 and
1978 (per cent)

	1952	*1978*
Workers:		
coastal	60.5	46.3 (1984)
inland	39.5	53.7 (1984)
Value of fixed assets:		
coastal	72.0	43.9
inland	28.0	56.1
Value of industrial output:		
coastal	69.4	60.9
inland	30.6	39.1
Capital–output ratio:		
coastal	0.45	0.54
inland	0.40	1.08

Source: SSB, *ZGGJJTJZL*, 1985, p. 137.

that led to the development of a distinctively 'self-reliant' pattern of industrial development. First, there was China's huge size and the low level of development of the transport system. Moreover, the Third Front policy meant that a large share of investible resources was allocated to expanding the transport system in areas with low returns. For example, new railways built to the west of the Beijing–Guangzhou railway (i.e. in the inland areas) accounted for 84 per cent of the total investment in railway construction in the period from 1963 to 1978 (Yu Guangyuan, 1984, p. 168). However, a further feature was the political turmoil over the country for long periods, most notably during the Great Leap Forward (1958–59) and the Cultural Revolution (1966–1976). This increased the desire of administrative units for self sufficiency since they were not able to rely on normal networks of trade, but also made it easier for the central authorities to retain some semblance of political order. In a feudal fashion, lower level leaders were made responsible for all activities – social, political and economic – within their boundaries, minimising contacts of ordinary citizens with the outside and making a direct and easy chain of command in all respects from higher to lower level authorities.

These features of the setting in China helped to produce a high degree of 'self-reliance' at every level of the economic system, far beyond that normally characteristic even of a command economy. Indeed, self-reliance (*zili gengsheng*) became a watchword of the whole Maoist system. Writing in 1972 Audrey Donnithorne commented: 'Countless independent or relatively independent production centres are being set up throughout the country.... This emphasis on self-reliance is applied to units, large and small, but units in the sense of enterprises, and also local units of administration down to the production teams.... Self sufficiency may be within an enterprise, a unit of local administration or a commune. Even individual counties and municipalities have been urged to "build small but complete local industrial systems by self-reliance".... The growth of enterprise self-reliance is particularily marked in regard to machinery' (Donnithorne, 1972, pp. 608–10).

Small plants   The policy of self-reliance alone tended to cause the number of small plants to rise rapidly. A further powerful pressure leading to an expansion of the role of small plants in the Maoist economy was the production of modern farm inputs in the countryside. After the disaster of the Great Leap Forward, China sought rapidly to expand the supply of modern inputs to the farm sector. At the centre of this process was the rapid growth of output from rural small scale plants. A large fraction of China's farm machinery was supplied by these plants by the mid-1970s. Small local iron and steel plants increased their share of total investment in iron and steel from 8 per cent in the mid-1950s to no less than 52 per cent in the mid-1970s (Yu Guangyuan, 1984, p. 156). By the mid-1970s around 45 per cent of total nitrogen output and around one-half of total cement output was produced in small rural plants (Perkins (ed.), 1977, pp. 156, 178).

As in pre-reform USSR, by the end of the Maoist period large plants dominated the industrial economy. Unlike the USSR, there was a very large number of small plants. Data for the mid-1980s show that within the factory sector ('independent accounting enterprises'), there were 286,000 small enterprises (68 per cent of the total number) with less than one hundred workers per enterprise (the average was 35 per enterprise) which produced just 9.6 per cent of the gross value of industrial output from factories (SSB, *ZGGYJJTJNJ*, 1988, p. 293). In addition, data for 1979 show there were no less than 580,000 miniscule enterprises (62 per cent of the total number of industrial enterpises in China) at the brigade or team level, employing an average of only 17 workers per plant, which produced just 3.4 per cent of the total industrial output value (World Bank, 1981(b), pp. 20–1).

The small and medium enterprise sector occupied an especially small part of the Soviet industrial size structure of establishments (Table 5.7). A successful reform was likely to have led to rapid growth of output and employment in this sector, which is typically quick-gestating and labour intensive. In the Soviet state sector, in which most workers were employed, there were wide differences in income and standard of living between occupations and sectors. Moreover, there were quite wide differences in average income and large differences in labour force growth rates between regions. As new employment opportunities emerged outside the large-scale state sector during a successful economic reform programme, it is not difficult to imagine how workers might have begun to migrate between sectors, occupations and regions. This could have happened in many ways, including the following: (i) direct bidding of full time permanent labour out of the state sector through higher wages; (ii) 'part-time' work in the non-state sector by state sector workers; (iii) state sector workers might retain their right to work in the state sector enterprise but cease to be paid wages from that enterprise, and being allowed to more or less permanently work full time in the non-state sector; (iv) workers in the state sector could be allowed to retain their rights to work in the state enterprise and their social security benefits from it in return for some form of fee paid to their original enterprise; (v) state enterprise could themselves invest in new enterprises (either directly or as joint ventures with capital from other sectors) in the production of goods and services for which demand was growing rapidly, allowing the re-deployment of surplus labour from the original enterprise. Some form of all these arrangements occurred in China during its reforms, but the rapid growth in the new entrants to the workforce and the huge rural labour surplus in farm employment tended to reduce the extent of migration from the state to the non-state sector.

Results of China's distinctive policies The combination of resource allocation to inland areas, 'self-reliance' and the proliferation of small plants had some benefits. The benefits it provided were as a legacy for future change. These were, most notably, a relatively widespread technical capacity in rural areas, with learning effects associated with the production of a large amount of machinery in small batches in rural settings. A second benefit was a reinforcement of the role local governments as a key economic agent over a wide array of activities rather than simply an administrator of agriculture.

However, the strategy also had high costs. China's industry failed to benefit from economes of scale and the advantages of specialisation and exchange, beyond those normally experienced in a command economy. A large proportion of the output produced under this strategy was of low quality, using, for example, large amounts of power and requiring frequent maintenance. Costs of production were widely acknowledged to be very high in a large portion of the small factories, since they were so often producing capital goods which are normally characterised by strong economies of scale at the plant level. For example, in the late 1970s in the production of the 2T Beijing–130 model of truck, the Beijing No. 2 vehicle plant produced around 8,000 trucks per annum, with a cost per vehicle of 10,000 yuan, while the Harbin Motor Vehicle Plant produced 50 trucks per annum, with a cost per vehicle of 33,000 yuan (Yu Guangyuan, 1984, p. 94). A large reason for China's extraordinarily high consumption of power and other material inputs per unit of output (see Chapter 3) was the high fuel costs of the small plants (Perkins (ed.), 1977, pp. 72–6).

Like the USSR, China faced large tasks in restructuring the large scale industrial sector. However, it faced a special problem in that it needed also to undertake a large scale restructuring of its small-scale sector. A central task of the reform was to restructure Chinese industry, 'turning scattered and all inclusive economic units into "economic integrations" organised according to the principles of specialisation, coordination, and economic rationality' (Yu Guangyuan, 1984, p. 108). In 1978, Yu Qiuli outlined the large tasks facing the small-scale machine-building sector as follows (USCJEC, 1978). He said that a new emphasis was to be placed upon specialisation, standardisation, and serial production, starting with agricultural machinery and equipment. He announced a medium-term plan to convert most small-and medium-sized plants from general equipment producers of specialised components under contract to large plants. As in every sector, strategic planning, not privatisation, was the *leitmotif* of the reform policies.

Technical progress

Both China and the USSR achieved low returns in terms of civilian technical progress from their investment in human capital in science. One reason was the isolation of scientific research workers in institutions and universities. However, the more fundamental reason was the lack of interest in industry in employing the skills of scientific workers to improve industrial performance either directly in the plant or indirectly through acquiring the fruits of their research. Indeed, enterprise managers had a strong interest in resisting technical progress, let alone attempting themselves to pursue it:

In the USSR innovation has to be 'introduced'. The Russian word
vnedreniye implies that it requires effort, a push from above. In the
West, on the contrary, one had industrial espionage, and efforts had
to expended to prevent one's rivals learning about one's innova-
tions. The reason for the contrast must be competition, which exists
in the West even in sectors (such as the chemical industry for instance) in which giant monopolists may seem to be dominant; whereas
in the USSR it is no accident that many plays and novels feature
the obstructionist director who resists innovation: he has very little
incentive to do otherwise. (Nove, 1983, 76)

By introducing the profit motive to industry, large increases in output
could in principle be achieved from existing scientific personnel. Even
in relation to their level of income it is likely that the potential for the
USSR to reap windfall gains from this aspect of reform was considerably greater than for China.

A further important part of the unrealised scientific potential was
accounted for by the large share of expertise allocated to the military
sector. In both cases the share was large. This reflected on, the one
hand, the frontline position of the USSR in the Cold War and, on the
other hand, it reflected the 'war on two fronts' against both the US
and the Soviet Union that China fought from the late 1950s up until
the early 1970s. In the early 1980s it was estimated that Soviet defence expenditures amounted to around 15 per cent of GNP, and that
the defence sector absorbed 16 per cent of domestic machinery production (USCJEC, 1982a, p. 306). Moreover, the defence sector claimed
a disproportionately large share of the best resources (USCJEC, 1982a,
p. 340). China's defence sector was much less advanced than that of
the USSR in the 1970s, with a much greater reliance on sheer numbers of military personnel. However, the share of industrial resources
preempted by the military sector was even greater than in the USSR.
It was estimated that in 1980 China's defence sector accounted for no
less than 21 per cent of total industrial output (USCJEC, 1975, p. 477).
In both cases there existed a very large 'peace dividend' from the end
of the Cold War which could release scientific and material resources
for civilian use. This dividend could be especially large if the end
of the Cold War coincided with well-devised policies to introduce
competition to industry leading to the intensive use for making profits
of scientific skills and capital stock formerly tied up in the military
sector.

Despite the 'turn to the West' in the 1970s, resulting in increasing

Soviet imports of foreign technology, equipment imports still accounted for only around 2 per cent of total domestic equipment investment (Hanson, 1978, p. 31). A leading expert in the field concluded that Soviet technology imports had played a 'limited' role in Soviet growth (Hanson, 1978, p. 43). The vast bulk of China's technology imports had orginated from the Soviet bloc in the 1950s. In the 1960s 'self-reliance had become the watchword . . . and imports of equipment and technology were reduced to the selective acquisition of the most advanced technology . . . The stock of Soviet equipment was rapidly becoming obsolete and domestically produced equipment was primitive' (USCJEC, 1978, p. 311). Both China and the USSR possessed an especially large opportunity for technical catch-up, provided the foreign exchange could be generated to pay for technology-enhancing imports. China was in a less favourable position than the Soviet Union to take advantage of this opportunity, since its scientific capabilities had been so badly damaged during the Cultural Revolution.

5.2.7 Agriculture

Differences

Climate and yields The sharp difference in climate produced a fundamentally different pattern of agriculture in China and the former USSR. The Soviet Union's harsh climate dictated that under any institutional system it was likely to be based on much more extensive agricultural practices, with a very different balance of grain and meat products from that in China. The cultivated area per person in the USSR was about the same as that in the USA, around 0.8 hectares per person, while that in China is only around 0.1 hectares per person (SSB, *ZGNCTJNJ*, 1989, pp. 417–18). Chinese grain yields per sown hectare are considerably above the world average, standing at around 4.0 tons, compared to only 1.9 tons in the USSR.

It is difficult to evaluate the degree to which low Soviet grain yields are attributable to climatic as opposed to other factors (discussed below). While Soviet grain yields are much below those in the USA (grain yields per sown hectare in the USA are around 4.7 tons), they are not a great deal below those in Canada (2.4 tons per sown hectare), where climatic condition more closely approximate those of the main grain-growing areas in the USSR. Moreover, careful studies of areas of the USA and the USSR with similar climatic condition showed remarkably little difference in yields per hectare (USCJEC, 1979, p. 37).

Table 5.9   China's 'Green Revolution'

	1957	1978	1992
Arable area:			
total (m. ha.)	112	99.5 (1979)	95.4
per capita (ha.)(index)	0.173 (100)	0.103 (58)	0.081 (47)
Irrigated			
area (m. ha):	27.4	45.0	48.6
% of arable area	(24.5)	(45.2)	(50.9)
of which:			
mechanically	1.2	24.9	26.3
irrigated (m. ha)	(1.1)	(25.0)	(27.6)
% of arable area			
Mechanically			
ploughed area (m. ha)	2.6	40.7	51.5
% of arable area	(2.3)	(40.9)	(54.0)
Farm			
machinery (m. kwh)	1.21	117.5	303.1
Large/medium			
tractors ('000s)	14.7	557.4	758.9
Walking tractors (m)	—	1.37	7.51
Combine			
harvesters ('000s)	1.8	19.0	51.1
Farm-use trucks ('000s)	4	74	642
Chemical fertiliser			
use (m. tons)	0.4	8.8	29.3

Source: SSB, *ZGTJNJ*, 1993, pp. 341 and 349, and World Bank, 1981c, p. 61.

The main shortcomings in Soviet agriculture were not so much in poor growth performance or yields per hectare, but rather in the large amount of resources needed to achieve these results.

Population pressure on farmland   China occupies less than 7 per cent of the world's cultivated area, around 10 per cent of the pastoral area, and less than 3 per cent of the forested area, but its population is around 22 per cent of the world's total. The former USSR occupied around 17 per cent of the world's cultivated area, 12 per cent of the pastoral area, and 23 per cent of the forested area, but accounted for only 6 per cent of the world's population (SSB, *ZGNCTJNJ*, 1989, pp.

Table 5.10 Arable area per capita in China and other selected countries in 1979 (hectares)

China	0.10	
within which:		
East	0.08	Shanghai, Jiangsu, Zhejiang, Anhui,
within which:		Fujian, Jiangxi and Shandong
'densely populated		
eastern provinces'*	0.05 (1992)	Jiangsu, Shanghai, Zhejiang, Fujian
Northeast	0.19	Liaoning, Jilin, Heilongjiang
Northwest	0.18	Shaanxi, Gansu, Ningxia, Xinjiang
Southwest	0.07	Sichuan, Guizhou, Yunan, Tibet
Central-South	0.08	Henan, Hubei, Hunan, Guangxi,
		Guangdong
North	0.15	Beijing, Tianjin, Hebei, Shanxi,
		Inner Mongolia
Other countries:		
Japan	0.04	
USA	0.86	
India	0.26	
USSR	0.89	

Source: SSB, *ZGNYJJGY*, 1982, pp. 12–13, SSB, *ZGTJNJ*, 1993, pp. 83 and 332.

Note: *Total population in 1993 was 156 million.

417–18). China's total population grew from around 650 million in the mid-1950s to almost one billion in the late 1970s. Alongside this vast growth in numbers, the total arable area shrank substantially, by about 14 per cent from 1957 to 1978 causing an alarming 40 per cent fall in the amount of farmland per person (Table 5.9).

By the late 1970s, the amount of farmland per person was among the lowest in the world, much below that even of India (Table 5.10). Moreover, within China, the regional differences are pronounced, with the main centres of economic activity in East and Central China having levels well below the national average (Table 5.10). Unlike in Japan, a significant part of China's farmland is located in inhospitable areas. In the densely populated eastern provinces, which have a considerably larger population than Japan, the amount of farmland per person is about the same as that in Japan (Table 5.10).

Even with the tough measures taken to control population growth (see below), China population total grew by over 200 million from 1978 to 1992. Moreover, the pressures of succcessful industrial growth

Table 5.11   Size of collective and state farms in China and the USSR
(average per farm)

	USSR (1985)*		China (1980)	
	Collective farms	State farms	Production teams	Production brigades
number of workers	488	529	56	449
sown area (hectares)	3485	4766	26	206
large animals	1930 (cows)**	1850 (cows)**	17	134
pigs	1109**	1163**	55	430
sheep/goats	1666**	2921**	33	263
large/medium tractors	20	57	0.1	1.1
walking tractors	—	—	0.3	2.6
combine harvesters	14	19	negl.	negl.
farm-use trucks	44	26	negl.	0.2
agricultural water pumps	—	—	0.8	6.4
mechanical theshers	—	—	0.5	3.5
grain husking machines	—	—	0.5	4.3
fodder crushing machines	—	—	0.3	2.0
rubber tyred carts:				
animal-drawn	—	—	0.4	3.4
hand-drawn	—	—	6.4	49.6

Notes: *In 1985, state farms occupied 179 million hectares of sown area,
and collective farms occupied 143 million hectares of sown area.
**Publicly owned

Source: Liu Nanchuan, 1989, pp. 287, 289, 303; SSB, *ZGNCTJNJ*, 1985,
pp. 232–3, 244; SSB, *SYC*, section 3.

further helped reduce the arable area. By 1992 the amount of farmland
per person had fallen by one-fifth compared to the late 1970s (Table 5.9).

Capital   Despite the Green Revolution in China, the stocks of large
farm machinery was vastly below that in the USSR. China's production brigades were around the same size as Soviet collective farms and
state farms in terms of the number of workers, but the stocks of tractors,

trucks and combine harvesters were vastly greater in the USSR (Table 5.11). Moreover, a large fraction of China modern inputs was easily divisible. The importance of large, lumpy farm inputs was much greater in the USSR than in China (Table 5.11). In the pre-reform Soviet Union there was an average of around 20 tractors, 14 combine harvesters and 44 trucks per collective farm (Table 5.11). In the comparable level of farm ownership and organisation in China, namely the production team, the average number of such large means of production was negligible. Indeed, even at the higher level, the production brigade, the numbers of large means of production also were negligible.

In the USSR, only a small fraction of total farmland was irrigated (around 7 per cent in the late 1970s) (Li Renfeng, *SLNYTJZLHB*, 1981, pp. 6, and 446). A major reason for China's ability to feed such a huge population on such a limited arable area was the high development (achieved over millenia) of its irrigation works. Already by the late 1950s, around one quarter of China's farmland was drained and irrigated (SSB, *ZGNYJJGY*, 1982, 133). Through huge efforts by the communes to mobilise labour for irrigation construction, China's drained and irrigated area rose from 27 m. ha. in 1959 to 45 m. ha. in 1978, raising the proportion of arable area that was drained and irrigated to 45 per cent by 1978 (SSB, *ZGNYJJGY*, 1982, p. 133). Given that much of China's farmland is in semi-arid areas, this was a high proportion. Even Japan's irrigation ratio in 1979 was no higher than 66 per cent, and the ratio in India, a country closely comparable with China in terms of the heterogeneity of climatic conditions, the ratio stood at just 21 per cent (SSB, *ZGNYJJGY*, 1982, p. 134). In advanced east coast provinces such as Jiangsu and Zhejiang, where conditions closely resembled those in Japan, the irrigation ratio stood at around 80 per cent of the arable area in the late 1980s (Table 5.12).

China's high labour input per unit of farmland, high irrigation ratio, and rapid advance in farm modernisation after the 1950s (Table 5.9), enabled China to attain high yields per unit of land sown. Moreover, about half of China's grain land was cropped more than once: China's Multiple Cropping Index, that is the ratio of sown area to arable area, in 1980 stood at 1.45 (SSB, *ZGTJZY*, 1990, p. 56, and SSB, *ZGNCTJNJ*, 1989, p. 251), so that annual yields per unit of arable land were considerably above yields per crop. By 1987 China's grain yields per sown hectare stood at 4.0 tons, compared to 2.4 tons in Bangladesh, 1.8 tons in Mexico, and 1.5 tons in India (SSB, *ZGNCTJNJ*, 1989, p. 419). Even in Japan, with more favourable natural conditions and much greater amounts of modern inputs per unit of farmland, yields per sown hectare

Table 5.12   Agricultural conditions in selected provinces in China, 1988

Province	Chemical fertiliser per arable hectare (tons)	Drained and irrigated area as per cent of arable area	Grain yield (tons per sown hectare)	Average net income per peasant (yuan)
China	0.93	46	3.6	545
Jiangsu	1.90	77	5.0	797
Zhejiiang	2.54	86	4.9	902
Sichuan	1.12	44	4.0	449
Gansu	0.27	24	2.1	340
Shanxi	0.52	30	2.6	439

Source: SSB, *ZGNCTJNJ*, 1989, pp. 111, 225, 252, 255, 263 and 272.

of grain (5.7 tons per hectare in 1987) were only 40 per cent above those in China as a whole (SSB, *ZGNCTJNJ*, 1989, p. 419). Japan's yields per sown hectare of grain land were just marginally above those of the most advanced provinces of China, such as Jiangsu and Zhejiang (Table 5.12).

China's limited arable area and the fact that a high level of yields had already been achieved meant that the technical constraints on raising farm output were greater than in many developing countries. Faced with growing population and growing incomes leading to improvements in diet, China in the 1980s needed to make large investments in agriculture in order technically to sustain the required large growth of farm output. At the start of its reform process, not only was China's level of food intake vastly below that of the USSR, but it was a long way behind that of the most relevant comparator country in Asia, namely Japan (Table 5.13). China's consumption of high quality foods was a long way behind that in Japan. China's reforms resulted in large increases in per capita income which were in turn reflected in increased demands for superior foodstuffs, taking China's food consumption towards that of Japan. As can be seen from Table 5.9, the 'Green Revolution' continued throughout the reform period, leading to large increases both in fixed assets and current inputs. This necessitated a great deal of investment, pre-empting investment funds from other uses.

It is incorrect to argue that China's farm output growth from the late 1970s to the early 1990s was achieved simply through making better use of existing resources, or 'taking up the slack'. Although the efficiency with which resources were used was much greater than in the Maoist period, a huge effort of saving and investment was needed

Table 5.13   Nutrient intake in China (1978), USSR, USA and Japan
(1988–90) (per capita per day)

	China	(China as per cent of Japan)	Japan	USSR	(USSR as per cent of USA)	USA
calories	2311	(79)	2921	3379	(93)	3642
of which:						
animal	142	(23)	616	949	(86)	1107
vegetable	2169	(94)	2305	2430	(96)	2535
protein (grams)	71	(75)	95	107	(97)	110
of which:						
animal	4	(8)	53	57	(81)	71
vegetable	67	(160)	42	50	(128)	39
fats (grams)	30	(37)	81	106	(68)	155
of which:						
animal	14	(37)	38	71	(89)	80
vegetable	16	(37)	43	35	(47)	75

Source: SSB, SYC, 1983, p. 509; SSB, ZGTJNJ, 1993, p. 896.

to sustain the growth of farm output in the face of underlying supply side constraints in order to cope with the large increase in demand for farm output.

At the start of its reform, the USSR's level of consumption of farm products per person was vastly above that in China (Table 5.14). Indeed, the difference in level of consumption between the USSR and the USA was quite small (Table 5.13). Moreover, the USSR's population was growing slowly. In other words, even a large growth of per capita income in the USSR would not lead to a large growth in demand for farm produce. China's task in reforming the farm sector was both to improve efficiency and substantially increase farm output. For the USSR, the task in reforming the farm sector was mainly to increase efficiency rather than to increase output.

Size of collective farms   The basic level of ownership of the means of production, of work organisation and income distibution in China was the production team. This contained only around 50–60 workers on average, and farmed just 26 hectares of sown area. The basic level of ownership, work organisation and income distribution in the USSR was the collective farm and the state farm (though technically the state farm did not own the means of production). The Soviet collective farm averaged no less than 38 workers and encompassed 3485 hectares of sown area. Only very late in the pre-reform period, using the 'link'

Table 5.14　Output per capita of different farm products in the USSR and China in 1985 (kilograms)

	Japan	China	USSR
grain	144	364	734
vegetable oil	0.4	6.3	6.7
meat	29	19	62
milk/milk products	61	3	354
eggs	18	5	16
aquatic products	95	7	36
sugar	8	4	30
fruit	49	11	66

Source: Ministry of Agriculture (ZGNCJJTJDQ), 1989, pp. 706–7.

system, were efforts made to lower the unit of work organisation and income distribution to a lower level, and even this had not spread throughout Soviet agriculture.

Labour force: growth　By the 1980s, the USSR's farm population was virtually stagnant. However, despite the efforts to control population growth, China's total population grew by more than 200 million from 1978 to 1992, and the rural workforce grew by more than 130 million over the same period, an increase of over 43 per cent.[14] Despite a successful programme of rural industrialisation and labour absorption, the agricultural labour force increased by no less than 65 million, or 25 per cent over the same period. The amount of farmland per person fell by around one quarter in these years (from 0.35 ha. to 0.27 ha. per person). Both economies began their reform process with large amount of surplus labour consequent upon the shortcomings of the Stalinist command economy. However, China faced much greater problems than the USSR in absorbing surplus labour due to the huge pressure of population growth which constantly added to the total numbers for whom employment needed to be found. In Japan at a roughly comparable stage in its development, the rate of growth of population (just 0.7 per cent per annum between 1850 to 1900) was much below that in China alongside a growing total area of farmland. Between 1900 and 1950 population growth accelerated somewhat (to 1.3 per cent per annum), but the area of farmland was growing quite fast (at around 0.7 per cent per annum) (Macpherson, 1987, Chapter 7).

Labour force: skill level　A sharply rising share of the Soviet rural workforce was technically qualified. Alongside a fall in the total rural workforce from the 1950s through to the 1980s went a steady rise in the number of technically skilled personnel. By the late 1970s, there were 1.4 million 'high-level and middle-level farming experts' and 4.2 million drivers and repairers of farm machinery (Li Renfeng, 1981, pp. 498–9), totalling over 22 per cent of the number of rural workers. The proportion of illiterate workers was negligible.

In China in the mid-1980s, a mere 0.05 per cent of the rural workforce was reported to have high-level specialist education. Only 8.8 per cent had even been to upper middle school. Fully 21 per cent were reported to be illiterate (SSB, ZGNCTJNJ, 1985, p. 232), while another survey from from the mid-1980s reported that 28 per cent of the rural workforce was either illiterate or semi-illiterate (SSB, ZGNCTJNJ, 1991, p. 244). The World Bank considered that the Cultural Revolution had badly damaged China's rural research and extension service: 'The numbers of qualified staff, especially at the senior levels, are severely limited . . .' (World Bank, 1981(c), p. 46). It believed that the agricultural education system had still in the late 1970s not recovered from 'the long period of closure and anti-professional bias' and that currently there were 'critical shortages of staff at all levels' (World Bank, 1981(c), p. 46).

Similarities

The institutional setting   The socialist economies all based their agricultural policies on the erroneous assumption, following Marx and Lenin, that agriculture, like industry, contained wide possibilities for economies of scale in all aspects of the farm process. This was a central rationale behind the decision to collectivise agriculture. Although the Soviet collective and state farm was much larger than the Chinese production team, the latter was still a very large insitution compared to farms under capitalist systems. Moreover, the basic form of work organisation and income distribution followed the Soviet model closely.

There are deep problems with the collective and state farm method of farm organisation (Nolan, 1988). It is unusual under capitalism to find farms with more than three or four workers: in the USA in the 1960s there was an average of just 1.9 workers per farm (Nolan, 1988, p. 41). The reason is to be found mainly in the peculiar difficulty of labour supervision in agriculture. The difficulties arise from the sequential nature of tasks over the course of the agricultural cycle (making it difficult to identify the labour contribution of individuals to a given piece of farmland), the spatial dispersion of work over a wide area

Table 5.15   A comparison of Soviet and US agriculture, 1974–5

	USSR	USA
Farm workers:		
total no. (m.) (1978)	27	4.1 (annual average)
share of total workforce (per cent)	26.3	3.7
Share of total national		
investment (1971/5) (per cent)	26	<5
Agriculture's share of GNP (per cent)	17.6	2.6
sown area (m. ha.)	217	137
Fertiliser application (m. tons)	15.0	17.5
Stocks of farm machinery:		
tractors: total no. (m.)	2.3	4.4
farm workers/tractor	12	0.9
farm trucks: total (m.)	1.3	2.9
farm workers/truck	20	1.4
combine harvesters: total no. (m.)	0.7	0.7
farm workers/truck	40	5.9
Comparative yields:		
Grain output per ha. (centners): foodgrain	13	21
feedgrain	16	38

Source: Li Renfeng, 1981, p. 67; USCJEC, 1976, pp. 578 and 585.

(leading, for example, to difficulties in evaluating the labour requirements of different pieces of land), and the large role played by weather
changes, necessitating flexible responses from workers. The sum impact of these factors was to produce large managerial diseconomies of
scale (measured by the number of workers, not the amount of capital)
in most aspects of the direct tasks of cultivation. However, there is
large scope for economies of scale, and hence benefit from co-operation,
in the ancillary aspects of the farm process, such as research, irrigation, crop spraying, processing, and marketing. Agriculture under capitalism is, typically, characterised by small units of production in the
main farm tasks, but with large amounts of co-operation in ancillary
activities.

A further serious set of problems affected agricultural performance.
These included the regular issuance of inappropriate, centrally determined instructions on agricultural technology and labour organisation,
tight government control over marketing of farm produce, and poor
quality and no choice for farmers in the selection of industrial inputs
for agriculture. Both Chinese and Soviet experience abounds in difficulties
stemming from this source.

Waste of resources   Far from economising on human labour and capital, the communist approach to agricultural organisation resulted in massive waste of resources. In 1980 in the USSR at least 14 per cent of the workforce was in agriculture, compared to only 6 per cent in the industrial market economies, and a broader definition estimates that proportion to have been as high as 26 per cent (Table 5.2) while in China 71 per cent was employed in agriculture, a similar proportion to that in the least developed countries in the world (Table 5.2).

In both cases agriculture grew at a moderate pace only through absorbing a large share of investment. In the USSR the farm sector's share rose from 17 per cent of total national investment in 1959–65 to over 20 per cent in the 1970s, compared to around 5 per cent in the USA (USCJEC, 1979, p. 40; see also Table 5.15). In China agricultural investment accounted for around 11 per cent of state investment in the early 1970s (Lardy, 1983, p. 130). However, a great deal of investment was organised and financed by collectives themselves, so that its final share was considerably above this figure. The World Bank estimates that agriculture's share of total national investment in the late 1970s was around 20 per cent (World Bank, 1981(a), p. 50). The farm sector's purchase of agricultural inputs grew rapidly, averaging almost 12 per cent per annum from 1957 to 1978 (Nolan, 1993a, p. 245). The rural sector's share of consumption of total steel products rose from 8 per cent in 1957 to 17 per cent in 1977, and its share of cement increased from 9 per cent to 25 per cent over the same period (Nolan, 1988, p. 60).

Importance of lumpy inputs   It has been shown above that in the prereform Soviet Union the importance of the main lumpy inputs was vastly greater than in China. In Soviet reform an important problem was the difficulty of devising a method through which individual farmers would continue to have secure access to large, lumpy inputs that were beyond their individual resources.

However, there was a wide range of more easily divisible mechanical inputs that played an important role in Chinese agriculture. These included walking tractors, mechanical threshers, and grain-husking and fodder-crushing machines. Most of these assets were more expensive relative to average Chinese peasant income in the late 1980s than a truck or tractor was to the Soviet collective farmer. In the early stages of reform in China the bulk of many important means of production remained in collective ownership, e.g. in 1984, it was still the case that over one-half of the stock of mechanical threshers and over two-thirds of the stock of water pumps was collectively owned (SSB, *ZGNCTJNJ*, 1985, pp. 242, 251). Only as incomes rose did the share of privately-owned assets in machinery become more dominant (by 1990, the share of privately owned farm machinery had grown to 75 per cent of the total value) (SSB, *ZGNCTJNJ*, 1991, p. 251).

However, even more important than this was the role of lumpy inputs in irrigation. It has been seen that irrigation occupied only a small role in Soviet agriculture. Irrigation was at the heart of China's high yields, with the irrigated area standing at over 45 per cent of the total arable area in the early 1980s. In 1985, 47 per cent of China's irrigated area was organised in 'irrigation districts' varying in size from 600 hectares to very large projects of over 30,000 hectares. Indeed, over 28 per cent of China's irrigation was provided by schemes which each contained over around 7,000 hectares (SSB, *ZGNCTJNJ*, 1991, pp. 256, 265). In addition, 36 per cent of China's irrigated area was irrigated by reservoirs (SSB, *ZGNCTJNJ*, 1991, pp. 256, 265), the vast bulk of which were far beyond the resources of individual farmers. Thus, in China's rural reform a critically important part of the process of maintaining farm efficiency was sustaining also the access of individual farmers to large, lumpy inputs that were beyond the resources of individual farmers.

Quality and variety of farm inputs   In both the Chinese and the Soviet case there is a large literature on the detrimental effect upon farm productivity of poor quality and variety of farm inputs. Both systems suffered from decisions about farm inputs being taken in offices remote from farmers, so that the resulting product was more or less inappropriate to local conditions. Both systems suffered from the poor quality and consequent frequent breakdown of mechanical inputs produced in state enterprises and supplied to a sellers' market. In both cases, a well-devised industrial reform could have created the potential for a large reduction in capital needs per unit of output for the farm sector through the supply of better and more approriate inputs.

Sale of farm output   In both the USSR and China a large share of farm marketings was controlled by state compulsory purchases. One important consequence of a well-designed introduction of increased freedom of choice for farmers about what to produce was the efficiency benefits to be derived from greater specialisation.

Role of the private sector   In both China and the USSR the private sector provided an important area for individual decision-making by farmers. In China the sector was subject to many more vicissitudes than in the USSR, with periods when it came under severe atttack. However, as in the USSR for much of the time there was some scope for private farming activity. In the early 1970s it is estimated that between ten and twenty per cent of commune members' income came from the private sector, depending on the region in question (Nolan and White, 1983, p. 252). At its peak in the USSR the private sector reached a level of importance much beyond that in China. In 1950 for example, it produced 73 per cent of Russian potato output, 44 per cent of vegetable output, 67 per cent of meat output, 75 per cent of milk products, 89 per cent of eggs and 21 per cent of wool output (Li Renfeng, 1981, 373). While the proportion produced by the private sector later declined somewhat, figures for the late 1970s showed that this sector produced over two-thirds of potato output, and around one-third of the output of vegetables, eggs, meat, and milk products (Li Renfeng, 1981, p. 384). Thus, in neither China nor the USSR had rural dwellers lost touch with individual farming. Indeed, private sector activity was the main source of supply for many of their most important food products.

Implications

In both cases relatively simple institutional changes had the potential to produce large improvements in efficiency, and to release labour and a much increased share of investment for employment elsewhere in the economy. These represented potentially large windfall gains for the reforming communist economy. Moreover, improvements in farm performance could have had beneficial effects on light industrial growth through the supply of industrial inputs, and on overall economic performance through the incentive effect of improving an essential element in people's livelihood even in a relatively advanced economy such as the USSR was in the 1970s. In addition, it might have had beneficial balance of payments effects through reducing food and raw material imports.

The most important and simplest institutional change was contracting farmland out to individual households, allowing households to take the main decisions about organising the means of production, and permitting them to make the key decisions about saving and investment within the framework of a stable tax environment. This 'land reform' alone should have been able to reverse the profound managerial diseconomies of scale associated with collective agriculture and state farms, and radically improve peasant incentives. If such a reform were associated also with simple changes in the way in which farm inputs were supplied and with a move towards the profit motive in industry, then there would also have been a possibility for profit-seeking farm households to begin to be more demanding in their selection of inputs in respect both to their quality and type.

The largest problem was lumpy farm inputs. Soviet agriculture at first sight appears to have been characterised generally by far greater 'lumpiness' than Chinese agriculture with large numbers of huge pieces of farm equipment. However, Chinese agriculture also had an important area of 'lumpiness' which did not apply in Soviet agriculture, namely the high degree of dependence of farm production on irrigation and drainage facilities. Even quite 'small' scale water conservation facilities could be well beyond the reach of individual households. The solution to the post-reform organisation of these inputs is not in principle very complicated. In advanced capitalist countries a large part of lumpy inputs, from processing facilities through to combine havesters and crop spraying aeroplanes, are owned either by non-farmers and hired out by specialist suppliers to individual farmers, or are co-operatively owned alongside individual farm operation. In principle, the land contract process could be combined with a maintenance of a large part of more lumpy inputs in the hands of profit oriented co-operatives or state machinery and irrigation companies.

5.2.8   Natural resource endowment

The former USSR was much the largest country in the world in terms of land area. Its territory accounted for no less than 29 per cent of the world's total. It had massive reserves of timber (around one quarter of the world total), coal (around one half of the world's total), oil and natural gas. It also contained the world's largest gold reserves, a fifth of the world's diamond reserves, the world's second largest deposits of copper, iron ore, nickel, and zinc, as well as an abundance of other rare raw materials. Even the Russian Federation is vastly the world's biggest country in terms of land area, still accounting for 13 per cent of the world's land area, almost twice the size of the USA and China.

China is a huge country. Like the former USSR it has huge coal reserves. However, it has not yet located large oil and natural gas reserves. China's continued need to depend heavily on coal as the main source of energy was a substantial burden during the reform period, since coal requires such large investments in transport per unit of power produced. Despite large foreign investment in oil exploration in the South China seas in the 1980s, no significant reserves were discovered. It remains a matter of conjecture whether central Asia will reveal large oil and natural gas reserves in China. China's timber reserves are tiny for a country of its size, and its precious metals and minerals do not compare with the size of Russia's deposits.

The willingness with which international oil companies were prepared to invest in exploration in China during its reforms demonstrates the ease with which the former USSR could have also attracted a large amount of foreign investment to enable natural resource production to modernise and grow. The necessary conditions were political stability, secure property rights and a guaranteed share of the income from the investment. This would have provided a relatively easy path with which, through simple institutional reform, to raise export earnings and greatly enlarge imports.

5.2.9 Population pressure

China in the 1980s and 1990s faced the problems a high age-specific fertility rate (in the absence of government measures to control fertility) common to most developing countries. In addition it confronted the special problem of a large age cohort entering the reproductive ages. China's system of basic needs guarantees under Mao left it peculiarly liable to explosively high rates of population growth in the absence of tough state action to control reproduction. In the 1960s, death rates had fallen to low levels but birthrates were high during a period in which the government was too preoccupied with other matters to pay attention to policies to control reproduction. Throughout the 1960s, birth rates remained at well over 30 per 1000, and in 1963 reached as high as 43 per 1000 (SSB, *ZGTJNJ*, 1990, p. 90). This exceptionally large cohort was moving through into the marriageable age groups in the 1980s and 1990s.

Under the people's communes China was successful in the 1970s in raising the average age of marriage. This, combined with greatly increased availability of contraception and strong sanctions helped to reduce sharply the overall birth rate in the late Maoist years (from 36 per 1000 in 1968 to 23 per 1000 in 1975) (SSB, *ZGTJNJ*, 1990, p. 90). Although the age of marriage and the proportion of the population using birth control remained high throughout the 1980s,[15] the bulge in the proportion of the population in the reproductive ages still presented large difficulties in controlling overall fertility.

If the Chinese government had not taken measures to control population growth rates in the 1980s, then China's population would have
grown even more rapidly than it did, presenting large problems for the
rate and structure of investment, which in turn would have slowed
down the rate of growth of income and output.

5.2.10 Inflationary potential

The rate of inflation in China under reform was higher than was re-
ported in the Maoist years, and it fluctuated considerably (Table 5.16).
However, compared to the rate of inflation in Russia under reform
(Table 5.16) or, indeed, in most developing countries (see Chapter 2),
China's inflation rate was modest. Did China have an easier task in
controlling inflation than did Russia?

It has been argued that Yeltsin's government inherited a legacy of
substantial repressed inflation which was a special difficulty for Russia's reforms. China also, in common with the other communist economies, inherited a large problem of repressed inflation from the Stalinist
period, not least the large excess demand for many goods and services
in short supply under the administered economy. These problems were
no less severe in China in 1976 than in the USSR in 1985. Of course,
as will be seen later (Chapter 7), in Russia after 1985 the problems of
repressed inflation rapidly intensified, but this was a direct result of
Gorbachev's political reforms These were in turn the fundamental element of the transition orthodoxy: the 'necessary' political democratisation before economic reform was possible.

In China also there were large structural pressures associated with
reforming the planned economy, such as bottlenecks in infrastructure,
which tended to stimulate inflation. Moreover, the bottlenecks only
intensified with the successful achievement of a rapid rate of growth,
with surges in demand for slow-gestating capital goods products.

In a country of China's size, there were peculiarly strong inflationary pressures in the reform period associated with the need to decen-
tralise many economic functions of government. In the absence of a
comprehensive reform of the financial system, there was, in a 'pris-
oner's dilemma' fashion, little incentive for local authorities or banks
to control the supply of money in the interests of control over the
national rate of inflation.

In sum, China's success in combining a reasonable rate of inflation
with rapid growth cannot be interpreted as mainly a matter of good
fortune in the inherited inflationary potential. It was a peculiarly difficult

feat to accomplish simultaneous accelerated growth, large structural transformation and a reasonably controlled rate of inflation.

5.3 NON-ECONOMIC FACTORS

5.3.1 Culture

China is the birthplace of Confucianism, which appears to have been a powerful vehicle of industrialisation elsewhere. At least some parts of China had a substantial entrepreneurial culture, dating back many centuries (see e.g. Wu *et al.*, forthcoming). Moreover, capitalism flourished in some parts of China in the twentieth century before the revolution (Bergere, 1986), allowing Chinese people in the reform period to build on a strong memory of capitalism. The fact that many of the Asian Newly Industrialising Countries were Confucian revived theories linking culture and economic development, long neglected after Max Weber's attempt to explain the rise of capitalism in Western Europe by the Protestant ethic. Confucianism emphasises hard work, education, meritocracy, and hierarchy, which fits the popular conception of an efficient corporation, if not a prosperous national economy. Consequently, many have tried to find the explanation for East Asian success in Confucian culture. It is tempting to add China to the list of countries whose growth can be explained by Confucianism. It certainly relieves the burden of explanation from the realm of policy choice. However, there are problems with this argument.

First, 'culture' is not a given factor. 'Culture' is continually being reconstructed either consciously and unconsciously. For example, the Japanese 'culture' of industrial harmony did not emerge spontaneously. Rather, as is frequently the case, it was deliberately invented. What needs to be explained is why and how the old culture of Confucianism was reconstructed in Japan in a form amenable to industrial development in East Asia.

Secondly, it is not clear that any type of Confucianism promotes economic development. Morishima (1982) has argued that Japan modernised while China failed to do so, because, unlike the Chinese or the Korean variety, Japanese Confucianism emphasised hierarchy and loyalty over individual edification. Moreover, a long scholarly tradition argues that China's variety of Confucianism constitutes a large handicap to economic development, due to long-ingrained habits of familism, nepotism and corruption. Indeed, Levy's classic account argued that in 'traditional China the economic aspects of life as well almost all others were predominantly family oriented, and business relationships were patterned on the family' (Levy *et al.*, 1949, p. 12). Levy argued that the value system of Chinese, family-oriented Confucianism was fundamentally opposed to that of the modern business corporation, due to its emphasis upon 'particularism and functional diffuseness' (Levy *et al,*, 1949, p. 12). Pessimism about China's economic prospects based on the deep-rooted problems of traditional cultural factors was a persistent theme of writing on China in the 1980s. This led many observers to doubt the real basis of alleged 'progress' in China's economic reforms, and to be pessimisitic about the future prospects for the economy.

Thirdly, the contrast between former Stalinist countries in the strength of the legacy of an entrepreneurial 'culture' is not nearly so clear-cut as some would wish to argue. As was seen above, the large growth of capitalism in pre-1914 Russia is inconsistent with a thesis of cultural incompatibility between 'Russianness' and capitalism. The vibrant black and grey market in the USSR showed that the entrepreneurial culture was not killed in Russia, a fact that was vividly confirmed by the rapidity with 'entrepreneurship' sprang into life after the mid-1980s. On the other hand, few countries have gone so far as China did under Mao Tsetung in attempting to obliterate entrepreneurship entirely: 'capitalism' was likened to 'a dog in the water to be beaten and drowned'.

5.3.2 Administrative capacity of the bureaucracy

Both China and the USSR had a long tradition of centralised bureaucratic rule. They each had a huge Party apparatus,[16] which was closely interwoven with the system of state administration. It cannot be argued that the Chinese bureaucratic apparatus or tradition of centralised rule was weaker than that of Russia. It would be hard also to argue to sustain an argument that the Chinese Communist Party apparatus was any less corrupt or any more professionally effective than that of the USSR in the late 1970s. Indeed, the Chinese Communist Party and administrative apparatus was seriously damaged during the Cultural Revolution. Even more than usual in a communist country promotions in China during this period had been based on ideological rather than professional criteria (i.e. 'red' rather than 'expert').

There is a long tradition of political analysis in China which argues that the main reason for China's failure to build on its great medieval technical breakthrough and experience an industrial revolution is precisely the inhibiting power of the bureaucracy (e.g. Balazs, 1964). Indeed, Needham's magisterial analysis of Chinese science and civilisation argues that this was the key to China's failure to make further advance:

> Chinese civilisation was basically inhibited from giving rise to modern science and technology, because the society which grew up in China after the feudal period was unsuitable for these developments ... Ancient feudalism in China was replaced by a special form of society to which we have no parallel in the West. This has been called Asiatic bureaucratism, in which all the lords have been swept away except one – the Son of Heaven, the Emperor, who rules the country and collects all the taxes through a gigantic bureaucracy. (Needham, 1969, pp. 175–6)

A substantial body of informed opinion both inside and outside China in the 1980s felt that the strength of this stifling bureaucratic tradition would prevent China advancing towards a successful market economy. Su Shaozhi, for example, former head of the Marxism-Leninism Institute, argued:

> China is a country with a feudal-despotic history of 2,000 years. . . . The influence of feudal-despotism in the ideological and political fields is first expressed in privilege. The prevailing unhealthy trends, exemplified when party and government cadres and their children engage in commercial business and appoint people by favouritism, are without exception related to privileges. . . . Doing business and appointing people in such ways by no means reflect the enterprising spirit of capitalists or the commodity relations of capitalism. (Su Shaozhi, 1988, pp. 147–8).

The bureaucracy was regarded by almost all commentators as the major obstacle to the implementation of reform policies in communist countries. Most observers regarded it is as self-evident that the bureaucracy would be deeply opposed to economic reform, since reform would deprive them of power and status. Aslund (1991, p. 14) summarises this orthodox approach as follows: 'A reform reduces the power of the bureaucracy by definition and most of the administration will inevitably oppose reform. Therefore, a successful reform must break the power of the anti-reform bureaucracy. . . . To break the power of the party and state bureaucracy may be seen as the key problem of a reform.'

However, the possession of an effective, competent state bureaucracy is a central element in explaining the rise of almost every successful industrialising country since Britain. There were two logical possibilities to the problems of the old state apparatus. One was to regard it as hopelessly unreformable, inherently opposed to any kind of reform measure and to destroy it. A second, reformist approach was to attempt to change its goals and methods of operation. This would involve a gradual process of professionalisation, making the organisation more youthful, introducing more rationality rather than quasi-religious principles into its ethical foundation, and giving the members of the apparatus a central role in the process of reconstructing the Stalinist economy. In the reformist approach the Party members are less threatened and although their tasks alter greatly over time, they retain their dignity, status and remain relatively well-rewarded.

The Chinese leadership attempted to follow the second approach and were broadly successful in it. However, there is no reason to believe that the Chinese bureaucratic apparatus had any greater capacity to be transformed successfully in this reformist way than did the Soviet one. Indeed, many observers writing in the 1970s would have argued that the reverse was the case. Consider Miller's evaluation of the Soviet bureaucracy which Gorbachev inherited:

> The Party's quasi-military structure and traditions made it an effective and durable instrument in the hands of such a leader. It still produced officials who could serve a transformist cause with energy and selfless loyalty. It contained millions of others who would doggedly carry out orders even if they did not fully understand them- indeed who would accept surgery on the Party provided it was administered by one of their own. (Miller, 1993, p. 77)

5.3.3 Mass demands for political reform

Political outcomes are far from a matter of choice by governments. One line of argument is that the dramatic contrast in political outcomes in China and the USSR was not at all a matter of policy choice but was, rather, an uncontrollable consequence of the fundamental difference in political environment. The most important such propositions relate to mass demands for democracy on the one hand and the propensity for the respective countries to split into separate political units (their 'fissiparous' tendencies).

Mass demands for democracy

The Soviet Union in the late 1970s was, self-evidently, a much more highly urbanised society than was China. It also had a much more strongly developed interest in Western values among the intellectual community. It is probable that in the 1970s there was a more widespread hope in the USSR that Western democratic institutions might be put into place than was the case in China.

However, the Soviet political system appeared to most observers both inside and outside the country to be stable. It had survived relatively intact since the 1920s without fundamental disruptions. The system, even in the post-Stalin and post-Krushchev period, was still repressive, allowing only limited areas of individual freedom. Moreover, China's political system had only recently been through huge upheaval in the shape of the Cultural Revolution, which had deeply damaged the Communist Party for several years, unleashing a period of widespread anarchy. There is no counterpart in Soviet history. Moreover, the principal actors in the Cultural Revolution had been millions of young people, urged by the country's leader to 'dare to rebel'.

In the Soviet Union, hopes of fundamental political change may have been more widespread than in China, but expectations of such change were low. It was the policy decisions of Gorbachev with respect to *glasnost* and *perestroika* of the political system that turned the hopes into ardent expectations. In the sharpest contrast there was a near consensus among the Chinese leadership that political democratisation was not a part of the political agenda in the near future in China. A series of campaigns against 'bourgeois' values attempted to reduce expectations of change among the politically active population.

Fissiparous tendencies

In the 1970s both China and the USSR were huge multinational empires. However, the relative size of the 'national minority' population was a major difference between the two countries. The non-Russian population accounted for around one-half of the total Soviet population whereas the non-Han population in China accounted for well under 10 per cent of the total. Once the minority nationalities began to pursue their demands for independence in a serious fashion in the USSR the situation was more difficult to control than would have been the case in China.

Successful market and income growth is the most powerful force leading to the disintegration of ethnic differences. In both cases the non-market Stalinist systems had kept the forces of nationalism intact in a 'deep-freeze' beneath a veneer of new 'socialist man'. The national leadership of both countries perpetuated a public propaganda myth that the 'nationality' question belonged to the past. In both cases the 'national minorities' were disproportionately concentrated in more sparsely populated, remote, resource-rich regions. In both cases national liberation movements had been brutally suppressed. However, the severity of these struggles in recent times had been much greater in China than in the USSR. China fought major battles against the Uighur 'national minority' in Xinjiang province in central Asia over a long period, and conducted a protracted guerilla war against the Tibetan independence movement.

In the 1970s in neither country was the expectation of national minority groups high. However, the policies pursued by the national leadership were strikingly different (see below). In the Soviet case the environment of political *perestroika* greatly raised the expectation of national minority groups. In China national policy-makers repeatedly made it clear that attempts to break away from rule by Peking would be repressed brutally. A reform strategy that led to accelerated economic growth had the potential to greatly defuse nationalist sentiment by providing employment, raising incomes, stimulating migration out of 'minority' areas and changing values through commercialisation.

Effective central rule in a country may not be undermined only by nationalism. China's long history has been dominated by regular cycles of national disintegration and reunification, even among the Han people. No theme is stronger in Chinese political history than the need to maintain national unity in the face of a high intrinsic propensity for the 'sheet of loose' sand to spin apart. China is not an inherently unified state. National unity has only been maintained over substantial periods through effective government. Its modern history shows only too clearly the high propensity for central rule to fall apart.

5.4 CONCLUSION

This chapter has identified many important differences between the political and economic inheritance bequeathed to the leaders of the respective countries at the start of their reform programme. These included China's much lower level of farmland per capita, of per capita income, of urbanisation, of industrialisation, and of scientific skills.

The role played by small-scale industrial enterprises was much greater in China than in the USSR. China also had a much more important role played by poorly located areas in its structure of industrial assets. China had a much higher rate of population growth, and a more ancient tradition of entrepreneurship. National minority populations occupied a much smaller share of total population in China than in the USSR. China possessed much larger concentrations of capital in the hands of overseas citizens. Some of these differences tended to work to the advantage of China, but many of them did not. It is not apparent that on balance the inherited system differences made it more likely that well-chosen policies would tend to lead to faster growth in China than in the USSR.

However, there were also important similarities. Both countries in modern times had given evidence of large reservoirs of entrepeneurial skill. Both countries had a high potentiality for fissure into political anarchy and separate nation states. Both countries possessed relatively well-educated populations for their level of income and, in both cases, there was massive underfulfilment of human productive capabilites. The basic 'planning' methods of the command economy were the same. The key features of both farm and the non-farm institutions were the same. Both systems had relatively large amounts of technical skill and capital stock locked up in the military sector. In each case, the economic system was massively underperforming compared to the productive potential achievable with existing physical and human capital. In each case, relatively simple system changes were capable of generating an initial large improvement in system performance which could act as the springboard to further more fundamental change and improvement. In other words, despite important differences, both the former USSR and China possessed huge catch-up possibilities, as did most of the former Stalinist countries.

The main conclusion of this chapter is that the principal reason for the contrast in outcome to reform in China and the USSR must lie with the difference in policies selected. These policies relate both to narrowly economic issues, and to the relationship between economic and political change. The contrast in policies chosen was itself the result of complex historical factors leading to fundamentally different approaches towards the task of transforming the Stalinist system.

6 Reform in China

6.1 POLITICS AND REFORM

6.1.1 Political stability

It is widely thought that the post-Mao Chinese leadership's obsession with political stability was motivated purely by the desire to cling to power: 'Keeping power is the only issue for the party' (*Economist*, 28th November 1992). This is too simplistic. The Chinese leadership valued political stability both for its functional relationship with economic advance and as a goal of intrinsic value.

Modern China has endured a large amount of political disorder (*da luan*). In the late nineteenth century a succession of rebellions rocked the Qing government. Much the most serious of these was the Taiping Rebellion of 1851–1864, 'the greatest civil war in world history', which in 'sheer brutality and destruction' had 'few peers in the annals of history' (Ho Pingti, 1959, p. 238).[1] The collapse of the Qing in 1911 was followed by a long period of civil disorder: 'For a whole decade from 1917 to 1927 there were incessant civil wars in various parts of the country. . . . From 1928 on the Nationalists were repeatedly at war with the Communists. . . . These wars were brought to an end in 1936; then war with Japan broke out in July 1937. . . . [I]n August 1945 civil war between the Nationalists and the Communists was soon renewed. For over a generation, therefore, China was seldom at peace' (Ho Pingti, 1959, p. 249). Warfare limited the government's ability to collect revenue and ensured that a large share of its meagre revenues was diverted towards military purposes.[2] Such modernisation as occurred was confined chiefly to the safe havens of the Treaty Ports.

The collapse of political authority damaged the state's capacity to undertake infrastructure investment thereby increasing the farm sector's susceptibility to natural disaster, and reduced the state's ability to respond to impending famine situations. Between nine and thirteen million people died in the great drought famine in northwest China in 1877–88, while in the great famine of 1928, around three million people perished in the province of Shensi alone (Ho Pingti, 1959, pp. 232–233). Repeated floods in the Yangzi and Yellow River valleys were accompanied by large loss of life, of the which the worst was that of 1938 when the Yellow River changed its course, and around 1.8 million people perished (Ho Pingti, 1959, p. 235).

China's leadership in the late 1970s was dominated by old men. Deng Xiaoping was pre-eminent. Around him were powerful veteran politicians, such as Chen Yun, Li Xiannian, Ye Jianying, and Yang Shangkun. Most commentators regarded China's 'gerontocracy' as unequivocally 'bad' for China. They were repeatedly contrasted with the new generation of Soviet leaders, such as Gorbachev, Shevardnadze, Yeltsin, Popov, and Sobchak. These were, in Mrs Thatcher's words, people with whom one could 'do business' in marked contrast to the old dictators, and, latterly, the old 'butchers' in Peking. China's aged leaders had experienced the anarchy of political life for much of the 'Republican' period. They had witnessed the disaster of the Great Leap Forward, which caused as many as thirty million excess deaths. This disaster served as a dire warning of the dangers of ill thought-out policy 'leaps'. They had more recently been through the searing experience of the Cultural Revolution. Its 'idealistic' goals had temporarily badly damaged the communist party, harmed the economy and threatened ordinary citizens' safety.

Self-interest in clinging to power was, of course, a central motive determining the Chinese leadership's approach to political reform. However, an important, though indeterminable, part of their approach was also based in a hard-headed appraisal of the options facing China. China was indeed like a 'sheet of loose sand' (*sha pan*) which could easily fall apart.

6.1.2 Strategic pursuit of national power

The desire to lead the country towards rapid modernisation was at least as important a goal for the Chinese leadership as political stability. China's determination to build a strong and internationally powerful economy was intensified by more than a century of economic failure and national humiliation. For around two thousand years China had been the 'central kingdom'. It had achieved a medieval economic and technical revolution well before Europe.

China's humiliation had extended from defeat in the Opium Wars through to the forcible opening of the country in a succession of unequal treaties. It continued with the military defeat by Japan in 1895, which ushered in the phase of 'slicing the melon' in the 1890s when China was carved up into spheres of influence: 'The various European governments have already started to partition China. They are not doing it openly, but stealthily like thieves. They have begun to rob China as they would a corpse' (Lenin, quoted in Hu Sheng, 1955, p. 112). The humiliation continued with the crushing in 1900 of the Yi He Tuan (Boxer) uprising by foreign forces, and China's descent after 1911 into civil war, warlordism and widespread banditry. In the Treaty Ports, foreign powers ruled, and ordinary Chinese were treated as second-class citizens. The country descended into a 'land of famine' in the eyes of the world as disasters swept the country (Mallory, 1926). Japanese forces occupied Manchuria (Manchukuo) and occupied the main body of the country from 1937 to 1945.

The establishment of the People's Republic of China in 1949 did not see the end of China's humiliation. The Great Leap Forward produced disaster. The Cultural Revolution ended in anarchy. For a long period under Mao, China was viewed as a land of 'political madness'. The Maoist period saw many achievements but also a comprehensive failure to modernise the economy and advance living standards in the way that had been hoped. China mostly was isolated in the international community. Even after the thaw in relations with the USA under Nixon, China still was marginalised in world affairs.

From the late nineteenth century onwards, a succession of its East Asian neighbours had modernised their economies successfully, culminating in the success of the East Asian dragons. Their rise to economic power was deeply galling. Hong Kong and Singapore were miniscule city states, and Taiwan and South Korea had been China's enemies. Hong Kong and Taiwan were considered by the mainland government to be still part of China. All of them espoused an opposed ideology. Their success dramatised the failure of China's command economy 'socialism'.

No sentiment was more powerful in shaping the approach towards the reform process than the determination to succeed at last in making China economically powerful in order to strengthen its position in the world and to restore a sense of national self-confidence. The Third Plenum of the Party's eleventh Central Committee in 1978, which set the Party on course for reform, regarded the task of modernisation as a 'New Long March to make China a modern powerful socialist country before the end of the century' (Central Committee, 1978, p. 10).

The turn from inward-looking, xenophobic Maoist policies towards a growth-oriented, state orchestrated, politically authoritarian integration with the world economy, parallels the strategic modernisation of Japan under the Meiji Restoration after the centuries-long isolation under the Tokugawa. It also draws inspiration from the dominant strand in Chinese modernisation theory from the late nineteenth century, in the shape of such thinkers as Kang Youwei, Liang Qichao and Sun Yatsen, through to their modern manifestation in Chiang Kaishek and Lee Kuanyu. Deng's declaration of the potential damage that could be done to the 'Second Chinese Revolution' by American-style democracy with the separation of powers (Deng Xiaoping, 1987, p. 630), closely parallels the criticism made by Liang Qichao after his visit to the USA in 1903:

> [Liang believed that] over the long term, the gradual displacement of group interests by individual interests [in the US] could only lead to an uncooperative, conflictful and disunified nation, which Liang considered would be unable to compete with other nations. . . . Was it not in the best interests of the nation, Liang asked, for the state to rise above societal conflicts for the sake of maintaining order? In answer he asserted that there could be no compromise for China at this stage in her history: strong leadership and a strong state . . . were the major signposts to be followed along the Chinese road to development. (Twohey, 1995, ch. 2).

6.1.3 A strong state as a functional necessity for economic advance

The leadership which assumed power on Mao's death, and which quickly restored Deng Xiaoping to the centre of power, considered economic advance to be the central goal. Instead of Mao's emphasis on class struggle and the transformation of human consciousness towards selflessness and serving the people, the Dengist programme placed first emphasis on achieving economic growth. It embraced the 'economistic' philosophy that Mao had so heavily criticised, and for which Deng and his supporters had been attacked and persecuted by Mao. The Third Plenum declared formally that 'the fundamental task' was to 'develop the productive forces': 'The whole party must shift the emphasis of its work to socialist modernisation' (Third Plenum, 1978, p. 11).

Deng consistently maintained that the only feasible political setting in which to reform the command economy successfully, and to maintain and improve useful planning functions, was under strong, unified party leadership:

> Without the Chinese Communist Party, who would organise the socialist economy, politics, military affairs and culture of China, and who

would organise the four modernisations? In the China of today we can never dispense with leadership by the Party and extol the spontaneity of the masses. . . . If a handful of people are again allowed to kick aside the Party committees and make trouble, the Four Modernisation will vanish into thin air. This is not an exaggerated statement I am making in order to scare people; it is the objective truth corroborated by a wealth of facts. (Deng Xiaoping, 1979, p. 49)

The Chinese leadership regarded the reform process as a huge task of 'systems engineering' (Central Committee, 1985, p. 520), involving the complex balancing of the interests of different social groups. It felt that this complex task was incompatible with simultaneous transformation of the political system towards Western-style democratic institutions. They were obsessed with the possibility that Western-style democratisation would produce political disintegration and, indeed, disintegration of the nation-state.

This fear stemmed from the long sweep of Chinese history in which the end of dynasties had almost always been followed by prolonged periods of chaos. It stemmed also from strong personal memories of pre-revolutionary politics and of the Cultural Revolution. It was based on a realistic evaluation of the brittle nature of the communist political system. Moreover, it stemmed too from an onerous sense of responsibilty to the Chinese people, to not fail once again to guide China along the path of successful modernisation. The clarity of Deng's vision in contrast to the flaccid nature of that of Gorbachev is striking:

At present, when we are confronted with manifold difficulties in our economic life which can be overcome only by series of readjustments and by consolidation and reorganisation, it is particularly necessary to stress publicly the importance of subordinating personal interests to collective ones, interests of the part to those of the whole, and immediate to long-term interests. . . . *[T]alk about democracy in the abstract will inevitably lead to the unchecked spread of ultra-democracy and anarchism, to the complete disruption of political stability and unity, and to the total failure of our modernisation programme. If this happens then the decade of struggle against Lin Biao and the Gang of Four will have been in vain, China will once again be plunge into chaos, division, retrogression and darkness, and the Chinese people will be deprived of all hope.* (Deng Xiaoping, 1979, p. 55) (Emphasis added)

6.1.4   Professionalisation of the bureaucracy

China entered the post-Mao reform period with an aged leadership not only at the apex of the Party but right down through its ranks. It was quickly realised that a central task for modernisation was professional-isation of this vast bureaucracy:

> Most of the leading comrades of the provincial and prefectural com-mittees are over 60, and not a few of them have passed 70. The same is true of the leading comrades of the ministries and commis-sions of government. . . . Most of the leading comrades of the county party committees are about 50. . . . [We need] to set right now to training thousands and thousands of young and middle aged cadres who have both political integrity and professional competence and promote them to leading posts at different levels to temper them there. (Chen Yun, 1981, pp. 131–2)

The attempt to modernise the bureaucracy began early in the post-Mao period, spearheaded by Deng Xiaoping.[3] The intention was to dismiss into retirement the old guard of Party officials in the govern-ment administration who did not possess high technical qualifications. This effort parallels those of Bismarckian Germany and Meiji Japan in the late nineteenth century, or Singapore, Taiwan and South Korea in the 1950s, in which a key point of the modernisation drive was the creation of a professional government administration responsible to an unelected executive authority rather than to an elected parliament. Slow, but important progress was made in the 1980s: '[T]he speed of organisational turnover, and the relative ease with which it has oc-curred, has been impressive. . . . [T]he Chinese bureaucracy now has a greater ability and willingness to bring technical competence to bear on competing policy alternatives' (Harding, 1987, pp. 208–9).[4] By the early 1990s it was obvious to anyone dealing with Chinese govern-ment institutions that there had been a great advance in the level of competence.

China's bureaucracy grew considerably during the reform period, the numbers employed full time in government and Party institutions rising from 4.7 million in 1978 to 11.5 million in 1992 (SSB, *ZGTJNJ*, 1993, Table 4.2).[5] while the number of Party members grew from 35 million in the mid-1970s to 50 million in the early 1990s. Although the methods of operation of the government altered substantially, with a gradual increase in the autonomy of economic agents, there remained wide areas for bureaucratic interference and corruption. Even in the mid-1990s, there still were large areas of government intervention in the workings of the market which provided opportunities for corrupt behaviour and the exercise of power over others. Despite Deng's injunction that 'bureaucratic' behaviour should be overcome, his 1980 description is valid for any point in the whole reform period:

> Bureaucracy remains a major and widespread problem in the political life of our Party and state. Its harmful manifestations include the following: standing high above the masses; abusing power; divorcing oneself from reality and the masses; spending a lot of time and effort to put up an impressive front; indulging in empty talk; sticking to rigid ways of thinking; being hidebound by convention; overstaffing administrative organs; being dilatory, inefficient, and irresponsible; failing to keep one's word; circulating documents endlessly without solving problems; shifting responsibility to others; and even assuming the airs of a mandarin, reprimanding other people at every turn, vindictively attacking others, suppressing democracy, deceiving superiors and subordinates; being arbitrary and despotic, practising favouritism, offering bribes, participating in corrupt practices in violation of the law and so on. Such things have reached an intolerable dimensions both in our domestic affairs and in our contacts with other countries. (Deng Xiaoping, 1980, p. 84)

It is possible that the bureaucratic tradition is more powerfully developed in China than in other countries. However, China shares these problems with almost all countries in which the state has played a central role in economic life, including Taiwan, South Korea and Japan. The question is whether on balance the negative aspects of bureaucracy are outweighed at a particular juncture by the positive aspects of substantial state action.

6.1.5   From totalitarianism to new authoritarianism

Despite maintaining a monopoly of control over political life, and tightly controlling the boundaries of freedom, a large range of socio-economic decisions was removed from the direct control of Party administrators. China's political system moved gradually closer to that of Taiwan and South Korea in the 1960s and 1970s. The 1980s saw a clash between two forms of 'new authoritarianism' in Chinese politics. One branch saw sustained authoritarianism as the vehicle to facilitate a rapid transition to a free enterprise economy based on privatisation of assets. A key slogan in this approach was 'hard politics, soft economics'. In this view it was seen as necessary to enable the beneficiaries from this process to control mass discontent at the uncertainty, unemployment and inequality it produced.

The alternative view, and one which seems have been held by the consensus of China's leaders, was that authoritarianism was necessary to enable the government to move in a controlled, evolutionary way towards a more market-influenced economy. In this process the level of 'social tolerance' for change was given a high weight in evaluating reform policies. Moreover, in this approach a major reason for maintaining a strong state was in order to ensure that the benefits of growth would percolate down to the bottom segments of the income distribtution, and to prevent reform being accompanied by a drastic redistribution of income and wealth. In this approach 'fairness' (*gongping*) was centrally important in formulating policy. It was opposed to the simplistic, anti-growth levelling of Maoist policies, but, equally, was committed to serious measures to spread the benefits of progress:

> Socialism means eliminating poverty. Pauperism is not socialism, still less communism. The superiority of the socialist system lies above all in its ability to increasingly develop the productive forces and to improve the people's material and cultural life. . . . The socialist system can enable all the people to become well off. This is why we want to uphold socialism. (Deng Xiaoping, 1984, pp. 2–3)

6.2 ECONOMIC REFORM

6.2.1 Economic ideology

a. Planning and the transition

The relationship between plan and market in the transition from the command economy can be considered from at least two perspectives in relation to the Chinese reforms after 1976. One approach views China's success as simply a function of the way in which it organised the 'transition' to a market economy. In this view growth is viewed as a product simply of passively removing controls more or less well. This is the view of most mainstream economists who have argued for the superiority of the Chinese 'incremental' approach.

An alternative aproach views China's accelerated growth as a function also of successful state intervention to guide China from an 'upper poor' income country to a middle income country. This approach focusses on the positive actions the Chinese government has taken, rather than viewing the growth process in China as a simply a negative one of removing state controls. The first approach focusses on analysing the reform period in terms of 'comparative transition' experience. The second approach examines China's growth in terms of comparative growth experience of countries undergoing large structural transformation, whether or not they are communist. Both perspectives are relevant in evaluating the Chinese performance.

b. Caution and experimentation in reform

From the earliest days of the Chinese reform programme, China's leaders had to wrestle constantly with advice from experts who urged the 'economic logic' and common sense of a rapid, comprehensive system reform. However, the leadership, with unremitting internal debate, and a barrage of conflicting advice, maintained a consistent line, summarised by Liu Guoguang:

> A prevailing view among Chinese and foreign economists has been that the economy ought to be restructured in a package deal. That is, once work is started, it has to be done in a comprehensive way all at once with different parts of the new structure co-ordinated with each other. It would be a mistake, the economists thought, to do it step by step, bit by bit. . . . *A package deal started all at once without prior experimentation would cause great losses if something goes wrong*. Therefore the reform must start with experimentation – from minor reform to moderate reform, and from moderate reform to major reform. New conditions and new problems must be constantly studied and experience summed up. The work must be guided in the light of circumstances. . . . *The division of reform [into steps] is intended to bring about the complicated reform in an orderly way without committing too many errors, or doing the damage that can be caused by sudden and impractical reform* (Liu Guoguang and Wang Ruisun, 1984, pp. 119–20). (Emphasis added)

An important objective of the evolutionary approach was to give the leaders time to reflect upon each stage and consider carefully their results before proceeding further: 'The whole course of the structural reform should be so slow, steady and well oriented that it will help concentration of the leaders' energies on the readjustment and at the same time ensure healthy progress in the reform' (Liu Guoguang and Wang Ruisun, 1984, p. 142).

The word 'gradually' appeared with relentless repetition in policy documents in China's reform programme. A certain conviction that the old Stalinist economic system needed fundamental reform was combined with an equally certain conviction that change had to proceed 'step by step', 'touching stones cross the river'. Rapid reform without prior experimentation carried high risks, and, impressed by the dreadful failures of the past century or more, China's post-Mao leaders were determined to proceed slowly, whatever highly educated domestic and foreign technocrats might suggest. Moreover, while allowing cope for local experimentation with reform they intended to keep control of the overall process:

> All moves in reform have to be tested in practice through which new experience will be acquired. . . . We must not try to accomplish the whole task at one stroke. All major reforms which affect the whole country will be arranged by the State Council under a unified plan. All localities, departments and units should be encouraged to conduct exploratory and pilot reforms. Nevertheless, any reform involving the overall situation or one that is extensive in scope must first be approved by the State Council. (Central Committee, 1984, p. 424)

All the major reforms were characterised by the same procedure: local experimentation was combined with central investigation and approval. China's reforms were massively time consuming. Vast amounts of labour time of officials and experts were spent investigating, writing reports, organising work conferences, debating results and monitoring new policy initiatives. The contrast with the simplicity of approach under the transition orthodoxy could not be greater. In the latter, the task of 'reforming governments' is simply to remove themselves from intervention in the economy.

A variety of factors have been advanced to explain the Chinese leadership's near obsession with caution in reform. It is sometimes argued that the Chinese national character is inclined to caution and experimentation, in contrast to the 'moody and impulsive' national character of Russians.[6] This observation sits uneasily with the enthusiasm with which hundreds of millions of Chinese citizens, high cadres children included, participated in the mass collectivisation campaigns, the Great

Leap Forward and even the Cultural Revolution. More serious explanations are examined in the following paragraphs.

Absence of an agreed goal for system reform   Even the most serious reformers among China's leaders did not have a clear view of the final goal. Almost everyone at the pinnacle of power believed the command economy needed reform, but none of them believed that a US-style free market economy was appropriate for a country such as China. There was a consensus that the desirable balance between plan and market could only be found through experimentation, and system evolution, not through sweeping *a priori* propositions.

Caution made it easier to maintain a pro-reform consensus within the party   For almost all members of the communist party in China, learning about a market economy and developing trust in the usefulness of markets involved radical new modes of thought. The much repeated and apparently simple statement that planning needed to move away from direct commands towards increasing reliance on indirect 'economic' levers to guide economic activity concealed a massive change in outlook. This was realised in the early days of the reform.[7] A slower pace of reform made this adjustment much easier. Comrades who might have dug their heels in and opposed a large transformation at a single stroke ended up accepting just as large a final shift in the economic mechanism because they step-by-step adjusted their consciousness. Consequently, their skill and experience were put to the service of reform, not wasted in opposing the reform. This approach greatly reduced the possibility of the debate over reform descending into polarised camps as happened in the USSR:

> We must not divide the cadres and the masses by calling some people 'reformers' and others 'conservatives'. We should have faith in comrades who fall behind the developing situation for a time, confident that they will understand things bettter in the course of the reform. . . . Of course, not everyone was in favour of reform at the outset. In the beginning two provinces [Sichuan and Anhui] took the lead: We worked out the principles and policies of reform on the basis of the experiences accumulated in these two provinces. For one or two years after we publicised these principles and policies, some provinces had misgivings about them and others didn't know what to think, but in the end they all followed suit. The Central Committee's policy was to wait for them to be convinced by facts. (Deng Xiaoping, 1987, p. 627)

China had already experienced a succession of disasters by attempting policy 'leaps' The old men who returned to power in the late 1970s in China had lived through an attempt to create a 'great leap forward' in political economy. In 1958 Mao had promised that a communist utopia could be created overnight in China, and that within a few years massive economic progress could be achieved through revolutionised socio-economic relationships. The Great Leap ended in disaster, with a massive collapse in output and tens of millions losing their lives through starvation. This made them deeply sceptical of policy advice such as that given to the Soviet leadership by Western and internal advisors, suggesting that radical policy changes could quickly produce excellent results.

In the 1970s China was a poor country The leadership was deeply aware that in a low income country policy errors could create disastrous results, which they had witnessed during the Great Leap Forward. This contrasted sharply with outlook of the Soviet leadership, which could not conceive that things might quickly get worse. China's leaders did not imagine that they could quickly create the wealth of the USA or Western Europe. Rather, they had the modest hope of avoiding disaster and achieving some improvement through cautious change. As long as China gradually became more prosperous, then the reforms would be deemed to have worked: 'Don't worry about going forward slowly as long as you're going forward' (*bu pa man, jiu pa zhan*).

c. *Plan and market in a low income country with a massive population*

China's old generation had all experienced a market economy. In some cases, such as Deng Xiaoping's, they had lived abroad under impoverished circumstances. No-one who lived in the burgeoning capitalist economy of China's Treaty Ports before 1949 could fail either to be impressed with the dynamic power of market forces, nor dismayed at the social inequalities, exploitation, degradation and insecurity it produced.[8] Moreover, any perceptive observer could see the many ways in which well-focused state action might improve the performance of the economy, especially that of the vast countryside. Indeed, Taiwan's approach towards combining plan and market (a 'planned free market economy') after 1950 came from this earlier experience on the Mainland (Li, 1988, chs. 3–4). China's reform leaders were under no illusions that 'free markets' would magically solve China's problems. They had first-hand experience of deep market failure. Russia's reform leaders' were quite unprepared for the harsh side of primitive capitalism, with gross inequalities in wealth, widespread child labour and prostitution, harsh working conditions, job insecurity, and large economic fluctuations. They imagined 'capitalism' to be like the USA or Western Europe in the 1980s, not like Russia before 1914, contemporary Brazil or India. China's leaders did not have such illusions. They had lived in a primitive capitalist system.

The generation which came to power in China in the late 1970s mostly had fought against Maoist policies and suffered greatly for so doing. Deng Xiaoping had been reviled during the Cultural Revolution as the 'number two capitalist roader', and had famously said 'it doesn't matter if the cat is black or white as long as it catches mice'. In other words one should be pragmatic in one's choice of economic policies. Their suitability should be judged by whether or not they were, indeed, successful in achieving economic growth and national prosperity. Chen Yun, who came to be caricatured in the 1980s by most foreign observers as the main 'reactionary', 'hardline' force in the Chinese leadership, had himself opposed Mao in favour of a large role for markets and individual incentives (Lardy and Lieberthal (eds), 1983).

The old men who returned to power in the late 1970s in China may be likened to those in the Soviet Union in the 1920s who had championed the cause of a mixed economy (a 'socio-economic salad' in Bukharin's famous phrase) under communist party rule. Chen Yun had himself been likened to Bukharin. China's leaders shared the economic pragmatism of the Bukharinist wing of the Soviet communist party in the 1920s. In both the early 1950s and again in the early 1960s, China had pursued loosely NEP-type policies, and this group had been in the forefront in promoting such measures. In the USSR in the late 1980s, the NEP model briefly was resurrected, only to be discarded equally quickly as the political scene shifted. In Russia in the 1920s, NEP had been a temporary resting place on the road to the Stalinist economy. In China after 1976 NEP policies were the transitional form towards a progressively more market-oriented economy.

The centre of gravity in the ideology that bound together China's reformist leaders was moving ever closer to that of a much wider current of thinking in political economy in East Asia, stretching from Meiji Japan in the late nineteenth century, through to Sun Yatsen and the Kuomintang (initially on mainland China, and subsequently in Taiwan), through to South Korea and Singapore since the 1950s. This approach viewed political institutions functionally. It regarded the best arrangement as that which would more rapidly produce national prosperity in a world of hostile international competition. In economic policy, the free market and the Stalinist command system were regarded as equally irrelevant. The broad approach owed much to that of Friedrich List. Chiang Kaishek, the leader of the Kuomintang, in the midst of his party's struggle with the Chinese Communist Party wrote in 1947:

> *China cannot compete with the advanced industrial nations. She must therefore adopt a protectionist policy with regard to foreign trade, and a policy of economic planning with respect to her industrial development.* Private capital alone will not be sufficient to operate on a large scale, or to compete with the trusts and government operated enterprises of foreign nations. *This is the great weakness of laissez-faire economic theory and makes it unsuitable for China.* (Chiang Kaishek, 1947, p. 279) (Emphasis added)

Economic policy was interpreted as inseparable from wider considerations of national endeavour, with individual group interests firmly subordinated to national goals:

> Western economics is merely the study of private enterprise or of market transactions, whereas Chinese economic theory is not confined to private enterprise or market transactions but is a combination of the people's livelihoods and national defense. . . . [E]conomics is the study of how to make the nation rich and strong – to build a nation into a wealthy, powerful, healthy, and contented state. In essence it is the study of national economic development. (Chiang Kaishek, 1947, pp. 243 and 248)

In this view planning was an essential condition for raising a low income country out of poverty. K.T. Li, Taiwan's former Minister of Economic Affairs in 1981 described the Taiwan government's approach in the following way:

> Although the value of economic planning is still not accepted by some 'free market' economists, the impressive results that some countries have achieved through such planning cannot be denied. . . . [F]or developing countries, particularly those where the conditions required for the smooth operation of the market mechanism are absent or incomplete, the need for economic planning seems even greater than

in the developed ones. . . . In the face of uncertainties in international markets and increased friction resulting from accelerated structural transformation of the domestic economy, effective economic planning will become more important than ever.

Had the reforming Soviet leaders listened to Mr Li instead of Jeffrey Sachs or Janos Kornai they might have developed a different view of the role of the state in an economy undergoing large structural change.

d. Independence in policy-making

A striking illustration of the contrast between the Chinese and Soviet leadership perspective is the nature of the influence of the international institutions. The policy advice produced by the Bretton Woods organisations for the USSR was fundamentally identical to the standard stabilisation and structural adjustment programmes which they produced for a succession of Third World countries. As the USSR descended into political–economic disintegration they increasingly took the form of formal conditionality requirements. In China the major institutions encountered in the Chinese policy-makers a group that was confident of the broad correctness of its pragmatic political economy approach towards reform. Chinese government reform policies mostly flew in the face of the orthodox policies of these institutions. However, so strong was the Chinese government's sense of national purpose, so determined was it to pursue its own pragmatic approach towards the transition, that the IMF and the World Bank did not publicly make as radical suggestions for reform as were their stock in trade elsewhere. Indeed, it has been remarked that a sort of schizophrenia developed in the World Bank. Almost all those who worked in the China department became persuaded of the desirability of a more pragmatic approach towards reform than was advocated by those in other branches of the organisation.

e. Public sector dominance

Under Mao the private sector was villified. In the reform period the pure private sector was once again allowed to exist, initially under very tight controls, but gradually gathering pace as the reforms wore on. By the early 1990s around 55 million people were employed in the pure private sector, with individual ownership of assets (SSB, *ZGTJNJ*, 1993, p. 99). However, the majority of these, around two-thirds, worked in the small-scale non-industrial sector, principally in tertiary activities. It will be seen later that the nature of publicly-owned enterprises altered greatly during the reform period. However, throughout these years the state, through its gradually reforming material supply system and through the state-controlled financial sector, gave priority to the public sector for activities involving enterprises of any substantial size.[9]

The state sector's share of total industrial output (gross value) fell sharply during the reform, from 78 per cent in 1978 to 48 per cent in 1992 (SSB, *ZGTJNJ*, 1993, p. 412). However, the share of the collectively owned sector (i.e. the locally publicly-owned sector) rose rapidly, from 22 per cent in 1978 to 32 per cent in 1992 (SSB, *ZGTJNJ*, 1993, p. 412). Thus, in 1992, fourteen years after the reforms began, the publicly owned sector still produced over 80 per cent of industrial output. Even in Guangdong province, much the most market-oriented province in China, the publicly owned sector still in 1992 produced over 68 per cent of industrial output value (SSB, *ZGTJNJ*, 1993, pp. 415–16).[10] The pure private sector produced just over 5 per cent and the 'other' sectors, which were mainly joint ventures, usually with public sector firms, produced just over 26 per cent of industrial output (gross value) in Guangdong (SSB, *ZGTJNJ*, 1993, pp. 415–16).

Thus, during at least the first decade and a half of China's reforms, entrepreneurship was mainly employed in the service of some form of public enterprise.

6.2.2 Price reform

By the mid-1980s, the Chinese government came to the conclusion that price reform was 'the key to the reform of the entire economic structure' (Central Committee, 1984, p. 684). A strong school of thought within China's policy think tanks argued for rapid price liberalisation (Wang Xiaoqiang, 1993). However, as in other aspects of the reforms, after intense debate, the government resolved to proceed cautiously since 'the reform of the price system affects every household and the national economy' (Central Committee, 1984, p. 684). The method adopted to move relative prices towards market-determined prices was the dual-track system, with the proportion sold at free or floating prices gradually expanding in relation to those sold at state fixed prices, and with the latter gradually moving towards the former.

By the late 1980s the proportion of retail prices controlled by state price officials had fallen to around one-third, and in the early 1990s a further push resulted in the de-control of virtually all retail prices. In

Table 6.1 Proportion of products sold at different types of prices (per cent)

	1978	1986	1990	1993
Share of total retail sales sold at:				
state-controlled prices	97	na	29.7	5
state-guided prices	0	na	17.2	na
market-regulated prices	3	na	53.1	na
Share of total sales of agricultural products sold by farmers at:				
state-controlled prices	94.4	37	25.2	10
state-guided prices	0	na	22.6	na
market-regulated prices	5.6	na	52.2	na
Share of industrial capital goods sold at:				
state-controlled prices	100	64	44.4	15
state-guided prices	0	23	18.8	na
market-regulated prices	0	13	36.8	na

Source: Li Ping, 1992, p. 17; Tian Yuan, 1990, p. 143; and Niu Gengying, 1994.

the wholesale sector, the move towards liberalisation of prices was even more gradual. Still in 1990, over a decade after the reforms began, over two-fifths of industrial capital goods sales were at state fixed prices, and only just over one-third were at genuinely market prices. In the early 1980s, a further push forwards to market prices occurred. By 1993 only 15 per cent of industrial capital goods sales were reported to be at state fixed prices (Table 6.1). For example, it is reported that the proportion of steel products sold at state fixed prices fell from 100 per cent in 1984 to 40 per cent in 1992. In 1993, price control for most steel products was lifted, though the state still controlled the price of steel supplied to the military sector, defence industries, agriculture, irrigation and railways (Wardley Corporate Finance, 1993). In 1993 the Ministry of Prices was relegated to a 'second-tier' level of Ministerial importance, in recognition of the contraction in its functions.

6.2.3 Decentralisation

China is a huge country. There are large problems in trying to co-ordinate planning decisions from a central authority. There are also large problems in trying to sustain a coherent economic reform programme for such a gigantic system. The maintenance of a strong, relatively unified communist party was critical to combining cautious decentralisation of key economic functions with some form of overall control over the reform process and the regular conduct of economic affairs.

Decentralisation of decision-making to lower-level administrative units was an important element in the reform programme. This had a financial aspect, under which local authorities were given greater independence to collect revenues. The central authorities increasingly focussed their efforts on major infrastructure projects.[11] This was a large change in the conception of the planning functions of the central government. By the Seventh Five-Year Plan (1986–90) just 180 priority projects accounted for three-quarters of the central government's spending on 'large and medium scale projects', and of these 91 per cent were in the fields of energy, transportation and raw materials. Energy and transport absorbed around one-half of total state capital investment (World Bank, 1990, pp. 93–4).

Over the course of the 1980s, a steady widening of the source of investment funds occurred, with more and more being obtained from outside the scope of the formal channels of the budget.[12] The proportion of 'public revenue' which was under either the direct or tight indirect control of the central government fell sharply during the reforms. The share of the state's budgetary revenue in national income fell sharply from 37 per cent in 1978 to 23 per cent in 1991 (SSB, *ZGTJNJ*, 1993, p. 18). Alongside this went a sharp rise in the share of 'extra-budgetary revenue' in total state financial revenue from 31 per cent in 1978 to 86 per cent in 1990 (SSB, *ZGTJZY*, 1991, p. 35). Extra-budgetary revenues were subject to less stringent direct controls from the central and, even, local authorities, but they were, nevertheless 'within the orbit of state planning'.[13] Thus, the reform periods saw a great loosening of the degree of direct central control over resource allocation, but still in the early 1990s, 43 per cent if national income went through either the official budget or the 'quasi budget', subject to official supervision by the state planning procedures.[14]

Over the course of the reform period local authorities developed an intense interest in promoting the local economy, from which the local leadership derived a wide variety of benefits both financial and psychological. The World Bank concluded that during the reform period a large shift had occurred in the motivation of local authorities: 'Local government objectives are to enhance their revenue base and to develop an investment strategy that will foster growth. Both can be met by developing profitable industries' (World Bank, 1990, p. 95). China's provinces mostly are the size of large countries. Even a single county (*xian*) could embrace 500,000 people. Decentralisation alongside gradual growth of a market economy produced an intensity of desire to promote the local economy comparable to that of the nation-state in a setting of international rivalry.

Local authorities became deeply interested in finding ways of promoting the sale of their localities' goods in other domestic and in international markets, and in attracting inward investment from other areas, and especially, from abroad. Inland, impoverished localities even ran publicly-funded training courses for migrants and provided them with information about migrant job opportunities. *The Economist* summed up this mood: 'No matter where you go in China to-day, the most emphatic sensation you get is the intensity of the desire to modernise and grow. Governors, party secretaries, party representatives on boards of directors: their only interest seems to be foreign investment, trade and economic reform' (*Economist*, 28 November 1992). The granting of increased autonomy to localities as market forces grew was arranged in a planned fashion, gradually spreading out from the tiny 'special economic zones' to wider and wider array of areas.[15]

The policy framework within which all levels operated was determined by the central government. This was given practical meaning through the continued power of the communist party. Moreover, key policy variables continued to be directly set at the centre. Arguably the most important of these was the figure for total social investment (*quan shehui touzi*) at each level. The annual figure for each province was approved by the centre, and then the province in turn approved the figure of each lower level down to the county.[16] During the Maoist period, only relatively small investments within the approved total investment budget for any given unit or locality were able to be undertaken without specific approval from higher authorities. During the reform years, the relative size of the investment items which could be independently decided upon grew steadily, but still in the early 1990s relatively large items required approval from higher levels.

6.2.4 Population

a. Growth

In the absence of controls, China in the 1980s and 1990s would have had to face not only the problem of a high age-specific fertility rate common to most developing countries, but in addition the special problem of a large age cohort in the reproductive ages (an 'echo' effect from the extremely high birth rates in China in the 1960s). Throughout the reform period the Chinese government's policy was: to 'unswervingly persist in our efforts to control population growth . . . so that the living standards of the entire people can improve step by step and national construction can expand year by year. . . . All acts violating law and discipline in the enforcement of [family planning measures] must be firmly opposed and prevented' (Zhao Ziyang, 1981, pp. 242–3).

Under the people's communes, China was successful in the 1970s in raising the average age of marriage. This, combined with greatly increased availability of contraception and strong sanctions helped to reduce sharply the overall birth rate in the late Maoist years.[17] Although the age of marriage and the proportion of the population using birth control remained high throughout the 1980s,[18] the bulge in the proportion of the population in the reproductive ages presented difficulties in controlling overall fertility. Despite de-collectivisation of farmland, the government still had many channels through which the rural population could be coerced into controlling birthrates (Nolan, 1988, pp. 192–3). Villagers who refused to comply with the birth control plan could be fined and/or denied access to credit, irrigation water, electricity, chemical fertiliser and other state supplied farm inputs. These sanctions were used to great effect throughout the 1980s: national interest was unswervingly placed above individual interest. Even remote mountainous areas witnessed substantial falls in birth rates as a result. The strenuous efforts of the Chinese government to control population growth involved a deep infringement on individual liberties, especially of women. It was upon women that the main burden of birth control in the 1980s fell through the mechanisms of IUDs, sterilisation and abortion.

As a result of these strenuous efforts at population control, the overall birthrate rose only slightly in the 1980s.[19] China's population growth rate in 1980–89 was only 1.4 per cent per annum (Table 6.2).[20] If China's population in the 1980s had followed the solution offered by the free market and individual choice, then it is reasonable to assume that China's population would have grown at the same rate as other low income countries. Consequently, in 1989 China's population would have been around 1,300 million, or around 200 million larger than its actual size.[21] Among innumerable effects, this much larger total would have necessitated that a larger share of investible resources was allocated to agriculture. In addition, the higher dependency ratio would have shifted the composition of investment away from growth-enhancing sectors.[22]

Table 6. 2   Growth of labour force in China (millions)

	Total population	Total labour force	Rural labour force	Farm labour force	Rural non-farm labour force	Total non-farm labour force	Industrial labour force
1978	963	402	306	284	23	118	61
1991	1158	584	431	350	81	233	100
2025	1597	(800)*					
Change, 1978–1991: (Million)	195	182	125	66	58	115	39
per cent per annum	1.4	2.9	2.6	1.6	10.2	5.4	3.9

Source: SSB, *ZGTJNJ*, 1992, section 4, and World Bank, *WDR*, 1992, pp. 268–9.

Note: *Assuming no change in participation rates, and using World Bank's prediction of only a small change in the share of the working age population in total population, the World Bank predicts that the share of the working age population in total population will fall from 67.2 per cent in 1990 to 66.5 per cent in 2025 (World Bank, *WDR*, 1992, pp. 268–9).

b. Migration

Prior to the 1980s tight constraints were exercised over migration, especially from rural to urban areas. In the 1980s official attitudes mostly remained hostile to migration. A major part of this hostility was connected with the fear of urban instability should large numbers of people flood into the cities. The government retained the official residence registration system (*hukou*). Moreover, central government policy continued to be shaped by a philosophy that regarded it as undesirable that agricultural land even in high cost, marginal areas, was left to go uncultivated due to migration.[23]

However, *de facto* controls over migration relaxed sharply in the 1980s as a consequence of the reforms, an aspect of the shift away from a totalitarian command system to an authoritarian 'socialist market' system. The main factor was the rapid growth of a free market in food, since control over access to rationed food had been a major instrument of previous control over migration. In addition, the growth of a market economy and removal of ceilings on personal incomes provided much enhanced personal incentives to migrate. Improved incomes increased the ability to do so. Moreover, the fiscal decentralisation and growing responsiveness of local governments to local interests increased the incentives of local governments in relatively poor areas to encourage migration in order to help reduce poverty locally.

In the late 1980s the size of the 'floating population' grew rapidly, with perhaps as many as 70 million, mainly rural, migrants in this category (Banister, 1992, p. 20), rising above even this number in the early 1990s. The phenomenon of 'blind' migration of large numbers of rural dwellers was widely recognised both by policy makers and ordinary urban citizens who encountered migrants at every turn. Their pressure made itself felt in striking fashion with huge crowds milling around railway stations in large east coast cities.[24]

Much migration to more rapidly growing east coast areas was from within the eastern provinces themselves, mostly from the poorer parts of these provinces.[25] Moreover, considerable migration, often over long distances, occurred within the poor provinces themselves. However, the demand for migrant labour was growing much more rapidly in the east coast provinces than in the poor provinces or in advanced areas of the central Chinese provinces such as Sichuan.[26] Large numbers of migrants were, indeed, moving out of poor provinces in search of employment hundreds or even thousands of kilometres away.[27]

Many village communities in advanced areas subcontracted land to poor migrants. However, micro-level data suggest that in the early 1990s such subcontracting was still not on a wide scale.[28] Local communities in rich areas were reluctant to grant permanent settlement rights to migrants, fearing that this would impose a burden on local welfare resources. There was also a fear that migrants who cultivated land for a long period might gain *de facto* ownership rights and be hard to evict in the absence of clearly defined private property rights.

These fears did not affect the demand for migrant workers who work as agricultural hired labour. The availability of cheap migrant labour encourages farmers in richer areas to substitute labour for capital in order to meet peak season demands. Unlike many poor countries such as India, China does not have legislation to 'protect' rural hired labour by attempting to set minimum wages, nor have attempts been permitted to organise migrant labourers into trade unions. In other countries such well-meaning attempts to protect the rights of migrants have frequently backfired by encouraging 'capitalist' farmers to substitute capital for labour, thereby slowing down the growth in demand for migrant labour. Clearly, this does not apply to China.

6.2.5 Savings and investment

During the reform period, a number of underlying factors led to a
high rate of saving and investment in general and in industry in particular. These included: the country's political stability; relatively low
inflation; the large opportunities for making profits in a rapidly restructuring economy (e.g. the service sector, transport and housing);
the large potentiality for employing poorly used existing resources in
more profitable ways than before; the virtuous circle of high demand
growth; and the existence of a large pool of surplus labour which enabled relatively high profits to be generated in the non-farm sector.
The reforms generated high incentives for localities to promote the
expansion of their local economy. In dramatic contrast with Russia in
the early 1990s China maintained tight control over capital outflow so
that virtually the only outlet for savings was within the domestic economy.

Throughout the reform period the rate of gross domestic savings
and investment remained exceptionally high, both standing at around
30–35 per cent of gross domestic product throughout the reform period
(World Bank, *WDR*, various issues). China's households saved roughly
23 per cent of their disposable income in 1981–7, compared to 18 per
cent in Taiwan (1965–81), 21 per cent in Japan (1976–82), and just 8
per cent in the USA (1976–82) (World Bank, 1990, p. 126). In 1991,
China's gross domestic savings rate stood at 39 per cent and gross
domestic investment at 36 per cent of GDP (World Bank, *WDR*, 1993,
p. 254). The World Bank reports that from an already high rate of
growth of real gross domestic investment in the 1970s (7 per cent per
annum from 1970 to 1980), the rate accelerated to 12.4 per cent per
annum from 1980 to 1991, compared to 1.7 per cent per annum for
low income countries (excluding India and China), and –0.7 per cent
per anum for lower middle income countries (World Bank, *WDR*, 1993,
p. 252). The only country with a comparably rapid rate of growth of
gross domestic investment was South Korea (13.0 per cent for the same
period). Unlike the type of high investment experienced by the command economies, in China during the reforms a growing proportion of
this exceptionally high rate of investment was occurring in response to
market incentives. Less and less did it reflect 'investment hunger'.
More and more it reflected a 'hunger for profits'.

The state continued, either directly or indirectly, to have a large
influence on the allocation of China's national income between investment and consumption. Despite substantial organisational changes,
including the establishment of specialist banks for different purposes,

the banking system remained a state monopoly providing credit at below a competitive market rate.of interest. Throughout the reform period state-owned enterprises were given priority in the state's allocation of credit.[29]

6.2.6 The international economy

a. Overall perspective

The Chinese economy had been isolated from the world economy since the 1940s. In the reform period the Chinese leadership realised that deeper integration with the world economy was essential for modernisation. However, they were acutely aware of the possibility that hasty, unplanned integration could lead to large problems: 'Reforming the economic structure and opening to the outside world is our unswerving principle, but it must be executed with great care so as to ensure success' (Central Committee, 1985, p. 441). Instead of the 'close' integration[30] recommended by the reform orthodoxy with free trade and free movement of capital, the government's intention was planned, 'strategic' integration.[31]

b. Agriculture

In the 1980s there was intense discussion among Chinese policy-makers about the degree to which the country could depend safely on world markets for food, especially grain. In the long term, China may benefit from importing more land-intensive farm produce. However in the 1980s the government judged that there would be large risks involved in greater integration with world food markets, especially for a country of China's size and income level. They believed that if China was much more dependent upon world markets for its food supplies and an exogenous shock sharply reduced its ability to import foodstuffs, the results would be catastrophic. Farm output cannot be expanded overnight. Infrastructure needs to be built and farmers skills take time to acquire.

China could not be certain that the market for its manufactures would continue to grow rapidly. China still was not a member of the GATT. There were constant rumblings of discontent against China's exports, with lobby groups arguing that China should not be allowed continued 'most favoured nation' access to the US market, due to its human rights record and the allegation that it 'dumps'. Moreover, the government was concerned lest there was an exogenous shock from world food prices. Over the long term, technical progress in food production and distribution has tended to bring down world food prices, and will possibly continue to do so in the future. However, food prices are volatile.[32] Despite pressures from many advisors to greatly increase grain imports, as world grain prices fell in the 1980s, the Chinese government remained conservative. Compared to many developing countries China maintained a low degree of dependence on world grain markets.[33] This meant that the Chinese government needed to push and/or encourage China's farmers to grow more grain to maintain a higher degree of grain self-sufficiency than they would have done under free market conditions. This imposed high costs upon the Chinese economy. However, the government judged that the costs were worth bearing in reducing China's dependence on the international economy.

c. Foreign debt

Throughout the reform period, the Chinese government was cautious about foreign borrowing. Its approach was to 'borrow prudent amounts and keep a rational debt structure, taking into account the country's financial and material resources and its capacity to repay' (Zhao Ziyang, 1987, p. 658). China's foreign debt as a proportion of exports remained low throughout the 1980s,[34] despite the fact that for most of the period it was highly creditworthy on international markets and could easily have greatly expanded its foreign borrowings had it wished.

China's caution in foreign borrowing allowed it to remain completely independent in policy formation. The Bretton Woods organisations, which China quickly rejoined during the early years of reform, were welcomed to provide advice, but there no question of conditionality. China's reform path was almost entirely contrary to that recommended by these institutions in other developing countries, in Russia and in Eastern Europe.

d. Private foreign investment

From 1949 until the late 1970s no foreign investment was permitted in China. Under Mao it was inconceivable that the giants of world capitalism should be allowed to invest in the country. The passage of the 1979 Law on Chinese–Foreign Joint Ventures marked a major step away from Maoist–Stalinist isolationism. This was the first of numerous laws intended to encourage foreign investment. China went to great lengths to attract foreign capital. In striking contrast to Maoist hostility to foreign capital, the Chinese government assured foreign investors of the 'good investment environment', with 'stable social order and cheap labour', which would enable foreign businessmen to 'make money here' (*Beijing Review*, 33(44), 1991). Local governments pushed central government regulations to the limit in order to attract foreign investment to their area. Moreover, growth of foreign investment was encouraged indirectly by China's highly protectionist polices of the reform period, which limited the access of international manufacturing capital to the Chinese market via direct sales.

The main purpose was not to attract foreign investment in order to act as a supplement to domestic savings, since the savings rate was high throughout the period of the reforms (see above). Rather, it was to enable China more quickly to catch up technologically. This included technical progress in the narrow sense of importing modern equipment for manufacturing plants. However, it included much wider conceptions. The dominant form of foreign investment was the joint venture.[35] In the joint venture a rapid diffusion of foreign management skills occurred, with wide externalities in demonstrating to other sectors how management might be organised better.

Foreign investment enterprises almost all were linked to a wide network of indigenous suppliers, upon whom new standards of product quality, production methods, and business concepts were imposed. A study of the global business of Nike sports shoes found that it employs 9,000 people directly but 75,000 people work for its independent subcontractors (*Financial Times*, 27–28 August 1994). Similarly, a study of joint ventures in the Chinese soft drinks industry in the early 1990s found that a typical plant employed directly only around 500 workers, but over one hundred plants were engaged in supplying inputs needed to produce the final product. In total these employed over 10,000 'full time equivalent' workers (Nolan, 1994).[36]

A major function of foreign investment in the early phase of the transition out of the communist economy was as a channel of information about the demands of the world market for products for which there was as yet a very limited domestic market. This was a particularly important function served by investment in southern China by capital from Hong Kong and, increasingly, Taiwan. The proportion of China's exports which it is estimated were re-exported through Hong Kong rose from 7 per cent in 1979 to 36 per cent in 1990 (Sung, 1991). As the sources of foreign investment widened geographically and the total amount accelerated sharply in the early 1990s, it came

Table 6.3   Growth of foreign capital in the Chinese economy, 1979–93
            (US$ billion)

	Total foreign funds		Foreign loans		Direct foreign investment		Portfolio equity flows
	Contracted	Actual utilised	Contracted	Actual utilised	Contracted	Actual utilised	
1979–82	20.6	12.5	13.5	10.7	7.0	1.8	0
1985	9.9	4.6	3.5	2.7	6.3	2.0	na
1990	12.1	10.3	5.1	6.5	7.0	3.8	na
1993	122.7	36.8	11.3	10.8	111.4	26.0	1.19 (1992)

Source: SSB, *ZGTJZY*, 1994, p. 110; and World Bank, *WDR*, 1994, p. 204.

to have a further important function. This was to act as a vehicle pushing forward the process of corporatisation of large state enterprises, through imposing strict standards of company auditing, and demonstrating the necessity of clearly delineated property rights.

After quite cautious growth of direct foreign investment in the early 1980s, and a hiatus after the Tiananmen massacre, the pace accelerated remarkably in the early 1990s. By 1993, agreed foreign direct investment had exploded to over 111 billion US dollars, ten times as large as loans from international institutions (Table 6.3). By mid-1993 it was reported that 135,000 Chinese enterprises had overseas participation. Enterprises with foreign investment were estimated to produce around six per cent of Chinese industrial output (*Financial Times*, 15 September 1993). Moreover, speculative portfolio inflows were tiny compared with direct investment (World Bank, *WDR*, 1994). By comparison, the inflow of foreign direct investment into Russia was pathetic (a cumulative total of just two billion dollars in 1990–1993) (EBRD, 1994, p. 123), and was greatly exceeded by speculative portfolio investment.

Despite a large absolute rise in investment from the US and Europe, the Far East was still massively dominant, although a rapidly increasing proportion of this came from international capital channelled through Hong Kong. Around three-quarters of the total inflow of capital in the 1980s came from Taiwan and Hong Kong, and was strongly concentrated in the coastal provinces of southeast China, especially Guangdong and Fujian. These provinces effectively were being integrated with the dynamic economies of Taiwan and Hong Kong. As land and labour costs rose in the latter economies, it made good sense for capital from these countries to shift into the neighbouring parts of the mainland, given the huge change in the business environment in China compared to the Maoist years. By 1990, exports from plants with foreign direct investment accounted for 13 per cent of the national total (Sung, 1991).

However, the involvement of overseas Chinese capital was deeper than this figure suggests. In addition to direct foreign investment, a large amount of overseas capital went into loans to indigenous factories to help them to upgrade their technical level through the import of new machinery (Sung, 1991). These factories then undertook processing and assembly operations for the overseas Chinese capitalists. One careful estimate concluded that as much as 41 per cent of China's exports in 1991 consisted of exports from plants of this type (Sung, 1991). By the early 1990s, the Pearl River Delta in Guangdong province was beginning to look like a large-scale version of Singapore, with a mass of light industrial enterprises oriented towards the world market and a large share of investment attributable to 'foreigners'.

This explosive growth of foreign investment in China was the result of an increasingly positive evaluation by foreign investors of China's merits as place in which to invest. It reflected also an apparent decision by the Chinese government to give even greater weight than before to the role that foreign investment might make in China's catch-up process. The flow of investment into China was part of a wider process of capital movement out of the old industrialised countries into the Far East in general. The fact that this move occurred simultaneously with the recession in Europe and Japan led to a large re-evaluation of the prospects for the global division of labour (see e.g. *Financial Times*, 1994).

All foreign investments needed government approval. Substantial investment characteristically needed approval from the central government. Still in 1994, the central government wished foreign investment to take place in accordance with its plan priorities:

> We shall guide the orientation of foreign investment in accordance with the state's industrial policies, directing foreign investment towards infrastructure and basic industry construction, key projects and upgrading technology in existing enterprises, in particular towards projects to increase the export of foreign currency earning products. (Chen Jihua, 1994)

In order to gain access to the vast and rapidly growing China market[37], Boeing was required to assist the main Chinese aircraft manufacturer in Xian to successively establish a capacity to produce spare parts and then manufacture whole sections of aircraft, and finally to assist in the development of a capacity to produce complete aircraft within China (*Financial Times*, 9 August 1994). In order to gain the right to invest in car production in China, Ford Motor Company was required to first invest for several years in upgrading the technical capacity of the Chinese automobile spare parts industry through a sequence of joint ventures (IHT, 28 June 1994).

China's development strategy after 1978 contrasted sharply with that pursued by South Korea and by Japan at comparable phases in their economic growth, when they severely limited direct foreign investment. The Chinese government was confident that it would be able to control the conditions under which foreign investment occurred, and that the economy was so large that no individual foreign investor could exercise a large influence on the state: 'Our socialist economic base is so huge that it can absorb billions of foreign funds without shaking the socialist foundation' (Deng Xiaoping, 1984, p. 5). In the early 1990s the share of China in many multinational companies' worldwide total assets, sales, and employment was rising rapidly. Moreover, Chinese capital invested in joint ventures was growing fast. At some point in the not too distant future, China is likely become a larger market for many of these companies than their nominal 'home' market. Moreover, their ownership structure is likely to become increasingly 'Sinicised' as Chinese institutions and individuals increasingly acquire shares in these companies. It is not too fanciful to imagine that at some point global companies which today are 'based' in Europe or the US may become 'based' in China with Chinese directors and managers of these companies more influential than those from other parts of the world.

e. Foreign trade

Overall approach   China's attitude towards international trade altered radically after Mao's death. In sharp contrast to the prevailing conventional wisdom in the Bretton Woods institutions, China's attitude towards international trade was instrumental. Its approach had a lot in common with that of Meiji Japan, South Korea and Taiwan: 'In foreign trade our principle is to encourage exports and organise imports according to needs' (*Beijing Review*, 33(44), 1990).

Export promotion   Increasing export earnings played a central role in China's modernisation strategy: 'Our capacity to earn foreign exchange through exports determines to a great extent, the degree to which we can open to the outside world and affects the scale and pace of domestic economic development' (Zhao Ziyang, 1987, p. 657). Foreign exchange was needed to 'introduce technology from outside, import essential facilities and raw materials and repay the principal and interest of foreign loans' (Central Committee, 1985, p. 444).

Most straightforwardly, the Chinese government undertook a succession of devaluations of the *yuan*.[38] By the early 1990s the gap between the official and the black market exchange rate had been eliminated. However, the approach towards full currrency convertibility over the reform period was halting and experimental. It stood in complete contrast to the orthodox view on currency convertibility and economic reform. A wide variety of complex, more or less tightly controlled foreign exchange swap market arrangements was introduced. An equally complex and experimental set of arrangements for foreign exchange retention by domestic exporters also was introduced. However, the *yuan* still had not become fully convertible over a decade and a half after the reforms began.

The reforming Chinese government introduced a wide variety of measures to stimulate exports which ran completely contrary to the reform orthodoxy on trade policy.[39] Designated priority export sectors were allowed to retain a large share of foreign exchange earnings.[40] Exporting firms were given rebates of industrial and commercial taxes, and direct rewards. The Chinese government gave large exporting firms preferential access to imported techology. Part of the industrial strategy of trying to construct large multi-plant corporations was aimed explicitly at building multinational companies that could compete on world markets with the giant corporations of the advanced capitalist world. Export industries were given cheap credit for technical upgrading, and priority access to low price power and raw materials within that part of the material supply system that still remained within the state's direct control. Chinese exporters mostly enjoyed access to land at negligible prices by world standards. Large, potentially successful exporters increasingly were allowed to engage independently in foreign trade rather than go through the proliferation of foreign trade corporations that emerged to replace the old Stalinist system of monolithic state trading corporations.

Part of China's manufactured exports in the 1980s was being produced with zero or even negative net value-added at world market prices (Hughes, 1991; Vogel, 1989). The Chinese government believed that at China's stage of development, the static efficiency costs involved in such exports were exceeded by the dynamic gains resulting from access to technology-enhancing imports whose value to the economy was not fully reflected in their price.

Protection   In the post-Mao period China maintained a battery of protective measures. The government was explicit about its policy.[41] Its approach closely resembled that of South Korea and Taiwan during their early phase of industrial development. K.T. Li's comments on Taiwan's protectionist policies are close to the justifications for protection used by China's reformist government:

> The price of relying on protectionist measures is well known. . . . However, in the early years of Taiwan's development it was obvious that its industry could not compete with the advanced countries in terms of production scale, technology, and marketing. Without adequate protection there was little hope of establishing a firm industrial base. . . . As a result the government decided to adopt a high-tariff policy and other non-tariff protectionist measures such as import controls and restrictions on new plant registration. (Li, 1988, p. 47)

The Chinese government also considered it 'obvious' that a command economy which was technically backward, had not yet established a structure of modern firms, nor completed domestic price reform, not completely dismantled its material balance planning system, nor reformed its social security system, could not possibly compete effectively in open competition on world markets. Almost the whole of its industrial sector could be considered an 'infant industry', or, more accurately, 'out-of-condition middle-aged industry' that required revitalisation before it could compete openly on world markets.

The government allocated a large part of China's foreign exchange earnings to priority purposes. There was a wide array of quantitative restrictions, often with outright bans on imports of certain types of goods. High tariffs were maintained throughout the reforms[42] and they were structured so as strongly to encourage import substitution.[43] In addition, China adopted such protectionist measures as requiring rigorous inspection procedures for imports of certain types (Vogel, 1989, p. 375).

In the early 1990s China made it clear that it wished to join the GATT, and it seemed likely that it would be invited to become a founder member of the successor organisation to the GATT, the World Trade Organisation. There was great discussion outside China about the degree to which China would wish or be able to persist in its protectionist policies. Moreover, if China were to implement the conditions of the GATT, it was still far from clear what impact this would have on the Chinese economy.

For the first decade and a half of economic reform in China, its protectionist policies flew in the face of orthodox policies for the reform of both poor capitalist and communist countries. China's slow but cumulatively massive domestic system reforms were able to proceed without the threat of open competition from foreign producers.

6.2.7 Agriculture

a. The reforms

China began cautious experimentation with reform of collective farms almost as soon as Mao had died. The largest single reform, 'contracting land to the household', was not completed until 1983. The intervening period involved constant experimentation, debate and groping for a solution.

Land ownership and distribution Farmland was the most important asset in China's reform, affecting the daily lives of the vast majority of its population. Farmland was 'de-collectivised' in the early 1980s. This was not followed by the establishment of private property rights in land (Zhu Ling, 1992). Because the CCP wished to prevent the emergence of a landlord class, it did not permit the purchase and sale of farmland. Still in 1994, the Party 'adhered to the collective ownership of famland' (Central Committee, 1994, p. 24). The village community remained the owner, controlling the terms on which land was contracted out and operated by peasant households. It endeavoured to ensure that farm households had equal access to farmland, while the village government obtained part of the Ricardian rents from the land to use for community purposes. The Chinese government, through the communist party remained substantially in control of the de-collectivisation of farmland. Farmland was not distributed via a free market auction, which would have helped to produce a locally unequal outcome. Rather the massively dominant form was distribution of land contracts on a locally equal per capita basis. This huge 'land reform', affecting over 800 million people, was a remarkably orderly process. It was not a disorganised land grab in which strong members of villages squeezed out the weak.

The labour process   Alongside land reform went a revolution in the rural labour process. All the major decisions in the rural economy returned to the hands of the peasant household.

Non-land capital goods   The local authorities who were formally the owners of almost all farm machinery in the late 1970s did not immediately privatise all farm machinery. Rather, in the early 1980s, while most small 'collective' means of production were sold to individual peasants,[44] most larger means of production were not. Initially, peasants lacked the savings to buy them.[45] However, from early in the 1980s individual households began to buy increasing amounts of means of production themselves alongside the rapid rise in their incomes. Within the overall stock of farm machinery, the proportion owned by individual peasant households rose steadily.[46] Thus, the process of privatising farm machinery was gradual, evolving organically alongside rising peasant incomes, proceeding incrementally from small to large means of production. Moreover, even in the late 1980s an important part of key lumpy assets in the farm economy, which were beyond the financial resources of individual households, remained in local community ownership.

Prior to 1978, irrigation was almost entirely organised either by the state or the 'collective'. Alongside the de-collectivisation of farmland, the 1980s saw rapid growth in self-provision by individual peasant households and by groups of households.[47] In irrigation as in other farm activities, the share of the collective sector declined as individual purchases of the means of production expanded, permitting households collective funds to be diverted increasingly to other purpose.[48] An important part of pre-reform water conservancy funding had been from government above the village level. Still at the end of the 1980s, a relatively small number of huge state reservoirs accounted for over two-fifths of the total amount of irrigation provided by reservoirs of over 100,000 m³, while the huge number of small, mainly collectively-run reservoirs accounted for only about one-third.[49]

However, in the 1980s the central government reduced substantially its outlays on water conservancy, believing that increased rural prosperity should enable a larger share of funding to come from the rural population itself.[50] The rapid increase in peasant prosperity allowed a fast rise in peasant savings which might, reasonably, have been thought sufficient to finance the requisite level of rural capital formation. What the government did not anticipate was the explosive growth of the rural non-farm sector which attracted a large share of rural savings in the second half of the 1980s.[51] This policy was later admitted officially to have been an error. It was reversed sharply in 1990–91.[52]

Despite the incremental growth of investment by individual households, collective and local state activity remained a fundamentally important complement: 'We will develop diversified service organisations in line with the needs of the farmers, and from a service network composed of rural collective economic organisations, state economic and technological departments, and associations of the farmers themselves, such as specialised and technical services' (Central Committee, 1993, p. 24). Indeed, alongside the growth of indivdual households' accumulation went a large absolute growth in input provision by village (*cun*), township (*xiangzhen*) and co-operating households, providing inputs that were beyond the capacity of individual households (Ministry of Agriculture, 1991).[53] Finance for the expansion came mainly from fee income for providing services and from subsidies from the local government, often from income generated in the non-farm sector (see below). Still in 1990 individual households were supplying only an estimated 23 per cent of machine ploughing, 30 per cent of drainage and irrigation services, 15 per cent of plant protection, 48 per cent of seed supply and just 3 per cent of veterinary services (Ministry of Agriculture, 1991).

The institutional structure of post-Mao agriculture in China resembled the modern 'Japanese' path in its balance between activities undertaken by individual households and those undertaken by the village or the state. There was, unsurprisingly, a large regional variation in the fiscal capacity of the local government, depending especially, on the level of development of the rural non-farm economy (see below).

Credit In most poor countries a variety of factors has led a large part of the rural population to rely on informal, high-interest credit, thereby inhibiting the level of investment, especially among poorer but potentially efficient farmers, as well as binding poorer people into a network of dependency upon traditional money lenders.

In China during reform peasant savings grew rapidly alongside peasant income.[54] The vast bulk of this was deposited in official institutions, notably the credit co-operatives and the Agricultural Bank.[55] The official credit institutions provided security, and 'usury' was still discouraged even in post-Mao China. A massive growth of institutional credit occurred in rural China in the 1980s.[56] Credit allocation often was corrupt, especially as the interest rate generally was set at less than market-clearing levels. However, it is improbable that in a poor rural economy such as China's, purely private credit institutions would have been as successful as China's predominantly state and quasi-state institutions in encouraging peasant savings and making funds available to all strata of the rural population.

Marketing: sale of farm output   Despite the legalisation of private trade in the 1980s[57] an important part of farm produce remained under compulsory procurement throughout the 1980s, most importantly a large share of grain, cotton, and edible oil marketings.[58] Even in the early 1990s a substantial part of the key commodities, notably grain, and edible oil crops, was sold to state purchasing agencies through quasi-compulsory contracts. However, for a wide range of produce, peasants were free to choose the channels through which they marketed their produce.[59] However, in part due to the continuance of compulsory purchase for a proportion of output, and in part due to the backward nature of private purchasing channels which could not expand overnight (it frequently requires lumpy investment to set up a wholesale capacity, and, of course, there is a large element of risk), the bulk of farm output, even of that which was sold voluntarily, continued to be marketed through state channels.[60] The commercialisation of Chinese agriculture increased sharply in the 1980s.[61] The increased impact of a market economy upon agriculture was reflected in the rapid growth in personnel connected with farm marketing.[62]

Marketing: purchase of farm produce   In the Maoist period almost all farm inputs were purchased by 'collectives' from state supply networks. Individual peasants had little impact upon purchase decisions, which frequently resulted in the supply of inappropriate means of production (e.g. the infamous three-wheeled, two-bladed plough) and absence of commercial pressure upon suppliers to improve product quality. As individual peasants began increasingly to make the decisions about the purchase of farm inputs, new pressures developed upon suppliers of farm inputs. However, the state and the quasi-state 'supply and marketing co-ops', despite some limitation in their role, and despite the growth of trade in the re-sale of farm inputs in free markets, remained the dominant channel through which farm inputs were channelled to peasants.[63] This led to corruption in the allocation of inputs (since there was often excess demand for farm inputs at state prices). However, it provided an important channel of control through which rural cadres could exercise sanctions over peasants through which to induce compliance with policies which were in the interests of the wider local or national community (e.g. payment of taxes, contributions to collective funds, observance of family planning policy).

Relative prices   In the late 1970s, the state engineered a large improvement in the relative price at which farm produce was bought from farmers.[64] However, faced with political constraints on further improvements (due to the need to control the rate at which urban food prices were allowed to rise), the 1980s as a whole witnessed a much slower improvement in the 'price scissors' from the farmers' point of view.[65]

Over the course of the 1980s, the Chinese government allowed the overall retail price of subsidiary foodstuffs to drift upwards, under a growing impact of market forces, more rapidly than for grain.[66] The gap betwen the state and the free market retail price closed steadily for most subsidiary foodstuffs.[67] However, for grain and edible oil, the gap hardly narrowed.[68] By 1991, Chinese price planners felt in a sufficiently strong position to sharply raise the state retail price of grain (by around 50 per cent) and of edible oil (by more than 100 per cent). A combination of tight political control, an increased familiarity with price increases and a large rise in real income, enabled the large step forward towards free market prices for farm produce to be carried off without major protest.

In the early 1990s, the government moved even further towards liberalisation of urban food prices, with even grain prices 'basically freed' in most Chinese cities. However, it was sensitive to the need to intervene to prevent excessive rises in urban food prices. For example, in the winter of 1993–94 an unanticipated rise in grain prices caused the central government to issue a directive requiring local government to bring grain prices under control through 'both administrative and economic measures' (*China Economic Digest*, Summer 1994, p. 22).

b. Results of reform policies

Inputs   Despite a rapid rise in non-farm employment and a sharp fall in the rate of population growth, China's farm workforce rose by 66 million (23 per cent) from 1978 to 1991 (Table 6.2). Simultaneously, China's arable area contracted by 4.5 per cent from 1980 to 1992 (SSB, *ZGNCTJNJ*, 1989, p. 251, and 1993, p. 229).[69] This was especially serious because of China's acute shortage of farmland. The main reasons for the removal of land from cultivation were first, a continuous pressure of state construction associated with urban growth, and second, the changing structure of farm production: around one-half of the gross amount of land lost to crop production in the late 1980s was lost due to tree planting and conversion to animal husbandry (SSB, *ZGNCTJNJ*, 1989, p. 251). The drained and irrigated area remained roughly constant in the 1980s at around 44–45 million hectares rising to 48.6 million hectares by 1991 as the state increased its investment (SSB, *ZGTJZY*, 1994, p. 70). The proportion of the arable area drained and irrigated rose from 45 per cent in 1980, already a high figure, to 51 per cent in 1992 (SSB, *ZGTJZY*, 1994, p. 70).[70]

Without irrigation and drainage, it is impossible to expand the areas using Green Revolution technology. Advanced East Coast provinces already had high irrigation ratios and grain yields far above the national average. At least a part of China's agricultural strategy needs to involve expanding the irrigated area in less advanced farming areas, notably North Western China where irrigation ratios, chemical fertiliser use and grain yields are still much below the national average. However, these are poor areas, and it is in these areas especially that state investment is needed to expand the irrigated area. Yet, in the period 1980–88, the effectively drained/irrigated area in Gansu actually fell by 1.6 per cent and in Shanxi it fell by 1.2 per cent (SSB, *ZGNCTJNJ*, 1985, p. 248, and 1989, p. 273).

During the late Maoist years, China's agriculture rapidly increased its purchase of modern means of production: from 1957 to 1975, the real average annual growth rate of sales of agricultural means of production was no less than 11.4 per cent (Table 6.4). In the early 1980s, the growth rate slowed appreciably to 3.5 per cent per annum (1980–85), but from 1985 to 1992 the rate of growth rose again to 6.2 per cent per annum (Table 6.4). Both farm fixed assets and current inputs grew at a rapid rate in the reform period: from 1978 to 1993 the average annual growth rate of agricultural machinery (total motive power) was 6.8 per cent and of chemical fertiliser consumption 8.8 per cent (SSB, *ZGTJZY*, 1994, pp. 57 and 70). By the late 1980s China's chemical fertiliser application per arable hectare had risen to a level around twice the average for the advanced capitalist countries, and was rapidly approaching that of Japan (Table 6.5).

After the 1970s large changes occurred in the structure of agricultural fixed assets in response to the sharp alteration in the pattern of land utilisation.[71] The stocks of many large means of production, unsuitable to small parcels of land, hardly grew or even fell.[72] However,

Table 6.4   Growth rate of inputs and output in Chinese agriculture

| | Average annual growth rate | | | |
	1957–78	1978–92	1980–85	1985–92
(a) Sales of agricultural means of production (real)[1]	11.4	5.5	3.5	6.2
(b) Net value of agricultural output[2]	1.4	5.4	8.5	3.9
Ratio of (b) to (a)	1:8.1	1:1.0	1:0.4	1:1.6

Notes: (1) Data in current prices deflated by the price index for sales of agricultural means of production.
(2) At comparable prices.
Source: SSB, *ZGTJNJ*, 1993, pp. 34, 242 and 611.

Table 6.5   Chemical fertiliser consumption per arable hectare, 1970–1 and 1991–2 (grams of plant nutrient per hectare of arable land)

	1970–1	1991–2
Low income countries*	91	403
of which:		
China	410	3043
India	137	752
Egypt	1312	3437
Middle income countries	363	585
of which:		
South Korea	2450	4517
High income countries	1022	1160
of which:		
UK	2631	3171
Netherlands	7493	5807
Japan	3547	3837

Note: *excluding India and China.

the stocks of many other kinds of farm machinery, more appropriate to the new organisation of farming, grew extremely fast.[73] Rapid growth occurred also in investment in fixed assets associated with the non-crop sector.[74] Farm transport equipment grew especially quickly, reflecting the rapid increase in farm commercialisation during the reforms.[75] By 1990, it was estimated that about 40 per cent of agricultural work had been mechanised.

Table 6.6   Output per capita of major food products in China (kgs)

	Grain	Oilseed	Meat	Aquatic products	Fruit
1978	319	5.5	9.0	4.9	6.9
1980	327	7.9	12.3	4.6	6.9
1985	361	15.0	16.8	6.7	11.1
1990	393	14.2	22.1	10.9	16.5
1993	387	15.3	27.4	15.4	25.6

Source: SSB, *ZGTJZY*, 1994, p. 17.

Output   Over the long-term under Maoist policies, China's real growth rate of farm output (net value) averaged around 1.4 per cent per annum (1957 to 1978) (Table 6.4). In the late 1970s and early 1980s accompanying the wide-ranging institutional reforms, the growth rate exploded.[76] From the mid-1980s onwards, growth slowed down somewhat. However, even in the second half of the 1980s (1984–91) the real average annual growth rate of farm output (net value) still remained well above the growth rate of total population and more than twice the rate achieved in the Maoist period (Table 6.4).

A powerful, sustained trend throughout the reform period was that the rate of growth of non-crop farm output greatly exceeded that of crop production.[77] In just a decade the share of animal products in Chinese farm output rose from one-fifth to almost one-third.[78] This reflected the increased incomes which enabled Chinese people to improve their diet, which was in turn reflected through the market mechanism in changed relative profitability of different products. Over the course of the reform period from 1978 to 1991 output per person of meat rose inexorably from 9.0 to 27.4 kgs, and of aquatic products from 4.9 to 15.4 kgs, and fruit from 6.9 kgs to 25.6 kgs (Table 6.6).

The size of China's grain output is much disputed. Total reported grain output per person failed to rise in the late 1980s (Table 6.6), yet per capita output of meat, aquatic products, and eggs, all grew fast. Moreover, the total number of large farm animals by 1989 was 13 per cent greater than in 1985 (SSB, *ZGTJNJ*, 1990, p. 373). All of these increases in animal numbers required fodder, the most important of which is grain. Reported total personal consumption of grain remained at around 260–270 million tons from 1984 to 1990. Part of the explanation is the fact that the share of beef and mutton in total meat output rose relative to that of pork. This meant that the share of grazing animals to grain-fed meat animals rose in the 1980s. A further factor was the increased proportion of pork production originating in Sichuan, which had a lower grain-feed to meat ratio than the average for the whole of China.[79] However, it is probable that output of grain produced for consumption by farm animals was seriously under-reported in the wake of the rural reforms.

Efficiency The real gross value of crop output per arable acre rose by around three quarters over the reform period.[80] The average annual real growth rate of total value of net farm output per worker accelerated sharply from only 0.3 per cent between 1957 to 1978 to 4.3 per cent from 1978 to 1991 (Ministry of Agriculture, *ZGNCJJTJDQ*, 1989, pp. 14–15, and SSB, *ZGTJNJ*, 1992, pp. 23, 48 and 98).

It is difficult to produce a meaningful measure of the capital-output ratio in Chinese agriculture in the 1980s.[81] However, it appears likely that the reforms halted the long-run trend decline in agricultural capital productivity. In the period 1978 to 1992, the the real average annual rate of increase in peasants' purchase of farm inputs slowed down appreciably from the long-term growth rate since the late 1950s of around 11.4 per cent to only around 5.5 per cent per annum, while the real average annual growth rate of net farm output accelerated sharply from the long-term trend of only around one and a half per cent to over five per cent (Table 6.4).

Rural income and poverty The share of agriculture in total village gross income declined from 69 per cent in 1978 to 36 per cent in 1992, alongside the rapid of the rural non-farm sector (SSB, *ZGTJZY*, 1992, p. 54 and SSB, *ZGNCTJNJ*, 1993, p. 54). However, even in the early 1990s, the bulk of peasant household income came from agriculture,[82] and it was the progress in farm sector productivity that underpinned the large rise in rural income. Indeed, over the whole reform period from 1978 to 1991 real average rural consumption per capita rose by 6.5 per cent per annum (SSB, *ZGTJNJ*, 1992, p. 277), a remarkable performance. The late 1970s and early 1980s witnessed exceptionally fast growth of rural income as the large latent potential in the rural economy was released through simple, well-designed institutional reforms. It was in this period that the fastest growth rates of income were achieved.[83]

A combination of trickle-down from the rapid rural growth and explicit government policy to assist poor regions produced a remarkable reduction in poverty in China in the post-Mao period. The World Bank estimated that the total number of people below a constant poverty line fell from around 270 million in the late 1970s to around 100 million only one decade later (Table 2.3).[84] The reduction was mainly concentrated in the early and mid-1980s, coinciding with the period of maximum growth of farm output and income.

Social stability   The egalitarian land reform in the 1980s tended greatly to increase socio-economic stability. It provided equality of access to the use rights for the most important asset in China's villages. This provided security to the weakest members of the village since in the last resort land could be sub-let. The relative equality in local access to farmland was a major reason for the fact that the Gini coefficient of rural household income distribution remained so low.[85] It made public action easier to implement since villagers shared a common position in respect to the principal means of production. It provided a hugely egalitarian underpinning to rural, and indeed national, income distribution.

c. Conclusion

In the farm sector in the 1980s China moved experimentally away from administrative 'planning'. China's farm institutions shifted decisively away from Stalinism, but towards the Japanese or the Taiwanese institutional route to farm modernisation rather than towards free markets. State and collective continued to have a large role in undertaking activities that were beyond the capacity of individual farm households. If these institutions are to be evaluated by overall performance, then the reform period must be judged an outstanding success, with rapid growth of farm output providing an underpinning to the large improvement in the Chinese people's standard of living. The broad combination of market forces and state action under the post-1978 rural reforms was appropriate to the nature of market failure in agriculture in Asian developing countries in general and in China in particular. Although the growth rate of farm output after 1984 slowed down, growth was still not slow compared to other countries or to China's own past. Moreover, many sectors of the farm economy grew rapidly in response to changing patterns of demand as incomes rose.

The state's continued intervention in price and marketing was heavily influenced by wider strategic and political considerations, especially the need to maintain social stability. Moreover, in a broad sense the government did get relative prices 'right', in that there was sufficient incentive even in the second half of the 1980s for farmers to save and invest large amounts in agriculture and to sustain a rate of growth of farm output considerably in excess of population growth.

China's rural reform programme released the large potential for efficiency improvement and output increase latent in the irrationalities of the Stalinist institutions. It laid the basis for a much wider success with economic reform, providing the foundation for improvements in the standard of living and demand, especially in the early period of reform.

6.2.8 Industry

a. Overall policies

Investment   A large share of the high level of investment (see above) was consistently channelled into the industrial sector.[86] This high rate of investment meant China was able to turn over its manufacturing assets every six to seven years, 'a pace of technological transformation that cannot be matched by any other developing country' (Burki, 1993, quoted in Singh, 1994).

Science and industry   After the great damage inflicted by Maoist polices upon Chinese science during the Cultural Revolution, the reform period saw a fast increase in science at higher educational level. The basis on which scientific research was organised was allowed to change rapidly in response to emerging reforms, in a crash programme to extract the maximum economic benefit from available scientific resources. From relatively early in the reforms the government allowed and encouraged a rapid commercialisation of science.[87]

This affected drastically the basis on which formerly relatively isolated research institutes conducted their work. Research institutes which engaged mainly in applied research projects that yielded immediate practical benefit, were instructed to 'earn income and accumulate funds through such activities as contracting state planned research projects, undertaking research projects entrusted by other organisations, transferring technological achievements, operating joint ventures in technology development and export business, and providing consultancy services' (Central Committee, 1985, p. 451). Operating expenses provided by the state for these sorts of institutes was to be reduced gradually, with the aim of 'making most of these institutes basically self reliant in their operating budgets within three to five years' (Central Committee,

1985, p. 451). The state shifted the focus of its research funding towards basic research. Research institutes of almost all kinds were encouraged to set up partnerships with industry or even establish their own small businesses. The pace of growth of industrial output was so rapid under the reforms that the demand for applied scientists to work directly in one form or another industry increased quickly. A strong incentive to link science to business for profit developed rapidly.

In science as in the physical side of the production process, supply and demand interacted in a virtuous circle, with growth in output increasing the demand for capital goods, in this case 'human capital'. This in turn raised the capacities of the economy to respond with increased output and productivity.

b. State industry policies

A superficial view of Chinese industry in the early 1990s would conclude that little had changed compared to pre-1976. The 'state' was still the 'owner' of the bulk of the industrial capital stock and paid the vast proportion of industrial taxes.[88] However, a great deal had altered both within the state sector and in the role of the state sector within industry.

Material supply   The right of state enterprises to determine their product mix and their source of input supply was extended gradually from the early 1980s, with the liberalisation proceeding much faster and farther in the non-state sector. State de-control over material supply gathered pace alongside the acceleration of price reform in the mid-1980s, but followed the same incremental path. New networks of input supply gradually evolved as the information system that is the heart of a market was put slowly into place. By the end of 1986, the number of industrial products subject to mandatory planning was cut from 120 to 60. However, the lion's share of producer goods was still allocated by the state: sixty per cent of producer goods were allocated through the material balance supply system in 1986 (Guo Jiann-Joong, 1992, p. 116). The scope of material supply allocations continued to shrink over the subsequent years. By the late 1980s only about one-fifth of industrial products was allocated directly by the State Planning Commission (Dong Fureng, 1990, p. 66), though the figure for producer goods continued to be much higher than for consumer goods.

Despite great shrinkage in its scope and liberalisation of prices, mandatory planning continued to have an important role in the state industrial sector in the early 1990s. For example, in 1990 the state owned Guangzhou Shipyard's allocation of steel from the China State Shipbuilding Corporation (CSSC) still stood at 86 per cent of its total steel supplies, with prices charged standing at 46 per cent less than the market price. By 1992 the allocation from the CSSC had fallen to 59 per cent of the shipyard's steel supplies, and the price had risen to just 19 per cent below the free market price. The prediction for 1993 was that the allocation from the state would fall to 36 per cent of steel used in the shipyard, and that the price would be 18 per cent less than the market price (Peregrine Capital, 1993). In some key sectors the proportion of inputs supplied through the material balance planning system was even higher. For example, in 1992 Shanghai Petrochemicals still received 97 per cent of its crude oil allocation directly from the state 'at prices substantially below world market prices' (Merrill Lynch, 1993).

In the early 1990s large-scale upstream state industries continued to produce a large share of their output according to the state plan. For example, prior to 1992, virtually all of Shanghai Petrochemicals' output was through the state plan at state-determined prices. In 1992 the proportion fell to 59 per cent, and in 1993 the predicted figure was 37 per cent (Merrill Lynch, 1993). In Maanshan Iron and Steel Company, it was still the case in 1993 that the state prescribed annually 'the mandatory production requirement and within such requirement, the product mix and sales of steel products' (Wardley Corporate Finance, 1993). The pattern of product specialisation among the major steel producers still was 'under the framework of centralised state control' (Wardley Corporate Finance, 1993).

Foreign investment   It was seen above that foreign direct investment played a growing role in China's public sector industry in the 1980s, accelerating sharply in the 1990s.

Competition   State industry operated in an increasingly competitive environment. From early in the reform process, the non-state sector began to compete with the state sector, with fiercest competition taking place in those sectors characterised by small economies of scale and low capital requirements. It was seen above that by the early 1990s the allocation and price of most industrial products was market-determined. This had many consequences. One of the most important was that profit rates were now much more a reflection of an enterprise's economic performance than of bureaucratic decisions.

Table 6.7 Number of industrial enterprises (establishments) in China (thousands)

	1957	1965	Year 1978	1985	1991
Total	—	—	—	5185	8092
of which:					
(A) *xiang* level and above	170	158	348	463	506
of which:					
state	49.6	45.9	83.7	93.7	105
collective	119.9	111.8	264.7	367.8	391
other	—	—	—	2	11
(B) below *xiang* level:	—	—	—	4722	7586
of which:					
urban and rural					
individual	—	—	—	3348	6385
other collective	—	—	—	1374	1200
xiang-level and above:					
large	—	—	1.2	2.3	4.3
medium	—	—	3.2	5.6	10.6
small	—	—	344.1	455.3	491.6

Source: SSB, *CEY*, 1981, pp. 207–8; SSB, *ZGTJZY*, 1992, p. 70.

Size structure of establishments A large change occurred in the size structure of industry in relation to the size of establishment, partly by design and partly through allowing market forces to work. Two phases took place in the growth of non-state industrial establishments. Within the state sector the state concentrated its planning efforts on the relatively small number of enterprises in the large and medium scale sector. It allowed the small-scale sector to languish and be overtaken rapidly by non-state industries (see below). From 1978 to 1991, the number of large- and medium-scale industrial enterprises rose by around 250 per cent for each of these categories, while for small-scale state enterprises, the growth was just 43 per cent (see Table 6.7). Alongside a 150 per cent increase in state industrial output (real gross value) from 1980 to 1992, the total number of state industrial enterprises grew by just 45 per cent (see Table 6.7).

Within each sector state planners attempted increasingly to focus production upon those enterprises which were better able to achieve economies of scale. For example, in the motorcycle industry, in 1989 the state formulated a strategy to restructure the industry. The plan was to increase domestic production mainly by concentrating efforts on nineteen designated producers. These designated producers were guaranteed energy supply, assigned sufficient import licences for imported parts and components, and given preferential financing. From 1983 to 1992, motorcycle output rose from 290,000 units to 1.98 million units, while the number of enterprises fell from 100 to 80 (Bear, Sterns, 1993).

During the reform period, the rapid growth of output in the non-state industrial sector was achieved almost entirely at the expense of the small-scale state industrial sector's share of total industrial output. The share of the non-state sector, including both the collective and, latterly, the individual and foreign investment sector, rose dramatically, from 22 per cent in 1978 to 52 per cent in 1992 (SSB, *ZGTJNJ*, 1993, p. 412). However, this was almost entirely achieved at the expense of the small-scale state sector. The share of the large-scale and medium-scale industrial sector, which was almost wholly state-owned, remained remarkably constant, at around 43 per cent throughout the reform period (Table 6.8), and within the 'formal' sector its share was even higher (Table 6.9). Indeed, it seems likely that the small-scale state sector's share of industrial output (gross value) fell from around 36 per cent in 1980 to less than ten per cent in 1991.[89]

By the early 1990s, the structure of industrial output by size of establishment in China was gradually moving towards something like that of India, or of Taiwan in the 1950s. In these countries, the state was dominant in the large-scale sector, leaving non-state forms of industrial organisation to dominate other sorts of industrial production in which there were fewer economies of scale. In these sectors, vastly greater numbers of enterprises were needed to produce much smaller amounts of output.

Sectoral division of production The state increasingly concentrated on 'upstream' activities, allowing small-scale non-state enterprises or leased out small state enterprises to enter 'downstream' production. The share of state enterprises in total output was much higher in 'upstream' industries such as oil refining, ferrous metals, chemical fibres, coal mining, chemicals and machine building (Table 6.10). In 1989 in the formal sector, around 26,000 large- and medium-sized enterprises (just over six per cent of the total number of industrial enterprises) produced 65 per cent of total industrial output value (SSB, *ZGGYJTJNJ*, 1990, section 5). The state allowed the share of non-state enterprises to grow fast in those sectors with low economies of scale at the plant level. The share of state-owned large and medium plants was under 50 per cent of total output value in sectors such as

Table 6.8 Share of total gross industrial output produced in different types of enterprises (current prices) (per cent)

	1980	1985	1991
Total	100	100	100
Large	25.1	25.3	28.1
Medium	18.1	17.0	15.5
Small:			
xiang level and above	56.8	47.5	38.3
below xiang level	na	10.2	18.1

Source: SSB, *CEY*, 1981, p. 212, and SSB, *ZGTJZY*, 1992, p. 70.

Note: The criterion of 'size' used here is different in different sectors. In many sectors the criterion is based on the plant's output capacity. In steel, for example, a 'large' plant is one with an output capacity of over 10 million tons; a 'medium' one has an output capacity of 100,000 to 10 million tons, and a 'small' one has an output capacity of under 100,000 tons. In other sectors, the criterion depends on the value of the plant's fixed assets.

Table 6.9 Share of industrial output in the 'formal' sector produced in enterprises of different sizes (per cent)

	1980	1985	1991
Large	25.1	28.2	34.3
Medium	18.1	18.9	19.0
Small	56.8	52.9	46.8

Source: SSB, *CEY*, 1981, p. 212, and SSB, *ZGTJZY*, 1992, p. 70.

Note: 'Formal' sector here means enterprises of *xiang* level and above.

Table 6.10 Share of the state sector in different industries' output (gross value) in China, 1990 (per cent)

furniture	12.4	transport machines	71.3
non-ferrous metals	17.8	fodder	73.3
plastics	21.8	drink	74.6
metal working	26.0	chemicals	77.9
wood products	42.5	coal mines	78.8
electrical machinery	48.7	food	79.5
building	51.2	chemical fibres	84.5

continued on page 207

Table 6.10   continued

materials			
textiles	56.5	ferrous metals	86.6
instruments	61.2	oil refining	96.4
electronics	66.0	tobacco	96.5
machinery	67.5		
rubber	68.1		

Source: SSB, *ZGTJNJ*, 1991.

Note: These data are for 'independent accounting enterprises' only. These produced 78 per cent of the gross value of industrial output in 1990.

printing, furniture, wood and straw products, leather products, plastic products, food products, metal products, building materials, and drink (SSB, *ZGGYJJTJNJ*, 1990, section 5). It was in these sectors that the non-state enterprises advanced most rapidly under the post-Mao reforms.

The pace of growth of light industry accelerated sharply in the reform period. From 1968 to 1992, light industry (real gross value of output) grew at a reported rate of almost fifteen per cent per annum (SSB, *ZGTJNJ*, 1993, p. 58). However, in a relatively closed economy such as China's, such growth can only be sustained through simultaneous rapid growth of output from heavy industry to provide the inputs for light industrial products.

Consequently, alongside a boom in output of light industrial products often from the small-scale sector, went a simultaneous rapid growth of output from the heavy industrial sector. For example, three major 'upstream' products of the petrochemical industry are synthetic fibres, resins and plastics. These inputs were mainly produced in state owned large-scale 'upstream' enterprises. Synthetic fibres are used to produce textiles, canvas, clothing, sacking, ropes and fishing nets. Resins and plastics are used to make films, containers, sheeting, cable jacketing, houseware, toys, electrical appliances, automobile parts and construction coating materials.

The real growth rate of heavy industrial output was reported to be almost eleven per cent per annum over the period 1978 to 1992 (SSB, *ZGTJNJ*, 1993, p. 58). Detailed consideration of the growth of output of a wide range of 'upstream' products (Table 6.11) demonstrates, unsurprisingly, that large absolute increases took place in the large scale, 'commanding heights' of the Chinese economy, in which state firms were massively dominant. In these sectors 'entrepreneurship'

Table 6.11   Output of selected industrial products in China

Item	Unit	1980	1992
chemical fibres	10,000 tons	45	213
yarn	10,000 tons	293	508
cloth	100 million metres	135	191
toothpaste	m. tubes	783	2257
pharmaceuticals	'000 tons	40	281
plastic products	10,000 tons	114	537
household refrigerators	10,000	5	486
household washing machines	10,000	25	708
electric fans	10,000	724	6837
TV sets	10,000	249	2868
tape recorders	10,000	74	3232
motor vehicles	10,000	22	107
motor cycles	10,000	5	205
telephone sets	10,000	176 (1984)	1982
plastics	10,000 tons	90	331
mining equipment	10,000 tons	16	37
petroleum equipment	10,000 tons	6	19
chemical industry equipment	10,000 tons	7	24
power generating equipment	10,000 kwh	419	1297
numerically controlled machine tools	number	1,613 (1984)	7,450
roller bearings	10,000 sets	22,755	77,456
internal combustion engines	10,000 h.p.	2,539	9,253
pig iron	10,000 tons	3,802	7,589
steel	10,000 tons	3,712	8,094
rolled steel	10,000 tons	2,716	6,697
cement	10,000 tons	7,966	30,622
plate glass	10,000 standard cases	2,771	9,359
sulphuric acid	10,000 tons	764	1,408
coal	m. tons	620	1,116
oil	m. tons	106	145
electric power	billion kwh	301	754

Sources: SSB, *ZGTJNJ*, 1993, section 10; 1986, section 15; and SSB, *CEY*, 1981, section IV.

depended heavily on the co-ordinated application of science. Moreover, these typically required much large amounts of capital per unit of output, needed much larger plant sizes and much longer gestation periods than was the case for the products of light industry. Paradoxically, an economy which had shown large heavy industry bias under the communist command system continued to require rapid growth of output from the heavy industrial sector during the reform period. The inter-sectoral relationship under reform had shifted from unbalanced heavy industry growth to a balanced growth path, rather than to the emphasis of light industry to the neglect of growth of heavy industry. Indeed, between 1978 and 1992, China's ranking in total world output shifted from fifth to fourth largest in steel, from third to first place in coal, from eighth to fifth in crude oil, from seventh to fourth in electricity, and from fourth to first in cement (SSB, *ZGTJNJ*, 1993, p. 901).

Large multi-plant companies   Support for the idea of industrial groups became a central plank of government plans to reform state industry: 'The goal is to form competitive and independently managed industrial giants' (Yao Jianguo, 1992). The government realised that it was necessary to reduce the contribution of uneconomically small plants and reduce the degree of in-house production of a wide range of inputs in huge plants. However, it was firmly committed to preserving simultaneously a central role for large firms and large plants: 'The fact is that mass production is desperately needed by modern society' (Yao Jianguo, 1992). The industrial enterprise group was to be a key means to achieve these goals.

The government identified over fifty leading enterprise groups which had been especially successful. They were to be models for other groups, and were to be targetted for state assistance (Yao Jianguo, 1992). The vast bulk of these were in heavy industry.[90] Most of them had their own parent company and more than half had invested in new enterprises or purchased subsidiary companies. The parent enterprises were 'responsible for overall business management of the group', were 'in charge of personnel management' and 'responsible for maintaining and increasing the value of national properties' (Yao Jianguo, 1992). The subsidiaries were allowed to join the group through 'contracting or lend lease arrangements with the parent enterprise' (Yao Jianguo, 1992).

By 1991 there were almost 7,000 enterprise groups. Some were 'tight knit', some 'semi-cohesive' and some merely 'loose'. Sometimes groups of state enterprises joined together under a single famous brand in order to produce a more or less formal vertically integrated company.

Sometimes horizontal integration occurred within the same former administrative department. A common pattern was for enterprises to amalgamate with scientific institutions. Urban enterprises with advanced technology commonly amalgamated with or annexed rural enterprises to produce a vertically integrated company. Often rural enterprises took over the land-intensive, pollution-intensive and unskilled labour-intensive parts of the production process, while the urban side assisted in upgrading the rural enterprises' technical level. Coastal enterprises often combined with rural enterprises which supplied raw material to the parent company. Finally, large enterprises often expanded by simply 'using their investment funds whenever and wherever profitable through expansion and annexation' (Li Yuanchao, 1992).

One of most striking successes was the Guangzhou-based Wanbao Electrical Appliances Group. In the early 1980s it was a small heavily indebted plant with 300 employees. By 1991 it had grown into a multi-plant enterprise with several dozen constituent enterprises employing more than 10,000 people, and an annual output of over one million refrigerators, making it one of the eight largest manufacturers of refrigerators in the world.

The 1980s saw the establishment of 'several scores' of comprehensive and large electrical appliance production conglomerates, including the Jinxing Electrical Appliance Group in Shanghai, the Panda Electrical Appliance Group in Jiangsu, and the Peony Electrical Appliances Group in Beijing. China's output of black and white TV sets, refrigerators, washing machines, electric fans and irons has risen from negligible levels to become the largest in the world. At the centre of this process were large industrial groups benefitting from economies of scale and scope. In 1990 China's electrical appliance industry exported US$200 million dollars' worth of goods, and the scope of its exports had broadened to include increasingly sophisticated products. China had begun to penetrate some of the world's most competitive markets. In 1988, for example, China exported 800,000 electric fans to the USA.[91]

Wanbao provides an example of an enterprise group which grew up from an initially small enterprise. More typical were those that emerged by restructuring large enterprises. For example, in motor vehicles the government selected eight large producers to form the core of China's reformed automobile industry. Between them the 'Big Eight' comprised 85 per cent of China's automobile output in the early 1990s. The Dongfeng Automobile Group was based around the former giant No. 2 Automobile Plant in Hubei Province. By the early 1990s it had 'taken over' around 300 enterprises of different scale. The constituent plants reoriented production under the guidance of the parent company, which was also the conduit through which new technology was targetted. They re-specialised into a variety of products, such as assembly, special purpose car production and the production of specialised inputs (Yao Jianguo, 1992).

In addition to restructuring the core business of motor vehicle production, the State Council's China National Automobile Committee reorganised over 2,400 small-scale manufacturers of motor vehicle parts into appproximately fifty manufacturing groups (First Boston *et al.*, 1992).

In the light industrial sector, a detailed case study of the Hefeng Textile Plant in Ningbo (Jiang Xiaoming, 1993) showed the way in which the multiplant firm was emerging in response to incentives at the enterprise level and in co-operation with ambitious local government plans. By the early 1990s, Hefeng had developed into a complex three-tier structure fairly similar to the pattern commonly observed in Japanese industry. In the first tier the process of amalgamation began in the early 1980s, gradually becoming more formal over time. By the late 1980s, the Hefeng textile (fibre) plant had formally amalgamated through vertical integration with three cloth manufacturers and one cloth dyeing plant, as well as the Industrial and Commercial Bank of Ningbo and the Zhejiang province Textile College. The group had a common board of directors and they co-ordinated the production, marketing and growth of the company. In addition, the company had a second tier of joint ventures with township enterprises, which also began early on in the reform process. The Hefeng company had invested in each of six township enterprises mainly in related fields, in which it had become a part owner, with a share in profits proportionate to its investment. Finally, there was a third tier of enterprises, mainly in the garment business, with whom Hefeng developed a more informal relationship.

In the beverage industry in the 1980s there was an explosive growth in the total number of plants and firms, with a proliferation of small plants producing low quality, often dangerous produce at high cost in terms of intermediate inputs. The Ministry of Light Industry mapped out a strategy for inviting selected multinational firms to invest in the industry and assist in the process of technical modernisation as well as comprehensively restructuring the organisation of production, focussing on the creation of four large, brand name soft drinks firms, eliminating a large number of small producers (Yan Xiaoqian, 1993). By the mid-1990s a very rapid alteration in the corporate structure of the in-

Table 6.12   Subsidiaries of the Guangzhou Shipyard, 1993

Name	Date of establishment	Attributable equity interest	Principal activities
Kwangchow Shipyard Container Factory	1982	100	Container manufacture
Masterwood Company Ltd.	1992	75	Furniture manufacture
Xinhui City Nanyang Shipping Industrial Company	1993	70	Ship dismantling
Guangzhou Haizhu District Guanghua Machinery Factory	1990	65	Machinery manufacture
Maring and Industrial Ltd.	1992	25	Provision of special coating (paint services)
Contech International Container Company	1985	22	Repair and inspection services for containers

Source: Peregrine Capital, 1993.

dustry had occurred along the lines earlier mapped out, with a large and growing share of the market occupied by four major companies.[92] Each was based on the franchise system of a central plant supplying concentrate to a network of franchised bottling plants around the country.

A detailed account of the growth of the state owned Guangzhou Shipyard (Peregrine Capital, 1993) showed how over the course of the reform period a large multi-plant company could develop based on the gradual emergence of formal structures of ownership developed in response to the gradual growth of market opportunities. By 1993 the Guangzhou shipyard was the part-owner of a group of six subsidiaries each of which was in related lines of business, and had informal subcontracting arrangements with a further four enterprises (see Table 6.12). Initially loose relationships gradually became more formal as the reform period progressed.

Property rights   Throughout the long reform period the Chinese government spoke of devising methods of 'revitalising state enterprises', not of improving their performance through 'privatisation' (see, e.g. Chen Jihua, 1994). However, property rights are not a 'black-and-white' issue of 'state' and 'private' ownership. Rather, there is a wide gradation of rights attached to the employment of property and obtaining a stream of income, as well as exercising the power and enjoying the prestige that derives from the effective employment of capital. After the late 1970s in the state sector there occurred a halting and gradual process of expansion of property rights for economic agents other than central government officials and those who formerly answered directly to them at the local level. Over this period in the Chinese state industrial sector there emerged gradually a group of institutional, corporate entrepreneurs who began to operate capital in order to improve their own position through promoting the economic interests of the institution which employed them. In this evolutionary process, a complex iteration occurred between changes in law and quasi-law, and spontaneous actions of lower level agents seeking to push beyond regulations at each stage.

Many channels developed through which agents increased their 'use rights' (*shiyong quan*) over state property as the central authorities battled to improve the performance of state industry. The material supply system was dismantled gradually. Consequently, managers were increasingly able to purchase inputs from the source which most benefited the enterprise whose assets they managed. They were increasingly able to determine the product mix of their enterprise, and to sell their product in the market that was most advantageous to their enterprise. Advertising and sales departments had died under the Maoist system. Now they sprang back into life. The price system was reformed gradually so that managers were given more and more leeway about the price to set for their product. Still in 1994, there were virtually no rights to make workers redundant from state enterprises. However, state enterprises that were growing did have increased rights to employ extra workers. Although there still were many restrictions, a rising share of the enterprise's wage bill was allocated as bonuses in the distribution of which managers had increased leeway.[93]

Although hedged around by innumerable regulations, a large change occurred in the rights of enterprise managers to raise capital and to allocate the allocate the stream of income generated by the property under their control. By 1992, almost 47 per cent of state enterprises' investment in fixed assets was generated by 'self-raised funds' (SSB, *ZGTJNJ*, 1993, p. 146). Correspondingly, the share of fixed investment that state enterprises were allocated directly out of the state budget had shrunk to a tiny six per cent. In addition to enhanced independence to allocate funds generated by their own activities, state enterprises now raised around 30 per cent of their fixed investment needs from bank loans and 8 per cent from foreign investment (SSB, *ZGTJNJ*, 1993, p. 146).

A striking alteration in capital markets was the spontaneous emergence of inter-plant investment. Initially, the inter-plant connections were tentative and informal. As the reform period progressed, the links became more widespread and formal. By the early 1990s, a large number of state companies based on interlocking ownership between state enterprises had emerged and were explicitly supported by government policy.

In addition to funds raised by the enterprises themselves, and/or raised from banks, at least as large a source of capital for investment by state industrial enterprises was the huge variety of state bureaucratic institutions which employed their financial resources to generate more capital. A typical new large industrial investment project in the early 1990s would involve several institutional investors. The capital for the project capital typically might be contributed by any combination of the plant or firm itself, a foreign joint venture partner, a state bank, and central or local government institutions. The institutions participating in the investment were all more or less interested in maximising returns from their investment. The system was groping its way towards the joint stock company.

Even in the early 1990s the Chinese government still was cautious about the desirability of developing a system of industrial ownership based mainly on shares freely tradeable on a stock market. Although stock markets were allowed to open in Shanghai and Shenzhen, the issue of publicly tradeable shares was highly controlled. By the end of 1993, only around 150 companies had been allowed to issue shares on China's two stock markets. Much illegal and quasi-legal issuance of tradeable shares occurred during the reform period. However, the vast bulk of capital throughout the reform period continued to take the form of investment by institutions outside the framework of a stock market and tradeable shares.

Within the formal framework of state ownership, a large change had occurred in the nature of ownership of capital. The evolving system was one based mainly on multiple ownership by a diversity of institutional investors, dominated by various 'state' institutions. The role of individual ownership was small. In addition, as was seen above, large changes occurred in the way in which the use rights of capital were exercised in the state industrial sector.

As the reform process evolved, the various parties with ownership rights in state enterprises developed a strong interest in the selection of managers who would use the assets in which the institutions had invested to generate high returns from their investment. State enterprise managers became selected increasingly for their business skills since this would increase the likelihood of the enterprise earning profits for the institutions to which it was subordinate. The rewards of the managers became increasingly also to reflect the performance of the business over which they were given control.

It is not too fanciful to speak of a process of 'organic privatisation' of state enterprises over the decade and a half of reform. The most important constraints over the exercise of rights to manage state industrial assets were the inability to declare workers redundant and the associated commitment by the government at different levels to keep poorly performing state enterprises operating despite making losses.

Labour markets A competitive labour market began to emerge in the state sector. A rapid rise occurred in the number (10 million in 1978 to 24 million in 1988) and proportion of 'non-fixed' workers (from 14 per cent in 1978 to 24 per cent in 1988) (SSB, *ZGLDGZTJZL*, 1949–85, 1987, pp. 28 and 33; and SSB, *ZGLDGZTJNJ*, 1989, p. 203). These categories of workers had less rights and lower average wages than did existing state enterprise employees (on wage differentials, see SSB, *ZGLDGZTJZL*, 1949–85, 1987, p. 171).

The state industrial sector absorbed labour much less rapidly than the non-state industrial sector and less rapidly also than the tertiary sector.[94] Moreover, within the state sector, the new entrants were increasingly attracted to more profitable, faster-growing firms. Much the fastest growth rate of employment in the non-state sector was in the diverse categories involving foreign investment but in the early 1990s the total number still was relatively small.[95]

The rate of growth of money wages in state enterprises in the 1980s was rapid in relation to China's history since 1949 (around 11 per cent per annum in state enterprises from 1978 to 1989) (SSB, *ZGTJZY*, 1990, p. 41) but was well below the rate in most Latin American countries over the same period. China's workforce still lacked an independent, defensive trade union movement, and was unable to bargain for wage increases in the way that occurs in countries with democratic institutions.

Results China's experimental, evolutionary reform of state industry produced many problems. Despite the passage of the Bankruptcy Law in 1987 few state enterprises of any size were allowed go bankrupt. By 1993, over 30 per cent of state enterprises were making losses

(SSB, *ZGTJZY*, 1994, p. 85), requiring the pre-emption of large amounts of public funds to keep them afloat. The ratio of losses of industrial enterprises to profits and taxes of profit-making enterprises rose from just over two per cent in 1985 to 30 per cent in 1993 (SSB, *ZGTJZY*, 1992, p. 82, and 1994, p. 85). Investment decision-making had become diffused without the full rigours of market discipline acting to repress capital spending. The 'soft budget constraint' upon Chinese state enterprises was facilitated by decentralisation of rights to issue credit, but without a comparable responsibility for banks' branches to account for their balance sheet performance. Moreover, the lending behaviour of the banks' branches was heavily influenced by the local government.

Partial reform of state industry provided a ripe environment for corruption. Parallel markets provided enormous incentives for profit-seeking enterprises to direct output away from the plan. An elaborate structure of negotiation was involved in determining the proportion of output to be included in the state's mandatory plan, in deciding the share of profits to be retained by the enterprise, and in all the complex allocation of rights connected with foreign trade. These negotiations often were accompanied by bribes, and the income to be derived from them, either by units or by individuals, could be large by the standards of ordinary Chinese citizens.

State industry overall grew relatively slowly. Its share of total gross industrial output fell sharply (see above). Market forces operated earlier and more powerfully in the non-state sector. For many observers this provided strong evidence of the relative inefficiency of the state-owned sector, and demonstrated the high cost of a 'half-way house' reform of state industry.

However, there were many offsetting positive results. Losses in state industry were mainly confined to sectors with special problems in the transition. In 1991, 98.9 per cent of losses in state industry came from the coal, oil, non-ferrous metals, tobacco and military sectors (*Beijing Review*, vol. 35, no. 26, June 29, 1992, p. 6). Morevoer, the extent of 'losses' falls greatly if the huge state enterprise outlays on housing, health, education, unemployment pay, food subsidies, etc., are removed from the balance sheet. In the West these would be the responsibility mainly of the state or the individual. Profits became an increasingly important goal for state enterprise managers. The incentives for regional governments to assist and push the enterprises under their control to raise profits also greatly increased. Prices were increasingly market-determined. Enterprises and local governments did alter their behaviour in response to the sharp change in the economic environment.

During the reform period China's manufactured exports grew rapidly. Much of the increase came from the state sector. Even in Guangdong province, adjacent to Hong Kong 'state-owned enterprises led [the province's] post-1986 export growth, accounting for 83 per cent of provincial exports in 1987' (Vogel, 1989, pp. 374–5). Through competition on world markets a significant section of China's state industrial sector altered its operational methods. China's outstanding export performance provided a means to technologically upgrade state industry through the rapid growth of imports. China's total imports of machinery and transport equipment rose from an annual level of under US$ 2 billion dollars in the late 1970s to US$ 45 billion dollars by 1993 (Davie, 1986, p. 332, and SSB, *ZGTJZY*, 1994, p. 106). A large share of this new technology was directed towards the state industrial sector. China's government export incentives flew in the face of static resource efficiency considerations, but had large dynamic gains.

The rationality of the size structure of state enterprise improved. The rapid growth of the non-state sector's share of industrial output (see below) was largely at the expense of the small-scale state sector.[96] The large-scale state-owned sector grew at roughly the same (i.e. very rapid) rate as the whole industrial sector. Indeed, the share of large scale industrial plants in total gross industrial output remained constant at around 25–26 per cent throughout the 1980s (Table 6.8).

Meticulous estimates by Jefferson *et al.*, (1992), show that the real gross value of output per worker in the state sector grew by around 5.2 per cent per annum from 1980 to 1988 (Table 6.8). More importantly, they estimate that real gross value of output over unit of capital in state enterprises also rose, by around 2.1 per cent per annum over the same period (Table 6.13). This marked a striking reversal of the previous long-run trend decline in capital productivity in the state industrial sector (Jefferson *et al.*, 1992).

China's reforms of the 1980s reversed the sectoral pattern of industrial growth: from 1952 to 1978, heavy industry grew at 14 per cent per annum and light industry grew at 9 per cent per annum; from 1979 to 1990, heavy industry grew at 10 per cent per annum, while light industry grew at 14 per cent per annum (gross value of output at comparable prices) (SSB, *ZGGYJJTJNJ*, 1989, p. 11, and SSB, *ZGTJZY*, 1991, p. 3).

Conclusion China avoided the 'quick fix' approach to the reform of state enterprises. In part this was for ideological reasons. The 'Old

Table 6.13   Growth rate of output (gross value) per unit of input in Chinese industry, 1980–1988 (per cent per annum, constant prices)

State-owned sector		Collectively owned sector	
Labour	5.21	Labour	12.13
Capital	2.14	Capital	4.49
Materials	2.06	Materials	3.21

Source: Jefferson *et al.*, 1992, p. 247.

Guard' of Chinese leaders felt that it was betrayal of socialism to give up state ownership of industry. However, is is unconvincing to suppose that this was the only, or even the main, explanation. The same leadership had permitted the introduction of market forces into the lives of the peasantry. This was much more dangerous in terms of traditional Stalinist thinking, since the peasantry was three-quarters of the population, and had supposedly backward political thoughts associated with 'petty commodity production'. It permitted too the rapid growth of competitive, profit seeking, community-owned enterprises (see below). It allowed rapid growth of individual business. It permitted the state industrial sector to divest itself of a large number of small enterprises, greatly reducing the share of the state's 'commanding heights' in industry. It encouraged foreign capital to invest in Chinese industry. It reversed Stalinist hostility to international trade. A more plausible explanation is that the leadership understood the dangers of 'shock therapy' privatisation and wished to avoid these.

c. Rural non-farm enterprises

Policies   In former communist countries the IMF/World Bank recommended: 'rapid privatisation of small enterprises through outright sales to individual, co-operatives and others' with the assets sold 'as quickly as possible' (IMF, 1990, pp. 2 and 27). China followed a different path. In the 1980s it once again became legal to set up and run small businesses, and the pure private sector grew rapidly. By the early 1990s the total number of people working in individual rural non-farm businesses had risen from negligible levels to around 47 million (SSB, *ZGNCTJNJ*, 1993, p. 49). However, the rural collectively-owned sector still employed a much larger number of people, around 59 million in 1992 (SSB, *ZGNCTJNJ*, 1993, p. 49). Pure private business sector was mainly small-scale 'petty commodity production', located predominantly in non-industrial activities with small amounts of fixed asssets per business.[97] The collective sector occupied the 'commanding heights' of rural industry accounting for over 63 per cent of employees in rural industry in 1992 (SSB, *ZGNCTJNJ*, 1993, p. 49).[98] Its share of total rural fixed assets (i.e. including farm sector assets) stood at an estimated 53 per cent in 1992 (SSB, *ZGNCTJNJ*, 1993, p. 272), and its share of rural non-farm assets must have been considerably above even this figure. The rural collectively-owned sector was much larger than the urban one. Its output value in 1992 was 2.2 times larger than that of the urban collective sector (SSB, *ZGTJNJ*, 1993, p. 409).

China's 'collectively'-owned enterprises were not co-operatives in the normal sense of the word, namely each enterprise run by its owners. Rather, they resembled national state-owned enterprises, with the 'state' being the local community (*xiang* or *cun*), each of which typically owned multiple establishments.[99] These small local multi-plant public enterprises were monitored by an asset management agency, the 'rural enterprises department', responsible to the community government.

Chinese township (*xiang*) governments resembled mini nation-states. They had a strong interest both in using markets and in overcoming market failure to promote the local economy. Unlike a single workers' co-operative enterprise, whose interests often lie in restricting employment, limiting re-investment, and maximising wages, the Chinese system of local public ownership led to competitive behaviour by enterprise managers, even to the extent that they had a strong incentive to squeeze surplus value out of the workforce. The local government attempted to overcome market failure, in respect to growth of the local economy and provision of equitable life chances to the local population.[100] These included financing risky ventures, training and retraining the local workforce, improving public health provision, acquiring and providing information, and constructing the local infrastructure.[101]

The rural non-farm sector was more flexible than partially reformed state industry in adjusting its product-mix to rapidly changing markets. In the reform period competitive factor and product markets were established quickly in this sector. Trade unions hardly existed and the large reserve army of surplus labour placed downward pressure on rural wages. Whereas in the state sector the workforce was long established and used to a low pace of work, the workforce in rural non-farm enterprises was mainly first generation, lacking the privileges or organisational capacity of the state sector workers. Strikes tended to be socially stigmatised in that they might damage the performance of enterprises which were owned by the whole community. Rural non-farm sector product markets were liberalised quite rapidly. In 1986 70 per cent of the main material inputs of the rural non-farm enterprises were obtained from the market and over two-thirds of rural non-farm enterprises' marketings were sold at prices determined by the enterprises themselves (Economic Research Institute, 1987, pp. 11–13).

The reform dramatically changed the incentives for the managers of rural collective enterprises. The most important insitutional innovation was the contract between the enterprise and local government. The most important part of the contract was the profits target.

Rural collectively-owned enterprises became the key to prosperity for Chinese local governments in the 1980s. While agriculture grew rapidly over the decade, the explosive growth of the non-farm sector meant that its share of total rural output rose quickly (from 31 per cent of the gross value of rural output in 1980 to 64 per cent in 1992 (SSB, *ZGTJNJ*, 1990, p. 33 and SSB, *ZGNCTJNJ*, 1993, p. 54). Its capacity to absorb surplus labour was high, and the greater its success in this respect, the more approval local leaders won from their community, and from the governments at higher levels. Non-farm enterprises were vitally important, too, as principal contributors to local government revenue.[102] They not only handed over profit taxes but also were required to make substantial contributions to the local community through a variety of levies.[103] It was strongly in the interest of local governments to ensure the expansion of profits from enterprises within their jurisdiction.

Local governments played a large role in the growth of the rural community enterprises. The most important decisions in local capital markets were taken either directly by the local government or, typically, by them in collaboration with the local managers of financial organisations (Byrd, 1990, Chapter 9). The local government's rural non-farm enterprises department identified new opportunities for profitable investment and took the risks involved in setting up new enterprises. They also made the final decision to close down collective enterprises and transfer the human and physical resources to other uses within the community. The World Bank's own study concludes: 'Without the deep involvement of community governments, China's rural non-farm sector could not have grown as rapidly as it did in the late 1970s and early 1980s' (Byrd, 1990, p. 358).

Results If the transition orthodoxy's view of the relationship between property rights and economic incentives were correct, one would have expected that, whatever changes had taken place in the setting within

Table 6.14 Growth of output and employment in the industrial sector of China's township enterprises

	1978	1992	Av. growth rate p.a. (per cent)
Employment (million)	17.3	63.4	9.7
Gross value of output (index, constant prices)	100(a)	1745	22
Value-added (constant prices)(a)	100	967	17
Output of selected products:			
electricity (100 m. kwh)	28.7	163.8	
coal (m. tons)	100	424	
chemical fertiliser (m. tons)	0.38	0.38	
farm tools (100 m.)	6.7	11.3	
cement (m. tons)	3.3	103.8	
bricks (billion)	73.0	495.5	
pre-fabricated cement (m. sq. metres)	—	91	
silk goods (m. metres)	69.2	1048.1	
paper/cardboard (m. tons)	0.4	7.9	
leather products (m. units)	348 (1985)	739.7	
electric fans (m.)	—	32.1	
everyday porcelain (b. units)	—	1.5	
central heating radiators (m.)	—	138	
salt (m. tons)	1.5	5.3	
sugar (m. tons)	0.18	0.41	
edible oil (m. tons)	0.54	5.61	
processed grain (m. tons)	53.9	390.0	
arts and crafts products (b. *yuan*)	0.37	2.62	
fodder (m. tons)	—	27.7	
sanitary porcelain (m. units)	—	117	
beer (m. tons)	—	1.3	
garments (b. units)	—	3.3	
canned food (m. tons)	—	1.2	
silk (1000 tons)	3.9	34.1	

Sources: SSB, *ZGTJNJ*, 1993, pp. 395–7; and SSB, *ZGTJZY*, 1994, p. 73.

Note: (a) deflated by rural retail price index.

which China's rural non-farm collectively-owned enterprises operated, they would still have been unable to operate successsfully. Instead of stagnation, the 1980s witnessed phenomenal growth in rural non-farm industry in which the public sector was dominant. Between 1978 and 1992 total employment in the sector increased from 17 million to 63 million and the gross value of output rose by around 22 per cent per annum (Table 6.14). The share of the township enterprise sector in China's gross material product rose from 17 per cent in 1985 to 25 per cent in 1990 (SSB, *ZGTJZY*, 1991, p. 65). Between 1978 and 1992 its share of national output of silk products rose from 11 per cent to 43 per cent; of edible oil, from 30 per cent to 86 per cent; of machine-made paper and cardboard, from 10 per cent to 50 per cent; of raw coal, from 15 per cent to 38 per cent; of cement from 5 per cent to 34 per cent and of bricks, from 66 per cent to 84 per cent (SSB, *ZGNCTJNJ*, 1993, p. 161).

In addition to the growth of output and employment, in just five years between 1985 and 1990, exports from China's rural township enterprises rose from $US1.7 to 9.6 billion, and their share of China's rapidly-growing exports increased from 4.8 per cent to 15.2 per cent (SSB, *ZGTJZY*, 1991, p. 65). The share of China's rural township sector in total world exports from low income countries (including India and China) rose from 3.2 per cent in 1985 to 8.0 per cent in 1989 (SSB, *ZGTJZY*, 1991, p. 65, and World Bank, *WDR*, 1987, p. 220, and 1991, p. 230), a remarkable rise in such a short period. Had the export performance of a single developing country improved in such a dramatic way, teams of Western experts would have been dispatched to understand the cause of the phenomenon. Yet there was little serious outside investigation of the reasons for the explosive export growth of this predominantly publicly-owned sector.

Conclusion   China's experience shows that community ownership can be an effective way of overcoming market failure for an important segment of the rural non-farm sector. Privatisation proved to be an unimportant part of the explanation for the accelerated growth of this sector. The main factors were establishing a competitive environment in which the enterprises operated, and setting up asset management agencies which had a strong interest in pushing the enterprises to generate profits. China's rural publicly-owned enterprises were a form of 'municipal socialism'. China's local authorities were able in most areas to generate revenue from the rural non-farm sector, so that they were in a better position than might have been the case with privatised small businesses to undertake community welfare expenditures of benefit to the standard of living of the whole local community.

d. Overall results of industrial reform

Three important results of the reforms testify to the drastically increased

Table 6.15   Changes in the share of gross value of industrial production
in selected Chinese provinces (at current prices)

Province/city	Share of GVIO (per cent) in		Share of GVIO produced under different ownership systems*(per cent)			
	1978	1992	State	Collective	Individual	Other
Fujian, Shandong, Guangdong, Jiangsu, Zhejiang	23.8	38.0	31.9	49.2	6.7	12.1
Liaoning, Shanghai, Heilongjiang, Beijing, Tianjin	35.6	21.5	60.3	27.1	3.1	9.6

Notes: *unweighted average

Sources: SSB, *ZGGYJJTJZL*, 1949–84, 1985, p. 144; SSB, *ZGTJZY*, 1992,
p. 71; SSB, *ZGTJNJ*, 1993, pp. 415–16.

impact of market forces on the industrial economy of China after the
late 1970s. Each of them demonstrates the way in which factors of
production had shifted towards industrial activities which yielded a
higher rate of return.

Regional growth   Under the influence of the reforms of the 1980s a
substantial shift occurred in the regional pattern of industrial growth.
Owing to their locational advantages, the returns to industrial investment generally were substantially higher on the east coast (SSB, *ZGTJNJ*,
1990, p. 449). In the 1980s and early 1990s the coastal provinces of
central and southern China achieved exceptionally rapid industrial growth
rates: from 1979 to 1989 the reported growth rates of the gross value
of industrial output (at comparable prices) in Jiangsu, Zhejiang, Fujian
and Guangdong were between 17 per cent and 21 per cent per annum
(SSB, *LSTJZLHB*, 1990, p. 50). The total population of these rapidly
industrialising provinces is around 200 million, i.e. roughly three times
the combined population of the 'Four Little Tigers' (South Korea, Hong
Kong, Singapore and Taiwan) and one-third larger than Brazil. A large
regional shift in the structure of industrial ouptut took place. The share
of the five coastal provinces of Guangdong, Fujian, Zhejiang, Jiangsu,
and Shandong, rose from 22 per cent of total gross value of industrial
output in 1978 to 38 per cent in 1992, while the share of the old core
industrial provinces/cities of Shanghai, Beijing, Tianjin, Liaoniing, fell

from 36 per cent in 1978 to 22 per cent in 1992 (Table 6.15). The fastest growing provinces were those with the highest shares of non-state industry (Table 6.15).

Equalisation in profitability betweeen industrial sectors　At the start of the reform process, profit rates (profits and taxes relative to capital stock) among the 37 industrial sectors varied widely. By the late 1980s a dramatic reduction in the dispersion of sectoral profit rates had occurred. Naughton estimates that the coefficient of variation of industrial profit rates among industrial sectors fell from 0.78 in 1980 to 0.44 in 1989 (Naughton, 1992, p. 28). He argues that this sharp alteration was mainly attributable to much reduced barriers to entry to higher profitability activities, driving down the rate of profit in these sectors.

Equalisation of rates of return between the state and the collective sector　Research by Jefferson *et al.* (1992) suggests that there was a 'modest shift towards intersectoral convergence of returns to capital and labour' between the state and collective industrial sector during the reform:

> Industrial reform has brought a new system of profit retention and encouraged the development of formal and informal sources of investment capital outside the state planning system. These changes have allowed collective firms and small state enterprises to augment their stocks of capital rapidly despite their limited access to government funds. This process has narrowed differences between the capital intensity of small and large enterprises and contributed to the convergence of intersectoral factor returns (Jefferson *et al.*, 1992, p. 256).

6.2.9　Conclusion

a. The political-economic setting of the institutional reforms

Political stability　The maintenance of political stability was an obsession for the reforming government. The price of this was continued commitment to the old political institutions, chiefly the vast communist party. This inevitably produced a great deal of corrupt behaviour by officials. However, the maintenance of political stability under the communist party had positive consequences for economic performance. It enabled the state to remain comparatively effective fiscally. The achievement of political stability under communist party rule meant that the rules that governed the organisation of the economy were reasonably predictable. Investors might have to deal with a thicket of bureaucrats but, once agreed, contractual arrrangements were reasonably secure.

Clarity of reform strategy   The broad features of the reform strategy could be perceived fairly clearly from early on. From the late 1980s through to the early 1990s the Chinese government never wavered in its commitment to experimentalism in reform, with priority to pragmatic pursuit of policies that would lead to successful growth of output and incomes. Therefore, economic agents were confronted by a reasonably stable set of parameters upon which to base their decisions.

Ethical underpinnings   Throughout the reform period the government sustained a public commitment to key values. The first of these was nationalism. In striking contrast to the countries of Eastern Europe and the former Soviet Union, the former collectivist values were not abandoned in favour of individualism. On the contrary, policy after policy was publicly justified in the interests of building a powerful country. Repeatedly, the interests of the individual and different social groups were subordinated to those of overall national prosperity.

A second consistent core value was public commitment to 'socialism'. The crude belief that equated socialism with the non-market, command economy was jettisoned early on in the reforms. Thereafter, increasingly, 'socialism' came to be indentified with two concepts. Firstly, planning for economic growth through the use of markets. Secondly, combining individual incentives with preventing the rise of a dominant capitalist class with a large concentration of individual wealth and, conversely, providing opportunities to those in less advantageous socio-economic positions. These values, and the fact that they were moderately effectively put into practice in a variety of policies, helped ensure that during the reform period there was a reasonably effective trickle down of the benefits of growth. Also, in the sharpest contrast to the rupture of old values in the USSR, some sense of 'social coherence' was maintained during the reform period. This benefitted popular welfare directly through its psychological impact. It also helped cement social stability through giving citizens a sense of participation in a common endeavour.

China's class structure under reform may be thought of as evolving towards a kind of bureaucratic market economy, in which individual incentives were harnessed predominantly within a collective framework and the state stood at the centre of the accumulation process. One symbol of this public institution-based market economy is the fact that still in 1993 it is estimated that 99 per cent of Chinese automobile imports were paid for by institutional expense accounts (Yan, 1994, p. 67).

Inflation   The final part of the environment within which the reforms occurred, was the government's approach towards inflation. On the one hand the government was not prepared to sacrifice growth to the pursuit of zero inflation. However, it was equally concerned not to allow the rate of inflation to rise to a level sufficient to threaten social stability and to divert investment into speculation away from investment in physical assets. The result was a pattern of fluctuating growth out of the command economy, with the government prepared to intervene sharply to lower inflation, primarily through direct controls on government expenditure, once the rate crossed a critical threshold. The state's ability to control the inflation rate depended both on the effectiveness of the state apparatus in raising revenue, and its capacity to resist interest group pressure for inflationary increases in state expenditure.

b. Supply

A succession of experimental reforms was put into practice by the Chinese government after the late 1970s. They began in the farm sector, but quickly spread into the 'collective' non-farm sector and gradually began to take effect in the state sector also. Throughout the reform period right up to the present, the government made it clear that the bulk of property would remain in some form of public ownership. It sought to improve the way in which assets were used through contractual arrangements that devolved control over the 'use rights' (*shiyong quan*) for public property in return for income sharing along agreed lines. Once specified these use rights provided a reasonable degree of security to the party contracting to use the assets. The contract arrangement provided economic agents with a reasonably secure prospect in respect to the division of the income stream from the use of the publicly owned assets. Price liberalisation proceed cautiously along dual track lines with final liberalisation for capital goods only completed in the early 1990s. Simultaneous with this went a gradual liberalisation of the material supply system. However, even in the early 1990s, domestic producers remained substantially shielded from the effects of foreign competition.

These gradually introduced, experimental, supply-side reforms to the command economy contributed to improvements in labour productivity and incomes in various ways. At every level both of state administration and management of assets, profits became an important goal. Those who were directly responsible for the management of assets began to have an interest in squeezing more value added from the stock of fixed assets under their control, and in reducing the stock of working capital per unit of output. A growing proportion of new investment found its way towards projects yielding higher returns. Thus, at the margin, capital began to move towards those regions, sectors and enterprises that yielded higher returns. Not only did the returns from investment improve, but the rate of savings and investment was sustained at a high level. Many factors contributed to this. These included: the country's political stability; relatively low inflation; the large opportunities for making profits in a rapidly restructuring economy (e.g. the service sector, transport and housing); the large potentiality for employing poorly used existing resources in more profitable ways than before; and the virtuous circle of high demand growth. From extreme technical backwardness, China began to generate rapid technical progress. This was achieved, firstly, through fast growth of export earnings. This in turn enabled rapid growth of imports of technology enhancing products, for which the government allowed priority in its import controls. A second factor was the increased incentive for domestic producers to achieve technical progress themselves.[104] A third, increasingly important, part of the process was technology absorbed through private foreign investment.

The shift towards markets and profits caused large changes in the allocation of the workforce over the course of the reforms. A core of workers remained in state enterprises, with a rump of them located in loss-making enterprises, which the state continued to subsidise rather than risk the social explosion which would follow from their closure. However, even within the state sector important shifts occured, with new entrants and part of the existing workforce being drawn in to employment in those substantial number of state enterprises where output was growing rapidly, and into those areas and sectors that were attracting relatively large amounts of capital. Moreover, large changes took place in the overall structure, as workers were pulled into long neglected sectors such as small non-farm business. A large part of even the non-farm workforce was non-unionised. The 'Lewis model' of growth was able to operate with fast growth of non-farm employment generating large surpluses per worker for reinvestment, unhindered in much of the labour market by insitutional restrictions on conditions of employment.

c. Demand

Throughout the reform period the Chinese economy remained highly protected. Domestic producers could be certain that, for a long period ahead, their only serious competitors in most spheres were from within China itself. The nature of domestic demand altered greatly during the reform period. As domestic markets gradually liberalised, consumers of all products were able to chose more and more freely, and became progressively more discriminating purchasers. This applied most obviously in consumer goods markets. The quality of a wide range of consumer goods rose in obvious ways during the reforms, many of which could not be captured by statistics. The command economy led to such well-known problems as a narrowing of product range, negligible progress in the design of the product, low reliability of consumer durables, and large stocks of unwanted goods. These processes began to reverse in the reform period. Consumers used the market to express their preference for products that were in some way considered to be superior, and increasingly profit-seeking producers began to respond. Simply looking at the raw data on clothing production, for example, impressive as the growth had been, cannot adequately convey the extent of the welfare improvement consequent upon the reforms. However, these demand changes were not confined only to consumer goods production. The same processes began also to affect the production of capital goods. As market forces slowly began to take effect, so the purchasers of capital goods began to shift their demand to those products that in some way were considered to represent better value for money. The enterprises that prospered and grew fastest tended to be those that produced products that were in some sense, whether price, design, durability or energy consumption, considered to be superior.

The increases in labour productivity over the reform period generated by the experimental reforms enabled large increases in personal income to take place. These in turn stimulated a high rate of increase in demand for consumer goods and services. In the early 1980s, a large rise occurred in demand for food grain, with considerable improvements in the quality of grain, away from coarse grain towards 'superior' grains. As incomes rose, demand for superior foodstuffs took over from grain as the main source of increased demand for food produce. Demand for housing was sustained at a high level throughout the reform period. All communist economies could have expected this to have been a large source of demand growth if they had been able to generate increases in personal income, since housing was so consistently sacrificed to other goals under the command economy. In the early phase of the reforms the main source of increased demand for industrial consumer goods was relatively simple consumer durables, such as bicyles, radios, black and white TVs, fans, and sewing machines. As the reforms progressed, demand growth shifted to a new wave of industrial products, such as colour TVs, refrigerators, hi-fi equipment, mobile phones, motor vehicles, air conditioners and fashion clothing. Meeting this huge, fast-growing demand mainly from domestic producers induced corresponding investment in the farm sector and in the light industries.

However, in a mainly closed economy, meeting the demand for these products necessititated a large, corresponding rise in demand for capital goods and intermediate inputs. Demand from domestic producers for such products as steel, cement, chemicals, chemical fibres, plastics, a wide variety of machinery, and transport equipment, all grew in leaps and bounds in the reform period.

Thus, a constant symbiosis between supply and demand occurred in the Chinese reform. Incremental institutional changes released the latent productive potentialities embedded in the Chinese economy, as it was in all the communist economies. This allowed initial growth of income. This in turn generated demand for both consumer and capital goods. This stimulated the growth of investment in these activities. This in turn allowed modernisation of the capital stock and improvements in labour productivity. This in turn started the cycle again stimulating further rises in demand, investment and productivity. The economy was, in the words of one commentator, 'growing out of the plan'.[105]

7 Reform in Russia

7.1 INTENSIFICATION OF THE PROBLEMS IN SOVIET POLITICAL ECONOMY UNDER GORBACHEV

7.1.1 Politics

a. Risk assessment

The USSR entered the 1980s with an aged leadership.[1] The new generation of leaders which came to power in the mid-1980s had grown up entirely during the Soviet period and had not experienced the turbulence of the first phase of Soviet industrialisation. The bulk of their working life had been conducted in the relative stability of post-war recovery, post-Stalinist growth and, finally, post-Krushchev stagnation. They had not experienced an economy and society in disintegration. They could only imagine that the Soviet Union's reforms might lead to more or less rapid progress. It was beyond their comprehension that their policy initiatives might be responsible, in only a few years, for the disintegration, humiliation and impoverishment of their country. This contrasts strikingly with the high degree of risk aversion on the part of the Chinese leadership after the death of Mao Zedong.

b. Perestroika and the relationship between political and economic reform

In the early months in power, it apeared that Gorbachev was content to work within the traditional political set-up, attempting to introduce new, though still half thought-out, measures under continued communist party rule. However, in his first year in office he became convinced that serious economic reform necessitated a prior transformation of political life.

A key intellectual influence on Gorbachev was the 'New Thinking' (*novoe myshlenie*), which had begun to develop in the institutes of the Academy of Sciences under Andropov in the early 1980s (Miller, 1993, Chapter 4). This research was characterised by a new freedom to study foreign ideas. It was influenced deeply by the social sciences in the

USA. Contacts developed rapidly between leading Soviet and American research personnel and institutions. Many of the core of policy advisors to Gorbachev had spent time in the leading American institutions such as Harvard and Columbia. There they absorbed the orthodox perspective of mainstream American social science. A central conception of the New Thinking was that economic and political reform were inextricably interlinked. Alexander Yakovlev, the effective head of Party ideology and one of the principal architects of *perestroika* alongside Gorbachev,[2] subsequently argued:

We need a real economic reform and a free national economy. By dismantling the state monopoly, such a free economy will support freedom of thought and defend *glasnost* and democracy through the common sense of its development. Society will gain the effect of a synergism of politics and the economy. Without them, the moving force of democracy will be weak and incapable of clearing the space of our existence from the rubble of re-feudalism and newly animated idol worship. In whatever form, it will be hideous and inhuman. (Yakovlev, 1993, p. 79)

The mainstream American social science view in the 1980s was deeply hostile to the role of the state beyond the simplest of interventions to cope with limited areas of market failure. It was strongly supportive of the intrinsic value of Western liberal-democratic insitutions in all countries, whatever the level of development or problems they confronted.

Only in recent years has a 'New Political Economy' begun to gain a toehold in the mainstream of US social science, seeing a more complex role for the state in its evaluation of the historical record of the advanced capitalist countries themselves and in re-analysing the achievements of the successful Asian economies since the late nineteenth century (e.g. Deyo (ed.), 1987). Even today this is not the mainstream view. The mainstream orthodoxy was deeply opposed to the communist value system, which was hostile to private property, the profit motive and competitive individualism, and supported the ideals of co-operation and equality. A vast outpouring of critical works on Soviet economic performance was produced by the US Sovietological industry, most notably the stream of publications from the US Congress Joint Economic Committee.

These were based on high levels of scholarship. They were valuable descriptively. However, almost without exception, none of them explicitly addressed the question of how the Soviet system might best be transformed or towards what model the USSR might move should serious reform get under way. The underlying perspective of this mass of writing was that the only alternative to the Soviet system was that of the USA. In other words, there was an implicit policy recommendation that the only feasible approach towards changing the deep problems of the Soviet economy and political system was to leap straight into the Western (i.e. American) form of politics and economics.

An important part of the 'New Thinking' group, strongly influenced by the intellectual input from the US, concluded that the Soviet system was simply bankrupt and needed to be demolished. The account which the former head of Soviet ideology, Yakovlev (1993, especially pp. 70–80), gives of his own views of the Soviet Union is comprehensively bleak:

> From the perspective of history [Bolshevism] is a system of social lunacy, which physically destroyed the peasantry, noble and merchant classes, and whole classes of entrepereneurs along with the clergy, intellectuals, and intelligentsia. It is a sower of crosses in graveyards, it is the 'mole of history', digging mass graves from Lvov to Magadan, from Norilsk to Kushka; it is an exploitation of human beings by all forms of oppression and ecological vandalism. . . . Bolshevism is a land mine of monstrous power that almost blew up the world; it is an anti-human precept, hammered in with the ruthlessness of an ideological fanaticism that conceals its intellectual and economic nullity. (Yakovlev, 1993, p. 70)

Moreover, in Yakovlev's account as in that of the New Thinking overall, there was a complete absence of any sense of a transitional strategy. There was simply disgust with the existing system, and a deep, wholly uncritical admiration for the economic and political achievements of the 'West', which was taken to mean principally the USA rather than Germany or Japan, let alone Sweden. The decades of Bolshevik rule were viewed as a disastrous mistake. The USA was thought to have 'won' the Cold War and its sustained criticism been proved correct by history.

Gorbachev was heavily influenced by this perspective. A central thrust of his *perestroika* policy was that it would enable the USSR to return to world civilisation. Miller's meticulous account sums up the impact of this group upon Gorbachev as follows :

Gorbachev was unusual in that he saw and accepted the logic of human rights dissent, that it falsified the central assumptions of the regime he comanded. This 'New Thinking' of course, . . . was not his work alone. His contribution was to bring together the isolated and alienated intellectuals who orginated it, *to turn a dissident subculture into a policy and to work out a strategy for realising it.* (Miller, 1993, p. 206) (Emphasis added).

Indeed, the very word *glasnost* has a strong association with dissident culture. The Russian word for 'openness' is usually *otkrovennost*, while the word *glasnost* was used by dissident critics of the Soviet regime in respect to the 'making public of things formerly kept hidden', especially in relation to human rights abuses and the official distortions of Soviet history (Yakovlev, 1993, p. 103, footnote).

Nothing in Gorbachev's background prior to his election to the post of General Secretary of the Soviet Communist Party in March 1985 suggested a person who was to lead the USSR away from communism. Miller considers that prior to Gorbachev's becoming General Secretary he was simply one of a group of 'impatient "Young Turk" court officials', who was 'a representative of the Soviet ruling class', and shared many of its limitations (Miller, 1993, p. 64). In Miller's view, there is little evidence that Gorbachev's law degree or the ethnic diversity of the Soviet Union had had much impact on his thinking. Gorbachev was 'conventional in his use of patronage to gain advancement and muster political support' (Miller, 1993, p. 65). Neither Gorbachev's contact with the the ideas of the agricultural economist Nikonov, nor with researchers in Andropov's 'think tank', nor the in-house analysis of Polish Solidarity, in which Gorbachev as a full Politburo member must have taken part, left any noticeable mark on the way in which Gorbachev conducted his occupancy of the agricultural portfolio (Miller, 1993, pp. 64–7).

None of the serious studies of the Gorbachev period is certain whether he developed his revolutionary views during his first year in office, or whether 'he was always always a nonconformist in private, waiting to throw off his conventional mask' (Miller, 1993, p. 65). What is certain is that the first year or so saw little shift in policy compared to his most influential immediate predecessor and patron, Andropov. Standard histories of the Gorbachev years look back upon the spring and summer of 1986 as the critical turning point in Gorbachev's thinking:

The prima facie evidence is that he did not change until after the 1986 Party Congress. His earliest policies after he became General

Secretary were standard Soviet policies, piecemeal and reactive. The merging of ministries to create a giant State Agro-Industrial Committee showed a traditional belief in reorganisation as a panacea. The campaign against alcohol addressed symptoms but not the cause. The new versions of the Party Programme and Rules and his speeches to the April Plenum and 27th Congress were cautious and unadventurous. . . . It was only some time after this that an evolution in his public statements began to be noticed. (Miller, 1993, p. 65)[3]

It was only in the summer of 1986 that the distinctive features of the campaign for *glasnost* and *perestroika* made their appearance:

> In the summer of 1986 it became clear that Gorbachev had changed strategy. . . . He turned to *perestroika* of the political system and his language was radicalised. Now, Gorbachev put the emphasis on democratisation and struggle with the resistance against reform'. (Aslund, 1991, p. 33)

None of the commentators is certain of the degree to which this period saw a change in Gorbachev's thinking as opposed to the making public of thoughts he had held for some time. However, they are agreed that the Chernobyl nuclear accident played a critical role in the move towards his public espousal of *glasnost*. Miller evaluates the change in his thinking and its relationship to Chernobyl as follows:

> I would argue that the evolution apparent in his public statements after 1985 represents a real evolution in thinking. . . . Overall one has the impression of a person thinking aloud, needing to think aloud in order to progress, and not afraid of sounding unconvincing. . . . I believe he learned intensively on the job, acquiring by 1987–88 a qualitatively different, and much more impressive grasp of the task he faced and of the implications and inter-relatedness of their solutions. We should ask what kind of catalyst might have stimulated this learning? . . . [T]he nuclear disaster at Chernobyl stands out as the most likely challenge. . . . It is as if he crossed a personal Rubicon some time in early May [1986]. (Miller, 1993, pp. 64–70, 'The impact of office')

Hosking's standard reference work on Soviet history (Hosking, 1992, p. 457) also considers that the Chernobyl accident played a key role in the push towards *glasnost* in the summer of 1986:

[D]uring the summer and autumn of 1986, a real change took place, gradually but unmistakably, not just in the style but in the substance of Gorbachev's policies. . . . [T]he emphasis shifted radically from merely tightening up the system to changing it radically. . . . It may be that the explosion in the nuclear power station at Chernobyl in April 1986 was a turning point, dramatising as it did the mortally dangerous defects of a centrally administered economy with such secretive and slovenly irresponsibility. Chernobyl certainly brought home the damage wrought by restricted *glasnost* in arousing both hostility abroad and panic at home. (Hosking, 1992, p. 457)

There was great resistance to economic reform among both the Soviet Party leadership and the rank and file of Party members. However, this was so in China also as it began its post-Mao reform programme in the late 1970s. In neither case was there a clear conception of how the reform process should proceed. Many people within both sets of leaderships were fearful of the consequences of economic reform. It is debatable whether at the start of the reform process the balance of forces for and against more serious reform of the economy was any different in the respective leadership camps in the two countries. Instead of attempting gradually to introduce a programme of economic reform which would slowly win round more of the leadership and the Party rank and file to the benefits of eventual serious reform, Gorbachev made the fateful decision to push ahead with political reform prior to major economic reform. High-level opposition to the policy of *glasnost* was disarmed temporarily by the humiliation caused by the Chernobyl explosion.

Gorbachev's classic work *Perestroika* (Gorbachev, 1988) is vacuous. The contrast with the clarity of vision and firmness of purpose in the speeches of Deng Xiaoping in the late 1970s (a comparable time in China's reform programme) is dramatic. It is overshadowed by the desire to appear 'modern' and 'Western'. The book is devoid of concrete, clear policy proposals. Instead the loose concept of *perestroika* provided an open-ended invitation to all segments of society to question the legitimacy of the existing system. Writing at the beginning of the Soviet reform process, Gorbachev expressed his hopes as follows:

The main idea of the January [1986] Plenary Meeting – as regards ways of accomplishing the tasks of *perestroika* and protecting society from a repetition of errors of the past – was the development of democracy. It is the principal guarantee of the ireversibility of

perestroika. The more socialist democracy there is, the more socialism we will have. This is our firm conviction, and we will not abandon
it. We will promote democracy in the economy, in politics and within
the Party itself. The creativity of the masses is the decisive force in
perestroika. There is no other more powerful force. (Gorbachev, 1988,
p. 63)

c. Glasnost

The most immediately tangible result of *perestroika* was hugely increased freedom of information, broadcasting, and publishing. In the
ideological ferment of the late 1980s a swathe of new organisations
emerged. An explosively rapid acceleration occurred in the development of a genuinely independent civil society. Tens of thousands of
informal groups (*neformaly*) emerged. A wide range of quasi-political
groups, from the ultra-left to the ultra-right, quickly developed. A
powerful Green Movement sprang into life revealing the full extent of
the Soviet ecological disaster. Long oppressed religions emerged into
the light of day. A massive reassessment of Soviet history began,
examining such fundamental questions as the real extent and causes of
the Great Famine of the early 1930s (Davies, 1989). Open, independent workers' movements were formed. Unprecedented waves of strikes
occurred during the Gorbachev years, transforming industrial relations.
   These developments in turn interacted in a vicious circle (or a virtuous one, depending on one's perspective) with the rapid decline in the
confidence and effectiveness of the communist party. The rising tide
of criticism rapidly undermined the party's self confidence and capacities. The growth of civil society quickly filled the rapidly growing
vacuum being vacated by the Party. The contrast with China in the
1980s is very strong indeed. There, despite the ferment of new ideas
that accompanied the development of the market economy, the Party
leadership resolutely tried to sustain the confidence and effectiveness
of the Party organisation. Within all institutions the Party remained an
effective weapon. A succession of campaigns was waged against 'spiri-
tual pollution' to maintain the intellectual class under Party control.
'Democracy Wall' in Beijing was closed down and leading dissidents
such as Wei Jingsheng were given long jail sentences.
   A fitting symbol of the degree of transformation of the climate of
Soviet intellectual life was provided in 1990 at the May Day Parade,
which in the past had been the scene of the annual well ordered review of Soviet military might:

The columns included members of the Hare Krishna religious sect and anarcho-syndicalists, social democrats and anti-Stalinists and, at the front, a monk from the Russian orthodox monastery at Zagorsk, who held up a nearly life-size representation of Christ on the cross, and called out to Gorbachev [standing on the podium overlooking Red Square] "Michael Sergeyevich, Christ is risen". (*IHT*, 2 May 1990)

d. Destroying the Communist Party

In the early phase of *perestroika* it seems that Gorbachev had not yet decided to launch an attack on the Party. Whatever his early intentions may have been, the rapid development of the 'informal groups' (*neformaly*) had far-reaching consequences for the Party: 'By tolerating or encouraging *neformaly* he [Gorbachev] had an instrument for mobilising society that bypassed the Party. Give them *glasnost* and they were able to create a climate in which every Party worker became "a bureaucrat who stops people living well"' (Miller, 1993, p. 128).

By the spring of 1988 it had become clear that Gorbachev had indeed changed his mind. He led a direct assault on the most fundamental principle of Leninism, namely the leading role of the communist party. The most important of several large changes initiated in that year was the commitment to establish a parliament chosen by free, competitive elections, which would approve or reject legislation and appoint and dismiss the executive. The impact of this decision and its implementation in 1989 was revolutionary. Miller summarises its impact as follows:

> What became generally obvious after the 1989 elections will have been dawing on alert or well-informed Party members since 1988 at the latest: contested voting in elections and parliament was incompatible with *nomenklatura* practices; free parliamentary voting on issues was incompatible with Party steering and discipline and, therefore, with democratic centralism; constitutional review must mean (at the very least) publicity for hitherto secret operations. (Miller, 1993, p. 84)

The elections of 1989 were a momentous event. Although still a large majority of those elected were communist party members, many important party figures were defeated: 'here was was a symbolic humiliation that cut deep: it included a clean sweep of the top officials in cities like Moscow, Leningrad, Kiev, Minsk, Kemerovo or Alma Ata' (Miller, 1993, p. 116).

Moreover, the transformation in the Soviet Union was taking place against the background of revolution in Eastern Europe in 1989. This was itself a direct consequence of *perestroika*. The unleashing of *perestroika* in the USSR had produced a similar impact on social consciousness in Eastern Europe. Moreover, Gorbachev's wish for the USSR to 'return to world civilisation' dictated that the Soviet Union should make it clear that it would not intervene as it had done in 1968. The dramatic toppling of the communist party in country after country provide the final push to the rapidly waning confidence of the Soviet Communist Party.

In February 1990 the CPSU formally ended its monopoly of power, with the elimination of Article VI from the Constitution. No longer was the Communist Party to be 'the leading and guiding force of Soviet society and the nucleus of its political system, of all state organisation and public organisation'. No longer would the Party 'determine the general perspectives of the development of society, and the course of home and foreign policy of the USSR', nor would it 'direct the great construction work of the Soviet people, and impart a planned and systematic character and theroretically substantiated character to their struggle for the victory of communism'.

Immediately afterwards, a new, non-Party position of President of the Soviet Union was created. The President was given sweeping powers along the lines of the US Constitution to dismiss ministers of government, to suspend the working of acts of government, to issue presidential decrees, and to delay legislation for the Supreme Soviet. Gorbachev was elected to this position by the Congress of People's Deputies in March 1990, completing his transition from Party to civilian head of state.[4]

The attack on the Party by Gorbachev recalls the Chinese Cultural Revolution. This parallel was not far from Gorbachev's mind. Early in the process of *perestroika*, in a speech on the subject in October 1987 he had said:

> When I put the matter this way, I do not want it to be understood as an appeal – as was once the case during the years of the Cultural Revolution in China – to bombard the headquarters. No, comrades, that would be a serious mistake. (Quoted in Miller, 1993, p. 82)

In fact, Gorbachev's revolution was to prove even more effective than the Cultural Revolution in demolishing communist party rule. Miller's careful assessment concludes: *'[T]he prima facie evidence is compelling that he deliberately made trouble for the Party: that he criticised it, encouraged opposition to it, weakened it, and then cast it aside'* (Miller, 1993, p. 127) (Added emphasis). At a meeting of leading Party officials in July 1989 Gorbachev mocked the meeting for its trepidations about the changes they were witnessing:

> Revolution isn't comfortable. . . . We summoned [it] up by our own policy. Do you mean to say we didn't understand that when we considered it? . . .' Some comrades are treating the transfer of power to the Soviets as amounting to the collapse of the universe. Even if one concedes its a collapse, then its the collapse of a warped universe. (Quoted in Miller, 1993, p. 129)

The way in which he ridiculed hesitant comrades irresistibly recalls Chairman Mao's treatment of this own nervous comrades prior to collectivisation in 1955: 'An upsurge in the new socialist mass movement is imminent throughout the countryside. But some of our comrades, tottering along like a woman with bound feet, are complaining all the time, "You're going too fast, much too fast"' (Mao, 1955, p. 184).

The bureaucracy holds the key to any attempt to modernise and undertake a programme of large structural change. China and the USSR each was ruled by a huge, deeply conservative bureaucracy, with the communist party at its core. There were only two possible lines of reform. One was to attempt gradually to alter the nature of the Party through a programme of retirements, professionalisation, slimming down, and reorientation of Party work towards indirect rather than direct intervention in socio-economic affairs. This required a substantial period of time and a great deal of patient work by a clear-sighted leadership. The alternative was to attempt quickly to alter the behaviour of the bureaucracy by rapidly opening it up to public scrutiny, accountability and popular pressure. Gorbachev's reform programme resulted in just such an outcome. It was applauded universally by a chorus of Western social scientists and politicians:

> A reform reduces the power of the bureaucracy by definition, and most of the administration will inevitably oppose reform. Therefore, a succesful reform must break the power of the anti-reform bureaucracy. . . . *To break the power of the party and state bureaucracy might be seen as the key problem of a reform. It is difficult to perceive any other solution than a far reaching democratisation with a*

strong popular pressure and openness balancing the bureaucracy. Moreover, some degree of institutional pluralism is necesssary if enterprise directors are to dare to make independent decisions. Any well-functioning economy presupposes flows of reasonably correct information, which are difficult to achieve without a rather open society with independent criticism of incorrect data'. (Aslund, 1991, p. 14) (Emphasis added)

It is not obvious that it would have been impossible for Gorbachev to devise a coalition of reformers at the top of the Party. The very fact of the selection of Gorbachev as Party leader indicated that 'a majority of the Politburo had concluded that more vigorous reforms were unavoidable if further economic decline was to be prevented' (Smith, 1993, p. 99). In the mid-1980s, prior to Gorbachev's election as general secretary, a perceptive commentator such as Stephen Cohen recognised the serious possibility of a reform coalition emerging at the top of the Party:

Successful reform from above ... requires a coalition between reformers and conservatives in Soviet officialdom. ... Such a coalition is not impossible. A Czech Communist official remarked during the Prague Spring, 'The boundary between progressive and conservative runs through each of us' ... *Signs that such a consensus for change may be forming in the Soviet Union have already appeared*, largely in response to commonly perceived problems of a degraded countryside, declining industrial productivity, and social epidemics of alcoholism, abortion, and divorce. (Cohen, 1986, p. 156) (Emphasis added)

Naturally, a coalition would have needed to limit itself initially to the common ground of cautious reform policies. This was the case in China too, but, eventually, the evidence from the reform pushed the centre of gravity of the reform coalition in a more radical direction. This needed time and patience, not a 'great leap'.

Miller's evaluation of Gorbachev is representative of a wide body of informed Western social science opinion:

As for the end of the CPSU, this can already be seen as a major political accomplishment. ... [T]he mono-organisational Party has been broken and there seems little chance of such a power being reimposed. ... *This was surely Gorbachev's finest achievement.* (Miller, 1993, p. 205) (Emphasis added)

Yakovlev echoes Miller's judgement that there was nothing 'inevitable' about the transformation wrought under Gorbachev, but rather that the change was policy induced from the top down:

> [T]he turn towards glasnost *was not inevitable in those years. It was dictated more by the philosophy of* perestroika *and its initiators than by immediate necessity.* . . . The idea of *perestroika* had long been fermenting in the minds of intellectuals. But it began to be implemented by people belonging to the top echelon of the Party hierarchy. . . . [T]he object of change remained the Pary itself and all that it had created over the decades, most of all the state with its absolutist domination over society. (Yakovlev, 1993, pp. 104 and 212) (Emphasis added)

e. Nationalism

Arguably the most potent effect of *perestroika* was in destroying the very geopolitical integrity of the Soviet state. *Glasnost* legitimated the rise of publicly expressed nationalist sentiments. It allowed the public airing of a mass of grievances against the central authorities, opening publicly long-hidden wounds of mistreatment of the constituent nationalities of the Soviet state. The effect was all the more searing, since these events had been hidden from public discussion for so long. The decline in the Party's will and capacity to rule, provided an increasingly uncontrolled setting within which these sentiments could grow. An important area in which the informal groups (*neformaly*) grew in the late 1980s was in nationalist Popular Fronts opposed to central rule. Criticism of the history of the communist authorities' treatment of the the nationalities grew ever more intense. The Republican elections of 1990 resulted in certain cases in outright defeat for the communist party, and in many cases in substantial anti-communist, anti-Unionist representation in the new regional parliamentary assemblies. The rise of nationalist sentiment was given room to grow by Gorbachev's tolerance of the legitimacy of debate about redefining the relationship between the centre and the republics. Again, there is sharp contrast with the resolution with which the Chinese leadership in the reform period refused to countenance any redefinition of the political nature of the Chinese state's relationship with the provinces.[5]

A final forceful twist to the growth of nationalism was provided by the decision in 1990 to permit competitive elections for newly established parliamentary institutions in each of the constituent republics of the Soviet Union. The elections themselves and the subsequent parliamentary debates provided a hot-house atmosphere within which nationalist ideas could develop. Quentin Peel of the *Financial Times* reported the situation in the following terms:

> It is impossible to describe the turmoil in the Soviet Republics and among its nationalities in other than dramatic terms. . . . In the past three years the unshakeable unity of the Soviet state, the project of creating *homo sovieticus*, the central grip by Party and ministries on the economies and societies of the fifteen republics and 100 ethnic groups have been weakened to the point where these concepts and powers can no longer either be invoked or used, except *in extremis* as when Azeris and Armenian kill each other. (*Financial Times*, 12 March 1990)

The move towards disintegration of the USSR was given its final twist by the 'turn to the right' in the final months of the life of the Soviet Union. Having presided over the virtual destruction of the Soviet state which he inherited, at the eleventh hour, in 1991, Gorbachev supported a last ditch attempt to reassert central control, with retrenchment of economic reform, a new prominence to the military and the KGB in political life and an attempt to re-establish central government authority over the mass media. The movement culminated in the August coup, which attempted to establish a military government of national emergency. It wished to halt the passage of the Union Treaty (which would have turned the USSR into a loosely federal state from a unified state) and to reverse the programme of economic and political reform. The defeat of the coup resulted in an acceleration of the very process it had been designed to halt. The Communist Party was suspended. A new head of the KGB was appointed with the brief to dismantle it. The move of the constituent republics towards full independence occurred at high speed, as most of the Republics announced themselves to be fully independent states. The Soviet Union formally ceased to exist on 1 January 1992, shortly after Gorbachev's resignation as President.

The contrast with China is striking. The Chinese government waged a prolonged and bloody struggle against nationalist opposition in Tibet. Moreover, an important part of China's international relations in the reform period was dominated by the desire to *expand* the internationally accepted borders of the country to include Hong Kong and Taiwan. National unity was not so much a policy goal as an obsession of the Chinese government. China's violent actions to maintain national unity incurred wrathful condemnation from the international community. The advanced capitalist countries conveniently forgot their own violent struggles to create and maintain national unity. They turned a blind eye to equally violent state actions to maintain national unity in 'democratic' India.

The failed coup of August 1991 resulted in a massive transfer of power away from Moscow and formal establishment of independence for the former constituent republics of the USSR, most of which had been a part of Imperial Russia since at least the middle of the nineteenth century. From a country with fifteen constituent republics and 290 million people, 'Russia' was reduced to a country of 150 million people, and fourteen newly independent states were established. This is no more 'natural' a process than would be the break-up of India into many separate countries corresponding to historically separate political units and linguistic groups, or than the split of the USA into two separate states would have been in the nineteeenth century, had the North not fought a bloody and successful war to maintain the state of the union.

7.1.2 Economics

a. Economic Ideology

The Soviet leadership in the mid-1980s had no first-hand understanding of a market economy. The USSR's adversary in the Cold War was the USA. The USA stood at the forefront of the consciousness of Soviet policy-makers as the epitome of capitalist economics and politics. Moreover, American social science and funding dominated thinking in non-communist politics and economics, from academic journals through to the international institutions, notably the IMF and the World Bank. In the 1970s the mainstream of US-dominated social science thinking moved even further towards an anti-state position. Only in the late 1980s and 1990s, under the impact of the collapse of the USSR and the rise of China, to add to the success of Japan and the East Asian Newly Industrialising Countries, did the mainstream of American social science begin to realise that the role of the state is more complex than it was confidently portrayed as being in the 1970s and 1980s.

Soviet intellectuals were reluctant to consider East Asia as having any relevance to their own policy formation. A charitable view would suggest that this was mainly on account of their historical relationship with China: 'As the leader of the Socialist bloc, most Soviet officials did not like the idea of copying the Chinese. . . . Until about mid-1986 the Chinese reforms were bitterly attacked in the Soviet Union' (Goldman, 1992, p. 61). A less charitable, but probably more accurate, view, would attribute this to little short of racism.[6] Most Russians were reluctant to believe that any of the East Asian countries, Japan included, were in any way superior to them, and could have much to teach them. They were infatuated with the 'West', especially with the main adversary, the USA.

b. Change within the traditional system

The dominant approach of the early period of Gorbachev's rule was simply to continue the 'pressure' of the Andropov period (1982–4). In investment policy the goal was to force up the rate of investment by reducing the share of consumption. Retirement rates for equipment were to be increased in order to raise the pace of modernisation and the share of investment allocated to new machinery. Industrial technical progress was supposed to be accelerated by raising the share of investment allocated to machine building. As a result of this campaign 'shortages' and hoarding intensified. Product quality deteriorated still further (Aslund, 1991, pp. 75–7).

A severe anti-alcohol campaign was launched. Its successful prosecution testifies to the continuing power of the Party as an administrative mechanism. From 1985 to 1987 alcohol sales fell by 60 per cent. In the short term there was a large fall in alcohol-related crimes and accidents, and a big decline in drinking at work.

The successive attempts since the 1960s to reform the economy through more 'pressure' (see above) had resulted in a steady long-term decline in product quality. A fierce campaign to raise product quality by administrative decree began in 1986. However, the disruptive consequences upon the material balance plan of a large rise in rejection rates of substandard output led to the campaign being quickly dropped.

Changes were introduced to the wage system, aimed to raise incentives by widening wage differentials and providing greater rewards to those who made greater 'contributions'. The 'Shchekino' experiment, under which enterprises were allowed to shed labour but retain the same size of wage bill, was popularised.

These changes did nothing to improve the fundamental defects of the Stalinist planning system. They represented the final attempt to reform within the old system: 'The futility of these efforts taught many [people] that the traditional system had reached a dead end and that economic reform was necessary' (Aslund, 1991, p. 88).

c. Beginnings of fundamental system reform[7]

Leadership perspectives

There was wide agreement among the Soviet leadership by 1987–88 that fundamental reform was necessary. However, there was great disagreement and genuine uncertainty about the pace and eventual goal of the transition. This is unsurprising. The range of debate about economic reform closely parallels that which occurred among China's leaders at a comparable time in their reforms, namely around two years after the death of Mao Tsetung, by which point China itself had realised the dead end of reform within the framework of the Stalinist command economy.

Gorbachev and Schevardnadze were on the radical wing in the USSR. However, even they did not envisage a more radical reform than that of Hungary after 1968 or that which China was to put into practice in the 1980s. Indeed, the reform which Schevardnadze pioneered in Georgia in 1972–85 shared many features with those which Zhao Ziyang pioneered in Sichuan province in the late 1970s and early 1980s. Even the 'conservative' wing of the Soviet leadership, including people like Ryzhkov and Ligachev appeared to support fundamental system reform, albeit at a slower pace and with a stronger role for 'socialist' elements such as collective ownership of assets. Indeed, Ryzhkov was the initiator of important reforms, notably in enterprise management, the promotion of joint ventures with foreign capital and the establishment of Special Economic Zones.

Party and economy

From 1987 onwards the leadership drastically reshaped the relationship between the Party and the economy. The official goal became a shift from direct to indirect influence over the economy. A rapid change occurred in central Party personnel, with the promotion of an almost entirely new team of Ministers and key officials in the central economic policy-making apparatus. It was planned to reduce the number of Party cadres involved in economic administration. Indeed, by only 1988 a large reduction occurred in the number of Central Committee departments, from twenty to just nine, had taken place, mainly by pulling officials out of intervention in economic management, and cuts of the same extent were extended to provincial committees (Miller, 1993, p. 128). Moreover, there was a stated committment to professionalise the Party apparatus to enable it to better fulfill its much altered functions.

Enterprise reform

The service experiments These experiments began in 1984, prior to Gorbachev's election, but were allowed to expand rapidly and spread to many parts of the country, becoming widespread in the Baltic provinces and in Georgia. Expansion in the service sector usually required little capital, and filled a huge gap left by the communist command system. Enterprises in this sector were given operational autonomy and were required simply to hand over a contracted share of profits and allowed to retain the rest. Within the service enterprise itself, contracts of different kinds were permitted with subordinate units or even with individuals. The experiment was highly significant: '[It] marked a departure from Brezhnevian economics. *It augured the introduction of a new economic thinking. . . . Experimental co-operatives, leaseholds and individual enterprises were legitimised by the experiment. Its economic results were excellent*' (Aslund, 1991, p. 96) (Emphasis added)

Experiments with self-financing in industry and agriculture The scheme began at Sumy in 1985 and by 1988 it had expanded to enterprises accounting for over 60 per cent of industrial and agricultural output value. Its essence was a contract system, with enterprises allowed to retain a contracted share of profits to be divided into different funds according to centrally determined rules. The participating enterprises still were locked into the material supply system from Gosnab, and faced state-fixed prices. However, these inconsistencies in the reforms aroused new debate prompting calls from economists for reform of the wholesale trade and the price system. It was increasingly realised that reform of the Stalinist economy was a seamless web embracing all the key aspects of the setting in which the enterprise operated.

Agricultural experiments Slow but important progress occurred under Gorbachev in extending a contract system to agriculture. Throughout there was considerable conflict between those in the leadership who wished land to be privatised and those who wished to retain state or collective ownership as in the Chinese case. In some areas, notably the Baltic provinces, leasehold farms developed fast. In 1989 a law on leaseholds was finally passed, allowing long-term leases of 15 years, and giving security of tenure to leaseholders. In 1986 compulsory deliveries were stabilised for a five-year period. Production above the plan and 30 per cent also of the total planned production of potatoes, fruit and vegetables, were allowed to be sold freely by producing units in any market they chose. Compared to the Chinese rural reforms, a large area of policy inadequacy was the failure to provide a clear contract framework for leasehold farmers to have access to the services provided by large lumpy inputs such as crop sprayers, tractors, harvesters, and processing equipment, which are all mostly large scale in Soviet agriculture. Without a clear specification of the conditions under which farmers would have access to these services, it would have been risky for farmers to opt for the leasehold system.

Law on state enterprises   This law was promulgated in July 1987, and complemented by ten decress on major functions of the economic system (including planning, material supplies, prices and banking) all of which potentially affected the way in which the state enterprise operated. Instead of state orders absorbing the whole of the enterprise's productive capacity, the Law was designed to reduce gradually the share of enterprise output pre-empted by state orders. In 1988 Gosplan announced that the goal was to reduce the share of state procurement from enterprises from close to 100 per cent to around 65–75 per cent in 1989, falling to 50–65 per cent in 1990 (Aslund, 1991, p. 129). The failure of Gosplan to proceed as rapidly as the Law had specified gave rise to 'an extraordinary public reaction against Gosplan and the branch ministries for their failure to implement the reform' (Aslund, 1991, p. 128). Indeed, many enterprise refused to accept directives that contradicted the Law. Material supplies via Gosnab were intended to fall gradually. The head of Gosnab in 1985–89 (Voronin) announced in 1987 that the share of output to be distributed through the wholesale trade (i.e. output outside the material balance planning system) would rise from 60 per cent in 1988/90 to 75/80 per cent in 1990/92 (Aslund, 1991, p. 131).

Although Gosnab dragged its feet in implementing the proposal, the agreed direction of movement was clear. Prices were to be reformed via the introduction of a mixed system of centrally fixed prices, negotiated prices, and market-determined prices, though the precise pace and balance between them was left unclear. While the Law raised the possibility of bankruptcy, in fact only a tiny handful of banruptcies occurred. In late 1987 the first joint-stock companies with private ownership emerged. They were essentially joint ventures between the state and shareholders: 'Their foundation had the character of a grassroots movement and was not preceded by any legislation. . . . Surprisingly little ideological resistance surfaced in the Soviet press. On June 19th 1990, the government adopted a statute on joint stock companies' (Aslund, 1991, p. 137).

The international economy
The Ministry of Foreign Trade was deprived of its monopoly in this sphere in 1986, with the appointment of a new minister and an almost clean sweep of top officials (Aslund, 1991, p. 140). By 1988 the rights to engage in foreign trade had been spread over 200 associations, and nearly 2,000 by 1990, with a big rise in the role of local authorities, each trying to promote the foreign trade of 'their' area. From 1986 exporting enterprises were allowed to retain a share (30–50 per cent) of export revenues. A large devaluation of the ruble (70 per cent) took place in 1990. Joint ventures with capitalist countries' firms were permitted from 1986. Gradual experimentation took place in the terms offered to foreign investors, though only 66 joint venture agreements had been concluded by mid-1988.

By the end of the Gorbachev period the USSR had applied to join the GATT and had greatly softened its formerly hostile attitude towards the IMF and the World Bank. By 1990, the relationship between the Soviet government and the main international institutions had altered to such an extent that the IMF, the World Bank, the OECD, and the EBRD were able jointly to 'undertake a detailed study of the Soviet economy, make recommendations for its reform, and establish the criteria under which Western economic assistance could effectively support such reforms' (IMF *et al.*, 1990, p. 1).

Law on individual labour activity
A large private sector had existed in the Soviet economy before Gorbachev came to power. Its main areas were legal rural private plots and private trade, illegal, unregistered provision of private services (repair of cars, appliances, shoes, and houses), and the black market in wholesale trade. It is estimated that as much as 30–40 per cent of personal income came from the private sector. The Law on Individual Labour Activity (1986) marked a large shift in the regime's attitude towards the market economy. It made it legal to operate as an individual entrepreneur in a number of specified fields (notably handicrafts and consumer services): '*An impressively large range of private activities had suddenly become legal*' (Aslund, 1991, p. 165) (Emphasis added). Individuals operating in these sectors had the right legally to purchase materials, to rent work premises, and to charge market prices for their products. Legal private enterprises were liable to only moderate tax rates. By 1989 there were estimated to be over 300,000 legally registered individual workers.

Law on co-operatives

The Law on Co-operatives was passed in May 1988. This was the most liberal piece of legislation of the entire 'reform wave' of 1987–88. The co-operatives had their property rights legally guaranteed. They were self-managed and self-financed. The government encouraged them to compete with state enterprises (Ryzhkov, *Pravda*, 25 May, 1988, quoted in Aslund, 1991, p. 170). They could freely purchase material supplies and sell their output at whatever prices their produce could command. To be formally registered as a co-operative there needed to be a minimum of three members, but there was no ceiling to the maximum number. Hired labour was forbidden technically, but 'this appeared a mere ideological formality, as they could employ an unlimited number of members on a contract basis' (Aslund, 1991, p. 170). The co-operatives were encouraged by lower tax rates on co-operative earnings, but these were paid directly to the local authorities, giving them a strong incentive to encourage the growth of the co-operatives. The Law contained a number of 'amazingly liberal' stipulations, such as permission to co-operatives to issue shares or bonds, to chose banks, to set up banks, to form associations with other co-operatives, and engage in foreign trade.

After just two years of operation under the new terms there were more than 150,000 of them, employing five million people (3.7 per cent of the total workforce). They were already producing perhaps seven per cent of national income. Moroever, the co-operative sector was beginning to attract skilled staff from state factories and government ministries (Miller, 1993, p. 103). This strongly parallels the rapid development of 'collective' enterprises in the 1980s in China.

The rapid growth of co-operatives helped the concept of markets and competition to be accepted by those in the leadership who were still apprehensive about purely private property. In an environment of chronic shortage, co-operatives often were able to take advantage of the huge market imperfections to make large profits: 'As soon as they sense a market somewhere, they rush to that place and start work' (Aslund, 1991, p. 172). Unsurprisingly, a large amount of debate occurred both within the leadership and among the population more generally about the function of co-operatives.

d. Intensification of policy debate

Gorbachev was in power for just six years. The first couple of years were characterised by continued application of the old methods of reform. Serious institutional reform did not begin until 1987–88. The economic reform policies of the following brief period under Gorbachev, outlined above, were cautious and pragmatic. They appeared to be taking Soviet economic institutions down a similar path to that of China at a comparable stage in its reforms, namely, the late 1970s and early 1980s.

Debate about the pace and direction of reform intensified in the final months of Gorbachev's rule. The arguments for a continuation of the incremental reform path were summarised in the Abalkin programme of October 1989 and its successor, the programme produced jointly by Ryzhkov, Abalkin, and Valentin Pavlov in late 1990. This programme was unambiguous in its commitment to a genuine market economy, with market determined prices and multiple forms of ownership. However, it emphasised that the pace of transition should continue to be cautious. It did not commit itself to privatisation of state assets. Rather, the essence of reform was to be a combination of allowing new ownership forms to develop alongside efforts to improve the effectiveness with which state assets were operated. This programme was strongly reminiscent of the institutional structure of the Soviet NEP period. Indeed, it visualised a continuing strong economic role for the state, with an overall framework of a 'regulated market economy' (Aslund, 1991, pp. 206–29).

The Soviet reforms were taking place against the backdrop of the massive economic and political transformations in Eastern Europe. The radical reformers were given great impetus by the reforms in Poland, and by the rapid growth in contact with Western economists. The influence of 'progressive' economists increased quickly. They argued for much more radical reform along the lines of the Polish model, with massive, rapid privatisation as its essential component.

The concept of gradual reform and a 'Third Way' was increasingly ridiculed both inside and outside the Soviet Union. Powerful figures such as Janos Kornai argued that history and logic demonstrated the irrelevance of such a path. The radical reformers argued that the existing reform path was not guided by any overall logic, and that there was no clear conception of where the system would ultimately end up. There was a widespread perception that the Chinese attempt to reform incrementally had been a failure. Balanced, positive evaluations of China's reforms by such economists as Perkins (1988) were simply ignored. The perception that China's halfway-house reforms had failed was reinforced powerfully by the horrific massacre in and around Tiananmen Square in 1989. Gorbachev's own visit to China during the Tiananmen Demonstration must have reinforced strongly his feeling that the Chinese reforms had failed.

Against this background a 'progressive' group of economists within the government produced two closely connected programmes for rapid reform within the space of a few months. Their essence was indicated by the authors of the first of these programmes published in February 1990: *'The time for gradual transformations has turned out to have been missed, and the ineffectiveness of partial reforms has been proved by the experiences of Hungary, Yugoslavia, Poland and China'* (quoted in Aslund, 1991, p. 207) (Emphasis added). This most important product of this group was the famous Shatalin Plan presented to the government in September 1990: 'The essence of the Shatalin programme was a rapid stabilisation and a fast transition to a market economy coupled with large scale privatisations and a general delegation of powers to union republics. It was very concrete with a detailed schedule for the transition during 500 days' (Aslund, 1991, p. 208).

The programme was widely welcomed by Western experts as a 'genuine', 'progressive' reform in contrast to the lamentable 'half-way house' of the 'conservative hardliners'. The view of Anders Aslund, a deeply knowledgeable Soviet expert and advisor to the Soviet government, is representative:

> The Shatalin programme was far from perfect. [N]otably it insisted on import substitution and was excessively protectionist. *Still, as far as principles and basic intentions are concerned, it is difficult for a western market economist not to side with the Shatalin programme on all the major points of dispute....* [T]he Shatalin programme signified an understanding of the necessity of a quick change of economic system and the forging of a new kind of relationship between the constituent republics of the Soviet Union. *If the economy is in steep decline, gradualism equals prolongation of economic suffering. Therefore, a swift change of system is necessary for the population's welfare, which can only by boosted by future capitalism.* (Aslund, 1991, p. 221) (Emphasis added)

It is difficult to evaluate the precise degree of influence of Western advisors such as Aslund, Sachs, or Layard, or the precise effect of the views of the international institutions, such as those contained in the report of the IMF and World Bank (IMF *et al.*, 1990).[8] However, at the very least they played a large role in bolstering the confidence of those in the government who favoured 'progressive', 'radical' solutions to the problems of the Soviet economy.

The radical proposals were not adopted as government policy, since, in the final months of the Gorbachev government, the administration was influenced powerfully by the conservative backlash against the political consequences of *perestroika*. The policies remained those of cautious economic reform. The implementation of the 'radical' programme was not to happen until the fall of Gorbachev and the disintegration of the Soviet Union.

e. Results

Under Gorbachev Soviet economic performance continued to deteriorate. Official estimates of the growth rate of national product in 1985–90 show figures that were even lower than those of the early 1980s. Unofficial estimates suggest that growth had virtually ceased by 1987. All estimates agree that by 1990 growth had become negative (Aslund, 1991, Table 7.11). Indeed, a careful estimate by the highly respected economist and statistician, Grigorii Khanin, argues that national income fell by 13.5–14.5 per cent in 1990 (quoted in Smith, 1993, p. 35). It is widely agreed that national income fell by a further 15 per cent or so in 1991, making a total collapse in national product from 1989 to 1991 of roughly 30 per cent, which is greater than during the Great Depression in the USA (Smith, 1993, p. 35). It is important to bear this starting point in mind when considering the much greater decline that was to occur after 1991.

A virtual consensus view exists that the main reason for the failure of the economic reform efforts under Gorbachev is their 'half-hearted' nature, and the blocking of 'serious' system reform by 'hardliners'. In other words, the failure of economic performance to improve is taken as evidence that the correct solution to the huge problems faced by the Soviet economy was a radical reform of the Shatalin type. This was the lesson taken by the Yeltsin government in the RSFSR in the wake of the collapse of the Soviet Union in 1991.

However, the reality is much more complex. The period of serious attempts at system reform was short-lived, lasting only around three years in total. China's incremental reform programme is far from complete and it has already lasted a decade and a half. However, much more importantly, the background against which the Soviet reforms were enacted was extraordinarily turbulent, amounting to nothing less than a political revolution and national disintegration. This had immense economic consequences in precisely the period during which the reforms were being attempted.

Much the most important economic impact was on the material supply system. Despite the commitment to an incremental reform strategy, by the late 1980s the judgement of the IMF and the World Bank (IMF *et al.*, 1990) was that 'the traditional centrally planned system' had 'largely collapsed' (IMF *et al.*, 1990, p. 10). The reasons for this were essentially political. In 'normal' times the material balance planning system has a high propensity to produce mismatch of supply and demand, generating strong pressures for suction and hoarding, and enterprise and regional self-sufficiency, in the well-known fashion analysed by Kornai. This fragile mechanism was shattered by the political convulsion consequent upon *perestroika*:

> Over the subsequent three years [from 1988] the ability of the centre to enforce the planned allocation system has collapsed. The Communist Party had enforced deliveries to the state, and that mechanism, simply failed. As a result, enterprises refused to deliver their products to the state at low prices, and instead began selling them at market prices to whomever they pleased. *What began as a Chinese style experiment with capitalism on the margin transformed itself into a collapse of the central allocation mechanisms.* This collapse of socialist coordination greatly damaged state enterprises and may have led to aggregate output declines in 1990 and 1991 (Blanchard *et al.*, 1993, p. 42) (Emphasis added)

The Party stood at the centre of the planning process, but the reforms had drastically reduced the number of Party members working in the planning system. Moreover, the morale of those still working at these activities had been eroded seriously by *glasnost*. Even more seriously, the reforms dramatically reshaped the relationship betweeen the centre and the republics. In its 1990 report, the IMF and World Bank noted: '[P]olicy making in the republics has been characterised by growing autonomy. In a climate of growing shortages, republics have become increasingly unwilling to trade with each other except on a barter basis. . . . The trend towards autonomy and increased barter trade between the republics has recently been reflected in the establishment of border controls on trade' (IMF *et al.*, 1990, pp. 10–11). The role of inter-republican trade in the former USSR was large: with the exception of the Russian Republican the share of GNP of each republic delivered to the other republics ranged from 21 per cent to 41 per cent, while that of the Russian republic stood at 11 per cent (Table 7.1). The supply and demand side consequences for national

Table 7.1   Union republics: Trade as a percentage of GNP in former
Soviet states, 1990

| | Foreign trade | | |
	Total	Intra-regional	Intra-regional share of total
Armenia	28.4	25.6	90.1
Azerbaijan	33.9	29.8	87.7
Belarus	47.3	41.0	86.8
Estonia	32.9	30.2	91.6
Georgia	28.9	24.8	85.9
Kazakhstan	23.5	20.8	88.7
Kirgizstan	32.3	27.7	85.7
Latvia	41.4	36.7	88.6
Lithuania	45.5	40.9	89.7
Moldova	33.0	28.9	87.7
Russian Federation	18.3	11.1	60.6
Tajikistan	35.9	31.0	86.5
Turkmenistan	35.6	33.0	92.5
Ukraine	29.0	23.8	82.1
Uzbekistan	28.5	25.5	89.4

Source: World Bank, 1992, p. 121.

Note: The international trade figures are downwardly biased in the sense that they are calculated at the exchange rate prior to its massive devaluation in the early 1990s.

output of the disintegration of inter-republican trade were enormous. The net result of these developments was a serious fall in industrial output and efficiency.

A closely-related development was the decline in the government's fiscal position. The drastic decline in the capacity of the state had serious consequences on both the revenue and the expenditure side. The deterioration in the size and morale of the tax collection agencies, which were mainly staffed by Party cadres, reduced the government's capacity to raise revenue. In addition, the vicious circle of decline in industrial output reduced the ability of enterprises to hand over contracted profits to the state. The deterioration in the country's foreign trade position reduced the government's revenue from foreign trade taxes. Moreover, increasingly, the republics refused to hand over revenue to the central authorities. The national government's budgetary revenues fell from 48 per cent of GNP in 1985 to 44 per cent in 1989 (Aslund, 1991, Table 7.9).

On the expenditure side, the growing frailty of the government meant that in 'populist' fashion it was less and less able to resist demands for sustaining expenditure despite the decline in revenues as a share of national product. The government was deeply afraid of the consequences of allowing state enterprises to go bankrupt and in the face of growing insolvency, it maintained its expenditure to cushion enterprise losses and keep enterprises afloat. Moreover, in an atmosphere of growing inflation and intensifying shortages, the government sustained increased expenditures on food subsidies to maintain social stability. The net result of these processes was that state expenditure as a share of national product rose steadily from 50 per cent in 1985 to over 52 per cent in 1989.

The fiscal crisis intensified. The fiscal deficit widened from 2.3 per cent of GDP in 1985 to around 11 per cent by 1988, with the deficits 'almost exclusively financed by credit extended by Gosbank' (IMF *et al.*, 1991,7). The consequences for the growth of the money supply were serious. The growth of money supply (M2) rose from an estimated annual average rate of 7.5 per cent in 1981–85 to over 15 per cent by the end of the 1980s, alongside declining real output (Aslund, 1991, Table 7.6). Faced with a growing shortage of consumer goods, the 'monetary overhang' intensified, and consumer dissatisfaction mounted.

The political changes also had large consequences for foreign trade. Raw materials constituted a large share of Soviet hard currency exports. However, instead of generating increased foreign exchange the period saw a decline in oil production, export volumes and foreign exchange earnings.[9] In part this reflected the general squeeze on investment out of the state budget consequent upon the rise in the share of non-investment outlays (the share of investment in the national budget fell from 9.0 per cent in 1985 to just 4.3 per cent in 1990) (Aslund, 1991, Table 7.8). However, it also reflected the rise of industrial militancy, in which mine workers were especially prominent, as well as the reluctance of oil-producing republics to allow the export of products for which the central government would gain hard currency.

Soviet hard currency earnings to the West fell from 21 billion nominal currency rubles in 1984 to just 17 billion in 1990 (Aslund, 1991, Table 7.10). However, alongside this calamitous performance went a comprehensive failure to control imports. Instead of using the country's limited and declining foreign exchange to focus imports upon growth-enhancing products, the increasingly hapless central government sharply increased imports in large part in order to placate domestic consumers: '[T]he import-oriented policy looked like a populist drive to soothe popular dissatisfaction with consumer goods' (Aslund, 1991, p. 198).

The net result was a sharp deterioration in the foreign trade position, and a rise in the gross external debt from $29 billion in 1985 to $54 billion in 1989 (Aslund, 1991, Table 7.10). The Soviet Union now had foreign debt of Latin American proportions, and an important corollary of this was that it lost independence in forming economic policy since it now became subject to IMF conditionality.

f. Gorbachev's 'achievement'

By the mid-1980s the Soviet Union was in great economic difficulty. Fundamental reform was necessary to improve the way the system operated. Tinkering within the traditional framework by applying more 'pressure' had aggravated rather than improved the situation. However, the system possessed enormous unused productive capacities in both human abilities and capital stock. Moreover, the country possessed a huge domestic market, and massive natural resources. There was a high potential for rapid advance if the right set of political and economic policies could have been found. Under Gorbachev the leaders were groping towards an incremental economic reform strategy which would have eventually yielded good results. Within a few years the benefits of such an approach would have become manifestly clear from the Chinese experience, and the dangers of shock therapy have become equally clear from the Eastern European experience. This would have given added confidence to the leadership about the correctness of such a strategy.

However, to be successful, an economic reform strategy requires political stability and effective government. These are necessary to maintain the government's fiscal capacity and to achieve financial stability. They are necessary also in order to enable the government to move from undertake the necessary planning functions in the transition away from the command economy. Moreover, they are necessary in order for the government to provide a sense of social coherence to minimise social dislocation likely to result from the transition.

The Gorbachev regime inherited a country that was politically stable. The 'revolutionary' dissident movement was confined to a small intellectual minority. Moreover, it possessed a powerful administrative apparatus in the shape of the Communist Party. The severity with which national minorities had been dealt with by previous governments meant that the nationalist movements had low expectations about the possibility for national independence. Gorbachev's policies of *perestroika* and *glasnost* turned the ideas of the dissident minority and a hostile international community into national policy. They resulted in the destruction of the Communist Party without substituting a stable, effective democratic system. They resulted also in the destruction of the nation-state as it had existed basically since the eighteenth century.

The economic consequences of these changes were enormous. Their effects completely swamped the impact of the limited economic reforms that were tentatively begun in the 1987–88 reform wave. The bequest of the Gorbachev period to its successor was a government, a society and an economy in a catastrophic tail-spin. It is hard to imagine how any government which inherited power in the new Russian state in 1991 or, indeed, in any of the former republics, could have restored the situation even over many years. In fact, the policies adopted by the successor state made a bad situation much worse.

7.2 REFORM IN THE RUSSIAN FEDERATION

Russia had now become a much smaller country. However, in some ways it had a higher possibility for rapid growth than the predecessor USSR. The country was now much more ethnically homogenous. It had cast off a large part of low income central Asia, with its rapid rates of population growth and ethnic tensions. The Russian Federation was of much higher average income than the former USSR. It possessed the vast bulk of the former USSR's natural resources, especially because of its retention of Siberia, which still contains large uncharted resources. It contained a large share of the best farmland. It retained around two-thirds of Russia's industrial capital stock and produced over two-thirds of net industrial output. It included the main core areas around which post-communist industrial growth might be organised, namely the Leningrad and Moscow regions, and the Urals. It had ceased to bear responsibility for Eastern Europe.

Russia patently was in a time of severe national crisis. Under such circumstances the population might have supported a strategy of planned transformation in which the national interest was placed above individual interests, and the hardships were shared relatively equally as in wartime in most countries. There was no shortage of economists who argued for a carefully considered strategy of evolutionary, planned reform of the command system,[10] including carefully thought-out proposals for an industrial strategy building on the strengths of Russia's industry (e.g. Fal'tsman, 1993). However, these voices were to be swamped by the 'cavalry charge' to privatisation and the 'free market'.

7.2.1 Politics

a. Centre and localities

The collapse of the communist party caused a fundamental change in the relationship between the centre and the localities. There had been elections throughout Russia at the local as well as at the national level in 1990. This occurred without any alternative party system to that of the Communist Party having been established, but under circumstances in which the Party was disintegrating. At the local level, the bulk of those elected were Party members, albeit that they embraced a wide variety of views, frequently hostile to the Party. Local representatives were elected mainly on the basis of some dimly perceived personal quality rather than because of allegiance to a certain party with a clear programme. There was a high degree of continuity of local ruling personnel between the two epochs. Moreover, although the Party had collapsed as a centralised apparatus a powerful network of personal connections remained among local power-holders. Furthermore, fresh elections were a long way off and by the time they took place huge changes in the landscape of economic life had been accomplished. None of these changes appeared in the form of a party platform presented to the electorate. Neither parties nor electoral platforms existed at the time of the elections.

The collapse of the communist party and material balance planning system transformed the *de facto* nature of ownership rights over state assets. The centre ceased to have direct control over the bulk of state property. *De facto* control passed substantially into the hands of local authorities and those who worked in the enterprises.

b. Change in the ethical environment

In a disintegrating political environment, with massive uncertainty, the ethical climate of government also disintegrated. There was little incentive for any individual in office to act in a way that served the social interest. Social norms had collapsed and there was little probability of others in office behaving in a way that put the community's interests first. Moreover, in a highly unstable ethical and political environment, with massive economic changes under way, there were hugely increased possibilities for individuals to profit at the expense of the community:

> [In the early 1990s] there was a malignant growth pervading the economy, the banking system and the body politic. Millions of ordinary

citizens have succumbed, making off with state property, black marketing, swindling, buying or selling protection. Obviously they aren't all tied to the mafia. Russia is so chaotic and broke that hardly anybody can stay honest and survive . . . "You Westerners may call this corruption, but we say *nishinstvo* in Russian, a term describing a poverty so desperate that one loses one's shame and moral compass" said Moscow's police chief in that first tremendous year of freedom. (Sterling, 1994, p. 81)

It is not that Russians are especially cynical, or that decades of communism has made them more selfish. Rather, in order to operate in a way that serves the community, established norms that create a network of obligations and trust have to exist. These were destroyed by the speed and extent of the rupture with the old system.

c. Organised crime

The economic decline under Gorbachev and the collapse after 1991 caused a rapid deterioration in law and order. The morale of the police force as well as the government's ability to pay its members declined. The wider ethical atmosphere altered drastically as the old norms of communism disintegrated. The former arbiter of public morality, the Communist Party, no longer existed. From a state committed to collectivism and social protection, the atmosphere in just a few years became highly individualistic with social protection for the less able drastically reduced. The widespread decline in living standards and the increase in poverty also contributed to the change in moral values as sheer desperation forced large numbers of people into crime. The homicide rate was reported to have more than doubled under *perestroika* from 7.4 per thousand in 1986 to 15.2 per thousand in 1991, and by 1992 the figure had climbed to 22.8 per thousand (Ellman, 1994, p. 332). The homicide rate in 1992 placed Russia firmly in the category of 'high homicide' countries, with the rate standing at around double that for the USA, and above that for such countries as Mexico and Brazil (Ellman, 1994, p. 333).

A much more difficult issue to evaluate is the degree of importance of illegal organisations, loosely referred to as the 'mafia'. Strong criminal groups already existed under the communist regime, mainly operating in the black economy. These groups contained most of the largest concentrations of private wealth in the country, and were thus in a unique position to benefit from the privatisation process: 'When Russia began its lurch towards the market in 1992 these criminal gangs were among the few possessors of large amounts of capital. *They were presented with an opportunity not merely to subvert an existing structure, as the mafia did to the state in southern Italy, but to buy a state in the process of being rebuilt'* (*The Economist*, 9 July 1994) (Emphasis added).

The most important single channel through which large concentrations of criminal wealth accumulated quickly during the reforms was the export of raw materials, including oil, gas and precious minerals. In addition there was a vast stockpile of weaponry employed by an armed force that was was in a state of complete chaos and disillusion. Moreover, there was rapid growth in the production and export of drugs.

Government policies assisted this process. The first was the 'joint venture' under which 'foreign expertise and capital' was allied to domestic state industry to 'modernise' a given sector through the joint venture. This typically resulted in a near monopoly being granted in the production and trade of a given raw material. The second was the granting of 'concessions' to entrepreneurs to 'develop' a given natural resource in a given region. The third was the export licences which were needed for many rare metals. Still in 1994 Yeltsin refused to eliminate the system of export licences on the most important single product, oil:

> The credibility of the government's own promises to combine reforms with a fight against abuses has come into question following its recent decision not to abolish quotas on oil exports as promised before July 1. This crucial foreign trade reform which would have increased tax revenues and removed a big source of corruption, was postponed at least until January 1995 without explanation. . . . This was just too juicy a morsel to give up for certain interest groups, explains Professor Yevgeny Yasin, chief economic analyst for President Boris Yeltsin. (*Financial Times*, 16–17 July 1994)

Those who were able to obtain the necessary export licence from government officials were able to make a large profit. The fourth was the government's maintenance of low compulsory purchase prices in the case of many raw materials, most notably oil, ostensibly in order to ensure affordable prices to industry of key raw material inputs. In fact, it provided a hugely lucrative source of income from arbitrage.

A vast export of raw materials and precious metals, much of it illegal, developed during the reform period. By 1993 exports of raw materials, of which oil was the largest single item, made up 80 per cent of Russia's exports. Through the system of concessions, licensing and joint ventures, a large part of the windfall profits from this vast operation was channelled into the hands of a small number of individuals. Large concentrations of wealth were accumulated during the first few years of reform by this relatively simple route. Such people include Andrei Chuguyevsky, one of the richest men in Russia, who won a concession to exploit Russia's huge Udokan copper deposits (*Financial Times*, 27 May 1993). This process of capital accumulation is analogous to that through which one important aspect of capital accumulation occurred in Elizabethan England, with the granting of monopolies to trading companies (Dobb, 1947, ch. 5, 'Capital accumulation and mercantilism').

It is argued by some writers that criminal organisations, both domestic and international, stand at the centre of this process. One account argued: 'Of all the Russian mafia's occupations, the biggest by far had to do with plundering the economy through mulifarious, unbelievably lucrative fraud. . . . A prostrate country lay open to the international world. . . . A gluttonous horde of foreign carpetbaggers, speculators and assorted felons showed up as soon as Russia began to look to the West' (Sterling, 1994, p. 93). This account argues that the large-scale 'mafia' gangs had come to control large parts of Russian economic life: '[S]ingularily free from harassment, the political–criminal condominium called the mafia has in fact come to control the life of Moscow, and of all Russia and other Commonwealth states' (Sterling, 1994, p. 88). In 1993 Boris Yeltsin himself declared: 'organised crime has become a direct threat to Russia's strategic interests and national security' (quoted in *The Economist*, 9 July 1994, p. 19). The report on organised crime commissioned by Yeltsin concluded despairingly: '[Russia is] a lawless society in which "every, repeat, every owner of a shop or kiosk pays a racketeer"' (quoted in *The Economist*, 9 July 1994, p. 19).

d. Politics at the centre

The first two and a half years of politics in the new Russian state were dominated by the relationship between the President and the Congress of People's Deputies. The task of reconstructing an effective administrative machine of government was simply ignored alongside continuing struggle about the nature of the division of power under the new institutions. This was disastrous. Countries that successfully rebuilt their economies after great national crises, such as that of Japan after World War ll, South Korea after the Korean War (1953) or Singapore in the mid-1960s after its split with Malaya, had regarded the construction of an effective government adminstative apparatus as a central task.

The Russian Congress had been elected in March 1990 on a relatively democratic basis. There were no special seats reserved for special interest groups. Every deputy faced the electorate, and almost all seats were contested. The old screening process by which a local electoral commission judged which nominees to put on the ballot had been eliminated in 1990. Any candidates nominated by residents or in a factory or institute had their name put on the voting paper. By 1990 public hostility to Communist Party officials was at a high level. Candidates who ran against the Party on a ticket of anti-communism stood a high chance of winning even if they were formally Party members. By 1990 the Party itself had become a broad church, including social democrats, free market liberals, right-wing nationalists as well as Stalinists. A clear majority, perhaps two-thirds of the deputies, were in favour of market reform rather than trying to turn the clock back to the Stalinist economy, despite the fact that around 85 per cent of the deputies were nominally Party members.[11]

These elections did not provide voters with a clear choice. There did not exist large stable, national political parties which possessed programmes that offered clear choices to the electorate. Votes were cast essentially for a mass of individuals, about whom the electorate had poor knowledge. Almost everyone in Russia wanted 'reform'. However, 'reform' can come in a wide variety of packages. Meaningful voter choice requires clear identification of alternatives.

Congress itself took the step in spring 1991 to create the position of an executive presidency. When Yeltsin was elected president of the RSFSR in June 1991 he also was elected without a clear platform in either economics or politics. He was mainly elected because of his personal qualities and of the fact that he presented an alternative to Gorbachev: 'Yeltsin's main strength was not, of course, the adulation of his subjects, but the deep popular hatred for Gorbachev. It is difficult to imagine a man simultaneously detested by everyone, from professors to janitors, from Zionist to anti-Semites. Yeltsin embodied not only faith in the "benevolent tsar", (or more precisely, "wise despot"), but also hopes of getting rid of Gorbachev' (Kagarlitsky, 1992, p. 117). Throughout the period since the August coup, Yeltsin has conspicuously failed to create or operate with any political party. Right through to the time of writing (Autumn 1994) he has attempted to project himself as aloof from the cut and thrust of political organisation within the Congress of People's Deputies.

e. The international community

For a brief period in 1990 Gorbachev flirted publicly with the possibility of attempting to put into practice a 'shock therapy' programme of economic reform. As soon as Yeltsin became the president of an independent Russia he made clear that he regarded this as the correct path. He appointed radical young advisors such as Yegor Gaidar to senior positions around him. The international institutions were given a permanent and important role in shaping policy advice. 'Foreign aid' programmes from organisations such as the Ford Foundation and Swedish government paid 'independent advisors' such as Anders Aslund, Richard Layard, David Lipton, and Jeffrey Sachs, to work closely with Yeltsin's team of domestic economists to construct economic policy: 'Basically this is a form of technical assistance for the Russian government' (Aslund, quoted in *Transition*, vol. 3, no. 10, November 1992, p. 5).[12] The IMF team was closely involved. Following their advice now was a formal 'condition' of obtaining their financial support. The many reformist Russian economists who favoured a more cautious, evolutionary transition process with a strong role for the state were excluded from the policy-making process, accused of being 'hardliners' opposed to 'reform'.

There was a close relationship between many of the Russian policy-makers and the powerful group of foreign advisors. The foreign experts came to the problem with the high technical expertise of 'Western economics'. They came with high incomes, lap-top computers, expensive clothes, and the accumulated experience of having 'solved' the problems of large numbers of other 'ailing economies'. In the desperate crisis into which Russia had now sunk it required great strength of purpose to be able to resist the seductive line of thought presented by the 'experts'. It is not too fanciful to talk of an intellectual 'compradore' mentality in Russia among its economic policy-making circle, with those who followed the path of 'free market reform' able to expect visiting fellowships in Western institutions and other rewards as a part of an implicit contract for their help in legitimating the 'correct' policy line.

There was overwhelming support among both international advisors and the Russians appointed by Yeltsin for a radical 'shock therapy' approach to economic policy. This amounted to the putting into effect of the '500 Day' programme which had been floated in the penultimate phase of the Gorbachev administration.

f. Conflict between Yeltsin and the Congress

Unfortunately for Yeltsin, while the Congress contained a majority of deputies who wished to reform the economy, there was not a majority in favour of the 'shock therapy' that Yeltsin wished to put into effect. Consequently, the period was dominated by constant struggle over the economic programme. It affected the issue of appointment of ministers, of the budget and the permissable level of budget deficit, and the fundamentals of economic reform legislation.

The conflict between Yeltsin and the Congress escalated in the two years after the August coup. In March 1993 Yeltsin declared his intention to ignore the Congress and rule by presidential decree: 'In any meaningful language this is elective dictatorship. . . . It is Boris Yeltsin's 18th Brumaire, and in any other circumstances the reaction of the rest of the world would have been indignant and immediate' (Jonathan Steele, *The Guardian*, 28 March 1993). Yeltsin retreated from direct confrontation, but finally pressed forward again in September/October 1993 by first suspending the Congress and then bloodily attacking the White House.

There was unanimous support from Western political leaders for both the suspension of Parliament and the subsequent violent assault on the White House, in which around 200 people were killed. A clear link was drawn between the crushing of the Congress and the ability of Yeltsin to proceed rapidly with the 'necessary' economic reform which the 'hardliners' in the Congress were almost universally alleged to have obstructed. It was widely argued that the Congress was unrepresentative of the view of the mass of Russian citizens since it had been elected before the formal dissolution of the Communist Party's leading role in the USSR.

There was a remarkable homogeneity of views in their interpretation of the conflict and its resolution among the leaders of the Western powers, the heads of the major international institutions and the Western mass media. On 25 September 1993, following the suspension of Congress a meeting of the finance ministers of the US, Germany, France, Britain, Italy and Canada, 'expressed their very strong hope' that the political developments of the preceding week would 'help Russia achieve a decisive breakthrough on the path of market reform'. The ministers 'praised President Boris Yeltsin's commitment to pursue the path of market-oriented reform, which they saw as right for creating a better future for the Rusian people and integrating Russia into the world economy' (*Financial Times*, 27 September 1993). Immediately after the attack, the Russian finance minister visited Washington and 'encouraged both [the IMF and the World Bank] to hope for a decisive change of course in an economic policy which had gone badly off course in the preceding three months' (*Financial Times*, 6 October 1993). A raft of measures was announced in the Government's Plan for Economic Work in 1994: these centred on 'liberalisation of trade and energy prices, speeding up privatisation and protecting private property' (*Financial Times*, 6 October 1993). The government was confident that the elections in December would bring a pro-reform majority that would allow the smooth passage of the shock therapy programme which had been delayed by the recalcitrant Congress.

Following the violent attack on the Congress, Yeltsin took a wide array of measures to consolidate his personal hold on power. These included a ban on opposition newspapers and on many political parties (most of these were lifted before the elections later in the year), imposing his own nominees on the mass media, and attempting to alter radically the nature of local politics by ordering local councils to be disbanded and power handed over to 'Moscow-appointed regional administrators' until the elections. Most importantly of all, in a very short space of time Yelstin drew up a completely new constitution. It gave wide powers to the president in relation to the Congress (renamed the Duma). The president had the right to set 'the general direction of internal and foreign policy'. He had the right to name the Prime Minister and insist on keeping him even if parliament objected. If his government was challenged by a vote of no confidence against it in parliament he could now keep office for three months and then sack the parliament rather than the government if the vote was repeated. He could veto any law passed by a simple majority in the lower house and then require a two-thirds majority for it to be passed. The constitution was approved by the thinnest of simple majority votes (less than 60 per cent of those who voted) among the small proportion of those who voted in the referendum (53 per cent of the electorate) later in the year (i.e. less than one-third of the total electorate).

g. *The December 1993 elections*

Contrary to all Western expectations, the elections of December 1993 produced a disastrous result for Yeltsin. The choice of political parties had become clearer than in the previous elections to the Congress of People's Deputies in 1990. Now there was greater clarity of positions associated with something resembling Western political parties. 'Russia's Choice', led by Yegor Gaidar was the clear flagship of radical economic reform. *Yabloko* was also committed to radical reform and was an obvious potential coalition partner for People's Choice. The former received just 14 per cent of the popular vote and the latter just 7 per cent. This was a humiliating defeat for Yeltsin and the radical reformers. Parties appealing specifically to a much slower programme of economic reform, with much greater attention to the interests of the socially deprived, namely the Communist Party, the Agrarian Party and 'Women of Russia' between them received 28 per cent of the vote.

Vastly more disturbing was the huge positive vote, no less than 25 per cent, for the neo-fascist party of Vladimir Zhirinovsky. His programme was vague, promising to restore Russia as a great power, end crime and corruption, and 'give every citizen a guarantee of well being'. The vote for Zhirinovsky clearly was not a vote for continued radical reform. Above all it seemed to be a cry of anger at the humiliation that Russia had suffered over the previous years since Gorbachev began *perestroika*, and the suffering that had been inflicted on a large segment of the population. It showed how completely out of touch with the depth of the crisis most Western leaders, most of the Western media and those who work in the international institutions had been. The IMF and the World Bank, 'poised to support and to lend to a reformist government' were 'now left high and dry' (*Financial Times*, 14 December 1993).

h. Temporary retreat

In the immediate aftermath of the shocking result of the December elections, it appeared as if Yeltsin had sharply altered course. The 'shock therapy' supporters in the government were either sacked or 'resigned'. The most important departures were Gaidar, first deputy prime minister, and Fyodorov, minister of finance. Symbolic departures were made from the team of government advisors by the 'resignation' of Jeffrey Sachs and Anders Aslund. The Prime Minister, Chernonmyrdin, said that the new course contained 'only elements of western market economics', and that the 'mechanical transfer of western economic methods' had 'caused more harm than good' (quoted in the *Financial Times*, 22–3 January 1994). He said that the new economic programme would be based on the 'special characteristics of our state, people and Russian traditions' (quoted in the *Financial Times*, 22–3 January 1994).

In fact the retreat turned out to be only temporary. To a considerable degree this was because the most important change of all, mass privatisation of publicly-owned assets, had proceeded so far by the time of the December elections as to be virtually irreversible. Yeltsin's position had been strengthened by the new, much more authoritarian constitution. Moreover, he received a massive level of support from international leaders and international opinion to press ahead with the 'shock therapy' transition: 'The west should continue to support Russia's political and economic transformation. . . . The western friends [of Mr Yeltsin and his allies] must encourage them to persevere with reform, because *only accelerated reform offers any hope of delivering the economic benefits which may persuade Russians to resist the siren songs of communist nostalgia and nationalist escapism*' (*Financial Times*, leader, 14 December 1993) (Emphasis added). Most importantly of all, he had continued detailed input into policy making from the IMF and World Bank, which critically bolstered the resolve of Yeltsin and his chief advisors to press ahead with their reform path after the initial shock of the December election result had worn off.

i. Prospect and retrospect

At the time of writing (Autumn 1994) the situation was still highly unstable. Much of the country had been hugely shocked by the transition to the market under 'wild capitalism'. Much of the population had experienced a large fall in their real income. A hugely unequal process of mass privatisation has occurred (see below). Law and order had disintegrated. Everyone lived under much greater uncertainty than during communist rule. However, there had not been a social explosion. The level of political violence had been relatively small. Indeed, the year 1994 so far had been relatively calm. It was common to ascribe the calmness after the dramas of 1992/3 to popular exhaustion and bewilderment in the face of the magnitude of the changes that had occurred. Other analyses pointed to the fact that the change had left a large body of the population without clearly defined patterns of social organisation which could inspire organised social and political action. The new 'civil society' was still being formed.

In the Autumn of 1994 the opposition promised a 'long hot autumn' in parliament (*Financial Times*, 24–25 September 1994). Almost every opinion poll showed 'a turning away from democrats and growing or sustained approval of nationalist and communist themes, if not parties and individuals' (*Financial Times*, 24–25 September 1994). However, the truth was that the opposition now lacked a clear, credible alternative strategy. The state machine was in tatters. It now possessed few assets. It lacked the capacity to do much more than, at best, control the money supply. By contrast the government possessed a clear, simple 'reforming' vision, given massive psychological support by the IMF. In the government's mind it had gone so far there was now little point in turning back, and it hoped that the worst might be over.

However, Russia's economic situation was parlous. Even worse may be in store than has been seen in the past few years. If this were to be the case, then the political landscape might alter yet again in ways that are hard to predict. The possibilities range from the ever-present spectre of a national military dictatorship to still further fragmentation into even smaller states, returning 'Russia' to a political landscape analogous to that of the fifteenth century. Nor might this be the worst possible outcome given the dire state into which Russia has sunk. It might be easier to undertake the reconstruction of an effective state apparatus in smaller political units. The narrower divergence of vested interests within smaller units might make co-operative action easier to achieve.

7.2.2 Economics

a. The strategy

The impact of the IMF and the surrounding team of international advisors can only be guessed at for the period prior to the end of the Soviet Union. However, their role in the construction of Yeltsin's reform programme is crystal clear. The broad strategy was to attempt finally to put into effect the shock therapy ('500 Day') programme which was shelved at the end of Gorbachev's period in power. The policy was outlined in a speech by Yeltsin to the Russian parliament on 28 October 1991. More specific detail was published in the 'Memorandum on the Economic Policy of the Russian Federation', which formed the basis of Russia's letter of intent to the IMF (Smith, 1993, p. 177):

> *The policies outlined in the [February] memorandum* (and other policy documents) *incorporated the basic pillars for the rapid transition to a market economy* (price liberalisation, removal of bureaucratic constraints on economic activity, privatisation of state industry and macro economic stabilisation, together with an appeal for Western economic

assistance) *developed by Jeffrey Sachs, ... who has been a princi-pal advisor to both the Polish and the Russian governments. The proposals, which had the broad support of the IMF, were largely modelled on the policies adopted by the Polish government in Janu-ary 1990, which has been popularily referred to as 'shock therapy'.* (Smith, 1993, p. 177) (Emphasis added)

The main aim of the reform programme was to privatise state assets as rapidly as possible. Even price stability was considered to be of secondary importance. Richard Layard, a close advisor to the Yeltsin government during the reforms, comments:

In 1992 Russia rediscovered capitalism – one of the main events of the century. Yet many people say the reforms have failed, since inflation is still rampant. This line of thought is flawed. *For the aim of the Russian reform is to change from communism to capital-ism. Price stability is something else – one of the aims of any govern-ment, communist or capitalist. ... The Gaidar team's main aim was to privatise the economy.* If they also attempted an early stabilisation, they would have been thrown out of office within months. They compromised because of the trade-offs they faced. (Layard, 1993, pp. 15–16) (Emphasis added)

b. Price liberalisation

Following the transition orthodoxy, most prices were freed from govern-ment control on 1 January 1991. Essentially, only prices of power supplies remained controlled by the central government, while some price con-trols, such as on apartments, public transport and some foodstuffs, were retained by local authorities (IMF, 1994, p. 5). Introducing the pro-gramme of price reform President Yeltsin said:

The time has come for resolute, strict, unhesitating action. Everyone knows the starting base. The situation is tense. ... The one-time transition to market prices is a difficult, forced, but necessary measure. ... *Things will be worse for everyone for about half a year where-upon prices will drop and the consumer market will be filled with goods. But as I promised before the elections, the economy will sta-bilise and the standard of living will gradually improve by the autumn of 1992.* (Quoted in Rakitski, 1994, p. 32) (Emphasis added) *c. International trade*

The Yeltsin government inherited a 'complicated mixture of multiple exchange rates, import and export licences and quotas, differentiated retention quotas and limited foreign currency reserves to defend a convertible currency'(Smith, 1993, p. 188). It quickly put into place a series of measures designed to liberalise the international trade and payments system. In November 1992 full current account convertibility was established for residents, and the ruble was allowed to float fairly freely (there was a 'dirty float', not a true free market). In the ensuing period the ruble collapsed so dramatically against the dollar that, at the interbank exchange rate, Russian per capita income fell to less than 500 dollars (IMF, 1993, p. 85).[13]

In a brief space of time in 1992, following the transition orthodoxy, Russia's import regime was almost completely liberalised. Quantitative restrictions were abolished and licenses almost entirely done away with (IMF, 1993). A new tariff structure was introduced in mid-1992, with tariffs set at just 5–15 per cent for most products (IMF, 1993). The depth of the domestic crisis and the extent of depreciation of the value of the ruble were so large that the immediate effect of opening up the economy to international competition was not a large increase in imports and intensified competition for most of domestic industry. However, it did create great uncertainty among producers about their future markets, and thereby damaged investment prospects. In 1994 pressure to reintroduce substantial protection mounted.

Several important groups of goods were subject to export quotas. These included crude oil, petroleum gas and other hydrocarbons, natural gas, non-ferrous metals, raw materials for the production of non-ferrous metals and alloys, sulphur, coal, apatite, ammonia, and timber. These were ostensibly in order to control domestic prices. The rights to export were not mainly sold through auction but rather were 'for the most part distributed directly [by the Ministry of Economy] directly to enterprises or to regions' (IMF, 1993, p. 39). Moreover, after June 1992 it was necessary to have a licence in order to export 'strategic goods'. The definition of 'strategic goods' widened steadily over time, and included important raw materials, energy, and precious metals (IMF, 1993, p. 39). In addition the government itself began to reengage directly in export operations, purchasing goods in rubles directly from domestic suppliers, with the Ministry of Foreign Economic Relations directly determining which enterprises should be allowed to sell the goods abroad (IMF, 1993, p. 39).

These export controls ostensibly existed in order to protect the country from having its natural resources 'plundered'. In fact they provided a rich environment for benefit through arbitrage to those who obtained the rights to purchase and sell scarce products on world markets (see above).

d. Agriculture

It was seen in Chapter 5 that the farm sector in the USSR directly employed a much large share of the workforce and accounted for a much larger share of the total capital stock than in the advanced capitalist countries. It was seen also that in China an important impetus to reform overall was provided by successful reform in the farm sector. Even in the higher income USSR agriculture was a key sector for reform: in 1991 foodstuffs accounted for around two-fifths of Soviet consumers' expenditure (IMF, 1993, p. 69). An important part of inputs to light industry was supplied by agriculture, and an important part of industrial demand came from the farm sector. Even in the USA it is estimated that as much as 38 per cent of the total workforce is engaged in branches that produce, process, store, and sell agricultural products (Nefedov, 1994, p. 52).

However, the farm sector after 1991 suffered from a number of serious problems. Unlike in the industrial sector, where a sharp alteration of policy occurred soon after the Yeltsin government took power (see below), the property rights regime for farmers remained unclear until at least October 1993, when the Presidential Decree was passed which appeared finally to open the way for a radical sub-division of collective and state farms into private, individual farms (World Bank, 1994, pp. 26–7). The intervening period saw a long struggle over farm land ownership rights. In 1990 a law was passed which opened the way to the transfer of farm land from state ownership to ownership by the village community. In one form or another this was basically completed for most communities. The law also gave individual farmers the rights to take their 'share' of community land and other assets and set up private farmers on their own.

However, few farmers did so. By early 1993 a mere 8 per cent of farm land was privately owned (World Bank, 1994, p. 42). In some villages, the village government refused to allow farmers to take their share of village assets and leave. However other factors appear to have been more important. There was a wide array of legislation, often contradictory, about the condition on which private land could be operated, the passage of which reflected the intensity of debate about this issue. Conditions were attached at different points to the leasing and sale of land, to limits on farm size, bequeathing farm land to relatives, using farm land for mortgages, and the employment of wage labour in farming. Moreover, it was highly uncertain whether the political atmosphere would alter, and the whole complex edifice of legislation would again be overturned (Kiselev, 1994, p. 75). Only in October 1993 did it finally appear that a framework of unambiguous commitment to private property in farmland had been established.

The first three years of Yeltsin's rule was wasted over discussions about ownership rights rather than devoted to improving the way in which the assets were operated. As the Chinese experience demonstrated, it was not necessary to privatise farmland through auction or, as is likely to happen in the Russia through gifts of land titles to villagers. Rather, a large initial improvement can be obtained through devising contracts with individual farmers over the use-rights of farmland. Moreover, this approach has the advantage that it prevents polarisation of village asset ownership, and preserves a method of villages raising finance from villagers for the use of village land.

However, uncertainty over property rights in land was not the main factor preventing farmers leaving collective and state farms to set up individual private farms. Lack of access to machinery services and capital were reported to be the main factors preventing farmers leaving (World Bank, 1994, p. 3). Land is more easily divisible than are non-land fixed assets. In 1993 among new private farmers there were reported to be only 23 trucks and 55 tractors per 100 farms (Kiselev, 1994, p. 75).

Respondents to a survey by Goskomstat in mid-1992 listed the following factors as impeding the growth of peasant farms (percentage of respondents in brackets): high price of agricultural equipment and construction materials (80 per cent); shortage of special equipment, construction materials, seeds, fertilisers, and other material–technical resources (66 per cent); high interest rates on credit (51 per cent); uncertainty over the long-term character of land and agrarian laws (46 per cent); difficulty in obtainig credit (45 per cent); lack of legal protection of peasant farmers (42 per cent); lack of roads and communications, and of water and gas supply networks (41 per cent); obstacles on the part of collective/state farm leadership (23 per cent); difficulties in acquiring land (21 per cent); rural population's negative attitude towards individual farms (15 per cent); peasant farmers' own lack of special knowledge (15 per cent); difficulties with medical care, placing children in kindergartens and schools, lack of stores and so forth (14 per cent) (Kiselev, 1994, p. 75).

In the sharpest contrast to China's rural reforms, virtually nothing was done to attempt to develop ways of supplying lumpy inputs to farmers more effectively. Instead the policy assumption was that once the ownership question was solved all else would fall in to place. This approach is even more inappropriate in the farm sector than it is in the industrial sector. In both poor and rich economies, agriculture is characterised by large market failures. In this sector more than in any other under advanced capitalism there is a co-operative provision of a large range of physical inputs and services that are the beyond the capability of the individual farmer. A central part of China's farm reform was, not always with complete success, the attempt to maintain co-operative facilities above the level of immediate operation of farmland, and to search for ways to improve the effectiveness of their supply to farmers. These all loosely came under the contract system. Only part of the blame for the abysmal failure in this area in Russia can be attributed to lack of government resources due to the severity of the economic situation. If anything the Russian countryside had an abundance of non-land capital stock, albeit that there were many faults with its appropriateness and quality. The key to improving the supply side was devising ways of supplying services from existing inputs to farmers more effectively.

However, unfortunately, there were more problems for Russian agriculture in the reform period than shortcomings in institutions. As in the 1920s, the liberalisation of prices allowed the inter-sectoral terms of trade to shift against farmers. Farms were producing for a relatively competitive market in farm produce, but the more monopolistic condition of supply of industrial inputs allowed a large relative increase in the price of farm sector inputs (Nefedov, 1994, p. 56).

Moreover, there were serious demand-side problems. The collapse in average incomes in the reform period was accompanied by a sharp decline in average per capita consumption of farm produce. Output of most 'superior' foodstuffs, such as milk, eggs, fish and meat fell sharply in the early 1990s (Table 7.2, and IMF, 1994, p. 87). Inferior foodstuffs were substituted for superior ones. There took place an increase in the output of grain and potatoes after a long period of gradual decline (Table 7.2). Naturally, while food output fell sharply, the fall was less than that for non-food light industrial products, as consumers substituted basic foods for less essential non-food goods.

However, there were large problems also for demand for non-food products from agriculture. As the increasingly impoverished consumers substituted basic foodstuffs for other items in their consumption basket,

Table 7.2   Output of principal farm products in Russia, 1992 and selected
years

		Year of maximum volume			
		Year	Volume	1991	1992
meat	m. tons	1989	18.9	17.4	15.1
(carcass					
weight)					
	index		100	92	79
milk	m. tons	1990	101.5	94.9	84.8
	index		100	93	84
eggs	b. units	1988	81.4	76.4	67.5
	index		100	94	83
wool	'000 tons	1989	472	435	384
	index		100	92	81
grain	m. tons	1978	218	155	191
	index		100	71	88
potatoes	m. tons	1973	102	62	71
	index		100	61	70
raw cotton	m. tons	1980	9.1	7.8	6.5
	index		100	86	71
sugar beet	m. tons	1976	99	65	59
	index		100	65	59
sunflower	m. tons	1973	7.4	5.6	5.5
seeds					
	index		100	76	75

Source: Nefedov, 1994, p. 53.

demand for basic non-food products, such as footwear and textiles,
fell much more seriously even than for foodstuffs (Tables 7.3 and 7.4).
Consequently, large falls occurred in demand for, and output of, industrial inputs such as cotton and wool (Table 7.2).

Unsurprisingly, faced with uncertainty over property rights, with
hopelessly inadequate institutions to provide lumpy farm inputs, with
falling demand for most farm products, and with falling incomes for
most farmers, and the intersectoral terms of trade moving against the
farm sector, the farm sector's demand for non-farm inputs fell precipitously. In a single year (1991–2), CIS output of tractors and combine
harvesters fell by 25 per cent, of mowers and potato harvesters by 34
per cent, and flax harvesters, by 50 per cent (Nefedov, 1994, p. 56).
However, even more worrying than the fall in demand for farm machinery, was the drastic decline in application of chemical fertilisers.
Output in the CIS plummetted from 35.3 million tons in 1988 to just

Table 7.3 Index of industrial output in Russia, selected products, February 1992 (1989 = 100)

Motor cars	97	Sawn timber	75
TV sets	80	Paper	80
Washing machines	100	Cotton textiles	90
Shoes	78	Synthetic textiles	63
Machine tools	75	Ferrous metals	70
Trucks	80	Cement	80
Tractors	60		

Source: World Bank, 1992, p. 14.

Table 7.4 Output of selected products in Russia (1993 as a percentage of 1991)

Vegetable oil	93	Milk	42
Refrigerators	95	Machine tools	61
Televisions	89	Chemical fibres	69
Cars	99	Textiles	50
Natural gas	96	Shoes	44
Oil	77	Tractors	50
Steel	77	Videocassette	
Meat	65	recorders	84

Source: Goskomstat. quoted in *Economist*, 15 January 1994.

19.3 million tons in 1992 (Nefedov, 1994, p. 55). Moreover, around one-third of this output was exported (Nefedov, 1994, p. 55).

e. Privatisation in the non-farm sector

In the preceding section it was shown that because of the collapse of the Communist Party and the material balance planning system, a large change occurred in the late 1980s and early 1990s in the *de facto* control over industrial assets. Much control over the use of assets and distribution of the income stream from those assets passed into the hands of managers and local governments.

After great debate, the Law on Privatisation finally was approved in July 1992. Yeltsin expressed the official populist hopes for the privatisation programme as follows: '*We need millions of owners, not hundreds of millionaires*' (quoted in Weir, 1993, p. 2815) (Emphasis added). This was the key part of the radical structural reform package. Much assistance was given in the privatisation process by the International

Finance Corporation, the private sector investment arm of the World Bank (*Financial Times*, 27 May 1993). Russia's privatisation programme was to produce what Richard Layard, advisor to the Russian government, proudly called the 'fastest rate of privatisation in human history', in which 'in one month the Russian government is privatising more than Mrs Thatcher did in ten years' (Richard Layard, quoted in the *Financial Times*, 6 October 1993). By the end of 1994 it is estimated that 70 per cent of state property will have been transferred to private hands and 70 per cent of workers will work in the private sector (*Financial Times*, 20 June 1994).

Small and medium enterprises[14]   These were 'privatised' in a completely different way from large-scale enterprises. In the Russian Federation there was a total of just over 100,000 small-scale enterprises, and around 130–140,000 medium-sized enterprises (IMF, 1993, p. 48). Almost all the small enterprises were in the retail, consumer services and catering sectors. However, there was a subtantial number of manufacturing enterprises among the medium-sized enterprises.[15] Prior to privatisation most of these enterprises were owned by municipalities and it was by them that the privatisation was carried out.

Privatisation was carried out at high speed in less than two years. The privatisation was accomplished either through tender offers or auction. Under local privatisation, 'employees received extremely favourable terms for purchasing their firms including a 30 per cent discount on either the winning tender offer or auction bid, and a period of up to three years to pay 75 per cent of the purchase price' (IMF, 1993, p. 48). A large proportion (around 60 per cent) of the privatised enterprises were recorded as having been purchased by 'their workers' collectives' (IMF, 1993, p. 48). However, the IMF notes that 'in many of these cases, employees were not able to afford the 25 per cent down payment and simply served as agents for private investors who wanted to buy the enterprise at the generous terms offered to employees'(IMF, 1993, p. 48). Moreover, since they lacked sufficient financial assets few ordinary citizens were able to participate in bidding for that substantial part of the privatised small and medium businesses which were not sold to workers' collectives.

Obviously it is difficult to investigate the degree to which criminals participated in and benefitted from the privatisation process. However, there is wide agreement that criminals did play a significant part in it. This large transfer of assets was occurring at a time of massive breakdown of law and order. One account describes the privatisation of assets in Moscow as follows:

The rules for privatisation were fluid, bent officials were easy to come by, and most Russians had no money to speak of. In a matter of weeks the mafia had the city sewn up. . . . Where standard bribery failed in the course of the takeover, the mafia had only to apply a little force. To acquire a popular Gastronom in the capital it simply prevented the employees from bidding by locking them up for the entire afternoon . . . In the end the Moscow properties were sold off for only 200 million rubles, whereas the city had been expecting 1.6 billion. Asked how he felt about the whole larcenous affair, the head of the city council's privatisation committee replied: 'Why not? If the mafia guarantees law and order, food in the shops and washed floors then I'm all for the mafia'. (Sterling, 1994, p. 86).

Large enterprises The first step in the privatisation of large enterprises was rapidly to 'corporatise' them by converting them into 'joint stock companies' with publicly-traded shares and boards of directors. Initially the shares technically were to be owned by GKI, the State Property Fund. The privatisation proper was to consist of the division of the 'state' owned shares into two tranches. The first tranche, amounting to 50–60 per cent of the firm's share value depending upon the variant chosen, was to consist of shares allocated to all citizens, each of whom was issued with a 10,000 ruble voucher to allocate as they chose between enterprises or simply to sell if they wished. The second tranche was to consist of shares allocated free or at a discount to managers and workers in the enterprise. The process had many problems.

A first problem was that there was virtually no preparation of the public for this process of momentous significance for the country. A survey conducted simultaneously with the first issue of vouchers found that the government's explanation of the purpose and nature of the privatisation voucher was 'largely incomprehensible to the population at large' (Tapilina *et al.*, 1993, p. 27): 'The materials that people read, see and hear are frequently of an abstract, speculative nature. They are oriented either towards the functionaries of the incipient market infrastructure or towards the highly educated segment of the population. But the average resident is bewildered about what to do with the privatisation check he has received' (Tapilina *et al.*, 1993, p. 27).

A second problem was that the dominant form of privatisation in its idealised form had a strong element of worker/manager buy-out. Moreover, the worker/manager buy-out aspect of the process was increased due to the fact that at the point at which shares were auctioned to outsiders, 'insiders' had a large advantage in that they possessed superior knowledge of the enterprise's prospects, and could themselves add to their holdings by advancing themselves loans from the enterprise's funds. In case studies of privatisation undertaken in 1993, it was found that large increases occurred in the share of ownership by the 'insiders' during the public auction part of the privatisation process (Buck *et al.*, 1993). While there are advantages with the worker/manager buy-out, there are disadvantages also. It creates incentives to diversify in order to minimise risk rather than maximise profits. It may lead to a high incentive to minimise additional employment in order to maximise income per person for current members of the organisation. One World Bank official involved in the process is reported to have said: 'Privatisation is a step in the direction of private firms, but even in five years these "privatised" enterprises are not going to look like western companies' (quoted in the *Financial Times*, 27 May 1993).

Thirdly, this system had a large element of inbuilt unfairness. It allowed in its basic priniciples large gains for one segment of society relative to those who did not work for state industrial enterprises. They now reaped the benefit of having become the *de facto* owners of 'their' enterprises since the mid-1980s. The large share of assets allocated to them free or at discount (of the already undervalued price) constituted a massive transfer of wealth to the one-half of the population who worked in state industrial enterprises. At least one-half of the adult population did not, but consisted of pensioners, member of the armed forces, bureaucrats and service sector workers (Blanchard *et al.*, 1993, p. 67): 'the privatisation schemes in their three main variants 'show the extraordinary generosity of the Russian government towards the workers and managers − not out of the goodness of the reformers' hearts but out of the recognition of the political reality' (Blanchard *et al.*, 1993, p. 58).

A fourth problem was that privatisation happened at the level of the enterprise, establishment or plant. This is quite different from creating large, internationally competitive multi-plant companies. It may take a long time for a rational, competitive structure of *firms* to emerge from the old structure of *plants* operating under a vertical chain of command. The construction of competitive companies in a former communist economy involves both divesting former plants of many units of production formerly within the plant while simultaneously creating new links with other businesses in order to benefit from economies of scale and scope, and compete with the large firms on the international market. This is a most complex process, and one in which the state planning apparatus may have a useful function to fulfill. Purely 'passive' privatisation, especially in conditions of a collapsing national economy, may fail to create quickly a company structure that competes effectively with multinational giant companies.

Fifthly, there was the practical difficulty of asset valuation. In an atmosphere of massive uncertainty about the whole economic and political environment and in which some important prices were still set by the state, the initial valuation of the privatised assets was hard to determine. For example, a key determinant of the price of the assets in privatised enterprises was the degree to which the enterprises were likely to face foreign competition directly. After an initial phase of complete liberalisation of imports in 1991–2, the Russian government quickly reintroduced tariffs, but still (1992–3) at a generally low level. In early 1994 it was announced that 'stiff' tariffs would shortly be introduced on manufactured goods. It remained anyone's guess what the long-term policy framework would be. The contrast with the consistent, explicit commitment to protect industry through the long transition period in China could not be sharper.

A sixth problem was the intentional undervaluation of assets in order to provide financial gain for insiders. There is wide evidence that during the privatisation process there was heavy undervaluation of assets in relation to any reasonable estimate about their long-term value (Buck *et al.*, 1993; Blanchard *et al.*, 1993, p. 71). This resulted in large windfall gains for the new owners, with a vastly disproportionate share of these gains being obtained by 'insiders'. The army of foreign advisors from the West encountered a situation fundamentally different from the relatively ordered process occurring in a relatively effective legal framework, which surrounded the comparatively small amount of privatisation in their own countries in recent years. In Russia the price of the assets on privatisation was decided effectively by the local 'state' apparatus. This was a heavily politicised process. It was politicised in the narrow sense that the local government, much of which consisted of former communist party members with close connections with factory managers, determined key aspects of the pricing of assets. Moreover, the pricing of assets, like all other social processes in post-Gorbachev Russia, occurred without a framework of relevant law. Nor would such law have been enforceable even if it existed, since the public security apparatus had disintegrated: the KGB was 'in a state of penury and purge', while the militia 'struggles with ancient telephones, ageing patrol cars, no gas, no computers and no money' (Sterling, 1994, p. 87).

The political corrruption surrounding the process of privatisation of state assets existed at the very highest level of government, as can be seen from the case of the former mayor of Moscow, Gavril Popov:

In November 1991, the Mayor [Popov] had actually signed over an entire district of the capital to a French–Russian joint venture called UKUSO, in which he and his minister for the Municipal Economy were acused of holding 40 per cent of the shares. . . . The 'October' district covered 4 million square metres of choice real estate from the splendid Gorky Park to Gagarinsk Square, occupied by academies, monasteries, a hospital and 22,000 residents including Mikhail Gorbachev. It was worth around $30 billion, but UKUSO got it on a 99–year lease at $10 per year. . . . Popov resigned eventually. . . . [but] was never taken to court because, like two and a half million government office holders in the former USSR, he had official and unconditional immunity. (Sterling, 1994, pp. 86–7)

Viktor Ilyutkin, the chairman of the Duma's Security Committee claimed that criminals now control 81 per cent of the voting shares in privatised enterprises (quoted in *The Economist*, 9 July 1994, p. 19). It is difficult to define a 'criminal' and even more difficult to obtain accurate information on such a matter. However, it is certain that an important part of share ownership in the privatised enterprises has been taken over by more or less criminal elements. Many Russian 'investment funds' were simply fronts for 'mafia' activities, 'cash rich from arbitrage activities', able to buy shares in companies in order to take over management control (*Financial Times*, 5 April 1994).

A seventh problem was that privatisation took place in the middle of a massive economic collapse, with large falls in real income for a substantial proportion of the population. This creates a high incentive for short-termism in individuals' investment decisions. The situation was analogous to a famine (Sen, 1982), with increasingly poor people disposing of assets on a large scale in order to meet short-run consumption needs. A study conducted in August 1992 found that two-fifths of the people questioned had no idea what they would do with the privatisation vouchers. Fully two-thirds of those who did have an idea of what they would do intended to 'sell their vouchers and use the money to buy things they needed' (Tapilina *et al.*, 1993, p. 36). The over-supply of privatisation vouchers caused the price to fall, enabling those who possessed capital to accumulate rapidly even more underpriced assets to be realised in the longer term. There was a high incentive for impoverished people both inside and outside the privatised enterprises to sell their newly acquired shares at well below their long-run value in order to survive in the short run. It was reported already in 1993 that as many as one-quarter of all citizens had sold their privatisation vouchers on the open market for less than their face value (Weir, 1993, p. 2815). The vouchers traded at below their face value 'from almost the first day of trading' (IMF, 1993, p. 49). Despite the large undervaluation of assets, the traded price of privatisation vouchers in mid-1993 was only around half the face value (*Financial Times*, 27 May 1993). However, the fall in the nominal value occurred alongside a huge inflation of the general price level. In real terms the value of each voucher fell by about 90 per cent in the year or so after their first issue (IMF, 1993, p. 49).

This process enabled the rapid creation of a highly concentrated form of speculative share ownership as a small number of the new rich individuals and their investment companies[16] were able rapidly to accumulate ownership rights in privatised enterprises. This was quite different from the widely dispersed pattern of share ownership fondly imagined by advocates of the mass voucher scheme. For example, it was known that by the end of 1993, a single individual (Bendukidze) had bought 28 per cent of the shares in the giant Uralmash iron and steel complex, for a mere 300,000 dollars at the current rate of exchange.[17] In another notorious case, the director of the GAZ Plant, which makes Volga motor cars, used tax credits from the state earmarked for investment to build a controlling stake in the company. He made agreements with 15 proxy companies to buy shares at public auctions and thereby came to control 30 per cent of the company's shares (*Financial Times*, 23 February 1994). The Deputy Minister of Finance was reported to have said that Russia's antiquated legal code contained no criminal penalty for the violations committed by the GAZ director (*Financial Times*, 23 February 1994). However, the goal of the investment companies and individual large investors was not necessarily to run the firms into which they had purchased in the difficult environment of Russia in the early 1990s and in a business about which they may have known very little, but often was simply to strip the companies' assets. Those who were in a position to accumulate assets were on average able to do so at staggeringly low prices in relation to the probable long-term value of the assets.

By the middle of 1994 public support for the privatisation programme had collapsed. According to a poll carried out by the Russian Academy of Sciences, the majority of those polled considered that privatisation was 'legalised theft'. Between one-third and two-thirds of respondents believed that privatisation was 'undertaken for the benefit of the *nomenclatura* and criminals' (*Financial Times*, 9 May 1994).

Primitive capitalist accumulation   The Deputy prime minister responsible for privatisation, Anatoly Chubais, said: 'privatisation itself is the creation of a Russian *bourgeoisie* '(quoted in the *Financial Times,* 27 May 1993). This was indeed, the result of the privatisation process. However, the nature of the new bourgeoisie had much more in common with that which emerged from the 'age of plunder' in Elizabethan England (Hoskins, 1976) than with the widely dispersed pattern of bourgeoisification that was dreamed of by the enthusiastic advocates of voucher schemes for the privatisation of public property in the former communist countries. In the course of only a couple years, Russia had gone through the process of 'primitive capitalist accumulation' which took centuries in Western Europe as capitalist property ownership emerged from feudalism. Marx's famous description of that process was widely referred to in Russia during privatisation:

> The economic structure of capitalistic society had grown out of the economic structure of feudal society. The dissolution of the latter set free the elements of the former. . . . The so-called primitive accumulation is nothing else than the historical process of divorcing the producer from the means of production. . . . In actual history it is notorious that conquest, enslavement, robbery, murder, briefly force, play the great part. In the tender annals of Political Economy, the idyllic part reigns from time immemorial. Right and "labour" were from all time the sole means of enrichment, the present year always excepted. As matter of fact the methods of primitive accumulation are anything but idyllic. (Marx, 1887, pp. 714–5)

The methods of primitive accumulation in Russia in the early 1990s also were 'anything but idyllic'. They left the country with a massively unequal distribution of assets from which to set out on its journey into capitalism. As always, the 'tender world' of economics could simply take these as the 'givens', the parameters of the economic system. Also, as always, economists could pretend that the resulting grotesque inequalities in the distribution of income and life chances were the consequence of differences in ability and effort, the consequence of citizens exercising their 'freedom to choose'. They could comfortably forget the odorous way in which the 'original accumulation' had occurred. They could get on with objective analysis of the economic process now that the 'smelly bit' was out of the way. Marx's description seems as apt to-day in describing the Russian situation as it was in describing the British process of primitive capitalist accumulation:

[P]rimitive accumulation plays in Political Economy about the same part as original sin in theology.... In times long gone by there were two sorts of people; one the diligent, intelligent, and above all, frugal elite; the other, lazy rascals, spending their substance, and more, in riotous living.... Thus it came to pass that the former accumulated wealth, and the latter sort had nothing to sell but their skins. And from this original sin dates the poverty of the great majority that, despite all its labour, has up to now nothing to sell but itself, and the wealth of the few that increases constantly although they have long since ceased to work. (Marx, 1887, p. 713)

Many analysts in Russia itself, including even many of the new capitalists who benefitted from it, recognised the period as one with the characteristics of 'primitive accumulation':

The reform that has been under way in Russia since the end of 1991 has been given many precise names: 'reformist breakthrough' (B. Yeltsin), the 'leap into the market' (E. Gaidar), and 'economic genocide against the people' (A. Rutskoi). This reform is also called the 'robbery of the robbed'. A more precise scientific definition is initial capital accumulation. (Rakitskii, 1994, p. 32)

The high-speed process of primitive capitalist accumulation eerily recalls W.G. Hoskins' comments on the dissolution of the monasteries in sixteenth century Britain: 'The spoilation of the Church during the greater part of the sixteenth century is one of the most fundamental divides in English history. Some called it the Great Sacrilege ... more modern historians refer placidly to the Great Transfer; I prefer to label it the Great Plunder, and to see in it that conspiracy of rich men procuring their own fortunes in the name of the commonwealth, whatever brand of the Christian faith they publicly or privately professes, and however they wriggled from one side to the other when the political wind veered round unexpectedly' (Hoskins, 1976, p. 122).

What kind of capitalism?   The mere establishment of private property is not a guarantee of rapid growth. Private property rights can exist in a wide variety of forms and settings, some of which are more favourable to growth than others. There is no precedent for the way in which capitalism has been created in Russia since the mid-1980s. Never before has there been such a rapid, lawless process of primitive capitalist accumulation, occurring moreover in the midst of the deepest economic collapse seen by any country in peacetime in the modern world. The market economy that has been brought into being has been decribed as more of an 'eastern bazaar' than a true market (Starikov, 1994): 'If [the] boorish bazaar features are now affirmed in economic life, there will no manner of mellow civilised "afterward": the triumphant criminal subculture will beat down and smother all the shoots of the civilised market, and will become our economy's unique genetic code for long decades, for centuries' (Starikov, 1994, 17).

f. Housing

House privatisation did not move rapidly, perhaps because it is the most sensitive of all privatisations. However, even in 1992, around eight per cent of apartments were privatised. The vast majority of these were 'given to residing tenants at no cost' (IMF, 1993, p. 50). The fastest pace of 'progress' in housing privatisation was recorded in Moscow, where 20 per cent were reported to have been privatised in this fashion in 1992 alone (IMF, 1993, p. 50). This method of privatisation means that the local authorities forego the possibility of income from increasing rents or from selling the property. Moreover, it provides a large windfall gain to those who were former *apparatchik*, since the allocation of housing was broadly in proportion to political power. Thus, on the one hand, a high ranking ex-Party member with an apartment (albeit small) in the middle of Moscow or St Petersburg, received a real transfer of perhaps $200,000 which might be the international value of his/her apartment. On the other hand, a janitor in a state factory on the outskirts of the city, with a single room in a dirty, poorly located apartment, in a decrepit tenement block, would receive a transfer of wealth that was only a small fraction of this amount. Moreover, more impoverished people would be more likely to sell or mortgage their property in order to survive the current difficulties.

g. The collapse of inter-republican trade

The Soviet industrial structure, with a fairly high share of large specialised plants, resulted in a relatively high degree of trade between regions (Table 7.1). The unweighted average of inter-republican trade in the former USSR as a proportion of GNP in each republic was around 29 per cent. However, the figure for the Russian Federation was only 11.1 per cent. These figures compared to an unweighted average for intra-EC trade of around 21 per cent (World Bank, 1991, p. 121).

It was seen above that the collapse of the CPSU and the disintegration of the Soviet state into separate political entities precipitated a collapse of inter-republican trade. This had disastrous consequences for those republics that were particularily highly dependent on inter republican trade. Industrial plant is not like 'putty' and cannot immediately be usefully switched away from producing inputs for a distant factory to producing substantially different output. Moreover, once trade disintegrated, multiple problems followed, such as the fact that a large portion of industrial plants immediately operated at below their full capacity, thereby driving up costs of production. Moreover, they found it difficult physically to obtain input supplies for their existing factories. This waited upon the re-establishment of trade and payments systems between the republics. The considerably lower degree of integration of the economy of the Russian Federation with those of the other states meant that the problems were much less severe for it than for some of the most trade dependent republics such as Belorussia and the Baltic states.

h. Inflation

The political pressures that allowed a sharp acceleration of inflation in the last years of Gorbachev's rule intensified in the period after the failed August coup. In a fashion that strongly resembled that in much of Latin America (Dornbusch *et al.*, 1991), the government was unable to tax effectively and unable to resist the pressures for continued large scale budgetary expenditure to keep ailing enterprises afloat in the midst of a collapsing economy and thereby prevent large increases in politically dangerous open unemployment. Alexander Khandruyev, a deputy governor of the Russian central bank, put the situation bluntly: 'If we simply stop credit emissions, then our government would face mass strikes to-morrow' (quoted in the *Financial Times*, 27 May 1993).

The Yeltsin government after August 1991 was well aware that its monetary policies were fuelling high inflation. However, up until late 1993–4 the political situation prevented them from taking the tough decisions necessary to control government spending and limit inflation. Richard Layard, one of the advisors to the Russian government, put the situation bluntly: 'Democracy rules out the Chinese solution. . . . When workers can strike and producers can fix their own prices, everything changes. Inflationary forces are unleashed that, if they meet with any degree of fiscal and monetary restraint, cause falls in real demand and then falls in output' (Layard, 1993, p. 26). In Layard's view, given the transformed political situation, the only way to solve the inflationary problem was huge rises in open unemployment: 'In the West it is the level of unemployment that determines the degree of inflationary pressure, and the same seems to be true in Russia. *There has to be enough unemployment to control inflation*' (Layard, 1993, p. 28) (My emphasis, P.N.).

The paradox of this view is that it leads back to more or less explicit support for authoritarianism. It is possible that only a 'Pinochet-style' government would have the political will to strictly limit government spending and accept the consequences of open unemployment rising rapidly. This is what in essence the 1993 Constitution attempted to do: namely, establish the framework for a Latin American, Pinochet-style New Authoritarianism. Even if the parliamentary majority attempted to block the measures, under the new constitution the President could, if need be, push through to the end with mass privatisation and control the money supply, even if this meant massive unemployment.

The argument had come full circle. The initial reason for the West supporting Gorbachev's reforms was supposed to be the ending of 'dictatorship in the Soviet Union'. It was argued then that only under democratic institutions could 'real reforms' be introduced. Now the argument went: 'only under an authoritarian Constitution can "real reforms" be finally pushed through to their sticking place'.

Despite the anti-Yeltsin vote in the December 1993 elections, the Russian Parliament was left with neither an organised opposition nor a government majority. Moreover, so much momentum had already been built up in the privatisation programme, that it was impossible to consider reversing it. The sheer pace of change and the exhaustion of the previous years' political in-fighting had taken the wind out of the sails of opposition in Parliament. Moreover, the Russian government came under renewed and intense pressure from the IMF. Only by meeting the IMF's financial targets would the government have access to desparately needed funds. Russia had by now ceased to have an independent economic policy. It had sunk to the level of a heavily indebted third world country, forced to comply with the conditions imposed by the international institutions and endure lectures from the finance ministers of the advanced capitalist countries:

At a meeting of with finance ministers and central bank governors from the Group of Seven leading industrial countries, Russian officials were told they must deliver on their promise to reduce the budget deficit to 6.5% of gross domestic product this year from 8% in 1993

and reduce the expansion of credit by the monetary authorities . . .
'We must have decisive implemention of budget and monetary poli-cies by Russia', said Mr Theo Waigel, the German finance minister.
According to UK officials, *the message was echoed by Mr Kenneth Clarke, the Chancellor, who said the Russians must keep up their reform policies if they were to obtain more assistance.* (*Financial Times*, 25 April 1994) (Emphasis added)

A 'spectacular change' occurred in Russian monetary policy in this period. The IMF's director, Michael Camdessus commented: 'a few months ago, the IMF had the impression that Russia had no monetary policy' and 'no such thing as a budget'. Now, however, Russia had 'a "very tough" monetary policy with very high real interest rates'. The central bank had ceased distributing subsidised credits. Institutions were in place to push down inflation (*Financial Times*, 22 April 1994). Inflation was rapidy brought down from over 20 per cent per month in 1993 to less than 10 per cent per month in the first half of 1994.

In the summer of 1994 the Russian government was under intense pressure from the Bretton Woods institutions to continue its tough monetary policy, maintain financial stability and apply the strictest hard budget constraint to state industries. The mounting inter-enter-prise debt crisis in 1994 was widely seen as a final step in the Rubicon to be crossed on the road to 'a market economy'. The World Bank and the IMF were involved closely with trying to shore up the government's resolve to face the inevitable wide wave of bankruptcies that would follow a decision to press on with the policies begun at the behest of the IMF early in 1994. If the government persisted with these policies, they would lead to the final *coup de grace* for state industry already in desperate decline. Tentative signs that the government was capitulating to internal pressure from lobbyists to soften monetary policy were met with exasperation from the Bretton Woods organisations: '"It is very disconcerting" an official said, "They are breaking the rules of the game established with Mr Camdessus [IMF managing director] this spring"' (*Financial Times*, 19 August 1994). In the face of intense IMF pressure and the self-evident need to bring hyperinflation under control, the government steeled itself to press ahead with the chosen path of restricting inflation and 'achieving macro-economic stability'. The government's fiscal capacity had shrunk des-perately low. Moreover, the revenue base had shrunk hugely because of the massive depression. Its revenue for 1994 seemed likely to be only one-half of the planned figure. The inexorable logic of bringing down the rate of inflation led to a further drastic cut in government spending. The situation was one of deep tragedy. The succession of political and economic choices made over the preceding decade had followed closely the transition orthodoxy: political reform followed by instantaneous price reform, 'close' integration with the world economy, and high-speed mass privatisation. These had brought Russia to the point at which the final *coup de grace* delivered to Russian industry did have an eerie logic. Under the given conditions, which were the result of following the transition orthodoxy's policies, there was no other way of bringing down hyperinflation. Without this, no economic progress was possible from the awful pit into which the economy had sunk. Yet implementing this policy would deliver the final *coup de grace* to the corpse of Russian industry and propel huge numbers of people out of regular wage employment into impoverishment in the 'informal sector'. Not only industry was affected. In order to stay within the limits agreed with the IMF the government 'slashed expenditure on everything. . . . Huge areas of Russian public life – health, social security, law and order, education, are starved of funds, and the bodies responsible for these areas are reduced to patching things together, taking bribes, or just giving up. . . . Great Soviet institutions [like Moscow State University and the Bolshoi ballet] have become ruined hulks' (*Financial Times*, 24–25 September 1994).

i. Foreign investment

Foreign direct investment conspicuously failed to be attracted to the new Russia. The reported total for 1993 was just $1.5 billion, falling to a predicted figure of only $1 billion in 1994. The cumulative total in mid-1994 was reported to be only $2.7 billion (*IHT*, 28 June 1994). The reported figure for foreign direct investment in China in 1993 alone was $22 billion (*Financial Times*, 24 January 1994). There were numerous reasons for such a poor performance in Russia.

The economic prospects were bleak. Even the deputy mayor of St Petersburg, the optimistic Alexei Kudrin, in an interview with the *Financial Times* told the interviewer that he did not think the 'economic crisis' would be over before 1996 at the earliest (*Financial Times*, 17 May 1994). This scenario was hardly likely to entice foreign investors to the city to make long-term investments in its collapsing industry.

The most fundamental features of the economic environment were uncertain, including such key parameters as the future level of protection.

Furthermore, even after 1991 the legal framework changed repeatedly: 'From the viewpoint of foreign investors, almost monthly changes in conditions of operation was the basic shortcoming of the reform' (Astapovich and Grigori'ev, 1994, p. 88).

The easiest area in which foreign direct investment might have been attracted was oil and natural gas. The international oil companies were salivating at the prospect of investing in Russia, 'one of the last great exploration opportunities for them'. However, prices remained controlled and much below those on the world market. Ownership rights were unclear, with 'pervasive uncertainty as to who is responsible for what' combined with 'rampant corruption'. The tax regime for the industry was 'punitive and constantly changing'. Thus, inflows of direct investment into this industry in the early 1990s were derisory. Output of oil slumped from 600 million tons at the peak in late 1980s to just 350 million tons in 1993: 'Nothing would do more to help the economy through the storms of the next few years than an increase in production and exports of oil, still Russia's largest export earner by far. Nothing, unfortunately, could seem more remote' (*Financial Times*, 27 May 1993).

For the foreign investor everything hinges on the political complexion of a future government. For most of the period after the establishment of the Russian Federation as an independent country, the political situation was highly unstable. Foreign investors feared the accession of a fiercely nationalistic government which would damage their interests: 'The high potential of investments in Russia for Western companies is obviously cancelled out by the political and commercial risk connected with the general political and economic instability, and by the insufficient development of legal and administrative norms' (Astapovich and Grigori'ev, 1994, p. 86).

In addition, the simple fact of the breakdown of law and order, and the rise of organised crime made the environment a difficult and dangerous one in which to operate. Foreign investors' employees and their families lived in much greater danger than in most countries.

Insofar as foreign investment did occur after 1991 it was primarily portfolio and speculative investment, hugely assisted by the massive depreciation of the international price of the ruble, which made Russian assets incredibly cheap in international terms. Richard Layard put the position succinctly: 'Shares are cheap. If you spend $1,000 to buy "vouchers" and exchange these for a portfolio of shares, you will end up owning capital that produces $20,000 of output each year (at present exchange rates). The comparable output figure for shares bought on the London stock market would be about $5,000' (Layard, in *Financial*

Times, 3 June 1994). The head of the Credit Suisse First Boston branch in Moscow commented as follows on the valuation at privatisation of shares in the Unified Energy System, the world's largest integrated Energy System as follows: 'A similar company, producing that number of kilowatts, would be worth about $49 billion in the US, over $30 billion in central Europe. Here, it was worth $200 million. *The world has not yet woken up to the fact that Russian assets are extremely cheap*' (quoted in *Financial Times*, 5 April 1994) (Emphasis added). By the Autumn of 1994 it was reported that there was around $200 million per month in 'foreign' portfolio invstment (*Financial Times*, 24–25 September 1994). By no means all of this was pure 'foreign' investment. An unidentifiable part of it was from capital recycled by Russian 'businessmen'. They were buying assets (nuclear fuels, precious metals, oil, natural gas, drugs, military equipment) in rubles and either legally or, often, illegally exporting them, with the proceeds 'invested' in a 'foreign' business. They then used foreign exchange to buy rubles and 'reinvest' in Russia by purchasing low priced assets in rubles, to start the cycle all over again. A combination of cheap rubles, under-priced assets and an unformed market economy was irresistible for speculators: 'Given the existing ruble exchange rate, both foreign and domestic speculators find it profitable to buy property for subsequent resale. [I]t may take a whole epoch for an effective proprietor and corporate control to evolve' (Astapovich and Grigori'ev, 1994, p. 99).

The contrast with China could not be greater. Domestic demand boomed for a decade and a half behind high and stable protectionist barriers. The government devised reasonably stable laws for foreign investors. The broad framework of political economy was clear and relatively stable. The country was relatively safe with fairly effective forces of law and order.

Far from the reforms generating a net inflow of capital to Russia, there is no doubt that in the early 1990s there was a large net outflow of capital. Within the country, hyperinflation, the collapse of mass purchasing power, extreme uncertainty about the long-term political environment, and the concentration of a large body of investible funds in the hands of speculators were all deeply inimical to long-term investment. Much of the capital flight was illegal. One careful estimate for 1992 believes that almost one-half of the capital drain out of Russia was in the form of illegal exports (Khanin, 1993(a), p. 19). Even if it had wished to, the government lacked the resources to monitor international capital movements closely. The Institute of International

Finance estimates that in 1993–4 at least one billion dollars per month was leaving Russia (*Financial Times*, 2 February 1994). However, due to 'lack of support from the Russian government', the Institute was not able to complete its investigations of capital flight from Russia: one investigator in the team said: 'Undoubtedly, our report turned out to be more political than was anticipated' (*Financial Times*, 2 February 1994). Numerous purchases of high-priced houses in London in the early 1990s were made by individual Russians, though the dividing line between 'company' and individual purchases was a thin one: 'Vladiir Gusinsky, head of the Most construction group, has bought property in London and Portugal registered as company-owned to minimise his tax bill. He is, he says, particularily fond of the Chelsea area' (quoted in *Financial Times*, 2 February 1994). Cartier, the luxury goods shop, said it had seen 'a big increase in Russian clients in the last year, buying watches, jewellery and other luxury goods – almost always with cash' (*Financial Times*, 2 February 1994).

j. Results

Investment In the early 1990s investment collapsed to less than one-half of its level in the late 1980s (Table 2.6). Khanin estimates that in 1992 alone investment fell by 50 per cent (Khanin, 1993a, p. 17). The decline accelerated into 1994, with a reported fall of 27 per cent in investment in the first half of 1994 alone (*Financial Times*, 14 July 1994) This was a consequence of the extremely high rate of inflation, the disintegration of institutions which could usefully employ new capital, the collapse of demand and the emergence of huge excess capacity. The drastic fall in investment caused serious acceleration in the average age of the country's capital stock. Instead of rapidly modernising its capital stock as China did, the first decade of post-Stalinist reform saw the capital stock steadily becoming more outdated and run down.

Trade In the sharpest contrast to China's reform programme, the reforms in Russia failed to generate economic institutions that could successfully compete on world markets. The recorded dollar value of the country's exports slumped from around 63 billion in 1990 to only 35 billion in 1994 (predicted) (Smith New Court, 1994). Unlike China, which was able rapidly to upgrade the technical level of industry through expanding imports, the value of Russia's imports slumped even more precipitously than the value of exports, from $84 in 1990 to just $30 billion in 1994 (predicted) (Smith New Court, 1994). In 1992 alone, there was a real fall of 40 per cent in equipment imports (Khanin, 1993b, p. 15).

Output   A poor economic performance simply disintegrated after the dissolution of the Soviet Union. Output plummeted, with net national product in 1993 reported to be less than 60 per cent of its level in 1989 (Table 2.6). Some estimates show an even greater fall. Khanin, for example, considers that national product in 1992 was less than one-half of the 1989 level (Khanin, 1993a). In 1994 it was predicted that net national product would fall a further 16–18 per cent (*Transition*, July–August, 1994).

Demand for energy fell drastically. Oil production in Russia fell from 10.9 million barrels per day in 1985 to just 7.0 million in 1993 (*Financial Times*, 19 August 1994). Moreover, this was alongside a sustained physical volume of oil exports. Domestic demand for oil fell by 19 per cent in 1993 alone (*Financial Times*, 19 August 1994).

Industrial output by 1993 had fallen to less than 70 per cent of the 1989 level (Table 2.6) and in 1994 was set to fall by a further 25–28 per cent (*Transition*, July–August, 1994), leaving total output at one-half or less of the 1989 level. Even this level of output was only sustained by a huge rise in inter-enterprise debt in 1994, which could not be sustained indefinitely.

Large falls occurred in the capital goods industries alongside the collapse in fixed investment. Already by 1993 output of machine tools had fallen to three-fifths of the level of 1991 (Table 7.3). In the first half of 1994, for example, output in the engineering industry fell by no less than 44 per cent (*Financial Times*, 14 July 1994). It was predicted that the output of the machine-building industry would fall by between 42 and 44 per cent for the whole year (*Transition*, July–August, 1994).

It was not the case that the 'dead wood' of the old heavy industrial sector was being cut out in a 'surgical operation'. Rather there was a deep, simultaneous decline in the production of both heavy and light industry. Output of key industrial consumer goods fell precipitously, reflecting the large fall in ordinary people's living standards. Production of sugar, shoes, fabric and clothes fell by 'between one-third and one-half in the first quarter of 1994' (*Financial Times*, 9 May 1994) after already large declines in 1991–93 (Tables 7.4 and 7.5).

Russia was experiencing explosive deindustrialisation. By the first half of 1994, it was reported that the 'service' sector was already producing over 50 per cent of GDP (*Financial Times*, 14 July 1994). The

Table 7.5 Retail price index in China and the former USSR (percentage change over the previous year)

Year	China	Former USSR
1978	0.7	0.7
1979	2.0	1.4
1980	6.0	0.7
1981	2.4	1.4
1982	1.9	3.4
1983	1.5	0.7
1984	2.8	−1.3
1985	8.8	0.7
1986	6.0	2.0
1987	7.3	1.9
1988	18.5	2.3
1989	17.8	2.3
1990	2.1	5.4
1991	2.9	98.4
1992	5.4	1,292
1993	13.0	1,226
1994	—	457*

Source: China: SSB, *ZGTJNJ*, 1994, p. 237 and *BR*, 14–20 August, 1994, vol. 37 (11). Former USSR: UN, *Economic Survey of Europe, 1989–90*, 392 and IMF, *World Economic Outlook*, May 1994, p. 119.

Note: *predicted.

shift into service sector 'employment' was an invevitable consequence of the collapse of the industrial sector. Real wage rates in the manufacturing sector slumped in the early 1990s. A large part of the workforce had their jobs and relative income redefined as the squeeze on the enterprises grew tighter. By 1993–4, large swathes of manufacturing industry had ceased paying wages altogether or were only paying them intermittently. Although technically still employed in state enterprises a large portion of the industrial workforce had effectively moved out into employment permanently or temporarily in the 'service' sector.

Structure of employment It is commonly argued by Western economists that the negative effects upon real income of the collapse of Russian industry have been exaggerated because this ignores the positive effect of the large rise in employment in the 'service' sector for which data are poor. This argument completely miscontrues the nature of most of such expanding service sector activity in Russia in the early 1990s. Indeed, the 'argument' is simply a tautology: if regular wage employment in industry collapses, and there is no 'social safety net', then to survive, people must 'work' in the 'service' sector even if, in the last instance, that means simply standing on a street corner for many hours each day begging. The 'social safety net' hardly exists in Russia. For example, a survey carried out by CARE in 1992 found that on average pensions were below the World Bank estimated minimal nutritional support level. A high percentage of those surveyed had chronic medical or dental problems that impaired eating (quoted in Ellman, 1994, p. 341). With such a low level for the 'social safety net' everyone who had any labour power to sell was forced into the labour market. That basically could only mean the 'service sector', since neither industry nor agriculture was expanding investment and employment.

A very large share of the new 'service' sector consisted of activities with pathetically limited amounts of capital, extremely low labour productivity and incomes, no effective labour law, and a high degree of uncertainty for those thereby 'employed'. Moreover, crime and vice were major new 'service' sector activities. The service sector in the new Russia had much more in common with the 'informal' sector of underdeveloped countries than with the high labour productivity service activities in which much (though far from all) of the recent expansion of 'service' sector had occurred in the advanced capitalist economies. It is hard to imagine how a high income, prosperous service sector can exist on a wide scale in a country the size of Russia in which the manufacturing sector has fallen to pieces.

Average incomes   The collapse in output was accompanied by a deep decline in average real incomes. It is estimated that real average incomes in 1991 stood at 74 per cent of their level in 1986, and by August 1992 stood at just 57 per cent of their 1986 level (Rakitskii, 1994, p. 40). Khanin estimates that in 1991/2 personal consumption fell by 29 per cent (Khanin, 1993b, p. 14). The World Bank estimated that in the year 1992/3 alone average real income fell by around one-fifth (reported in Weir, 1993, p. 2811). These were, of course, all very rough estimates indeed. The decline in average incomes was reflected in the drastic fall in output of products consumed by the mass of citizens, including basic industrial consumer goods, such as shoes and textiles (Tables 7.3 and 7.4), the fall in output of superior foodstuffs (Table 7.2), and the change in the share of consumption allocated to food. It is estimated that the share of food expenditure in average income rose from 33 per cent in 1986, to 45 per cent in 1991, and after leaping to 77 per cent in February 1992 in the immediate aftermath of price liberalisation, still stood at 57 per cent in August of the same year (Rakitskii, 1994, p. 40).

Income distribution   For a large portion of the population living standards collapsed alongside a massive unequalising change in the distribution of income and wealth. The journal *Ekonomika i zhizn* estimated that the range of incomes between the top and the bottom decile of income distribution rose from a multiple of 4.5 in December 1991 to 11.0 by December 1993 just two years later (quoted in Banerji, 1994, p. 1154), and was reported to stand at 13.0 in mid-1994 (*Transition*, July–August, 1994). Statistics are, of course, unusually problematic in such a turbulent time. The perceptions of impartial and experienced observers are much more impressive. In one of his final articles, Alec Nove (1994) wrote:

> It is not necessary to be a socialist to criticise the vast gulf that has formed between the rich and the poor in Russia.... People are getting rich from deals, from buying things and reselling them. Initial accumulation? But it should be followed by the investment of accumulated resources in production. This is not happening yet. What is happening is that enormous profits are piling up in foreign banks or are being spent on various foreign labels. (Nove, 1994, p. 46).

Alongside the rise in absolute poverty (see below) went an explosive growth in the real income of the new capitalist class. *Newsweek* estimated that by 1993 there were perhaps 100,000 (0.6 per cent of the total population) who had incomes equivalent to $2,000 a month or more (15 February 1993). *Kommersant*, the leading business newspaper, commissioned a survey which found that about three million Russians (around 2 per cent of the total population) were able to live at a typical middle-class European level (quoted in Weir, 1993, p. 2813). However, the most powerful of the new rich certainly escaped the inadequate statistical networks and their income was visible mainly in the proliferating new large houses on the outskirts of major cities, and in the expensive imported consumer goods. Alongside the huge number of homeless people (estimated to be around 300,000–400,000 in Moscow alone) went a huge rise in the consumption of imported Mercedes Benz motor cars, with Russia buying more new top-of-the-range models than in the whole of Europe combined (reported in Weir, 1993, p. 2813).

Poverty It is widely acknowledged that the early 1990s saw a large rise in absolute poverty (see, for example, Ellman, 1994, p. 341). The journal *Trud* estimated that in 1993 around 15 million (10 per cent) of the Russian population lived 'far below the poverty line', while a further 40 million people (around one-third of the population), lived at or slightly above subsistence level (quoted in Weir, 1993, p. 2813). In 1993/4 the dimensions of poverty accelerated alarmingly. The Russian Ministry of Labour's Living Standard Centre reported that the proportion of the population in poverty rose from 29 per cent in the fourth quarter of 1993 to 39 per cent in the second quarter of 1994 (*Transition*, July–August, 1994).

Public health Public health provision fell sharply. State budgetary outlays on health care were estimated to have fallen from around 4 per cent of GNP in the mid-1980s to just over 1 per cent in 1993 (Weir, 1993, p. 2812). In 1991 alone, real government spending on healthcare was estimated to have fallen by 39 per cent (*Financial Times*, 26 August 1994). A large part of access to health services had been privatised *de facto* as health practitioners coped with drastically falling personal remuneration from the state by supplying their services through the black market. A profound consequence of the combined fall in real incomes, decline in public health care provision and deep psychological disorientation, was a remarkable rise in death rates.

A meticulous recent study concludes that since the collapse of the USSR, 'the mortality situation in the successor states has rapidly and significantly worsened': between 1991 and 1993 the crude death rate in Russia rose by 26 per cent (Ellman, 1994). As a result, by 1993 the life expectancy at birth of Russian men had fallen to about 59, which was about 6 years below the level of 1987 (Ellman, 1994). By 1993, male life expectancy at birth in Russia had fallen below the level of the medium income countries and probably fallen to a level about that of Indonesia in the second half of the 1980s (Ellman, 1994, p. 352). The author explains this 'remarkable phenomenon' as follows:

Provisional, tentative and necessarily speculative analysis of the main objective, ultimate reasons for the increase in age-specific death rate and disease in the successor states since the break up of the USSR are: impoverishment; state failure in the Soviet period, followed by

State desertion in the post-Soviet period; inadequate financing for medical staff and medical facilities, lack of medicines and other medical supplies, and the introduction of user payments for medical services; a deterioration in public hygiene, food contamination and the quality of drinking water; economic, social and political disintegration; an increase in the length of the working week; and mortal conflicts ranging from murder via gang wars to civil wars and major interstate military conflicts. (Ellman, 1994, p. 352)

Psychological crisis The prospects for most Russians are bleak. The pace and nature of the transition from communism has had the most profound psychological consequences with the mass of citizens experiencing deep disorientation. Researchers at the Central Economic Mathematical Institute concluded 'The crisis which the country is in, is not only economic and political, but also social-psychological. Such psychological phenomena as apathy, cynicism, disappointment, are no less precise indicators of the crisis than inflation and the fall in production' (quoted in Ellman, 1994, pp. 148–9). The political consequence of this trauma was the vote for Zhironovsky and against the liberal reform programme of the Yeltsin advisors. Such was the level of disillusion that in St Petersburg, the vanguard city of economic reform, the elections for the city council in April 1994 were almost annulled. The turnout only reached the required minimum of 25 per cent when polling was extended for an extra day (*Financial Times*, 17 May 1994).

Human resources The human 'capital stock' was run down rapidly as the state of the nation's housing, health provision, diet and education drastically declined. The capacity of the labour force to undertake effective work was reduced by widespread psychological disorientation. Even the change in ethical values towards ultra individualism reduced the co-operative capacities that are necessary even for most capitalist organisations to function well.

However, there were even simpler senses in which the human capital stock was being run down. Large numbers of people with specialist skills were transferring their skills to completely different activities in order to survive. Huge numbers of people were shifting out of the (now) low paid or non-paid labour in the public sector into often unrelated activities in the private economy, so that a large part of their training was wasted. Moreover, a large emigration of skilled labour was occurring due to lack of demand for their services within the collapsing domestic economy. By 1993 there were estimated to be over

400 Russian scientists and engineers 'working for the prosperity of the South Korean economy' with many more invited to go in the near future (Starikov, 1994, p. 17). It is estimated that around a quarter of million workers with high skills will leave the CIS annually in the 1990s (Starikov, 1994, p. 18).

Prospects   Under Gorbachev, the Russian economy moved from stagnation into deep recession. In 1991–93, the situation declined into the most profound depression witnessed in any country in peacetime in the modern world. In 1993–4 the economy entered free fall. A report to the German government from three leading think tanks on the Russian economy considered that even worse was in store for the Russian economy, believing that the most likely scenario was for 'a complete collapse of industrial production' with 'mass unemployment inevitable' (*Financial Times*, 11 May 1994).

The 'gleam in the eye' of the Russian government and its advisors in the IMF was that if the inflation rate could be kept genuinely low indefinitely and the currency stabilised, then the economy could begin to grow again by around 1996. In the view of the *Financial Times*: 'it is not wholly utopian to imagine that Russia could end the millenium as one of the world's fastest growing economies' (*Financial Times*, 24–25 September, 1994). However, this was, at best, a hope which may well not come to fruition. Moreover, even if it were to turn out to be true it would have come at the end of over a decade of failure, great hardship for most Russians, and huge unequalising changes in the class structure.

7.2.3 Summary

The fundamental cause of the Russian collapse lies in the destruction of the nation-state and the state administrative apparatus under Gorbachev. This process was substantially the result of appalling policy errors by the Soviet leadership. This in turn is explicable to some degree by deeper forces in modern Soviet history. However, the policy choice was attributable also to the massive pressure directed against the Soviet government, and Gorbachev in particular, in the final phase of the Cold War. It was, moreover, influenced by the impact that contacts with Western, especially US, Sovietological institutions had upon key figures surrounding Gorbachev. The overthrow of the Soviet state was almost universally applauded in the Western media, by Western academics and, especially, by Western politicians. The overthrow of the communist state was the central building block of the transition orthodoxy.

Once the state apparatus had collapsed, the range of options for any successor government was reduced greatly. The depth of the political and economic difficulties bequeathed to the Russian government in 1991 made it difficult to devise a successful economic strategy for the country in the early 1990s.

The nature of the political problems after August 1991 was such that it was difficult for the government to pursue any kind of consistent policy. The composition of the new parliamentary institutions rendered it impossible to get agreement on a consistent economic policy. The state's fiscal capacity had been deeply undermined by the political changes, giving a high built-in propensity towards inflation. The framework of law and order had already begun to break down. This deeply undermined the security of property rights, and made it likely that the distributional consequences of any move towards privatisation would be heavily affected by criminal power. The government's confidence was shattered by the political disintegration of the USSR, the overthrow of the Communist Party of the Soviet Union, and by the swift collapse of communism in Eastern Europe. Moreover, the government was desparate for international financial support. These events helped push the government towards the international instititutions for advice on how to try to shape its economic programme.

The path that was adopted was one which produced the worst of all possible worlds. The 'Shock Therapy' of instantaneous price liberalisation and wild, high-speed privatisation occurred without an effective framework of law and order, or government administrative strength. It occured in an economy with hyperinflation and collapsed government fiscal capacity. The main purpose of the government in this period (1992/4) was not to minimise the human cost of the transition, but to maximise the speed with which capitalist institutions were created. The most important such institution was regarded by the government as a capitalist class. There was the clearest view that the short-term costs were worthwhile in the interests of creating the efficiency and growth-promoting insititutions of capitalism. The result was a process of brutal and massively unequal primitive capitalist accumulation, the 'creation of markets in circumstances of total chaos', as Mr Soskovets, the deputy prime minister, expressed it (*Financial Times*, 23 August 1994). The policy of rapid privatisation was supported strongly by a large part of the circle of foreign advisors and by the international capitalists with whom government officals had contact.

Without a coherent, effective state apparatus, no strategy for transition from the communist economy in Russia after August 1991 could succeed. In the absence of such an apparatus it was impossible to follow an 'East Asian' approach to the transition. However, the initial orientation of the Yeltsin government and the advice it received from the international institutions was directed away from trying to reconstruct a strong state. The destruction of such a state was widely regarded as the great achievement of the Gorbachev epoch. A tragic attempt to re-construct a 'strong state', with explicit Western support, commenced only as the economy entered free fall in 1993–4.

The disaster of the Soviet transition from communism demonstrates the folly of attempting a comprehensive Great Leap of the entire system of politics and economics. The result was a drastic worsening of the conditions of life for a large part of the Soviet population, and the construction of a hugely unequal distribution of assets and economic power. Russia's economic situation cannot deteriorate for ever. The optimisic scenario visualises the economy beginning to stabilise within a couple of years. It is even possible that it may begin to achieve reasonable growth towards the end of the century if inflation remains low and political calm is maintained. However, the costs incurred during their period, which will have lasted around fifteen years, even on the optimistic scenario, will have been high. Policy choice has been the central reason for this outcome. Tragically, the Soviet economic system had a large potential for improvement under a suitable set of incremental reforms. It was not necessary that there be a period of 'surgery' and steep decline of output and living standards before improvement set in. However, successful implementaion of such policies required the maintenance of a strong and effective state apparatus. Moreover, the 'optimistic' scenario may be incorrect. Russia's decline may still have a long way to go, and it is quite possible that the political system will see fresh transformations.

When Deng Xiaoping talked in the late 1970s and in the 1980s of the dangers of descent into political chaos in China if the communist party were overthrown, he was regarded by a large fraction of the intellectual democratic movement in China as at best foolish and at worst malign in whipping up an unreal danger in order to justify prolongation of a vile regime.[18] Political correctness and passionate rhetorical gestures are not a good basis for policy.

It can now be seen the communist system was brittle, especially in the huge empires of Russia and China. There was no possibility for careful, controlled reform, gradually releasing the 'safety valve' of political control. The choice can now be seen all too clearly from the Russian case in a way that few imagined a decade or so ago. The only alternative to continued communist party rule in Russia and China during the transition to some form of market economy was indeed political chaos. The establishment of a stable democratic system was something that could only be accomplished after the market economy had been developed and the habits of life necessary for stable democracy established. Unfortunately, political chaos creates the worst possible conditions for producing just such an advance in the market economy in a reforming Stalinist system.

8 Conclusions

8.1 SUMMARY

Overall

After the late 1970s China slowly moved away from totalitarian, command economy communism. It moved towards a nationalistic, state-guided, bureaucratic market economy, with a high emphasis on harnessing individual entrepreneurial energies within a collectivist framework. The reforms harnessed the potential latent in the old system and set in motion a virtuous circle of growth out of the command economy. China became ever more powerful internationally. In Russia, the reforms quickly destroyed the old state apparatus, but failed to construct an effective successor state. They allowed the creation of a highly unequal and deeply disorienting process of primitive capitalist accumulation. The resulting inequalities in asset ownership will fix the parameters for economic life for many decades to come. The reforms caused a disastrous decline in investment and industrial output, setting in motion a vicious circle of economic collapse. Russia became ever weaker internationally, to the point that its policies were constructed at the direct instruction of the major international capitalist institutions. In the brief space of just a few years it had been humiliated and broken as a great power.

This book contains two implicit counterfactual propositions. First, the selection of different policies in Russia could have produced rapid growth of output and a large improvement in popular living standards. Secondly, the selection of a different set of policies in China could easily have produced a political and economic disaster, with a large decline in popular living standards.

There is currently a great deal of interest in Russia in the 'Chinese solution' to Russia's deep problems. The analysis in this book does not lead logically to the easy conclusion that Russia ought now to follow 'the Chinese path'. This was a path out of the communist command economic system, using the still extant institutions of communism, working with a unified nation-state, and reorganising an existing system of publicly-owned assets. It began with the establishment of a virtuous circle of growth leading to a whole sequence of interconnected improvements in performance. The state apparatus in Russia is destroyed. The nation-state is destroyed. There are few assets left in the public sector. The economy is in the deepest decline. It is a fantasy to imagine that one can simply reconstruct the old nation state, the old administrative apparatus, and the old publicly-owned economy. Careful study of China's reform path would have been relevant to devising a reform strategy for the country in the late 1980s. It is not much relevant to Russia's current situation. This requires thinking afresh from the present conditions. The 'Chinese solution' is no more an answer to Russia's current disastrous situation than were 'free markets' and 'democracy' an answer to the problems of the communist command system.

Chapter 2

The contrast in performance under reform policies is breathtaking. Almost every major indicator in the two countries moved in an opposite direction. At every stage of China's reform programme commentators predicted that the growth shortly would run out of steam. Instead, its economic boom continued almost uninterrupted right through to the mid-1990s. Morever, the most important indicators of all, those concerned with the physical quality of life, almost all showed substantial improvement alongside the accelerated growth of output and real income. In Russia, the poor performance in Gorbachev's early years turned into a very poor performance in the late period of his rule. It became nothing less than a disaster in the 1990s. Output declined precipitously. While foreign direct investment poured into China it shunned Russia. Most important of all, the indicators of the physical quality of life showed a sharp downturn, with a large rise in death rates. The rest of this book tried to explain and evaluate this contrast.

Chapter 3

Some commentators critical of the outcome of post-communist reform have argued explicitly or have implied that the most that was needed with the communist system was tinkering in order substantially to improve its performance. Others have argued that the command system served a useful function in the early stages of development, but had outlived it usefulness.[1] This chapter argues that both these views are incorrect. It suggests that the basic concepts of the command economic system were fundamentally flawed from the outset. Moreover, it argues that in both cases systemic problems were intensifying. However, neither system was on the verge of collapse. Dangerous reform experiments cannot be justified in hindsight as rescuing the systems from impending disaster. They needed system reform to rescue them from stagnation. The questions were: how fast, in what manner and towards what goal should reform proceed? Most importantly, what should be the relationship between political and economic reform?

Chapter 4

This chapter evaluates the arguments that were made in principle about how to reform a communist system. Until the reforms began in China, little was written on the subject. The 'policy' content of the vast bulk of the writing on the communist systems consisted simply of contrasting the shortcomings of these systems with the alleged advantages of capitalism. In other words, the implicit 'policy' recommendation was simply: 'establish a capitalist system and Western democratic institutions'. Even in the early 1980s the literature on the principles of reforming communist systems was small. Only in the late 1980s, and especially after the overthrow of communist systems in Eastern Europe in 1989, did a large 'transition' literature begin to emerge. This was relevant not only to the post-communist countries of Eastern Europe, but also to still-communist countries of the USSR, China and, much less discussed, the smaller communist countries in Asia.[2]

A large consensus quickly built up in the Western literature,[3] and was deeply influential in the remaining communist countries. It was a combination of the political principles of advanced capitalism and the economic principles of British colonialism. This transition orthodoxy was constructed around a number of key propositions.

It was held that serious economic reform was only possible after the communist party was overthrown. It was accepted as self-evident that the overthrow of communism was intrinsically desirable since it added to the welfare of the citizens of the communist countries by giving them political freedom. Moreover, it was 'twice blessed' since it was believed to be the only way in which serious economic reform could be brought about. The belief in the intrinsic and functional virtues of democratisation was buttressed by the shift within the international institutions towards democratisation as a means to improve the situation in poorly performing developing countries, especially those of Africa.

'Transition' economists mostly believed that reforming communist countries could only achieve rapid improvement in their economic performance if they quickly moved towards a free market economy. The policies recommended were simply a more extreme version of the 'stabilisation and structural adjustment package' that had been implemented in so many developing countries under the supervision of the Bretton Woods institutions. The intellectual lineage of the transition orthodoxy extends back to the economic liberalism of the utilitarian economists which underlay the economic policies of the British empire. It was 'laisssez-faire' in modern dress. Its key elements were tight monetary policy, price liberalisation, abolition of protection, and privatisation of state-owned enterprises. These policies were almost inseparable from the proposition that a 'half-way house' solution of incremental system reform was a path to economic failure – worse perhaps, even, than the command economy. The notion that there was a 'Third Way' which combines the virtues of plan and market in some form of 'market socialism' was ridiculed by the most influential reform 'theorists', such as Kornai, and parroted by less influential figures.

The 'transition orthodoxy' was seriously flawed. It underestimated the capacity of communist governments to introduce serious market reforms. It underestimated the difficulty of producing a stable political environment in the wake of the anti-communist revolution. This problem was especially acute in large countries with wide regional diversities. It underestimated the importance of effective government of whatever political complexion for the conduct of economic life and for citizens' security: communist 'law' and communist administration is preferable to lawlessness and widespread criminality. The transition orthodoxy greatly underestimated the problems that would be caused by attempts to introduce rapid system change. It failed to anticipate the degree to which it would be necessary for the state to undertake a wide range of functions where the market 'failed' during the complex period of the transition away from the communist command system. These failures were in respect both to the achievement of growth and stability but also distribution of assets and income. Painfully little thought was given to the consequences for the resulting distribution of assets under a programme of rapid privatisation under conditions of shock therapy.

The central thesis of this book is that the contrasting outcomes in China and Russia stem from the sharply different approaches taken by the respective leadership in the two countries towards the transition orthodoxy. These consensus views were held not only among academic social scientists in the advanced capitalist countries. They played a central role in the formal advice and informal influence of the powerful international institutions, notably the IMF and the World Bank. They were important also in the approach adopted by domestic social scientists and policy 'think tanks' once they began to gain some independence of thought. Even in China the orthodoxy gained influence rapidly among policy advisors as contacts with the international community grew apace in the 1980s. It required enormous intellectual courage for a young Chinese economist sent for training at the World Bank, the IMF or in a Western university to resist the ideas presented by the vastly richer and more sophisticated teachers. Most of the teachers they encountered had contempt for socialism and planning. They also considered the 'economics' of the Chinese reforms as primitive. They also regarded the Chinese leaders as immoral in their approach to politics.

The Chinese leadership resisted these pressures and adopted policies that were quite contrary to those of the orthodoxy. Its economic policies were criticised widely as leading to a dead end: 'up the creek to nowhere'. Its political approach was condemned to the extent that an important part of the international community wished to punish China for not observing the internationally acceptable norms of political behaviour. Gorbachev and his immediate advisors comprehensively embraced the central tenets of the mainstream reform consensus, initially in their approach to political reform and latterly in their attempt to reform the economy. Under Yeltsin there was an even more explicit commitment to the transition orthodoxy.

Chapter 5

To what extent was this contrast in results caused by the large differences in the political and economic conditions in the two countries at the start of reform? There was, indeed, a wide range of differences between the two systems. These included the geopolitical location, level of per capita income, industrialisation and urbanisation, relative importance of small-scale industry, the strength of the ancient roots of entrepreneurship, the availability of capital in the hands of overseas citizens, population pressure on farmland, relative size of the scientific community, cultural outlook, and relative size of ethnic minorities. However, there were many areas of fundamental similarity. These included the way the core of industry was organised; the relative importance of heavy industry within the industrial structure; the level of mass education relative to the country's income level; entrepreneurial capabilities as revealed in the modern period; the relatively large role of the military sector; and the huge common underachievement in relation to existing human and physical resources. In both cases there was a large potential for well-designed institutional change to produce a substantial and continuing improvement in economic performance.

Many of the differences between the systems suggested *a priori* not that China would be likely to perform better than the USSR under a well-designed reform programme, but rather, the reverse. China's extraordinarily successful performance under reform was to a considerable degree despite, not because of, its legacy from pre- and post-revolutionary history. Its special handicaps for accelerated growth included the location of a large proportion of industry in remote inland areas; a low level of scientific personnel relative to both the population size and the level of income; a relatively large proportion of industrial output produced in small-scale, technologically backward plants; a miniscule amount of farmland per capita; and a high rate of population growth.

Many of the factors that are now identified as 'advantages' for China, such as the large amount of capital in the hands of overseas Chinese and the availability of a huge rural labour surplus, could only be taken advantage of because the policies adopted enabled them so to be. In the absence of policies that stimulated investment in the non-farm sector, the large and rapidly growing rural population would have been a huge liability, not an advantage, with ever-falling labour productivity in agriculture. Overseas Chinese capital would likewise have not been prepared to invest in China unless the chosen policies made it advantageous for them to do so. Had the Chinese system of political economy disintegrated in the way that the Soviet Union's did, investment by overseas Chinese would have been only a small fraction of that which actually occurred.

Chapter 6

During system reform the Chinese government was obsessed with maintaining social and political stability. The continued commitment to the old political insitutions allowed a great deal of official corruption to occur. However, the maintenance of a strong communist party enabled the state to remain comparatively effective fiscally. It meant that the rules governing the organisation of the economy were reasonably predictable and contractual arrrangements were reasonably secure. The Chinese government was unwavering in its commitment to experimentalism in reform, with priority to policies that would lead to growth of output and incomes. Economic agents were confronted by a reasonably stable set of parameters upon which to base their decisions. The government sustained a public commitment to key ethical values. The former collectivist values were not abandoned in favour of individualism.

The interests of the individual and different social groups were subordinated to building a powerful country and common prosperity. The term 'socialism' was redefined gradually but not jettisoned. In 1994, the Chinese government still considered the country to be a socialist, rather than a capitalist, market economy. 'Socialism' came to be indentified firstly with planning through the use of markets. It was identified secondly with combining individual incentives with limitations on asset accumulation by individuals and, thirdly, with providing 'fair' opportunities to those in less advantageous socio-economic positions. These values, and the associated polices, helped ensure that during the reform period there was a reasonably effective trickle-down of the benefits of growth. A sense of 'social coherence' was maintained during the reform period. This benefitted popular welfare directly through its psychological impact. It also helped cement social stability through giving citizens a sense of participation in a common endeavour.

The Chinese reforms aimed to improve the performance from publicly-owned assets through the devolution of control over the 'use rights' (*shiyong quan*) in return for income sharing along contracted lines. Price liberalisation proceeded cautiously along dual track lines. Simultaneously, the material supply system was gradually liberalised. However, even in the early 1990s, domestic producers remained shielded from foreign competition. These gradually introduced, experimental, supply-side reforms improved labour productivity and incomes. Capital began to move towards those regions, sectors and enterprises that yielded higher returns. Not only did the returns from investment improve, but the rate of savings and investment was sustained at a high level. The 'Lewis model' of growth was able to operate with fast growth of non-farm employment generating large surpluses per worker for reinvestment, unhindered in much of the labour market by institutional restrictions on conditions of employment. From extreme technical backwardness, China began to generate rapid technical progress. Fast growth of export earnings enabled rapid growth of imports of technology-enhancing products. The reforms provided domestic producers with increased incentives to achieve technical progress themselves.[4] Private direct foreign investment acted as an increasingly important channel for modernisation.

Throughout the reform period the Chinese economy remained highly protected. Domestic producers could be certain that for a long period ahead, their only serious competitors in most spheres were from within China itself. As domestic markets gradually liberalised, consumers of all products were able to choose more and more freely, and became progressively more discriminating purchasers. This applied most obviously in consumer goods markets. The quality of a wide range of consumer goods rose in obvious ways during the reforms, many of which could not be captured by statistics. The same processes began also to affect the production of capital goods. The enterprises that prospered and grew fastest tended to be those that produced products that were in some sense, whether price, design, durability or energy consumption, considered to be superior. The large increases in personal income caused a large increase in demand for consumer goods and services. An initial large rise in demand for food grain, shifted to increased demand for superior foodstuffs. Demand for housing was sustained at a high level throughout the reform period. In the early phase of the reforms the main source of increased demand for industrial consumer goods was relatively simple consumer durables, such as bicyles and sewing machines. As the reforms progressed, demand growth shifted to a new wave of industrial products, such as colour TVs, refrigerators, hi-fi equipment and fashion clothing. Meeting this huge, fast-growing demand mainly from domestic producers induced corresponding investment in the farm sector and in the light industries. In a substantially closed economy, meeting the demand for these products necessitated a large, corresponding rise in demand for capital goods and intermediate inputs. Demand from domestic producers for such products as steel, cement, chemicals, a wide variety of machinery, and transport equipment, all grew by leaps and bounds.

A powerful symbiosis between supply and demand took place. Incremental institutional changes released the latent productive potentialities embedded in the Chinese economy, as it was in all the communist economies. This allowed initial growth of income, which generated demand for both consumer and capital goods. This stimulated the growth of investment in these activities, which allowed modernisation of the capital stock and improvements in labour productivity. This in turn started the cycle again – stimulating further rises in demand, investment and productivity. China was 'growing out of the plan'.[5]

Chapter 7

The fundamental cause of the Soviet collapse lies in the destruction of the state administrative apparatus and the nation-state under Gorbachev. This was mainly the result of policy choices made by the Soviet leadership. This in turn was influenced by deeper forces in modern Soviet history. The policy choice was attributable also to the massive pressure directed against the Soviet Union in the final phase of the Cold War. Once the state apparatus had collapsed, the range of options for any successor government was reduced hugely. The depth of the political and economic difficulties bequeathed to the Russian government in 1991 made it difficult to devise a successful economic strategy for the country in the early 1990s. The political problems after August 1991 were such that it was difficult for the government to pursue any kind of consistent policy. The composition of the new parliamentary institutions rendered it impossible to get agreement on a consistent economic policy. The state's fiscal capacity had been deeply undermined by the political changes, giving a high built-in propensity towards inflation. The framework of law and order had already begun to break down. This undermined the security of property rights, and made it likely that the distributional consequences of any move towards privatisation would be heavily affected by criminal power. The government's confidence had been shattered by the political disintegration of the USSR, the overthrow of the Communist Party of the Soviet Union, and by the swift collapse of communism in Eastern Europe. These circumstances pushed the government towards the international institutions for advice on how to try to shape its economic programme.

The path that was adopted was one which produced the worst of all possible worlds. The 'Big Bang' of instantaneous price liberalisation and rapid privatisation occurred without an effective framework of law and order, or government administrative strength. It occured in an economy with hyperinflation and collapsed government fiscal capacity. The main purpose of the government in this period of privatisation (1992–4) was not to minimise the human cost of the transition, but rather to maximise the speed with which capitalist institutions were created. The most important such institution was regarded by the government as a capitalist class. There was the clearest view that the costs incurred were worthwhile in the interests of creating the efficiency and growth-promoting institutions of capitalism. Such a perspective was supported strongly by a large part of the circle of foreign advisors and by the international capitalists with whom government officials had contact. This resulted in a process of highly unequal primitive capitalist accumulation, the 'creation of markets in circumstances of total chaos' (Mr Soskovets, the deputy prime minister, quoted in the *Financial Times*, 23 August 1994). Without a coherent, effective state apparatus no strategy for transition from the communist economy in Russia after August 1991 could succeed. In the absence of such an apparatus it was impossible to visualise an 'East Asian' approach to the transition. Destruction of the state apparatus was regarded widely as the great achievement of the Gorbachev epoch.

The disaster of the Soviet transition from communism demonstrates the folly of attempting a comprehensive Great Leap of the entire system of politics and economics. The result was a drastic worsening of the conditions of life for a large part of the Soviet population, and the construction a hugely unequal distribution of assets and economic power. Russia's economic situation cannot deteriorate for ever. Nevertheless, the decline may still have a long way to go. Moreover, the costs incurred by the mid-1990s already were very high. Policy choice was the central reason for this outcome. Tragically, the Soviet economic system had a large potential for improvement under a suitable set of incremental reforms. It was not necessary for there to be a period of 'surgery' and steep decline of output and living standards before improvement set in. However, successful implementation of such policies required the maintenance of a strong and effective state apparatus.

8.2 IMPLICATIONS FOR ECONOMIC PRINCIPLES AND POLICY

Evolution versus revolution

A policy of attempting to achieve a comprehensive revolution in all the parameters of socio-economic life is a risky method of trying to improve the performance of economic systems. The Popperian principle of experimentation is much sounder. The natural sciences provide a good guide to improving socio-economic systems. Paradoxically, the move out of communism in Russia parallels the move into communism in the same country in 1917. Both were massive, revolutionary, 'historicist' experiments, stimulated by a desire to leap into a better future at a single bound. It is deeply ironic that the end of communism in the former USSR should have paralleled the way in which the system was brought into being: it was created by a utopian revolution and it ended with a utopian revolution. It is hard to imagine that reflection upon the contrast in outcomes from the different reform paths in China and the former USSR will not reinforce the position of those, who, like Popper, argue for the evolutionary approach towards economic policy.

Political economy

Economists have refined enormously their understanding of relatively small problems by modelling and statistically investigating them while taking the broad parameters of economic life as given. However, when it came to thinking about the huge question of how the communist countries might best make the transition towards a system that would provide a better life for their long-suffering citizens, most economists forgot how little their analysis had taught them about the large issues. Instead they plunged into advising about how best to reform the communist systems with great confidence bred from their improved understanding of relatively small problems. They leapt from the complexities of their own special fields into grand simplistic generalisations in areas about which they often had painfully limited knowledge, and for which their training had served them ill. The deep questions about the way in which the parameters of economic life impact upon economic performance are outside the scope of most economics courses. They involve attempting to understand the way in which culture, politics, psychology and social structure interact with the economy. This branch of the subject has been steadily squeezed out of economics.[6] It is the stuff of political economy in the sense in which the term was understood by the classical economists. If ever an issue called out for real political economy it was the transition from communism.

Plans, commands and markets

'Planning' became progressively more unfashionable from the 1960s onwards. Much of the blame for this derived from a misidentification of 'planning' with the economic methods of the communist countries. The communist economy was not planned. It was a command economy, at least as anarchic in its own way as capitalism. The comparison of the experience of China and Russia's reforms confirms that, at certain junctures and in certain countries, effective planning is a necessary condition of economic success. It was precisely during the transition that the communist countries urgently needed good planning. These necessary planning functions had some elements common to most of the reforming communist countries. They included a need for the state carefully to conduct reform experiments; to co-ordinate the interrelationship between different parts of the reform programme; to maintain social stability by cushioning the impact of the growth of market forces upon different social groups; to protect domestic industry while market forces were being introduced; to support the growth of powerful new firms that could compete internationally; raise resources (either directly or indirectly) for necessary investment in transport, health, education, transport, and power generation; to supervise the reorganisation of the use of public assets so as to prevent the emergence of a deeply unequal distribution of asset ownership; to sustain public involvement in, and understanding of, the complex tasks of the transition. However, many of the necessary planning functions in the transition were country-specific, such as the necessity in China for the state to control population growth and to undertake large investments in farm infrastructure.

Unfortunately, the reforming government of the USSR misidentified planning with commands. It destroyed the command economy and failed to put into place a planned transition away from that system. The Chinese government realised that, in the transition from a command to a more market-oriented economy, a great deal of planning was needed. China's transition from the communist economy is an example of outstandingly good 'planning' in the classic sense in which the word 'planning' was used by Tinbergen (1964), Chakravarty (1987) and Lowe (1965).

The degree to which and the manner in which planning is needed is not the same in all countries at all stages of development. The market 'fails' in respect to growth, distribution and the environment much more in some circumstances than in others. Even the extreme cases of 'free markets', such as Hong Kong since 1949, Britain in the Industrial Revolution, and the USA in the nineteenth century, on close inspection turn out to involve much more state intervention than is commonly supposed. The free market has rarely, if ever, provided the means for countries to undertake successfully large structural transformation. Good planning involves recognition of the special way in which the market is failing in the particular country concerned, and then devising flexible, pragmatic solutions to the failures.

Turning points and cumulative causation

Correct and incorrect policy choices at key points can set in motion large processes of either positive or negative cumulative causation that may take a long time to reverse. The reform process in the China and Russia can now be seen to have been a knife-edge situation. It was perfectly possible, if different policies had been chosen, for the results to have been completely the reverse of those which actually came to pass. The wrong policies could have sent China spinning backwards

for an indefinite period. The experience of China before 1949 and in
the Great Leap and the Cultural Revolution testified to the real possibility of this happening. Conversely, the correct policies could have
liberated the latent productive capacities in the Soviet economy, and
ushered in a period of accelerated growth. Once each country set out
on its distinctive path away from the command economy, a whole sequence of virtuous and vicious circles of politics and economics was
set up, which helped to reinforce the path along which the respective
countries were travelling.

On the one hand, in China initial success in releasing latent productive potentialities in turn encouraged demand growth, which encouraged new investment, both domestic and foreign. This in turn provided
increased employment opportunities and permitted technical progress,
which in turn allowed further productivity and income growth, all of
which in turn contributed to greater social stability, which in turn encouraged further investment.

On the other hand, in Russia initial failure to implement policies
which released latent productive capacities, but destroyed the old system while not replacing it with a functioning new system, caused a
severe recession. The resulting demand downturn greatly discouraged
new investment, which in turn damaged opportunities in regular wage
employment, thrusting those thereby made unemployed in the regular
wage sector into low productivity, 'informal' sector employment, and
prevented technical progress. This in turn stopped productivity and income
growth, all of which in turn contributed to greater social instability,
which in turn further discouraged investment.

Role of demand

The generation of economists brought up during or soon after the inter-
war depression was, naturally, preoccupied with the demand side of
the economy. In the post-war period, economics became increasingly
preoccupied with the supply side. The transitional orthodoxy gave virtually no place at all to the role of demand. It made the implicit assumption that the reforming economies faced an unlimited world demand
and that domestic demand had no special function. The contrast between the Chinese and the Russian reform process emphasises the importance of the demand side in general and, under certain circumstances,
of domestic demand in particular.

The Chinese-style economic reform strategy created a rapidly growing internal demand which made it possible to adjust out of planning

through growth. Improved productivity was achieved through demand-induced investment in new, higher productivity activities while old ones were allowed to atrophy, rather than ruthlessly shut down as part of a 'surgical operation'. The growth-oriented 'Chinese path' transitional process contributed to improved productivity by quickly expanding the share of the total capital stock that operated with new techniques. The Russian approach produced a sharp contraction of demand which in turn caused a rapidly shrinking total capital stock towards a small core of currently profitable activities.

Infant industry protection

It has long been recognised that countries with much lower levels of economic development need to protect their infant industries from more advanced economies. However, the question of what constitutes an 'infant' industry is complex, especially in the reforming socialist economies. An 'infant' industry does not just include an industry which did not exist in any form at some prior point such as, for example, the electronic calculator industry in China before the 1980s. An 'old' industry which is hopelessly out-of-date and uncompetitive on international markets, but which is in the process of being modernised and restructured, can be considered to have the same characteristics as an 'infant' industry. It is rational that an industry, or a section of it, which today is uncompetitive and would be bankrupted in open international competition, but which is thought likely to become competitive, be given protection. The increased competitiveness might come about through the industry's own response to changed conditions of competition within the domestic economy and/or through measures undertaken by the government. The measures through which the industry's competitiveness might be increased include foreign investment, outlays on new technology, changed management practices, improvements in product design, changes in the size structure of industry and changes in the spatial location of industry. All of these things are likely to occur rapidly in a seriously reforming socialist economy without its being comprehensively and rapidly opened up to international competition. This is, indeed, what occurred in Chinese industry in the 1980s. Industries which are today viable and becoming increasingly internationally competitive would not exist if the Chinese economy had been opened up at a single stroke to international competition in the late 1970s.

After decades of complete protection from both domestic and international competition, the socialist countries which opened themselves up to unrestricted international competition, saw a large part of their industry devasted. Yet in the long run, given the huge changes taking place within the domestic economy to which the firms might be expected to respond and with suitable anticipatory efforts by industry and government, much of these industries might have become competitive behind protective barriers. In other words, it is logical to apply the infant industry philosophy to appropriate sections of industry in the former socialist countries. One of the key functions of planning is to identify sectors that are likely to become internationally competitive in the long run and to take measures to assist them to become so.

Ownership

Transferring ownership of a vast array of state assets is hugely time-consuming, and is unlikely to be accomplished equitably if it is done hastily before a market economy has been established. Moreover, it may well result in a structure of asset ownership which impedes investment. However, in the transitional economy moving out of the command system, large improvement in performance did not require privatisation of ownership. Large improvement in economic performance of publicly-owned assets can be obtained by devising incentives to use property effectively via contracts governing use rights. In small-scale enterprises, local public ownership can be compatible with incentives for effective use of publicly-owned resources. In the farm sector large improvement in the effectiveness of resource use can be obtained within a framework of public ownership of farmland. It is likely that China will eventually move towards a form of private ownership economy, but for almost two decades it was possible to obtain sustained improvements in economic performance in all sectors based on a form of mainly public ownership of assets.

On reflection, this is unsurprising. A large part of the capitalist system generates strong incentives to effective use of resources without the immediate stimulus of private ownership. The essence of capitalism is much more the existence of contracts that encourage effective use of resources by the manager of those resources, than it is the direct interest of the manager of resources being stimulated by the fact that they own those resources. A large fraction of farmland and small retail outlets is rented from the owner. The vast bulk of managers within large companies are stimulated to effective performance by appropriate contracts and by non-pecuniary motivation, rather than by ownership. Even if capitalist managers do own shares, their own performance is rarely likely to increase the price of the shares they own, since the fraction of the total is so small.

A wide variety of property rights regimes can now be seen to be compatible with effective economic performance. In between 'all-people' and individual private ownership is a great variety of property rights arrangements, which may be more or less compatible with strong incentives for managers of those assets to use them effectively to earn income and expand the value of the resources under their disposition.

Distribution of wealth

The myth of individal 'freedom to choose' is central to the ideology of free market capitalism. Daily reality continually confounds this naive view of the way in which life chances are structured, to say nothing of the profound differences in life chances between people in different nations. The origins of class differences in life chances and capacities to benefit from economic opportunities are conveniently forgotten in much of the work that economists undertake. The clarity with which the new, hugely unequal class structure of Russia was created in the early 1990s – that is to say the process of primitive capitalist accumulation – brings home vividly the importance in all societies of class-based differences in the distribution of wealth and income in determining the differences in people's life chances. People's 'freedom to choose' is comprehensively constrained by their class position.

Trickle-down

A consistent 'leftist' view in development economics and in the study of the economic history of the advanced capitalist countries has been that 'trickle down' doesn't work. In this perspective, the main path through which to improve the condition of poor people is through redistribution. On the other hand, a consistent theme of much 'free market' analysis has been that growth is the best guarantor of 'basic needs'.

Badly-designed redistributive polices, such as many of those in Maoist China, damage the incentives necessary for growth and, in the long run, prevent the mass of the population from increasing their income beyond a certain level. China's reforms since the late 1970s show that fast growth independently creates through the market large oppportunities for improvement in the welfare of the poorest people. However, it shows also that it is possible to devise polices for redistribution which generate faster improvements in popular welfare than would come from the free market, while simultaneously maintaining incentives for sustained growth. However, China's Maoist past, especially the disaster of the Great Leap Forward, demonstrates that even the most egalitarian of redistributive systems cannot avoid a huge decline in popular welfare if output falls to a sufficiently large degree.

Under Russia's reform programme, there occurred a massive redistribution of income away from the bottom deciles of the population. The top decile or so of the income distribution grew richer in absolute terms at a rapid rate and rapidly increased their share of income and wealth alongside a disastrous deterioration in output and average income. This was the reverse of 'trickle-down', with both output decline and redistribution away from the bottom deciles of the distribution. A fairer sharing of the burden of the economic collapse, such as occurred during wartime in Britain, could have greatly reduced greatly the extent of suffering for the bottom deciles of the population.

Good government and economic performance

In recent years 'good government' has increasingly been considered to be important in determining economic performance (Reynolds, 1985). However, there was a strong tendency to equate 'good government' with democratic government. This was most explicit in the case of conditionality from Western governments in their aid to African states. However, the contrast between the reform process in China and Russia vividly illustrates the inadequacy of such a perspective. China's government under Deng Xiaoping was widely thought to be 'bad', oppressing its people under continued communist political dictatorship, and stubbornly refusing to let go of the planning system. On the other hand, Gorbachev's government was widely thought to be outstandingly 'good' for promoting welfare-enhancing destruction of the Communist Party and trying to push forward with large reform of the 'planned' economy. It is now obvious that this view was wrong. China's communist dictatorship was vastly 'better' at governing China than the Gorbachev or Yeltsin governments were at governing the USSR and the Russian Federation respectively. The reforming Chinese government was vastly superior to its Russian counterpart in selecting and implementing 'good' policies that would release the system's productive potentialities and enhance the welfare of the vast bulk of the population.

Human rights, political choice and economic policy

Prior to the end of communism, narrowly political rights, especially the ending of one party totalitarian dictatorship, was given high weight as a policy goal both inside and outside the communist countries. This was so for a variety of reasons.

Some regarded the overthrow of communism as the primary policy goal, whatever the consequences this might have for the welfare of the citizens of the communist countries. These 'capitalist triumphalists' regarded this as the successful conclusion of the seventy-year struggle between communism and capitalism. For some of these this was a great moral victory and for others simply a moment of sweet revenge.

Others thought that the overthrow of communism was in itself a massive improvement in welfare for the citizens of the communist countries. The intoxicating ether of 'freedom at last' was thought to be much the most important item in the citizen's welfare function. Many people within the communist countries, including both China and the former USSR, held this view.

Others thought that the overthrow would lead to large improvements in economic performance and mass incomes. Some thought this would happen quickly, while others did believe, more realistically, that the countries would need to travel through a difficult period before things improved.

However, 'human rights' include a wide range of rights other than the right to vote in elections and to air opinions freely. They include the rights to food, housing, security of employment, access to health services, and personal security. It can now be seen, with much greater clarity than before the reforms, that at a certain juncture there may be a trade-off, at least over a reasonably long period, between the achievement of narrowly political rights and the achievement of other human rights.

The relationship between choice of economic policy by a government and voters' rights is complex. Even under relatively stable democracies there are difficulties. Obvious problems include the fact that political parties' platforms embrace a wide range of policies, both economic and non-economic. Parties may be elected because a majority of voters supports the non-economic part of the programme rather than the economic part. In a first-past-the-post system, it is perfectly possible for a government to be consistently elected by a minority of the electorate and to implement a programme with which the majority of the electorate disagrees. However, the larger the set of changes that the government proposes to implement, the more problematic the relationship of political choice to democracy becomes.

The 'right to vote' in a 'free and fair' election is only as meaningful as the choices which the electors are given. In elections in the advanced capitalist countries electoral platforms almost always involve incremental changes whose effects are reasonably predictable. The most radical changes in democratic politics within modern developed countries may well have been those which occurred in the 1980s under Mrs Thatcher in Britain. The programme of successive Conservative governments was undoubtedly 'radical', but it was still incremental and fairly predictable. The main planks of the programme were trade union legislation and privatisation of clearly identified sections of the nationalised industries. The outcomes were reasonably close to those predicted in the manifestos.

The wider were the choices offered to the electorate of a reforming communist country the more unpredictable were the outcomes for voters. It was impossible for voters to calculate the full effects of revolutionary programmes of system transformation upon either the country or upon themselves individually. Moreover, the more revolutionary was the reforming programme, the less reversible would be the policies by the time the next election occured. Therefore the electorate was deprived of meaningful choice and simply voted in the dark, with vague sentiments governing the choices they made. Whether this amounted to more 'democracy' is debatable.

Before the overthrow of communism, under circumstances of guaranteed employment, low rents, low or zero price education and health provision, subsidised food, and effective law and order, many citizens would have given a relatively high importance in their welfare functions, to political liberty. However, after a period of falling incomes, employment insecurity, and collapsing social order, their preferences can be expected to be greatly altered. If they had known before the overthrow of communism that it would lead to an economic and social disaster for a large part of the population, then their support for the change might be expected to have been a great deal less.

Notes and References

1 Introduction

1. The precise figure is dependent on the way in which a 'communist' country is defined.
2. The closest one gets to such an account is Amalrik (1980). He identified war with China as the catalyst that would initiate the collapse of the Soviet state. However, even he did not anticipate the rise of China.
3. To the best of my knowledge, it is the first book on the subject. Doubtless, many will be written in years to come.
4. The most substantial study I have located is the article by Sachs and Woo (1994).

2 The Results of Reforms in China and Russia

1. Local studies such as Lyons' on Fujian province, confirm the huge achievement in the 1980s: 'Unless Fujian is grossly unrepresentative, China has indeed prosecuted a war on poverty of remarkable dimensions – and certainly one deserving of greater attention than it has received to date' (Lyons, 1992, p. 64).
2. From 1978 to 1992, the reported average annual growth of real per capita consumption was 6.7 per cent for rural dwellers and 5.9 per cent for urban dwellers (SSB, *ZGTJZY*, p. 49).
3. In fact, unofficial estimates of output suggest that the downturn began before 1989, and there may well have been negative growth of national product over the whole 1985–1990 period (Aslund, 1991, 200).
4. The journal *Trud* estimates that from 1989 to 1992 consumption of meat fell by 21 per cent, dairy products by 34 per cent, sugar by 13 per cent, and fruits by 32 per cent. Consumption of bread rose by 22 per cent (reported in Weir, 1993, p. 2812).
5. A full comparison of death rates requires analysis of age-specific death rates rather than overall death rates.

3 The Need for Reform of the Chinese and Soviet Systems of Political Economy

1. Avrich estimates that there were around 10,000 casualties on the Soviet side, and perhaps around 2,000 on the side of the occupants of the fortress (Avrich, 1970, pp. 210–11), though some estimates are far higher. The struggle was drawn out, lasting in total over three weeks, with great ferocity in the final assault.
2. From an essay written by a leader of one of the Democracy Movement's leading organisations shortly before his arrest in May 1979.

3. Only one of these, Lin Biao, may have been killed by the leaders, and even that possibility is much debated.

4. Paradoxically, the rate of progress in modern computing is only now beginning to make feasible the study of some of the less complex aspects of this process.

5. Chen *et al.* (1988) estimate that from 1957 to 1978 capital productivity fell by around 0.8 per cent per annum in the state industrial sector.

6. Newly added fixed assets minus depreciation plus additions to the 'circulation fund' in the material sectors (SSB, *CEY*, 1981, p. 510).

7. Non-productive construction refers to 'residential quarters, public health centres, public utilities and other administrative organs that cater to cultural and material needs of the people' (SSB, *CEY*, 1981, p. 517).

4 The Transition Orthodoxy and its Problems

1. At the time of publication of this article Alfred Steinherr was Director of the Financial Research Department of the European Investment Bank, Luxembourg.

2. See, for example, the discussion in Chang, 1994, p. 124, and 'Introduction' in White (ed.), 1988.

3. See especially White (ed.), 1988 and Amsden, 1989.

4. This is not always the case. Hong Kong, for example, enjoyed specially advantageous conditions (particularily on the supply side) necessitating less extensive (though still very significant) state intervention. If interventions are more in response to vested interests than in the interests of the overall accumulation process, then state intervention may in the end produce a worse result than the free market. It is wrong to say that 'state failure' has almost always been worse than 'market failure'. Deepak Lal is a forceful exponent of this view (Lal, 1983). However, in framing development policy one needs to be alert to the possibility of 'state failure', and in the last resort it is, indeed, possible for 'state failure' to be worse than 'market failure'.

5. In each of the Asian NICs, but most strikingly in South Korea and Taiwan, successful development policies resulting in large increases in *per capita* output and income were followed by mass demands for democratisation of political life. Moreover, all the advanced capitalist countries followed a similar sequence of rising income followed by mass demands for democratisation of political life, which governments eventually found impossible to resist.

6. On the 'populist' roots of Latin American inflation, see Dornbusch *et al.*, 1991.

7. In 1992, net foreign direct investment in communist China was reported to be $11,145 million (World Bank, *WDR*, 1994, p. 204). In the same year net foreign direct investment in the whole of post-communist Eastern Europe totalled just $2,825 million while Yeltsin's post-communist Russia received just $100 million for Russia (UN, 1993, p. 239).

8. In August 1862, President Lincoln declared: 'My paramount object in this struggle is to save the Union, and is not either to save or destroy Slavery'. In the struggle to prevent Southern secession, which took place

between 1861 and 1865, over 600,000 soldiers lost their lives.

9. The main areas so designated were those ruled by Japan for a substantial period (principally Manchuria and Taiwan), and the Treaty Ports with foreign gunboat-backed order.

10. One could add a very long bibliography of economists who advocated high speed as the only 'logical' way to achieve a successful transition. Kornai's account (Kornai, 1986) of the 'failure' of Hungarian reform was deeply influential in the early days of thinking about reform in the post-communist countries.

11. Compared to the neighbouring Czech Republic, the Hungarian stock market is 'smaller, better regulated and often peripheral to the economic transformation of the economy' (*Financial Times*, 21 September 1994).

12. In the period 1990–1993 Hungary attracted 44 per cent of the cumulative total of foreign direct investment in Eastern Europe and the former Soviet Union (EBRD, 1994, p. 123).

13. I do not wish to imply that the serious problems in Russia today are as great as those in the Soviet Union in the early 1930s.

14. For a graphic account of insider dealing by officials under 'wild privatisation' in the Czech Republic, see the *Financial Times*, 21 September 1994.

15. In the UK, for example, the share of net output produced by firms with under 20 employees rose from 16 per cent in 1963 to 25 per cent in 1987 (Hughes, 1993, p. 30).

16. This tendency has been especially pronounced in the metal-working industries. In the US, for example, the share of small- and medium-sized firms (under 500 employees) in the metal-working sectors rose from 30 per cent of total sales in 1976 to 40 per cent in 1986 (Acs and Audretsch, 1993, p. 72).

17. Indeed, the share of the top 100 firms in manufacturing output in the UK has remained remarkably stable over a long period of time, at around two-fifths of total net output value since the mid-1960s (Hughes, 1993, p. 31).

18. This is not the place to enter a discussion about the impact upon life chances of region, race or gender.

19. It must be admitted that the seriousness of the depression was not anticipated.

20. See Yotopoulos (1989), for a meticulous account.

5 'Catch-up' Capabilities Compared

1. The most substantial analysis to date is probably Sachs and Woo, 1994.

2. Eastern Europe and the former Soviet Union.

3. The total value of imports for the seven largest Western European economies in 1991 was $1155 billion, compared to $506 billion for the USA and $234 billion for Japan. The total value of exports from the Four Little Tigers in the same year was $314 billion US dollars (World Bank, *WDR*, 1993, pp. 264–5).

4. The share of the US in China's exports rose from around 5.4 per cent in 1980 to around 8.6 per cent in 1991 (SSB, *ZGTJNJ*, 1981 and 1992).

5. According to an estimate of credit risk by the Economist Intelligence Unit, based on 11 factors, including indebtedness, current-account posi-

tion and political stability, Russia was the second riskiest country in the world in the second quarter of 1993, next to Iraq. China, despite having been recently downgraded on the basis of its overheating economy, ranked between Malaysia and Thailand (*The Economist*, 21 August 1993, p. 88).

6. In the period 1980–85 the growth rate of net value of farm output (compound annual growth rate, at constant prices) was 8.6 per cent compared to 10.0 per cent for national income, and in the period 1985–91 the comparable rates were 3.7 per cent and 7.6 per cent (SSB, *ZGTJNJ*, 1992, p. 33).

7. The *Financial Times* reports, for example, that in 1994, western institutional investors, anticipating a fall in stock market prices were able to 'get out in time'. However, in addition to this capital flight, between $50–150 million of domestic capital 'flowed into the coffers of western merchant banks' (*Financial Times*, 21 September 1994).

8. The USA's tariff rates (average unweighted average) for manufactured imports were as follows: 1820 = 40 per cent, 1875 = 40–50 per cent, 1913 = 25 per cent (World Bank, 1991, *WDR*, p. 97).

9. A major problem, even for China's primary and secondary education, was the disruption caused by the Cultural Revolution, which led to schools being closed across much of the country for two to three years and, even when they reopened, ideological education took a high priority in the curriculum.

10. This is the main reason why it is so rare under non-socialist agriculture to find units of production which employ a large number of workers.

11. See, e.g. Pipes, 1977, Chapter 8, 'The missing bourgeoisie'.

12. For a detailed discussion of the many different forms which the black economy could take in the USSR see, especially, Grossman, 1979.

13. In the advanced industrial economies in the late 1970s around 70 per cent of total industrial output was composed of 'heavy' industrial products, and of this over one-half consisted of intermediate inputs (chemicals, rubber, plastics, non-metalic minerals and building materials, metallurgical and metal mining, petroleum and coal extraction, and electricity (World Bank, 1981b, 90).

14. The Chinese data in this paragraph are all from SSB, *ZGTJNJ*, 1983, pp. 81, 97–98, 115.

15. The average age of first marriage for women remained at 22 from 1980 to 1987, and the proportion of the population using birth control rose from 51 per cent in 1980 to 58 per cent in 1988 (SSB, *ZGRKTJNJ*, 1989, p. 134).

16. The Chinese Communist Party in the late 1970s numbered about 38 million, or around 3.5 per cent of the total population, while the Soviet Communist Party numbered about 18 million, or around 6.7 per cent of the total population.

6 Reform in China

1. China's population is estimated to have fallen by no less than 84 million from 1851 to 1871 (Perkins, 1968, p. 212).

2. In the years 1928–35 it is estimated that 40–48 per cent of government expenditure was on the military (Feuerwerker, 1968, p. 58).

3. The need to professionalise, reduce in size and make more youthful

China's government bureaucracy was a central theme of Deng's speeches in the early 1980s (Deng, 1984).

4. Harding (1987, pp. 204–11) provides a careful account of the large increase in the proportion of technically qualified bureaucrats and the substantial decline in their average age during the early and mid-1980s.

5. A wider definition would put the number of government bureaucrats in the early 1990s at around 30 million.

6. This proposition has been put to me more than once at seminars I have given on this subject.

7. The Third Plenum concluded: 'Carrying out the four modernisations requires great growth of the productive forces, which in turn requires diverse changes in those aspects of the relations of production and the superstructure not in harmony with the growth of the productive forces, and requires changes in all methods of management, actions and thinking which stand in the way of such growth. Socialist modernisation is a profound and extensive revolution' (Central Committee, 1978, p. 10).

8. On the former see Rawski, 1989 and Bergere, 1981; on the latter see Anderson, 1928, and Gamble, 1921.

9. In 1992, for example, in the urban industrial sector, only around 1.3 million people worked in the individually owned, pure private sector, compared to 2.4 million in joint ventures, 18.6 million in the 'collective' sector, and over 45 million in state enterprises. In the countryside in the same year, *xiang*-run and *cun*-run industrial enterprises employed around twice the number as were employed in individually owned enterprises (43 million, compared to 20.3 million) (SSB, *ZGTJNJ*, 1993, p. 99; SSB, *ZGGYJJTJNJ*, 1993, p. 413; and SSB, *ZGNCTJNJ*, 1993, p. 232).

10. 35 per cent in the state sector and 34 per cent in the collective sector (SSB, *ZGTJNJ*, 1993, pp. 415–16).

11. 'From now on, the central authorities should gradually diminish the scope for their financial investments and concentrate them on energy, transport, and new industries. Projects involving short investment cycles and yielding fairly large profits, should be undertaken as far as possible by local authorities or by enterprises' (Zhao Ziyang, 1981, in *Major Documents*, 1991, p. 229).

12. Source of funds for total social investment in fixed assets

	1978	1985	1992
State budget	62.2	16.0	4.3
Domestic credit	1.7	20.1	27.1
Foreign investment	4.2	3.6	5.5
Self-raised funds	31.9	60.3	51.2
Other			12.0

Source: SSB, *ZGTJNJ*, 1993, p. 24.

13. Funds which compose extra budgetary revenue are 'those funds which each locality, ministry, enterprise and administrative unit itself collects and uses in accordance with the scope fixed by the state. These funds are a supplement to the funds in the state budget. . . . The uses to which

such funds are put are within the orbit of the plan and cannot be blindly expanded.' These funds include such locally raised items as supplementary industrial, commercial and agricultural taxes, and supplementary levies for local public works. They include also such items as extrabudgetary funds handed over to higher authorities for keypoint construction of power and communications construction (SSB, *ZGTJNJ*, 1993, section 6).

14. To establish the precise degree to which official central and local control over extra-budgetary revenue changed over the course of the reform period would be a specialist study of great complexity, involving examination of all the manifold categories under which extra-budgetary revenue was channelled. Only in 1994 did the state appear to be ready to renounce all control over the extra budgetary funds, simultaneously with a large tax reform. The former was, presumably, conditional upon successful implementation of the latter.

15. 'The coastal area has a population of over 200 million. With good foundations in industry and agriculture, a comparatively developed commodity economy, fairly advanced science, culture and education, convenient transportation and easily available information, it had extensive connections with foreign countries in history and and occupies a decisive position in construction at present. . . . The reform of our economic structure and opening up to the outside will advance step by step from the coastal area to the hinterland through our exploration and practice in developing firstly the special economic zones, then the open cities along the coastal areas and then the open zones in the coastal area and finally the hinterland' (Central Committee, 1985, pp. 443–4).

16. I am indebted to the research of Mr Tang Zhimin for his investigations of this question.

17. The birthrate fell from 36 per 1000 in 1968 to 23 per 1000 in 1975 (SSB, *ZGTJNJ*, 1990, p. 90).

18. The average age of first marriage for women remained at 22 per 1000 from 1980 to 1987, and the proportion of the population using birth control rose from 51 per cent in 1980 to 58 per cent in 1988 (SSB, *ZGRKTJNJ*, 1989, p. 134).

19. The birthrate rose from 18 per 1000 in 1980 to 21 per 1000 in 1990 (SSB, *ZGTJZY*, 1991, p. 14), and the natural growth rate remained below 15 per 1000 throughout the decade (the peak was 16.6 per 1000 in 1987, falling to 14.4 per 1000 in 1990) (SSB, *ZGTJZY*, 1991, p. 14).

20. This compared with 2.7 per cent per annum for developing countries as a whole (excluding India and China) and 2.1 per cent per annum for India (World Bank, *WDR*, 1991, p. 254).

21. If China's population had grown at the same rate as India's it would have been about 100 million people larger than its actual size by 1989–90.

22. By 1985 China had a remarkably low dependency ratio (population under 15 and over 64 years as a proportion of the working age population aged 15–64) compared to other developing countries (0.54 compared to 0.65 in 'medium human development' countries, 0.72 in India, and 0.95 in other 'low human development' countries) (UNDP, 1990, p. 166), and the ratio fell throughout the 1980s. The number of 'non-workers'

per worker fell from 1.40 in 1978 to 1.02 in 1989 (SSB, *ZGTJNJ*, 1990, pp. 89 and 113).

23. '[T]he prevailing official attitude seems to be that China has so little cultivated land that all of it must continue to be tilled, even the poorest agricultural land. So, for example, instead of rejoicing when residents of poor mountain villages spontaneously move to nearby developed plains, the semi-official media laments the abandonment of the formerly cultivated mountain fields' (Banister, 1992, p. 22).

24. The Pearl River Delta (narrowly defined) in 1989 was reported to have 2.2 million migrant workers, the Yangzi Delta had 1.7 million, and the Bohai coastal area had 1.8 million migrants (Research Group on Migration, 1989, p. 15). These were large numbers in absolute terms, but small in comparison with the total rural labour force–even in poor areas.

25. Vogel (1989) estimates that, by 1987, 60 per cent of the more than three million migrant workers in the Pearl River Delta, Canton, Shenzhen and Zhuhai Special Economic Zones, were from mountainous areas within Guangdong province itself (Vogel, 1989, pp. 265–6).

26. The proportion of the urban population 'waiting for work' is a reasonable indicator of the degree of tightness of the local labour market. Offical data show significantly higher proportions in inland and poor provinces than in the booming coastal areas (SSB, *ZGLDGZTJNJ*, 1990, section 2). The proportion nationally 'waiting for work' in urban China in 1989 was 2.6 per cent while in impoverished Gansu province the figure was 5.5 per cent (SSB, *ZGLDGZTJNJ*, 1990, p. 49). Moreover, in impoverished parts of the province the figure was even higher. In Linxia city, for example, in the mountainous minority area to the south of Lanzhou, the provincial capital, the figure was no less than 17.5 per cent (SSB, *ZGLDGZTJNJ*, 1990, p. 70).

27. Rough estimates by officials involved in anti-poverty work suggest that in 1991 around 6 million people migrated out of Sichuan province, around 3 million from Henan, and around 3 million also from Gansu (personal communication, 1991). As many as 20 million migrants may have made the trek from western to eastern China in search of employment in 1990 or 1991.

28. For example, a study of ten villages in Zhejiang province showed that less than five per cent of migrants were working in agriculture (Rural Policy Research Department, 1988, pp. 28–30).

29. Singh and Jefferson report that in the first half of 1993, for example, almost nine-tenths of total investment in industry was channelled into the state-owned sector (Singh and Jefferson, 1994, p. 8).

30. For an extensive evaluation of the Chinese government's approach towards integration with the world economy in terms of 'close' versus 'strategic' integration, see Singh, 1993.

31. 'Our aim in expanding economic and technological exchange with foreign countries is to enhance our ability to be self-reliant and to promote the development of the national economy' (Hu Yaobang, 1982, p. 287).

32. The average unit price of China's grain imports plummetted in the early and mid-1980s (by 51 per cent from 1981 to 1987) before rising explosively in the late 1980s (increasing by 67 per cent in 1987–1989) (SSB,

ZGTJNJ, 1983–1990).

33. At their peak in the early 1980s net grain imports amounted to only 4 per cent of domestic output; in the mid-1980s, China even became a small net grain exporter and, in the late 1980s, net grain imports remained at only around 2 per cent of domestic output (SSB, *ZGTJZY*, 1983–1990, and SSB, *ZGTJNJ*, 1983–1990).

34. In 1991 for instance, the figure stood at 87 per cent compared to an average of 308 per cent for other low income countries (excluding India and China), and 160 per cent for middle income countries (World Bank, *WDR*, 1993, p. 284).

35. To a considerable degree this was because foreign companies preferred to deal with the vast Chinese bureaucracy via a native enterprise, and through who it might gain access to the still unreformed domestic market system. For the foreign partner the joint venture allowed a channel through which to have access to a strange culture, a way through continuing bureaucratic controls and access to the 'mothers-in-law', the commissions and bureaux that still stand above Chinese industrial enterprises: 'These "mothers-in-law" represent the best route to the permissions, tax concessions, "locked in" customers and central funding they need' (*Financial Times*, 2 February 1994).

36. Workers engaged only part of the time in producing inputs for the joint venture have their labour time converted to 'full-time equivalents'.

37. It is estimated that China will be the world's third largest market for airliners by 2010.

38. The value of the yuan fell from 1.7 per dollar in 1981 to 6 per dollar in 1992.

39. 'To encourage exports and increase foreign exchange earnings we should adopt the following measures. We should organise and expand the supply of export commodities. Except for a few major commodities vital to the national economy and people's everyday life, whenever there are conflicts between export and domestic sales, priority should be given to the needs of exports. We should step up the construction of bases for the production of export commodities and, where conditions permit, set up export commodity processing zones with distinctive characteristics and the ability to earn foreign exchange. We should improve the system by which foreign exchange earnings are distributed. A fund should be established for an export development award. Economic awards should be given to regions, departments and enterprises which have scored outstanding achievements in expanding exports and increasing foreign exchange earnings. It is particularily important for us to use such economic levers as pricing, exchange rates and customs duties to encourage the production of export commodities' (Central Committee, 1985, p. 511).

40. E.g. by 1987, producers of electrical machinery and instruments were allowed to retain 100 per cent of export earnings.

41. 'Maintaining balance between the acquisition and use of foreign exchange is a difficult, long-term task. We must emphasise economic efficiency in the use of foreign exchange, which should promote domestic technological progress and enhance our ability to earn more foreign exchange. We should readjust the mix of import commodities in ac-

cordance with his principle, giving priority to computer software, advanced technologies and key equipment. It will be necessary for us to import certain means of production and consumer goods which are badly needed on the domestic market. However, we should in no case support an excessive rate of production or overextended scale of construction by using large sums of foreign exchange over a long period of time to import raw materials. Nor should we stimulate domestic consumption by importing too many high grade consumer goods. *We should make every effort to produce at home such goods as we can and refrain from blindly importing them, so as to protect and stimulate the development of the domestic industries.* In assembly-line industries that use imported parts and accessories, we should gradually substitute ones of our own manufacture. We must see to it that the technologies introduced are applied, mastered and developed and that they gradually become standardised. In order to centralise guidance and control in this area the state should draw national plans and policies for the importation and integration of technologies and should initiate a licence system to avoid duplication of imports and lack of co-ordination between imported technology and domestic research and development' (CCP Central Committee, 1985, in *Major Documents*, 1991, pp. 511–512).

42. For example, in 1991 China levied a 120 per cent *ad valorem* tariff on the import of beer (China Development Finance, 1993), and there were tariffs on most imports of petroleum products, intermediate petrochemicals, resins, plastics and synthetic fibres, ranging from 9 per cent to 80 per cent of the import prices (Merrill Lynch, 1993).

43. For example, tariffs on the import of motorcycle components varied from 25 per cent to 120 per cent *ad valorem*, with tariff rates rising in relation to the proportion of proportion of imported inputs in the final product (Bear, Sterns, 1993).

44. By 1984, individual households owned over 90 per cent of carts and over 80 per cent of small walking tractors (SSB, *ZGNCTJNJ*, 1985, p. 242).

45. In 1984, the 'collective' sector still owned 56 per cent of large and medium-sized tractors, 51 per cent of mechanical threshers, 48 per cent of farm trucks, and 65 per cent of drainage and irrigation machinery (SSB, *ZGNCTJNJ*, 1985, p. 242).

46. By 1988, peasant ownership of large and medium-sized tractors had risen to 65 per cent, to 74 per cent for mechanical threshers, 68 per cent for farm trucks, and 50 per cent for drainage and irrigation machinery (SSB, *ZGNCTJNJ*, 1989, p. 268).

47. Their share of total drainage and irrigation machinery (in terms of horsepower) rose from 35 per cent to 50 per cent between 1984 and 1988 (SSB, *ZGNCTJNJ*, 1985, p. 242; 1989, p. 268). The number of pumpsets sold by the state and by supply and marketing co-ops in the 1980s rose rapidly from 510,000 in 1980 to 1.1 million in 1988 (SSB, *ZGNCTJNJ*, 1989, p. 187), and the share of total stocks owned by individual households rose from 39 per cent to 62 per cent between 1984 and 1988 (SSB, *ZGNCTJNJ*, 1985, p. 242; 1989, p. 268).

48. Far from weakening, as has been asserted by many authors, the ca-

pacity of the local government to obtain income from the rural economy grew in the wake of the agricultural reforms: the share of total 'collective retentions' from total rural net income rose from 4.6 per cent in 1983 to 10.6 per cent in 1987, and the share of individual household net income contributed by households to 'collective retentions' rose from 3.3 per cent in 1984 to 4.2 per cent in 1989 (SSB, *ZGTJNJ*, 1985, p. 290; 1986, p. 221; 1990, p. 393).

49. In the late 1980s, for reservoirs of over 100,000m., 0.4 per cent of the total number accounted for 41 per cent of the area irrigated, while over 80,000 small reservoirs, mainly run by collectives, accounted for 33–4 per cent of the total area irrigated (SSB, *ZGTJNJ*, 1983, p. 201, and 1990, p. 35). In addition to these 'small' reservoirs, China has several million mini-reservoirs (6.3 million in 1982) (SSB, *ZGTJNJ*, 1985, p. 201).

50. The share of expenditure on basic construction investment in waterworks in total budgetary outlays plummetted from 1.63 per cent in 1983 to just 0.87 per cent in 1988 and, in real terms, outlays may well have fallen by around one-fifth (SSB, *ZGNCTJNJ*, 1989, pp. 293–5, and SSB, *ZGTJNJ*, 1990, 254) from 1983 to 1989. There is a 22 per cent fall from 1983 to 1989 if budget outlays on capital construction are deflated by the retail price of agricultural means of production.

51. In 1989, individual peasant households accounted for 84 per cent of the deposits in credit co-ops, but 52 per cent of the outstanding loans were to rural non-farm enterprises (SSB, *ZGTJNJ*, 1990, p. 668).

52. The amount spent by the central government on water conservation works appears to have risen by more than 50 per cent from 1987 to 1990 (4.7 billion yuan in 1987, 7.3 billion yuan in 1990)(*BR*, 28 January to 3 February 1991, p. 17).

53. Growth of different forms of service provision for Chinese agriculture provided by 'socialised service groups', 1986–1990 (average per village [*cun*])

	1986	1990
Area supplied by machine ploughing socialised service groups: (*mu*)	1053	1377
Area irrigated by socialised service groups (*mu*)	1128	1361
Amount of seeds provided by socialised seed supply service groups (tons)	8.4	11.4
Area with plant protection provided by socialised service groups (*mu*)	1811	2174
Amount of chemical fertiliser provided by socialised service groups (tons)	87.4	123.3
Animals treated by socialised veterinary service groups (number)	6627	8451

Source: Ministry of Agriculture, 1991

Notes: The data are drawn from a survey of 5,389 villages (*cun*) in 205 *xian* in 29 provinces, autonomous regions and directly administered municipalities (excluding Tibet and Taiwan).

Socialised service organisations include the following:
(1) *xiangzhen* (township) technical departments (agro-technology stations, agro-machinery stations, plant protection stations, etc);
(2) *xiang* and *cun* collective economic organisations (including *cun* service companies, service stations and teams set up the *cun* people's committee and *cun* people's small groups);
(3) different specialist service groups (including specialist associations, research associations, joint service groups, specialised households and different forms of popular co-operative groups).

54. Throughout the 1980s peasants saved roughly 13–15 per cent of their current income (SSB, *ZGTJNJ*, 1990, p. 312).
55. Deposits in the credit co-operatives rose from 27 billion *yuan* in 1980 (15 *yuan* per peasant) to 167 billion in 1989 (263 *yuan* per peasant).
56. Outstanding loans from the rural credit co-operatives rose from 8.2 billion *yuan* in 1980 to 109.5 billion *yuan* in 1989 (SSB, *ZGTJNJ*, 1990, p. 668), while outstanding loans from the Agricultural Bank rose from 19 billion *yuan* in 1980 to 83 billion *yuan* in 1988 (SSB, *ZGNCTJNJ*, 1989, pp. 293–5). Outstanding loans from the two institutions together amounted to 34 *yuan* per peasant in 1980, and had risen to 315 *yuan* in 1988 (i.e. around a fourfold increase in real terms).
57. From 1978 to 1989 the number of markets in the cities grew from a negligible level to over 13,000, while in the villages the numbers grew from 33,000 to over 59,000 (SSB, *ZGTJZY*, 1990, p. 94). In rural free markets the volume of trade increased roughly fivefold in real terms from 1978 to 1989 (SSB, *ZGTJZY*, 1990, p. 94, and SSB, *ZGTJNJ*, 1990, p. 250).
58. It was still the case in 1988 that 95 per cent of cotton, 91 per cent of grain and 80 per cent of edible oil marketings were sold through state commercial channels or the quasi-state channel of the 'supply and marketing co-operatives' (SSB, *ZGNCTJNJ*, 1989, pp. 160–1).
59. For example, by 1988, only 57 per cent of pork sales, 63 per cent of tea sales, 36 per cent of fresh egg sales and 42 per cent of aquatic products were sold to the non-farm sector through state or quasi-state marketing channels, whereas in 1978 all of the marketed output of these products had been sold to state or quasi-state agencies (SSB, *ZGNCTJNJ*, 1989, pp. 160–1).
60. The proportion of farm sales to the non-farm sector which was outside state channels rose from just 5.6 per cent in 1978 to 19.9 per cent in 1989 (SSB, *ZGTJZY*, 1990, p. 94).
61. The proportion of the gross value of farm output marketed rose from 40 per cent in 1978 to 52 per cent in 1989 (SSB, *ZGTJZY*, 1990, pp. 7 and 94).
62. The number of people working in supply and marketing co-operatives rose from 268,000 in 1980 to 394,000 in 1988 (SSB, *ZGGXHZSTJZY*, 1949–1988; 1989, pp. 17 and 20), and the total number of rural non-farm workers in 'transport, communications, post and telecommunications' rose from 2.2 million in 1980 to 6.1 million in 1989 (SSB, *ZGTJZY*, 1990, p. 51).

63. Still in 1988, almost 100 per cent of chemical fertilisers, pesticides and herbicides, and nearly three-quarters of 'walking tractors' were sold via state commerce or supply and marketing co-ops (SSB, *ZGNCTJNJ*, 1989, pp. 187 and 271; SSB, *ZGTJZY*, 1990, pp. 74–5).
64. The 'price scissors' (index of farm purchase prices as a proportion of index of retail prices of industrial products in villages) moved in favour of farm produce by 13–14 per cent per annum from 1978 to 1980 (SSB, *ZGTJNJ*, 1990, section 7).
65. The average annual rate of improvement from 1980 to 1989 fell to around 3 per cent (SSB, *ZGTJNJ*, 1990, section 7).
66. The average retail price of meat and eggs rose 157 per cent from 1983 to 1989, and the increase for aquatic products was 197 per cent compared to 78 per cent for grain (SSB, *ZGTJNJ*, 1990, p. 251).
67. For aquatic products the average gap between the two fell from 59 per cent in 1980 to 22 per cent in 1988, for meat and eggs from 22 per cent to 14 per cent, and for fresh vegetables from 65 per cent to 11 per cent (SSB, *ZGNCTJNJ*, 1989, p. 179).
68. Still in 1988, the difference was 70 per cent for edible oil and 98 per cent for grain (SSB, *ZGNCTJNJ*, 1989, p. 175).
69. From 99.9 million hectares in 1980 to 95.4 million hectares in 1992.
70. The evidence on the quality of irrigation is ambiguous. The proportion of the irrigated area irrigated by machine rose from the already high figure of 56 per cent in 1980 to 59 per cent in 1988 (SSB, *ZGTJZY*, 1990, p. 64). Other official indicators (area with water logging, soil erosion and alkaline-saline problems solved) also showed some improvement during the 1980s (SSB, *CEY*, 1983, p. 201; SSB, *ZGTJNJ*, 1990, p. 350). However, the second half of the 1980s witnessed above-average crop losses in every year through natural disasters. The area with over 30 per cent crop losses due to natural disasters in 1985–1989 averaged 23.0 m. ha., compared to 16.6 m. ha. in the years 1981–4 (SSB, *ZGTJNJ*, 1990, p. 389). Equally, of the total area affected by natural disasters, the proportion which did suffer serious crop losses rose only marginally, from 48 per cent in 1981–4 to 50 per cent in 1985–9 (SSB, *ZGTJNJ*, 1990, p. 389), suggesting that the main cause of the increased impact of natural disasters was the normal cycle of weather conditions.
71. For the data in this paragraph, see SSB, *ZGNCTJNJ*, 1989, p. 262 and 1993, p. 243.
72. For example, stocks of large and medium-sized tractors and combine harvesters hardly grew at all during the 1980s and, indeed, the number of large and medium-sized tractors fell by 5 per cent from 1985 to 1990. The number of rice transplanting machines fell precipitously (from 82,000 in 1980 to 14,000 in 1988).
73. The number of small and hand-operated tractors grew from 1.9 million in 1980 to 7.0 million in 1990, the number of mechanical threshers grew from 2.5 million in 1980 to 4.5 million in 1988, and the number of small mechanical harvesters grew from 74,000 in 1980 to 210,000 in 1988.
74. For example, the stocks of motorised fishing boats used by farmers grew from 61,000 in 1980 to 265,000 in 1988.
75. Stocks of trucks for agricultural use rose from 1.4 million in 1980 to

5.9 million in 1988, stocks of motorised transport boats rose from 108,000 in 1980 to 319,000 in 1988, and the number of rubber-tyred hand-pulled trucks rose from 35 million in 1980 to 66 million in 1988.

76. The growth rate of real gross value of output reached over 8 per cent per annum between 1980 and 1985 (SSB, *ZGTJZY*, 1990, p. 53).

77. From 1978 to 1991 the average annual growth rate of crop production was 5.9 per cent, compared to 8.9 per cent for animal husbandry, 12.7 per cent for sidelines, and 10.6 per cent for fishing (SSB, *ZGTJZY*, 1992, p. 55; and SSB, *ZGTJNJ*, 1992, p. 33) (all figures gross value of output).

78. The share of crop production in the gross value of farm output (current prices) fell from 71.7 per cent in 1980 to 57.2 per cent in 1991, while that of animal husbandry rose from 18.4 per cent to 26.4 per cent, and that of fishing rose from 1.7 per cent to 5.9 per cent (SSB, *ZGTJZY*, 1992, p. 55).

79. I am indebted to Andrew Watson for both this and the previous point (personal communication).

80. Output per acre rose by 31 per cent in the early period, from 1978 to 1985, and by a further 34 per cent from 1985 to 1992 (SSB, *ZGNCTJNJ*, 1985, p. 171, and 1993, p. 188; and SSB, *ZGTJNJ*, 1993, p. 238).

81. Not least because it is impossible to disentangle the proportion of village assets used for agricultural and for non-farm work.

82. The proportion in 1991 was 61.2 per cent (SSB, *ZGTJNJ*, 1992, p. 307).

83. The average annual growth rate of rural per capita income in 1978–84 was over 11 per cent (SSB, *ZGTJNJ*, 1992, p. 277).

84. Local studies, such as Lyons' on Fujian province, confirm the huge achievement in the 1980s: 'Unlesss Fujian is grossly unrepresentative, China has indeed prosecuted a war on poverty of remarkable dimensions – and certainly one deserving of greater attention than it has received to date' (Lyons, 1992, p. 64).

85. The Gini coefficient of rural household income distribution reportedly rose from 0.21 in 1978 to 0.26 in 1985 (Zhao, 1990, p. 193).

86. The share of industry in 'basic construction investment' stood at 45 per cent in the Sixth Five Year Plan (1981–85) and 52 per cent during the Seventh Five Year Plan (SSB, *ZGTJZY*, 1992, p. 24).

87. 'The intellectual industry had emerged as new trade. The technology market constitutes an essential component of China's socialist commodity economy. The practice of uncompensated transfer of technological achievements by purely administrative means should be eliminated in favour of the exploitation of the technology market that serves to unclog the channels of the flow of technology to production' (Central Committee, 1985, p. 453).

88. The 'independent accounting sector' in China is roughly analogous to the 'organised' sector in other countries. In 1992 it acounted for 75 per cent of the gross value of industrial output in China in 1992 (SSB, *ZGTJNJ*, 1993, p. 419). In the same year within this sector state-owned enterprises accounted for 78 per cent of the total value of fixed assets, produced 69 per cent of pre-tax profits and accounted for 77 per cent of the taxes paid (SSB, *ZGTJNJ*, 1993, p. 419).

89. Derived from SSB, *CEY*, 1981, p. 212, and SSB, *ZGTJZY*, 1992, p. 70.
90. The distribution of the 55 key industrial enterprise groups is as follows: machine building and electronics: 16; metallurgy: 4; textiles: 1; energy: 7; communications: 2; chemicals: 4; construction materials: 4; forestry: 4; aeronautics and astronautics: 6; foreign economic relations and trade: 2; medicine: 2; civil aviation administration: 3 (Yao, 1992).
91. The information in this paragraph is from *Beijing Review*, vol. 34, no. 23, June 10–16, 1991.
92. These were the Guangdong based Jianlibao group, the Tianjin-based Jinmei group, and the joint ventures of Coca Cola and Pepsi Cola.
93. The share rose from 2.3 per cent of the wage bill in 1978 to 20 per cent in 1992 (SSB, *ZGTJNJ*, 1993, p. 127).
94. Number of workers in different sectors (million)

	1981	1993	1993 (as percentage of 1981)
state industry	34	46	135
non–state industry	24	61	254
tertiary sector	59	123	208

Source: SSB, *CEY*, 1981, p. 107; SSB, *ZGTJZY*, 1994, pp. 20–21.

95. Between 1985 and 1992 the total number employed in various foreign-owned and joint foreign firms rose from 436,000 to over 2.8 million (SSB, *ZGTJNJ*, 1993, p. 109).
96. Its share of total gross value of industrial output falling from 35 per cent in 1981 to just 14 per cent in 1989 (SSB, *ZGTJNJ*, 1983, pp. 220–3, and SSB, *ZGTJZY*, 1990, p. 68).
97. 57 per cent of employees in rural individual enterprises were in the non-industrial sector (SSB, *ZGNCTJNJ*, 1993, p. 49).
98. Rural industry in turn accounted for the bulk of total rural non-farm output, accounting for over 75 per cent of rural non-farm gross value of output in 1992 (SSB, *ZGTJZY*, 1994, p. 71).
99. In 1992 there was an average of 12 establishments per xiang (SSB, *ZGNCTJNJ*, 1993, p. 47).
100. This is not, of course, inconsistent with a great deal of corrupt behaviour.
101. Of course, the capacity to do these things varied enormously between different parts of the country, principally in relation to the degree of success in developing the non-farm economy.
102. In 1992 *xiang*-run enterprises reportedly paid out 22 per cent of their net income in state taxes and kept 29 per cent as 'collective retentions' for further expansion of the business, which would in turn provide increased employment opportunities to the local community (SSB, *ZGNCTJNJ*, 1993, p. 197).
103. For example, in 1993, *xiang*- and *cun*-run enterprises used 14.1 billion *yuan* of their retained profits for 'expanded reproduction', compared to 16.4 billion yuan for 'village construction', including support for village welfare, education, and small town contruction, and a further 3.8 billion yuan for support for agriculture (SSB, *ZGTJZY*, 1993, p. 71). In

addition, prior to the payment of state taxes, a further 10 per cent of the enterprises' net income was deducted for supporting various rural construction projects (SSB, *ZGTJZY*, 1994, footnote to table, p. 71).

104. In the same way as Japan at a comparable stage of development this focussed more on borrowing and adapting international technology rather than undertaking primary research.

105. Naughton, 1994.

7 Reform in Russia

1. 'The most striking characteristic of [the top leadership stratum] is its advanced age . . .; the coming succession will inevitably bring about massive replacement of the leadership stratum, and will compress the turnover into a relatively short time span' (Bialer, 1983, p. 400).

2. Yakovlev was head of the Propaganda Department in the early 1970s and again, under Gorbachev in the late 1980s, he became the head of Soviet ideology, rising to become a member of the Politburo in 1987. He had been an exchange student at Columbia University in 1958–9 and Soviet ambassador to Canada from 1973 to 1983.

3. A fundamentally similar evaluation is given by Hosking's standar reference work (Hosking, 1992, p. 457).

4. The original agreement was that the President would be elected by a national ballot, but Gorbachev sidestepped this possibility through a consitutional sleight of hand.

5. It did, of course, substantially alter the economic relationship between the centre and the provinces.

6. Striking public examples of this are Solzhenitsyn's Nobel Prize acceptance speech, which contains references to the 'Yellow Peril', and Stalin's contemptuous attitude towards the Chinese, recorded in Krushchev's memoirs.

7. I found the extremely careful, scholarly account of the Gorbachev economic reforms in Aslund (1991) most useful in writing this section. I disagree profoundly with the overall evaluation that Aslund makes of the relationship between economic and political reform, and his evaluation of the desirable nature of economic reform in formerly centrally planned economies.

8. See especially the discussion in section V, entitled 'Alternative approaches to reform' (IMF *et al.*, 1990, pp. 16–19).

9. It should be noted that the decline in world oil prices had been reversed by 1986.

10. See e.g. Khanin, 1993a.

11. See especially, the careful acount given by Jonathan Steele in *The Guardian Weekly*, March 1993.

12. See for example the discussion in *Transition*, vol. 3, no. 10, November 1992, p. 5.

13. Of course, in purchasing power parity terms Russian national income per capita was much higher, around 3,400 dollars in the early 1990s (IMF, 1993, p. 85).

14. Small enterprises were defined as those having fewer than 200 employees

and a book value of fixed assets of less than one million rubles as of
1 January 1992. Medium-sized enterprises were defined as those enterprises having between 2000 and 1000 employees, or a book value of
assets of between one million and fifty million rubles as of 1 January
1992 (IMF, 1993, p. 47).
15. I have been unable to locate an exact figure.
16. There were about 100 'licensed investment companies' by January 1993
(IMF, 1993, p. 51).
17. Personal communication.
18. In my own debates with members of the Chinese democratic movement
I was attacked repeatedly for suggesting that the possibility of political
chaos had to be taken very seriously indeed, and for suggesting that
supporting policies that sound liberal but which lead to political chaos
will have disastrous results for the lives of most ordinary Chinese people.
For example, in debate with the 'Future of China Society' in New York
in November 1990 (the proceedings were subsequently published in Chinese) (Future of China Society, New York, 1993), and in the debate at
the Oxford Union on 4 May 1992, commemorating the Tiananmen Square
massacre.

8 Conclusions

1. This view is effectively the same as that in the reformist 'joke'. Question:
what is socialism? Answer: The transitional stage between feudalism and
capitalism.
2. These 'smaller' countries were not all absolutely small. In the late 1980s
the total population of Asian communist countries other than China was
around 120 million, compared to 110 million for European communist
countries (134 million if one includes Yugoslavia). Vietnam's population
is almost twice that of Poland (65 million versus 38 million), and Burma's population (around 40 million) is also larger than Poland's. In the
applied literature on transforming economies, there is a massive prepon-
derance of books and articles on the east European countries, yet the communist countries of Asia other than China contain just as many people,
and in the long run may well be more powerful economies than the former
communist countries of east Europe.
3. Notable exceptions to the consensus in the early stages of the process
were, from very different points of view, Galbraith (1990) and Walters
(1991 and 1992).
4. In the same way as Japan at a comparable stage of development this focussed
more on borrowing and adapting international technology rather than undertaking primary research.
5. Naughton, 1994.
6. This was acknowledged even by the mainstream Report by the US
Commision on Education in Economics (Report, 1991).

Bibliography

Abramowitz, M. (1986) 'Catching up, forging ahead, falling behind', *Journal of Economic History*, vol. 46, no. 2, pp. 385–406.

Acs, Z., and Audretsch, D. (eds) (1993) *Small firms and entrepreneurship* (Cambridge: Cambridge University Press).

Acs, Z., and Audretsch, D.B. (1993) 'Has the role of small firms changed in the US?', in Acs and Audretsch (eds), (1993).

Agarwala, A.N., and Singh, S.P. (1958) *The Economics of Underdevelopment* (New York: Oxford University Press).

Agenbegyan, A. (1988) *The Challenge: The Economics of Perestroika* (London: Hutchinson).

Amalrik, A. (1980) *Will the Soviet Union survive until 1984?* (Harmondsworth: Pelican Books, expanded edition).

Amnesty International (1987) *China: Torture and ill-treatment of prisoners* (London: Amnesty International Publications).

Amsden, A.M. (1989) *Asia's Next Giant* (New York: Oxford University Press).

Anderson, A.M. (1928) *Humanity and labour in China* (London: Christian Student Movement).

Aslund, A. (1990) 'Gorbachev, Perestroika, and Economic Crisis', *Problems of Communism*, January–April, pp. 13–41.

Aslund, A. (1991) *Gorbachev's struggle for economic reform* (London: Pinter).

Aslund, A. (1992) 'Aslund urges stronger Western involvement', *Transition*, vol. 3, no. 10, November.

Astapovich, A., and L. Gregoriev (1994) 'Foreign investment in Russia: Problems and solutions', *Problems of Economic Transition*, vol. 36, no. 10.

Avrich, P. (1970) *Kronstadt, 1921* (New York: Norton).

Balazs, E. (1964) *Chinese civilisation and bureaucracy* (New Haven: Yale University Press).

Banerji, A. (1994) 'Food shortages in Russia', *Economic and Political Weekly*, vol. 29, no. 19, May 7.

Banister, J. (1987) *China's changing population* (Stanford: Stanford University Press).

Banister, J. (1992) *Demographic aspects of poverty in China*, World Bank Working Paper (World Bank: Washington DC).

Baran, P. (1957) *The Political Economy of Growth* (New York: Monthly Review Press).

Bardhan, P.K. (1984) *The political economy of development in India* (Oxford: Blackwell).

Baring Securities (1991) *Shenzhen – China's economic superpower?* (Hong Kong: Hong Kong Research).

Barnett, D. (1974) *Uncertain passage: China's transition to the post-Mao era*, (Washington, DC: Brookings Institution).

Bater, J. (1987) 'St Petersburg and Moscow on the eve of the Revolution', in Kaiser (1987).

Bauer, P. (1981) *Equality, the Third World and Economic Delusion* (London: Weidenfield and Nicolson).

Bear, Stearns and Co. Inc. (1993) *Ek Chor China Motorcycles Co. Ltd.: Prospectus* (New York: Bear, Stearns and Co. Inc).

Bergere, M-C. (1986) *The Golden Age of the Chinese Bourgeoisie* (Cambridge: Cambridge University Press).

Bergson, A. and S. Kuznets (eds) (1963) *Economic trends in the Soviet Union* (Cambridge, Mass.: Harvard University Press).

Bergson, A. and D. Levine, (eds) (1983) *The Soviet Economy: Towards the Year 2000* (London: Allen and Unwin).

Berliner, J. (1983) 'Planning and management', in Bergson and Levine (1983).

Bialer, S. (1983) 'Politics and priorities', in Bergson and Levine (1983).

Blackwell, W. (1983) 'The Russian entrepreneur in the Tsarist period: An overview', in Guroff and Kasterson (1983).

Blanchard, O., M. Boycko, M. Dabrowski, R. Dornbusch, R. Layard and A. Shliefer (1993) *Post-Communist Reform* (Cambridge, Mass: MIT Press).

Blanchard, O., R. Dornbusch, P. Krugman, R. Layard and L. Summers (1991) *Reform in Eastern Europe* (Cambridge, Mass.: MIT Press).

Borenzstein, E. and M. Kumar (1991) 'Proposals for privatisation in Eastern Europe', *IMF Staff Papers*, vol. 38, June, reprinted in Kennett and Lieberman (1993).

Boserup, E. (1981) *Population and Technology* (Oxford: Basil Blackwell).

Brown, H.P. (1986) *The origins of trade union power* (Oxford: Oxford University Press).

Brown, A. and M. Kaser (eds) (1978) *The Soviet Union since the Fall of Khrushchev* (London: Macmillan).

Buck, T. Filatochev, I., and M. Wright (1993) 'Buy outs and the transformation of Russian industry', Nottingham University, School of Management and Finance, Discussion Paper.

Bukharin, N. and E. Preobrazhensky *The ABC of communism* (Harmondsworth: Penguin Books, 1969). First published in Russian, 1920.

Byrd, W. (1992) *China's industrial firms under reform* (London: Oxford University Press).

Byrd, W. (1990) 'Entrepreneurship, Capital, and Ownership', in W. Byrd and Q. Lin (eds), *China's Rural Industry* (Washington, DC: World Bank).

Byrd, W. and Q. Lin (1990) *China's Rural Industry* (Washington DC: Oxford University Press).

Byrd, W. and G. Tidrick (1987) *China's industrial reforms* (London: Oxford University Press).

Carr, E.H. (1979) *The Russian Revolution from Lenin to Stalin, 1917–1929* (London: Macmillan).

Carr, E.H. and R.W. Davies (1969) *Foundations of a planned economy, 1926–1929* (Harmondsworth: Pelican Books).

Central Committee of the CCP (1978) 'Communiqué of the third plenary session of the eleventh central commitee of the Communist Party of China', in *Major Documents* (1991).

Central Committee of the CCP (1984) 'Decision on reform of the economic structure', in *Major Documents* (1991).

Central Committee of the CCP (1993) 'Decision of the CCP Central Committee on some issues concerning the establishment of a socialist market economic structure', *Beijing Review*, vol. 36, no. 47, Nov. 22–28.

Central Committee of the CCP and the State Council (1985) 'Summary of the forum on the Changjiang Delta, Zhujiang Delta and Xiamen-Quanzhou Triangle in Southern Fujian', 18 February, in *Major Documents* (1991).

Chakravarty, S. (1987) *Development Planning: The Indian experience* (Oxford: Oxford University Press).

Chandler, A.D. (1990) *Scale and Scope: The dynamics of industrial capitalism* (Cambridge, Mass.: Harvard University Press).

Chang, H.J. (1993) *The Political Economy of Industrial Policy* (London: Macmillan).

Chang, H.J. (1994) 'Heaven or hell? Interpreting the Korean experience', manuscript, Cambridge.

Chang, H.J. and P. Nolan (1995) 'Europe versus Asia: Contrasting paths to the reform of political economy', in Chang and Nolan (eds) *The transformation of the communist economies: Against the mainstream* (London: Macmillan).

Chang, H.J. and P. Nolan (eds) (1995) *The transformation of the communist economies: Against the mainstream* (London: Macmillan).

Chapman, J. (1963) 'Consumption', in Bergson and Kuznets (1963).

Chen Derong (1993) *The contract management responsibility system in China*, University of Birmingham Doctoral Thesis.

Chen, Jihua (1994) 'Report on the implementation of the 1993 plan for national economic and social development', *Beijing Review*, vol. 37, no. 15, April 11–17.

Chen, Kang, G.H. Jefferson, T.G. Rawski, H. Wang, and Y. Zheng (1988) 'New estimates of fixed investment and capital stock for Chinese state industry', *China Quarterly*, June, no. 114.

Chen, Kang, G. Jefferson, and I. Singh (1992) 'Lessons from China's reform', *Journal of Comparative Economics*, vol. 16, pp. 201–225.

Chen, Yun, (1981) 'Training and promoting young and middle aged cadres is our urgent task', in *Major Documents*, 1991.

Chenery, H. *et al.* (1974) *Redistribution with Growth* (New York: Oxford University Press).

Cheung, Steven N.S. (1986) *Will China Go 'Capitalist?'*, Hobart paper 94 (London: IEA).

Chiang, Kaishek (1947) *China's destiny* (London: Dennis Dobson).

Clague, C., and G.C. Rausser (1992) *The emergence of market economies in Eastern Europe* (Oxford: Blackwell).

Cohen, S. (1986) *Rethinking the Soviet experience* (New York: Oxford University Press).

Cohn, S.H. (1982) 'Sources of low productivity in Soviet capital investment', in USCJEC (1982).

Conquest, R. (1986) *The Harvest of Terror* (Harmondsworth: Penguin Books).

Constitution of the People's Republic of China (1975) (Peking: Foreign Languages Press).

Council for Economic Planning and Development, Republic of China (1989) *Taiwan Statistical Data Book 1989* (Taipei, Republic of China: Council for Economic Planning and Development).

Dai, Yannian (1994) 'Spotlight on China's modern enterprise system', *Beijing Review*, vol. 37, no. 9, Feb. 28–Mar. 6.

Dasgupta, P. (1990) 'Well-being and the extent of its realisation in poor countries', *Economic Journal*, vol. 100, no. 190, pp. 1–32.

Davie, J.L. (1986) 'China's international trade and finance', in USCJEC, 1986.

Davies, R.W. *Soviet history in the Gorbachev revolution* (London: Macmillan, 1989).

Deng, Xiaoping (1979) 'The necessity of upholding the four cardinal principles in the drive for the four modernisations', in *Major Documents*, 1991.

Deng, Xiaoping (1980) 'On the Reform of the system of party and state leadership', in *Major Documents* (1991).

Deng, Xiaoping (1984) *Selected Works of Deng Xiaoping (1975–1982)* (Beijing: Foreign Languages Press).

Deng, Xiaoping (1987) 'We shall speed up reform', June 12, in *Major Documents*, 1991.

Derbyshire, J.D. and I. Derbyshire *World political sytems* (Edinburgh: Chambers).

Deyo, F.C. (ed.) (1987) *The Political Economy of the New Asian Industrialism* (Ithaca: Cornell University Press).

Dic Lo (1995) 'Economic theory and transformation of the Soviet-type system: The challenge of the late industrialisation perspective', in Chang and Nolan (1995).

Dobb, M. (1966) *Studies in the Development of Capitalism* (London: Routledge and Kegan Paul).

Dong, Fureng (1982) 'Relationship between accumulation and consumption', in Xu Dixin (ed) (1982).

Dong, Fureng (1990) 'Reform of the operating mechanism and reform of ownership', in Nolan and Dong (1990).

Dong, Fureng, C. Lin and B. Naughton (1996) *China's state owned enterprise reforms* (London: Macmillan).

Donnithorne, A. (1972) *China's economic system* (London: George Allen and Unwin).

Dornbusch, R. and S. Edwards (eds) (1991) *The Macroeconomics of Latin American Populism* (Chicago: Chicago University Press).

Economic Handbook of xiangzhen qiye (1989) (Beijing: Xin Shidai Chubanshe).

Economic Research Institute, Chinese Academy of Social Sciences (1987), *Reports on the organisation and growth of China's xiangzhen enterprises*, Economic Research Materials, no. 7.

Economist Intelligence Unit (1992) *CIS: Country Report (former USSR)*, no. 4.

Economist Intelligence Unit (1991) *Poland: Country report*, no. 1.

Edwards, S. (1992) 'Stabilisation and liberalising policies for economies in transition: Latin American lessons for Eastern Europe', in Clague and Rauser (1992).

Ellman, M. (1991) 'The contradictions of perestroika: The case of agriculture', *European Journal of Agricultural Economics*, vol. 18, pp. 1–18.

Ellman, M. (1994) 'The increase in death and disease under *katastroika*', *Cambridge Journal of Economics*, vol. 18, no. 4, pp. 329–356.

Ellman, M. and M. Kantorovich (1990) *The disintegration of the Soviet Union* (London: Routledge).

Erlich, E. (1985) 'The size structure of manufacturing establishments and enterprises: an international comparison', *Journal of Comparative Economics*, vol. 9, pp. 267–95.

European Bank for Reconstruction and Development (1994) *Economic transition in eastern Europe and the former Soviet Union* (London: EBRD).

European Community (1991) *The largest groups at world and community level*, mimeo.

Fal'tsman, V. (1993) 'Russia's industrial strategy in the period of transition', *Problems of Economic Transition*, vol. 36, no. 8, December, pp. 23–41.

Fan, Q, and M.E. Schaffer (1991) 'Enterprise reforms in Chinese and Polish state-owned industries', Research Programme on the Chinese Economy (London School of Economics: STICERD).

Feshbach, M. (1983) 'Population and labour force', in Bergson and Levine (1983).

Field, R.M. (1992) 'China's industrial performance since 1978', *China Quarterly*, no. 131, September, pp. 577–607.

Fields, G.S. (1980) *Poverty, Inequality and Development* (Cambridge: Cambridge University Press).

Fieleke, N.S. (1991) 'The liberalisation of trade and payments in Eastern Europe', *New England Economic Review*, March/April, reprinted in Kennett and Lieberman (1992).

Findlay, R. (1988) 'Trade, development and the state', in Ranis and Schultz, (1988).

First Boston, Merrill Lynch, and Salomon Brothers (1992) *Brilliance Automotive Holdings Limited: Prospectus* (New York: First Boston, Merrill Lynch and Salomon Brothers).

Friedman, M. (1982) *Capitalism and Freedom* (Chicago: University of Chicago Press). Selection reprinted in Kennett and Lieberman (1992).

Galbraith, J.K. (1990) 'The rush to capitalism', *New York Review of Books*, October 25, reprinted in Kennett and Lieberman (1992).

Gamble, S.D. (1921) *Peking: A social survey* (New York: George H. Doran Doran).

Gao, Shangquan (1992) 'New operating mechanism', *Beijing Review*, vol. 35, no. 24, June 15–21.

Gatrell, P. (1986) *The Tsarist Economy, 1850–1917* (London: Batsford).

Goldman, M. (1992) *What went wrong with* perestroika? (New York: Norton).

Gomulka, S. (1989) 'Shock Needed for the Polish Economy', *Guardian* (London), 19 August.

Gomulka, S. *The theory of technological change and economic growth* (London: Routledge).

Goodman, D. (ed.) (1981) *Beijing Street Voices* (London: Marion Boyars).

Gorbachev, M. (1988) *Perestroika* (London: Collins).

Government of India, Planning Commission (1961) *Third Five Year Plan* (New Delhi: Government of India).

Granick, D. (1967) *Soviet metal fabricating* (Madison and Milwaukee: University of Wisconsin Press).

Grossman, G. (1979) 'Notes on the illegal economy and corruption', in USCJEC, (1979).

Guo, Jiann-Joong (1992) *Price reform in China, 1979–86* (London: Macmillan).

Guo, Shuqing. *et al.* (1990) 'On accumulation in China in recent years', *Economic Research (Jingji yanjiu)*, January, no. 1.

Guroff, G. and F.V. Kasteson (eds) (1983) *Entrepreneurship in Imperial Russia and the Soviet Union* (Princeton NJ: Princeton University Press).

Hahn, F. (1984) 'Reflections on the invisible hand', in F. Hahn, *Equilibrium and macroeconomics* (Oxford: Basil Blackwell).

Halliday, J. (1975) *A political history of Japanese capitalism* (London: Monthly Review Press).

Handelman, M. (1994) *Comrade Criminal* (London: Michael Joseph).

Hanson, P. (1978) 'The import of Western technology', in Brown and Kaser (1978).

Harding, H. (1987) *China's second revolution* (Washington, DC: The Brookings Institution).

Hay, D. and G.S. Liu (1992) 'Cost behaviour of Chinese state-owned manufacturing enterpises during the reform period, 1979–87', Applied Economics Discussion Paper, no. 134, Institute of Economics and Statistics, Oxford University.

He, Xin (1990) 'Scholar discusses democracy and other issues', *Beijing Review*, vol. 33, no. 34, 20–26 August.

Heston, A. (1983) 'National Income', in Khumar and Desai (1983).

Hicks, G. (ed.) (1990) *The broken mirror* (Harlow, Essex: Longman).

Hinton, W. (1991) *The privatisation of China* (London: Earthscan).

Hirschman, A. (1977) *The passion and the interests* (Princeton, NJ: Princeton University Press).

Ho, Pingti (1959) *The Population of China* (Cambridge, Mass.: Harvard University Press).

Hobsbawm, E. and T. Ranger (eds) (1983) *The invention of tradition*, (Cambridge: Cambridge University Press).

Hosking, G. (1992) *A History of the Soviet Union, 1917–1991* (London: Harper Collins).

Hoskins, W.G. (1976) *The Age of Plunder*, (Harlow: Longmans).

Hu, Sheng (1955) *Imperialism and Chinese Politics* (Peking: Foreign Languages Press).

Hu, Yaobang (1982) 'Create a new situation in modernisation', in *Major Documents* (1991).

Hughes, A. (1993) 'Industrial concentration and small firms in the UK: the 1980s in historical perspective', in Acs and Audretsch (1993).

Hughes, H. (1991) 'Constraints on export growth: foreign or domestic?'. Mimeo.

Hurd, D. (1990) Speech at the Overseas Development Institute, London, 6 June.

IMF (1993) *Russian Federation*, Economic Review, no. 8 (Washington DC: International Monetary Fund).

IMF (1994) *World Economic Outlook* (Washington DC: International Monetary Fund) May.

IMF, World Bank, OECD and EBRD (1990) *The Economy of the USSR: Summary and Recommendations* (Washington, DC: World Bank).

Jaquemin, A. *et al.* (1989) 'Horizontal mergers and competition policy in the European Community', *European Economy*, no. 40, May.

Jefferson, G., T. Rawski and Y. Zheng (1992) 'Growth, efficiency and convergence in China's state and collective industry', *Economic Development and Cultural Change*, vol. 40, no. 2, January 1992, pp. 239–66.

Jefferson, G., and Xu Wenyi (1991) 'The impact of reform on socialist enterprises in transition: structure, conduct and performance in Chinese industry', *Journal of Comparative Economics*, vol. 15, pp. 45–64.

Jiang, Xiaoming (1993) *Property rights an economic reform: A case study of the Hefeng Textile plant in Ningbo*, Cambridge University Doctoral Thesis.

Johnson, C. (1990) 'Foreword', in Hicks (1990).

Kagarlitsky, B. (1992) *The disintegration of the monolith* (London: Verso).

Kaiser, D.H. (ed.) (1987) *The workers' revolution in Russia, 1917* (Cambridge: Cambridge University Press).

Kennett, D. and M. Lieberman (eds) (1992) *The Road to Capitalism* (Orlando, Florida: Dryden Press).

Khanin, G.I. (1993a) 'The economic crisis in Russia: Possible ways out', *Problems of Economic Transition*, vol. 36, no. 2, pp. 23–27.

Khanin, G.I. (1993b) 'Russia's economic situation in 1992', *Problems of Economic Transition*, vol. 36, no. 7, pp. 6–24.

Khumar, D. and M. Desai (eds) (1983) *The Cambridge Economic History of India*, vol. 2 (Cambridge: Cambridge University Press).

Kiselev, S. (1994) 'The state and the farmer', *Problems of Economic Transition*, vol. 36, no. 10, pp. 67–81.

Kitching, G. (1983) *Rethinking socialism* (London: Methuen).

Korbash, M. (1984) *The economic 'theories' of Maoism* (Moscow: Progress Publishers).

Kornai, J. (1980) *Economics of shortage*, 2 vols (Amsterdam: North Holland).

Kornai, J. (1986) 'The Hungarian reform process: Visions, hopes, and realities', *Journal of Economic Literature*, vol. 24, pp. 1687–1737.

Kornai, J. (1990) *The road to a free economy* (New York: Norton).

Kornai, J. (1992) *The socialist system* (Oxford: Clarendon Press).

Kreuger, A. (1992) 'Institutions for the new private sector', in Clague and Rausser (1992).

Lake, D.A. (1988) *Power, protection and free trade* (London: Cornell University Press).

Lal, D. (1983) *The Poverty of Development Economics* (London: Institute of Economic Affairs).

Lane, D. (1978) *Politics and society in the USSR* (second edition) (London: Martin Robertson).

Lardy, N. and K. Lieberthal (eds) (1983) *Chen Yun's strategy for China's development* (Armonk, New York: M.E. Sharpe).

Lardy, N. (1983) *Agriculture in Modern China's Economic Development* (Cambridge: Cambridge University Press).

Layard, R. (1993) 'Stabilisation versus reform? Russia's first year', in Blanchard *et al.* (1994).

Lester, W. (1813) *The happy era of one hundred millions of the human race, or the merchant, manufacturer, and the Englishman's recognised right to an unlimited free trade with India* (no place or publisher).

Levy, M., and Kuo-heng Shih (1949) *The rise of the modern Chinese business class* (New York: Institute of Pacific Relations).

Lewin, M. (1975) *Political undercurrents in Soviet Economic Debate* (London: Pluto Press).

Li, K.T. (1988) *Economic transformation of Taiwan* (London: Shepheard-Walwyn).

Li, Ping (1992) 'Price reform the progressive way', *Beijing Review*, vol. 35, no. 18, May 4–10.

Li, Renfeng (1981) *Statistical Materials on Soviet Agriculture* (*Sulian nongye tongji huibian*) (Beijing: Nongye chubanshe).

Li, Yuanchao (1992) 'Enterprise groups in China: The present situation and future trends', *Social Sciences in China*, Summer, pp. 5–15.

Liberman, E.G. (1971) *Economic methods and the effectiveness of production* (New York: International Arts and Sciences Press).

Lin, C. (1981) 'The reinstatement of Chinese economics today', *China Quarterly*, March, no. 85, pp. 1–48.

Lipton, D. and J. Sachs (1990a), 'Creating a market economy in Eastern Europe: the case of Poland', *Brookings Papers on Economic Activity*, vol. 1, reprinted in Kennett and Lieberman, (1992).

Lipton, D. and J. Sachs (1990b), 'Privatisation in Eastern Europe', *Brookings Papers on Economic Activity*, no. 2, reprinted in Kennett and Lieberman (1992).

List, F. (1983) *The natural system of political economy*, first published in German, 1837. (English edition; London: Frank Cass, translated and edited by W.O. Henderson).

Little, I. (1979) 'An economic reconnaissance', in W. Galenson (ed.), *Economic Growth and Structural change in Taiwan* (London: Cornell University Press).

Little, I. (1982) *Economic Development, Theory, Policy and International Relations* (New York: Basic Books).

Liu, Guoguang, and Wang Ruisun (1984) 'Set-up of production', in Yu Guangyuan (1984).

Liu, Nanchuan, Chen Yichu, and Zhang Chu (1988) *Seventy years of Soviet economic growth*, (*Sulian guomin jingji fazhan qishi nian*) (Beijing: Jijie chubanshe).

Liu, Shaoqi (1939) 'How to be a good communist', in Liu, Shaoqi (1980).

Liu, Shaoqi (1945) 'On the party', in Liu, Shaoqi (1980).

Liu, Shaoqi (1980) *Three essays on Party-building* (Beijing: Foreign Languages Press).

Liu Suinain, and Wu Qing (1986) *China's socialist economy* (Beijing: *Beijing Review*).

Lowe, A. (1965) *On economic knowledge* (New York: Harper Row).

Lukichna, L. (1993) 'On poverty and defining the subsistence minimum', *Problems of Economic Transition*, vol. 36, no. 8, pp. 74–85.

Lyons, B. (1992) *China's war on poverty: A case study of Fujian province, 1985–1990* (Chinese University of Hong Kong: Institute of Asia-Pacific Studies).

Macmillan, J. and B. Naughton (1991) 'How to reform a planned economy', *Oxford Review of Economic Policy*, vol. 8, no. 1, pp. 130–43.

Macpherson, I. (1987) *The economic development of Japan c. 1868–1941* (London: Macmillan).

Major Documents of the People's Republic of China, 1991 (*Major Documents*) (Beijing: Foreign Languages Press).

Mallory, J.W. (1926) *China: Land of Famine* (New York: American Geographical Society).

Mao, Zedong (1949) 'On the people's democratic dictatorship', June, in Mao (1971).

Mao, Zedong (1955) 'On the cooperative transformation of agriculture', July, in Mao (1971).

Mao, Zedong (1959) 'Critique of Stalin's Economic Problems in the Soviet Union', in Mao (1971).

Mao, Zedong (1971) *Selected Readings from the works of Mao Tsetung* (Peking: Foreign Languages Press).

Mao, Zedong (1977) *Selected Works of Mao Tsetung* (Peking: Foreign Languages Press).

Marx, K. (1887) *Capital*, vol. 1 (New York: International Publishers, Aveling and Moore edition, 1967).

Merrill Lynch (1993) *Shanghai Petrochemical Company Limited* (Hong Kong: Merrill Lynch).

Miller, J. (1993) *Mikhail Gorbachev and the end of Soviet power* (Houndmills: Macmillan).

Ministry of Agriculture (1982) (ZGNYJJGY), *Outline of China's agriculture* (*Zhongguo nongye jingji gaiyao*) (Beijing: Nongye chubanshe).

Ministry of Agriculture (1988) *Statistical Abstract of China's xiangzhen enterprises*, (*Quanguo xiangzhen qiye tongji zhaiyao*), (Beijing: Xiangzhen qiye bu).

Ministry of Agriculture (1989) (ZGNCJJTJDQ) *Statistical Record of China's Rural Economy, 1949–1986*, (*Zhongguo nongcun jingji tongji daquan*), (Beijing: Zhongguo tongji chubanshe).

Ministry of Agriculture (1991) 'China's land contract management system and the operation of co-operative organisations in China in 1990', *Problems of Agricultural Economics* (*Nongye jingji wenti*), no. 8 and 9.

Mo Yan-ren (ed.), (1987) *The development history of township and village enterprises in Jiangsu Province* (Nanjing: Institute of Technology Press, China).

Morishima, M. (1982) *Why has Japan succeeded?* (Cambridge: Cambridge University Press).

Murrell, P. (1992) 'Evolutionary and radical approaches to economic reform', *Economics of Planning*, vol. 25, pp. 79–95.

Myrdal, G. (1956) *Development and Underdevelopment* (Cairo: National Bank of Egypt).

Naughton, B. (1992) 'Implications of the state monopoly over industry and its relaxation', *Modern China*, vol. 18, no. 1, pp. 14–41.

Naughton, B., 1994, *Growing out of the plan*, Cambridge, Cambridge University Press.

Needham, J. (1954) *Science and Civilisation in China* (Cambridge: Cambridge University Press).

Needham, J. (1969) *The grand titration* (London: George Allen and Unwin).

Nefedov, V. (1994) 'The agro-industrial complex of the CIS', *Problems of Economic Transition*, vol. 37, no. 2, pp. 50–62.

Nelson, R. and S. Winter (1982) *An Evolutionary Theory of Economic Change* (Cambridge: Harvard University Press).

Niu, Gengying (1994) 'China's economic reform in 1994', *Beijing Review*, vol. 37, no. 2, Jan. 10–16.

Nolan, P. (1988) *The political economy of collective farms* (Cambridge: Polity Press).

Nolan, P. (1993a), *State and market in the Chinese economy* (London: Macmillan).

Nolan, P. (1993b), 'Political economy and the reform of Stalinism: The Chinese puzzle', *Contributions to Political Economy*, vol. 12.

Nolan, P. (1993c) 'The causation and prevention of famine: A critique of A.K. Sen', *Journal of Peasant Studies*, vol. 21, no. 1, October.

Nolan, P. (1994a), 'Democratisation, human rights and economic reform: The case of China and Russia', *Democratisation*, vol. 1, no. 1, Spring.

Nolan, P. (1994b), 'Economic reform, foreign investment and the Chinese beverage industry', mimeo.

Nolan, P. and Dong Fureng (eds) (1990) *The Chinese economy and its future* (Cambridge: Polity Press).

Nolan, P. and G. White (1983) 'Urban bias, rural bias or state bias? Urban-rural relations in post-revolutionary China', *Journal of Development Studies*, vol. 20, no. 3, April.

North, D.C. (1990) *Institutions, institutional change and economic performance* (Cambridge: Cambridge University Press).

North, D.C. and R.P. Thomas (1973) *The Rise of the Western World* (Cambridge: Cambridge University Press).

Nove, A. (1968) *The Soviet Economy* (London: George Allen and Unwin).

Nove, A. (1983) *The Economics of Feasible Socialism* (London: George Allen and Unwin).

Nove, A. (1994) 'Once again on concepts of socialism', *Problems of Economic Transition*, vol. 37, no. 2, June, pp. 41–9.

OECD (1972) *The industrial policy of Japan* (Paris: OECD).

Office of the Mayor of St Petersburg (1991) *St Petersburg: Business Plan*. Produced for the office of the Mayor of St Petersburg by Coopers and Lybrand in association with Scottish Enterprise and the Leontief Centre of St Petersburg.

Olson, M. (1982) *The Rise and Decline of Nations* (New Haven: Yale University Press).

Peregrine Capital (1993) *Guangzhou Shipyard International Company Limited* (Hong Kong, Peregrine Capital).

Perkins, D.H. (1968) *Agricultural Development in China, 1368–1968* (Edinburgh: Edinburgh University Press).

Perkins, D.H. (ed.) (1977) *China: Rural small-scale industry in the People's Republic of China* (London: University of California Press).

Perkins, D.H. (1988) 'Reforming China's economic system', *Journal of Economic Literature*, vol. 26, June, pp. 601–45.

Perlamutrov, V. (1994) 'Towards a market economy or an economic catastrophe?', *Problems of Economic Transition*, vol. 37, no. 2, pp. 24–40.

Phelps Brown, H. (1983) *The Origins of Trade Union Power* (Oxford: Oxford University Press).

Pipes, L. (1977) *Russia under the old regime* (Harmondsworth: Peregrine Books).

Plant, R. (1986) *Equality, Markets and the State* (London: Fabian Society).

Polanyi, K. (1957) *The great transformation* (New York: Beacon Press).

Popper, K. (1957) *The Poverty of Historicism* (London: Routledge and Kegan Paul).

Popper, K.R. (1960) *The poverty of historicism* (London: Routledge and Kegan Paul).

Prais, S.J. (1981) *Productivity and industrial structure* (Cambridge: Cambridge University Press).

Prybyla, J. (1990) 'A broken system', in G. Hicks (ed.), *The broken mirror: China after Tiananmen* (London: Longman).

Prybyla, J. (1991) 'The road from socialism: Why, where, what and how', *Problems of Communism*, vol. XL, January–April.

Rakistkii, B. (1994) 'The condition of the population of Russia', *Problems of Economic Transition*, vol. 36, no. 10, pp. 32–43.

Ranis, G. and T.P. Schultz, (1988) *The State of Development Economics* (Oxford: Basil Blackwell).

Rawski, T.G. (1989) *Economic Growth in Pre-war China* (Berkeley: University of California Press).

Report of the Commission on Graduate Education in Economics (1991) *Journal of Economic Literature*, vol. 29, September, pp. 1035–1053.

Research Group on Migration and Employment of China's Rural Labour (1989) 'The current situation or rural employment in China and prospects', *Problems of Agricultural Economics* (*Nongye jingji wenti*), no. 7 (117).

Reynolds, B. (ed.) (1987) *Reform in China* (London: M.E. Sharpe).

Reynolds, L.G. (1985) *Economic Growth in the Third World, 1850–1980* (New Haven: Yale University Press).

Riskin, C. (1987) *China's political economy* (Oxford: Oxford University Press).

Rodzinski, W. (1988) *The People's Republic of China: Reflections on Chinese political history since 1949* (London: Collins).

Rosenberg, N., and L.E. Birdsell (1986) *How the West grew rich* (London: I.B. Tauris).

Rueschmeyer, D., E.H. Stephens, and J.D. Stephens, (1992), *Capitalist Development and Democracy* (Cambridge: Polity Press).

Rules of the Communist Party of the Soviet Union (1961).

Rural Policy Research Department, Zhejiang Province (1988) 'Transfer of rural workforce in Zhejiang', *Problems of Agricultural Economics* (*Nongye jingji wenti*), no. 1 (97).

Sachs, J. and W.T. Woo (1994) 'Structural factors in the economic reforms of China, Eastern Europe, and the Former Soviet Union', *Economic Policy*, vol. 9, no. 18, April.

Schapiro, J. (1970) *The Communist Party of the Soviet Union* (London: Methuen).

Scherer, F.M. and D. Ross (1990) *Industrial market structure and performance*, third edition (Boston: Houghton Mifflin).

Schram, S. (1974) *Mao Tsetung Unrehearsed* (Harmondsworth: Penguin Books).

Schroeder, G. (1979) 'The Soviet economy on a treadmill of "reforms"', in USCJEC (1979).

Schroeder, G. (1982) 'Soviet economic "reform" decrees on the treadmill', in USCJEC, (1982).

Schroeder, G. (1983) 'Consumption', in Bergson and Levine (1983).

Schurmann, F. (1964) 'China's "New Economic Policy" – Transition or beginning?', *China Quarterly*, no. 17, January–March, pp. 65–91.

Schurmann, F. (1968) *Ideology and Organisation in communist China* (Berkeley: University of California Press).

Sen, A.K. (1981) 'Public action and the quality of life in developing countries', *Oxford Bulletin of Economics and Statistics*, vol. 43.

Sen, A.K. (1982) *Poverty and famine* (Oxford: Clarendon Press).

Sen, A.K. (1989) 'Food and freedom', *World Development*, vol. 17, no. 6, 769–81.

Shen, Liren and Dai, Yuanchen (1990) 'The formation, shortcomings and origins of "the economy divided by dukes and princes under the emperor" in China', *Economic Research (Jingji yanjiu)*, no. 3, March.

Shmelyev, N. and V. Popov (1990) *The turning point: Revitalising the Soviet economy* (London: I.B. Tauris).

Singh, A. (1993) 'The plan, the market and evolutionary economic reform in China', UNCTAD, Discussion Paper, December, no. 76.

Singh, I. (1991) 'Is there schizophrenia about socialist reform?', *Transition* (Washington DC, World Bank, July–August).

Smith, A. (1976) *The Wealth of Nations* (Chicago: University of Chicago Press, Cannan Edition).

Smith, A. (1993) *Russia and the world economy* (London: Routledge).

Smith New Court Securities (1994) 'What tune is Yeltsin dancing to?', February, Russia/Ukraine/Kazakhstan.

Staley, E. and R. Morse (1965) *Modern small industry for developing countries* (New York: McGraw-Hill).

Starikov, E. (1994) 'A bazaar not a market', *Problems of Economic Transition*, vol. 37, no. 2, pp. 14–23.

State Statistical Bureau (SSB) (1984–93) *Chinese Economic Yearbook* (*Zhongguo tongji nianjian*) (ZGTJNJ) (Beijing: Zhongguo tongji chubanshe).

State Statistical Bureau (SSB) (1984–94) *Statistical Survey of China* (*Zhongguo tongji zhaiyao*) (ZGTJZY) (Beijing: Zhongguo tongji chubanshe).

State Statistical Bureau (SSB) (1985), *Statistical materials on Chinese industry, 1949–1984* (*Zhongguo gongye jingji tongji ziliao*) (ZGGYJJTJZL) (Beijing: Tongji chubanshe).

State Statistical Bureau (SSB) (1985–93) *Chinese Rural Statistical Yearbook* (*Zhongguo nongcun tongji nianjian*) (ZGNCTJNJ) (Beijing: Zhongguo tongji chubanshe).

State Statistical Bureau (SSB) (1986–93) *Economic statistics on Chinese industry* (*Zhongguo gongye jingji tongji nianjian*) (ZGGYJJTJNJ) (Beijing: Tongji chubanshe).

State Statistical Bureau (SSB) (1987) *Statistical materials on Chinese labour and wages, 1949–85* (*Zhongguo laodong gongzi tongjii ziliao*) (ZGLDGZTJZL) (Beijing: Tongji chubanshe).

State Statistical Bureau (SSB) (1987) *Statistical materials on investment in fixed assets in China, 1950–1985* (*Zhongguo guding zichan touzi tongji ziliao*) (ZGGDZCTZTJZL) (Beijing: Tongji chubanshe).

State Statistical Bureau (SSB) (1989) *Guangdong Statistical yearbook, 1989*, (*Guangdong sheng tongji nianjian*) (GDSTJNJ) (Guangdong: Tongji chubanshe).

State Statistical Bureau (SSB) (1989) *Statistical yearbook of Chinese popu-*

lation (*Zhongguo renkou tongji nianjian*) (*ZGRKTJNJ*) (Beijing: Kexue jishu wenxian chubanshe).

State Statistical Bureau (SSB) (1989) *Statistical materials on China's supply and marketing co-operatives, 1949–1988*, (*Zhongguo gongxiao hezuoshe tongji ziliao*) (*ZGGXHZSTJZY*) (Beijing: Zhongguo tongji chubanshe).

State Statistical Bureau, SSB (1990) *Jiangsu statistical yearbook, 1990, (Jiangsu sheng tongji nianjian*) (*JSSTJNJ*) (Jiangsu: Tongji chubanshe).

State Statistical Bureau (SSB) (1990) *Compendium of historical statistical materials 1949–1989 (Lishi tongji ziliao huibian*) (*LSTJZLHB*) (Beijing: Tongji chubanshe).

State Statistical Bureau (1991) 'Statistical Communiqué of the State Statistical Bureau of the People's Republic of China on National Economic and Social Development in 1990', *Beijing Review*, vol. 34, February 22.

State Statistical Bureau (SSB) (various years) *Statistical yearbook of Chinese labour and wages (Zhongguo laodong gongzi tongji nianjian*) (*ZGLDGZTJNJ*) (Beijing: State Statistical Bureau).

Steinherr, A. (1991) 'Essential ingredients for reforms in Eastern Europe', *MOCT-MOST*, no. 3, pp. 3–29.

Sterling, C. (1994) *Crime without Frontiers* (London: Little, Brown and Company).

Stern, N. (1989) 'The economics of development: A survey', *Economic Journal*, vol. 99, September, pp. 597–685.

Stewart, F. (1985) *Planning to meet Basic Needs* (London: Macmillan).

Stokes, E. (1959) *The English Utilitarians and India* (Oxford: Clarendon Press).

Su, Shaozhi (1988) *Democratisation and Reform* (Notingham: Spokesman Books).

Sung, Shangqing, and Chen Shengchang (1984) 'Set-up of production', in Yu Guangyan (ed.) (1984).

Sung, Yingwing (1991) 'The reintegration of southeast China', unpublished ms.

Surinov, A. (1994) 'How are we living? The dynamics of the population's money income in 1992', *Problems of Economic Transition*, vol. 36, no. 10.

Szamuely, L. (1974) *First models of the socialist economic system* Budapest.

Taplina, V.S., T.I. Bogomolova and A.R. Mikheeva (1993) 'What should one do with a voucher?', *Problems of Economic Transition*, vol. 36, no. 7.

Taylor, L. (1988) *Varieties of stabilisation experience* (Oxford: Oxford University Press).

Taylor, L. (1994) 'Economic reform: India and elsewhere', *Economic and Political Weekly*, vol. 29, 20 August, pp. 2209–11.

Therborn, G. (1977) 'The rule of capital and the rise of democracy', *New Left Review*, no. 103, May–June.

Tian, Yuan (1990) 'Prices', in Nolan and Dong (1990).

Tidrick, Gene and Chen Jiyuan (1987) *China's Industrial Reform* (Washington: Oxford University Press).

Tinbergen, J. (1964) *Central Planning* (London: Yale University Press).

Trotsky, L. (1977) *A History of the Russian Revolution* (London: Pluto Press). First published in 1934.

Twohey, M. (1995) 'New authoritarianism in China'. Cambridge University PhD thesis, forthcoming.

United Nations (UN) (1994) *World Investment Report* (New York: UNCTAD).

United Nations Development Programme (UNDP) (1990 and 1992) *Human Development Report* (New York: Oxford University Press).

United Nations Economic Commision for Europe (1993) *Economic Survey for Europe, 1992–3* (New York: United Nations).

USCJEC (1975) *China: A reassessment of the economy* (Washington, DC: US Government Printing Office).

USCJEC (1976) *Soviet economy in a new perspective* (Washington, DC: US Government Printing Office).

USCJEC (1978) *Chinese economy post-Mao* (Washington, DC: US Government Printing Office).

USCJEC (1979) *Soviet economy in a time of change*, 2 vols (Washington, DC: US Government Printing Office).

USCJEC (1982a) *Soviet Economy in the 1980s: Problems and Prospects* (Washington, DC: US Government Printing Office).

USCJEC (1982b) *China under the four modernisations* (Washington, DC: US Government Printing Office).

USCJEC (1986) *China's economy looks towards the year 2000* (Washington, DC: US Government Printing Office).

Vogel, E. (1989) *One step ahead in China* (London: Harvard University Press).

Wade, R. (1990) *Governing the market* (Princeton, NJ: Princeton University Press).

Walker, K. (1965) *Planning in Chinese agriculture* (London: Frank Cass).

Walters, A. (1991) 'Misapprehensions on privatisation', *International Economic Insights*, vol. 2, no. 1. Reprinted in Kennet and Lieberman (1992).

Walters, A. (1992) 'The transition to a market economy', in Clague and Rausser (1992).

Wang, F. (ed.) (1988) *Introduction to economics of xiangzhen qiye* (Beijing: Xin shidai chubanshe).

Wang, Hao (ed.) (1990) *Research into economic efficiency in different branches of the Chinese national economy (Zhonguo guomin jingji gebumen jingji xiaoyi yanjiu)* (Beijing: Jingji guanli chubanshe).

Wang, Jiafu (ed.) (1988) *TV Lectures on knowledge of xiangzhen enterprise economic law (Xiangzhen qiye jingji falu zhishi dianshi jingzuo)* (Beijing: Zhongguo zhengfa daxue chubanshe).

Wang, Xiaoqiang (1993) 'Groping for stones to cross the river: Chinese price reform against the"Big Bang"'. Cambridge University, Department of Applied Economics, Discussion Paper No. DPET 9305.

Ward, B. and R. Dubose (1972) *Only One Earth* (Harmondsworth: Penguin Books).

Wardley Corporate Finance (1993) *Maanshan Iron and Steel Company Limited* (Hong Kong: Wardley Corporate Finance).

Weir, F. (1993) 'Russia's descent into Latin America', *Economic and Political Weekly*, Special Number, vol. 28, no. 51, 18 December 1993.

White, G. (ed.) (1988) *Developmental States in East Asia* (London: Macmillan).

Williamson, C. (1960) *American suffrage: from property to democracy, 1760–1860* (Princeton: Princeton University Press).

World Bank (1981a) *China: Socialist development* (Washington, DC: World Bank).

World Bank (1981b) *China: Socialist development*, Annex D: *Challenges and achievements in industry*, Washington, DC, World Bank.

World Bank, (1981c), *China: Socialist development*, annex C, *Agricultural Development* (Washington, DC: World Bank).

World Bank (1981d), *China: Socialist Economic Development*, annex B, *Population Health and Nutrition*, Washington, DC, World Bank.

World Bank (1985) *China: Long-term Development Issues and Options* (Washington, DC: World Bank).

World Bank (1990) *China: Macroeconomic Stability and Industrial Growth under Decentralised Socialism* (Washington, DC: World Bank).

World Bank (1992a) *Russian Economic Reform: Crossing the Threshold of Structural Change* (Washington, DC: World Bank).

World Bank (1992b) *China: Strategies for reducing poverty in the 1990s* (Washington, DC: World Bank).

World Bank (1979–94) *World Development Report (WDR)* (Washington, DC: Oxford University Press).

World Bank (1994) *Land Reform and Farm Restructuring in Russia* (Washington, DC: World Bank).

World Commission on the Environment (1987) *Our Common Future* (New York: Oxford University Press).

Xu, Dixin and Wu Chengming, (eds) (1985) *China's Capitalist Sprouts* (*Zhongguo zibenzhuyi mengya*) (Beijing: Renmin chubanshe).

Xu, Dixin *et al.* (1982) *China's search for economic growth* (Beijing: New World Press).

Yakovlev, A. (1993) *The fate of Marxism in Russia* (London: Yale University Press).

Yan, R. (1994) 'To reach China's consumers, adapt to *Guoqing*' *Harvard Business Review*, Sept.–Oct.

Yao, Jianguo (1992) 'Experimenting with enterprise groups', *Beijing Review*, May 11–17, vol. 35, no. 19.

Yavlinsky, G. *et al.* (1991) *500 Days: Transition to Market* (New York: St Martin's Press, partially reprinted in Kennett and Liebermann (1992)).

Yotopoulos, P. (1989) 'The (rip) tide of privatisation: Lessons from Chile', *World Development*, vol. 17, no. 5, pp. 683–702.

Yu, Guangyan (ed.) (1984) *China's Socialist Modernisation* (Beijing: Foreign Languages Press).

Zaleski, E. (1980) *Stalinist planning for economic growth, 1933–1952* (London: Macmillan).

Zhang, Leying (1991) 'Evaluating the Chinese government's policy of encouraging foreign investment in manufacturing', London University PhD dissertation.

Zhao, Renwei (1990) 'Income distribution', in Nolan and Dong (eds) (1990).

Zhao, Ziyang (1981) 'Principles for future economic construction', in *Major Documents*, 1991.

Zhao, Ziyang (1987) 'Advance along the road of socialism with Chinese characteristics', in *Major Documents* (1991).

Zhdanov (1934) 'Soviet literature – the richest in ideas, the most advanced literature', August, in M. Gorky *et al.*, *Soviet Writers' Congress 1934* (London: Lawrence & Wishart, 1977).

Zhu, Ling, and Jiang Zhongyi (1993) 'From brigade to village community: the land tenure system and rural development in China', *Cambridge Journal of Economics*, vol. 17, no. 4, December, pp. 441–62.

Zong, Huaiwen (1989) *Years of Trial, Turmoil and Triumph* (Beijing: Foreign Languages Press).

Index